Trees in Towns and Cities

A History of British Urban Arboriculture

Mark Johnston

WIND*gather*
PRESS

Windgather Press is an imprint of Oxbow Books

Published in the United Kingdom in 2015 by
OXBOW BOOKS
10 Hythe Bridge Street, Oxford OX1 2EW

and in the United States by
OXBOW BOOKS
908 Darby Road, Havertown, PA 19083

Paperback Edition: ISBN 978-1-909686-62-5
Digital Edition: ISBN 978-1-909686-63-2

A CIP record for this book is available from the British Library

Printed in the United Kingdom by Berforts Information Press

For a complete list of Windgather titles, please contact:

United Kingdom
Oxbow Books
Telephone (01865) 241249
Fax (01865) 794449
Email: oxbow@oxbowbooks.com
www.oxbowbooks.com

United States of America
Oxbow Books
Telephone (800) 791-9354
Fax (610) 853-9146
Email: queries@casemateacademic.com
www.casemateacademic.com/oxbow

Oxbow Books is part of the Casemate group

Front cover: *One of the more impressive walks in London at The Royal Palace of St James's
next to the park (Larwood 1880).*
Back cover: *Tree in Cambridge Botanic Garden (photo: author).*

Contents

List of Illustrations

Preface

This book arose from a need to provide my degree students studying arboriculture and urban forestry with a convenient account of the history of urban trees in Britain. While there are some excellent books on the history of urban parks, gardens, and other open spaces, they often have limited information on trees or the development of urban arboriculture. Neither were there any book chapters or academic papers that gave adequate or concise coverage. In view of this, I decided to produce some notes myself with information gathered from various sources. These notes generated a lot of interest from both students and colleagues and it encouraged me to embark on a project to produce an entire book on the subject in the hope that this might fill a significant gap in the literature. Furthermore, I felt that this fascinating story could also appeal to a general readership of people interested in garden history, heritage landscapes and the natural and built environment.

When managing urban trees and greenspace, arboriculturists, urban foresters and other relevant professionals need to have a good understanding of the history and significance of those landscapes. Even in the harsh urban environment trees can live for a long time if given sufficient care and attention. For this reason, their impact on the urban landscape may continue for many decades, even centuries. For example, our current streetscapes are made up of many cultural and aesthetic influences, from the preference of the Victorian and Edwardian planters for their planes and limes, the popularity of flowering cherries in the 1950s, through to today's tailor-made trees. The wider urban landscape has also been subject to different 'fashions' through the years that still persist today, such as the high-maintenance formal Victorian landscapes and the more naturalistic 'ecological' landscapes of the 1980s. Examples of a range these influences can usually be found in most towns and cities. Do we protect those landscapes for what may be perceived as their heritage value or do we redevelop them into something which might be considered more appropriate for our needs today? Whatever management decisions are made, they should not be based on the arbitrary preferences of small pressure groups or a few powerful individuals. All of us, the professionals and the community, need to make an effort to understand where our urban landscapes have come from before we can make considered decisions, collectively, about where we want to take them in the future.

One of the difficulties in writing this book was to avoid producing yet another history of urban parks, gardens and other greenspaces and ensure that the text focused specifically on the trees and urban arboriculture. Nevertheless, in order to place the trees and woodland in context and give relevant background information, it has been necessary to give some of that broader history. I have also been conscious of the need to give a balanced view of this history that reflects the experience of the majority of urban dwellers at the time. Studies in garden and landscape history have often been preoccupied with those belonging to the rich and powerful. This book focuses particularly on working people and the extent to which they have been able to enjoy urban trees and greenspace.

In the research for this book I have done an enormous amount of reading on the historical aspects of urban trees and greenspace in Britain. Much of that has involved delving into some old and rare books that together have contained a wealth of information that seemed to have been long forgotten. I have also visited many historic landscapes, including parks, gardens and arboretums that I had not already seen during my career – and that was a particularly enjoyable part of this project. All this information from a range of sources was then filtered through my own knowledge and experience of urban arboriculture acquired over forty years. At times it seemed that each chapter could be a book in itself and what is presented here is the result of some drastic editing. The decisions about what to include and what emphasis to give this have been entirely mine.

Many people have played a part in the production of this book. These contributions have been wide-ranging and have included sourcing information, facilitating site visits, commenting on draft chapters or giving me some valuable support for my wider academic and research work. There are too many people to name individually but the following acknowledgements must be given. My thanks go to the authors of the many books and articles that I have read while gathering information and a perspective on this history. Generally, those authors that are referenced most frequently are those that I have found particularly useful. I wish to thank to Paul Elliott of Derby University for his early work with me in setting up this project and for the benefit of his excellent published research on British arboriculture in the nineteenth century. In the early stages of this project I was fortunate to share an office and many stimulating conversations on this topic with my colleague Andrew Hirons of Myerscough College. The Library staff at Myerscough College were very helpful in sourcing relevant academic articles that I was not able to obtain myself. Sue Griffiths of Birmingham Trees for Life made a valuable contribution at a point where I was struggling for inspiration and for interesting photos that were not just focused on London. Diane Heath, a neighbour and photographer in Belfast, played a crucial role in ensuring that my illustrations were of sufficient quality to be a real credit to the text. Lastly, but most importantly, I want to thank my wife Anne for the wonderful support she has given me throughout this project. Without her understanding and encouragement this book would never have been written.

Mark Johnston
Belfast, August 2014

1

The Rise of Professional Arboriculture

Since trees were first planted and cultivated in Britain's towns and cities, somebody has had to undertake this work. Those employed professionally on tree work have generally required a level of specialist knowledge, not least because of the risks involved in maintaining or removing mature trees in close proximity to people and built development. If that was not the case then this difficult and demanding work could be a particularly dangerous occupation, as many amateur tree workers down the years have found out to their cost.

Over the centuries, the planting and care of urban trees has been embraced by a range of different professionals (Figure 1). This has included horticulturists, landscapers, foresters, civil engineers and many others. Since the early twentieth century, the planting and care of trees for amenity purposes has come to be regarded as the province of arboriculture, although the original use of that term was almost synonymous with forestry (James 1982, 122). Modern arboriculture as a science and profession can trace much of its origins to both horticulture and forestry. Its approach to the planting and cultivation of trees is derived largely from horticulture. However, much of the equipment and techniques involved in mature tree maintenance have their origins in forestry.

FIGURE 1. Over the centuries various professionals have been engaged in the planting and care of trees, in both urban and rural situations. This woodcut of tree workers is from the title page of the 1656 edition of William Lawson's *A New Orchard and Garden*.

While the recognised scope of arboriculture focuses principally on trees, it can also embrace other woody plants (Wilson 2013, 9). Its emphasis has traditionally been on the so-called amenity benefits of trees, with much attention given to the aesthetic. Arboriculture generally focuses on individual or small groups of trees, in both urban and rural situations. Since the 1960s, the planning and management of tree populations throughout an urban area has become known as 'urban forestry' and the totality of trees and woodland in and around a town or city is now referred to as the 'urban forest' (Johnston 1996). In historical terms that is a very recent development.

This chapter explores the development of arboriculture as a professional activity concerned with the planting and care of amenity trees in urban areas. Some difficulties were encountered in the research process because of the historical changes in the meaning of the term 'arboriculture'. What might be described as arboriculture in many eighteenth century texts is now regarded as forestry and beyond the scope of this book. Furthermore, in dealing with the topic of professionalism in arboriculture it has been difficult to make any precise distinction between what is rural and what is urban. Therefore, in this chapter more than any other, we tend to cover more general aspects of arboriculture.

Early arboricultural practices

Perhaps the earliest arboricultural practices in Britain can be traced back to the Romans. They took some of the principles and practice of tree planting and care established by the Greeks and other early civilisations and adapted them to their own needs (Campana 1999, 6). Their achievements in general landscaping often exceeded anything seen before and provided a basic framework of tree culture, style and design that would survive the demise of the ancient world in Europe to emerge again in the Renaissance. The Romans were the first to give the tree worker a name: arborator. Used originally only for a tree pruner, mainly for fruit trees, it was later used to include all those who undertook planting and care with any trees. The name 'arborator' was still being used in this context by John Evelyn in the seventeenth century, although he more commonly used the term 'arborist' (Evelyn 1664, 75).

Following the end of the Roman occupation in the year 410, little progress seems to have been made in the theory and practice of arboriculture in Britain until the English Renaissance in the sixteenth and early seventeenth centuries (Hadfield 1967). During this period the development of arboriculture was characterised by a focus on a formal style of landscaping, the establishment of early botanical gardens and early forest management. The fashion for a formal approach to landscaping in the gardens of country estates and town residences, heavily influenced by continental European styles such as the Italian, French and Dutch, emphasised a desire to control and manipulate nature. This was reflected in the pruning and landscape use of trees where topiary was fashionable and there was a preference for ordered and symmetrical arrangements of trees. While the economic value of trees was still of primary interest in Britain, the aesthetic considerations of trees and woodlands were also receiving more attention. The landscape itself, both rural and urban, contained a significant mix of native and exotic tree species. This reflected the considerable numbers of trees introduced from overseas and planted out in a variety of landscapes for their economic and aesthetic benefit (Loudon 1838a).

Scholarly works relevant to trees were also being published as scientific knowledge continued to expand. Early in the seventeenth century the previously allied subjects of horticulture and botany, both particularly relevant to trees, began to split into separate fields of study (Campbell-Culver 2006, 17). During this period and for some time after, much of the British literature on trees reflected economic preoccupations and tended to focus on forest (timber) trees and fruit trees. Nevertheless, these usually contained important information about basic arboricultural practices such as planting and pruning. In disseminating information on tree care practices among the landed aristocracy, a number of publications were influential. The earliest British reference book of note was probably *The Book of Husbandry* by Anthony Fitzherbert in 1534, which included some aspects of arboriculture, although only in a rural context (Fitzherbert 1882). In 1563, Thomas Hill wrote the first English book on general gardening, *The Profitable Arte of Gardening*, and this included some references to trees (Henrey 1975, 57). Hill followed this in 1577 with a more extensive work entitled *The Gardener's Labyrinth* (Hill 1987). Leonard Mascall's *A Booke of the Arte and Maner Howe to Plant and Graffe all sortes of Trees*, first published in 1569, gave considerable detail on the techniques of planting and grafting for fruit trees, including information on the equipment used (Mascall 1569). This was not actually an original text as it was based on a translation of a French work by Davy Brossard (Henrey 1975, 63). By contrast, William Lawson's book *A New Orchard and Garden*, published in 1618, was based on the author's forty-eight years of experience in a northern garden (Lawson 1618). It included the first detailed account of general arboricultural practices of that era, including tree planting, moving, pruning, wound treatment and cavity filling. He was also one of the first writers to recognise that most absorbing roots were close to the soil surface. Ralph Austen's book *A Treatise of Fruit-trees*, published in 1653, ensured his reputation as one the most significant seventeenth century authorities on that subject (Austen 1653; Amherst 1896, 185) (Figure 2). Austen was also concerned with wider aspects of arboricultural knowledge with important contributions on the propagation, planting and care of trees.

Botanic Gardens began to be established in Britain from the seventeenth century, prompted in part by the steady introduction of new trees and shrubs (Loudon 1838a) (see Chapter 7). The oldest of these was the Oxford Botanic Garden (1621), followed by Edinburgh (1670) and Chelsea Physic Garden (1673). In his *Arboretum Britannicum* in 1838, John Claudius Loudon detailed the most important of these seventeenth century gardens and the trees and shrubs that were introduced during that time (Loudon 1838a). As the flow of

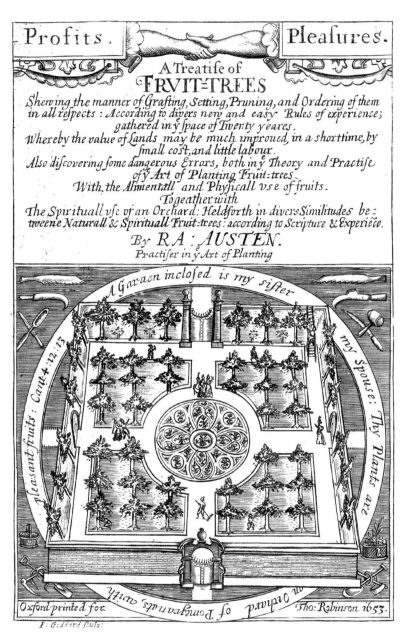

FIGURE 2. Ralph Austen's *A Treatise of Fruit Trees* in 1653 was not only a major work on pomology but also included general information relevant to practical arboriculture. However, its preoccupation with moral and religious matters probably limited its popular appeal. The title-page engraving is by John Goddard.

new tree introductions continued, these began to be recorded in learned books on the subject. The first fully illustrated encyclopaedia of trees to be published in Britain is likely to have been *Dendrographias, sive historiae naturalis de arboribus et fructicibus* (Johnson 2010, 48). This was written by John Johnston (Johannes Jonstonus) and published in Frankfurt in 1662. Had this remarkable work not been written entirely in Latin, it would have been more widely known in later years.

FIGURE 3. John Evelyn (1620–1706) was the author of *Sylva or a Discourse of Forest Trees*, regarded by many as the one of the world's greatest books on trees. This portrait of Evelyn was engraved by Francesco Bartolozzi and is from Hunter's 1776 edition.

John Evelyn's *Sylva or a Discourse of Forest Trees*, first published in 1664, is regarded by some authorities as one of the world's greatest books on trees in any language (Campbell-Culver 2006, 46) (Figure 3). *Sylva* is also widely recognised as the first text on forestry published in English that was also a passionate call to plant and restore woodlands for the nation's economic survival. Despite its title, it is not just about 'forest' or timber trees. Evelyn went beyond his original brief from the Royal Society and included the use of trees in gardens with a number of species of ornamental value (Evelyn 1664). While there is almost no mention of trees in towns, Evelyn's work is a remarkable source of information about early arboriculture. He was critical of tree work standards at that time and had this to say on the subject of poor pruning:

> For 'tis a misery to see how our fairest trees are defaced and mangled by unskilful Wood-men, and mischievous Bordurers, who go always armed with short Hand-bills, hacking and chopping off all that comes in their way; by which our trees are made full of knots, boils, cankers and deformed bunches, to their utter destruction.

Evelyn adds that good workmen should be ashamed of this unsatisfactory situation. He goes on:

> As much to be reprehended are those who either begin this work at unseasonable times, or so maim the poor branches, that either out of laziness or lack of skill, they leave most of them stubs, and instead of cutting the arms and branches close to the bole, hack them off a foot or two from the body of the tree, by which they become hollow and rotten.

Evelyn 1664, 74

According to Evelyn, pruning should be undertaken "...by cutting clean, smooth and close, making the stroke upwards and with a sharp bill..." to avoid the bark and branch tearing. His *Sylva* went through many further editions both in his lifetime and subsequently. Later editions included more information on arboricultural practices, including further descriptions and diagrams of tools and equipment required for the work. *Sylva*, or *Silva* as it was spelt in later editions, remained an authoritative work on trees and tree culture well into the eighteenth century.

In 1776, seventy years after Evelyn's death, a new edition of *Sylva* was published with extensive notes by Dr Alexander Hunter of York (Evelyn 1776). Hunter's edition revived the national ardour for tree planting that the first edition created (Henrey 1975, 110). It also came at a time when it was increasingly popular to use trees in a general plan for the embellishment of estates and so was purchased enthusiastically by landowners. Collectively, all the editions of *Sylva* have ensured that no other work on arboriculture written before 1800 exerted a greater influence on forestry in Britain. For many generations of arboriculturists and foresters, the first edition remains the most iconic British work ever written on trees. Others have been more critical of this early text and regard Hunter's edition with his own notes as more valuable (James 1981, 131).

A contemporary of Evelyn was Moses Cook, partner in the Brompton Park Nursery and gardener to the Earl of Essex (Hadfield *et al.* 1980, 79). He wrote *The Manner of Raising, Ordering, and Improving Forest-Trees, etc.,* published in 1676, which proved to be highly influential (Cook 1676). Not only did Cook explode some popular myths about tree cultivation but he also set out some basic principles of good arboricultural practice, particularly in relation to the use of trees in walks and avenues. Cook was well known to Evelyn and is often credited as being the source for the practical horticultural detail in Evelyn's works (University of Toronto 2012) (Figure 4).

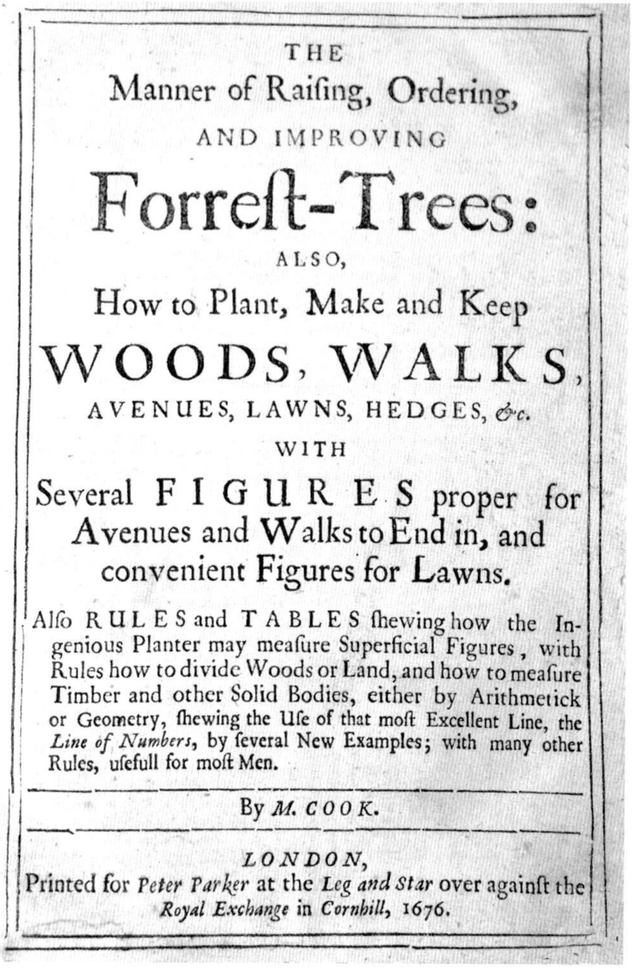

The most influential British garden designers of this period were George London and Henry Wise, whose services were in great demand by the aristocracy and landed classes (Quest-Ritson 2001, 83). Much influenced by the French formal style of André Le Nôtre (1613–1700), their garden designs represented the epitome of taste and they dominated the horticultural scene for nearly fifty years. London and Wise were originally in partnership as nurserymen at the celebrated Brompton Park Nursery in Kensington, London, where Moses Cook had been a partner. Brompton Park specialised in ornamental trees and shrubs and eventually covered 100 acres, making it by far the largest nursery in England. It was the first commercial tree and shrub nursery to achieve such a dominant position in the English nursery trade, in much the same way as Veitch of Exeter in the nineteenth century and Hillier of Winchester in the twentieth.

THE
Manner of Raising, Ordering,
AND IMPROVING
Forrest-Trees:
ALSO,
How to Plant, Make and Keep
WOODS, WALKS,
AVENUES, LAWNS, HEDGES, &c.
WITH
Several FIGURES proper for
Avenues and Walks to End in, and
convenient Figures for Lawns.

Also RULES and TABLES shewing how the Ingenious Planter may measure Superficial Figures, with Rules how to divide Woods or Land, and how to measure Timber and other Solid Bodies, either by Arithmetick or Geometry, shewing the Use of that most Excellent Line, the *Line of Numbers*, by several New Examples; with many other Rules, usefull for most Men.

By *M. COOK.*

LONDON,
Printed for *Peter Parker* at the *Leg and Star* over against the *Royal Exchange* in *Cornhill*, 1676.

FIGURE 4. In 1676, Moses Cook published his remarkable work *The Manner of Raising, Ordering, and Improving Forest Trees.* This has been largely overshadowed by Evelyn's *Sylva* but some authorities credit Cook as being the source of the practical horticultural detail in Evelyn's works.

Arboriculture in the 1700s

By the early eighteenth century, the British landed gentry and aristocracy were reacting against the formal garden style that was largely French-influenced. The popularity of these landscapes with their *parterres*, long radiating avenues of trees, and straight-edged canals was fading. Now, a more simple and natural approach was gaining favour that involved the extensive planting of trees as part of the 'improvement' of estates (Langley 1728a and 1728b). From this emerged the English landscape movement with its emphasis on creating green parklands with belts, clumps and groves of trees and serpentine lakes. This generated a revolution in the appearance of British gardens and estate landscapes throughout the eighteenth century that also impacted on urban landscapes. The revolution continued later in the century when the emphasis changed towards a wilder, 'picturesque' approach, which included trees and woodlands (Gilpin 1794).

Later in the eighteenth century as the Industrial Revolution gathered pace, there was a dramatic increase in wealth among the upper echelons of society, not only among the old landed aristocracy but also the *nouveaux riches* of industrialists, financiers and other entrepreneurs (Trevelyan 1951, 102–8). For these wealthy individuals, one very potent way of displaying their social status was through the symbol of the estate and the garden. The essential requirement was an extensive country estate together with a town house for the Season. There was much competition among the landed classes to be seen at the forefront of the latest innovations and taste. Trees provided much of the expression of this landscape movement, linking the man-made garden with its surrounding countryside. The emphasis on trees stimulated a demand for gardening expertise that had some arboricultural skills. The design of these new landscapes was generally the preserve of the architect or garden designer.

The workforces on the country estates and town gardens charged with delivering these prestige landscapes were led by Head Gardeners, who might occasionally be involved at the design stage (Musgrave 2007, 124). This was a position of considerable responsibility that took years of apprenticeship to achieve, with only a very limited number of gardeners rising from the ranks to those lofty heights. Gardeners were male, usually from a rural working-class background, and required considerable self-discipline and motivation to engage in many years of self-improvement through reading and study. While the eighteenth century saw a boom in horticultural publishing, books were often very expensive and beyond the means of ordinary gardeners. These books were invariable purchased by the landowner, who may have already paid a 'subscription' towards its publication, who then passed on the knowledge to their Head Gardener. Many of these new books on landscape and gardening had significant sections on the cultivation and management of trees, in urban as well as rural locations. In 1722, Thomas Fairchild published his influential book *The City Gardener*, the first British text on urban horticulture that included information about trees, shrubs and other plants which thrived best in London (Fairchild 1722) (Figure 5).

Around 1725, a society for gardeners residing in London was established, and Fairchild was among those who joined it (Chalmers 1812). Meeting every month they compared notes about plants they were growing and entered the information in a register. In 1730, this was published as *A Catalogue of Trees and Shrubs both Exotic and Domestic which are propagated for Sale in the Gardens near London* (Society of Gardeners 1730). The *Catalogue* has been attributed to Philip Miller, who was at one time secretary of the society and a leading horticulturist of the age. The work was more than just a catalogue and included useful information about propagation and cultivation. The preface to the work also listed 'the principal encouragers of planting and gardening in England, previously to and at that time'. In 1731, Miller produced the first edition of his classic work entitled *The Gardeners Dictionary*, at the time the most celebrated work of its kind and which included much information about cultivating and improving trees and other plants (Miller 1735). He had plenty to say about tree pruning and issued a warning against the damage inflicted on many trees by severe topping. The book went through many editions, the last dated 1768.

FIGURE 5. When Thomas Fairchild published his influential book *The City Gardener* in 1722 it was the first British text on urban horticulture. It also made extensive reference to the planting and care of urban trees. This frontispiece was engraved by John Clarke and shows the scene from an urban garden, possibly Fairchild's.

William Hanbury was Rector of Church Langton in Leicestershire from 1753 and used his natural genius for planting and gardening to develop extensive plantations and gardens in his parish. In 1758, he had published *An Essay on Planting, and a Scheme for Making It Conducive to the Glory of God and the Advantage of Society*, which set out his moral and religious view of working with trees (Hanbury 1758). In 1770, he published his seminal work entitled *A Complete Body of Planting and Gardening*, in two folio volumes and nearly 1000 pages (Hanbury 1770). This remains one of the most outstanding works on horticulture, arboriculture and forestry in the English language. Unfortunately, its limited circulation and sheer size has ensured it has not been widely read.

Towards the end of the eighteenth century, two further books were published that had a significant impact on the development of arboriculture. The first in 1775 by William Boutcher, a nurseryman from Edinburgh, was entitled

A Treatise on Forest-Trees (Boutcher 1775). Boutcher undertook numerous experiments in tree care to establish what was good practice. The second work was in 1785 by William Marshall, a landscape gardener from Yorkshire, entitled *Planting and Ornamental Gardening*, although later editions were called *Planting and Rural Ornament* (Marshall 1785). In the 'Advertisement' to his work, located at the start of the book, Marshall not only promotes his own arboricultural expertise but also gives his views of other writers on this subject. His comments on Evelyn's *Sylva* are typical of his forthright style:

> It is probably that, in the early part of his life, Evelyn was a practical planter upon his estate at Wotton in Surrey; but his book was written in the wane of his life, at Greenwich, during a long and painful fit of the gout. His *Sylva* contains many practical rules, valuable, no doubt, in his day, but now superseded by modern practice.
>
> Marshall 1785, vi

By contrast, Marshall was full of praise for Moses Cook who he describes as 'our first writer on planting'. He was also impressed by the work of Phillip Miller and particularly William Hanbury and laments that the writings of the latter were not more widely known. In their time, both Boutcher and Marshall were notable for advancing general knowledge on the pruning of trees. They may best be remembered for recommending top pruning when transplanting trees to ensure a balance between the root and shoot system when roots were lost during the transplanting process.

In 1794, Samuel Hayes, Irish MP, amateur architect and passionate planter of trees, wrote the first book on tree care and management in Ireland. Entitled *A Practical Treatise on Planting and the Management of Woods and Coppice*s, it

FIGURE 6. In 1794, Samuel Hayes' work *A Practical Treatise on the Planting and Management of Woods and Coppices* became the first book on trees published in Ireland. It covered various aspects of arboriculture and was well-received in Britain. The engraving by William Esdall shows the equipment and technique used by Hayes in transplanting semi-mature trees.

was based on his experience at Avondale, his estate in County Wicklow (Hayes 1794) (Figure 6). Much of the book deals with what we now regard as forestry but there are also a number of arboricultural subjects such as tree pruning, wound dressing and moving large trees. It is likely that the book was not just directed at Irish aristocrats and landowners but also to the larger audience of their counterparts in Britain.

Arboriculture in the 1800s

As the Georgian era entered a new century, interest in horticulture, including trees and shrubs, continued to increase. This was not just a fascination of the upper class on their country estates but also an increasing preoccupation of the expanding middle class of Britain's towns and cities. This was reflected in the formation of the first horticultural societies, comprising individuals who wished to exchange information and ideas about plants and gardening. In London in 1804, Sir Joseph Banks and John Wedgewood formed the Horticultural Society of London (Elliott 2004, 4–5). In 1821, the Society established an experimental garden in Cheswick which included an arboretum containing a great variety of trees. To encourage the introduction of new trees, shrubs and other plants, the Society began organising and sponsoring an extensive series of plant collecting expeditions to many different countries around the world (*ibid.*, 197–211). The Society's interest in trees also reflected a wider public interest in the nation's tree heritage, stimulated by books such as Jacob Strutt's *Sylva Britannica* (Strutt, 1830), In 1861, the Society changed its name to the Royal Horticultural Society when granted its Royal Charter and it has subsequently become one of the world's foremost horticultural organisations (Elliott 2004, 25).

To satisfy the growing public interest in trees and tree cultivation, more books were published and some of these charted significant advances in arboricultural theory and practice. In 1802, William Forsyth published *The Culture and Management of Fruit-Trees* based on his experience as a royal gardener (Forsyth 1802). Although focused on fruit trees, it set out some fundamental arboricultural techniques, particularly on wound and cavity treatment, that remained standard practice for another hundred years. Forsyth stressed the importance of cleaning out cavities thoroughly and for this reason some regard him as the father of tree surgery as a science (Campana 1999, 10). He devised a formula for filling tree cavities with cow dung, old lime, wood ashes and sand. Plate 13 of Forsyth's book illustrates a range of sixteen tools for undertaking tree work. With the exception of the cavity cleaning equipment, some would still be useful today (Forsyth 1802, 359) (Figure 7).

No sooner had Forsyth's recipe for wound treatment become known, it was widely criticised by others. Sir Arthur St Clair offered an alternative product, comprising hot tar in dusted chalk (Campana 1999, 10). Another critic was Walter Nicol, the son of a Scottish landscape gardener who gained experience in England before establishing himself in Edinburgh as horticultural designer and author. In the second edition of his book *The Practical Planter*, he challenged the Forsyth formula as less effective than tar (Nicol 1803, 180). Nicol also noted the need for an undercut when pruning limbs to prevent what he called 'laceration' (tearing). Although previous authors such as Evelyn had recommended this, Nicol was probably the first to use the term 'undercut'. Another researcher into pruning and wound treatment at this time was William Pontey, Nurseryman and Gardener to the Duke of Bedford (Pontey 1808a). In his book *The Forest Pruner or Timber Owner's Assistant*, first published in 1806, he is also critical of Forsyth for implying that wounds not treated with his own composition would fail to close. He noted "the astonishing and successful exertions of simple nature in healing the wounds of trees" (*ibid.*, 25). This insight into the ability of trees to close their own wounds was based on observation and it took another 170 years for arboricultural research to adequately explain the science behind this (Shigo and Marx 1976). In a companion volume around the same time entitled *The Profitable Planter*, Pontey also goes into considerable detail on equipment and techniques used in tree planting (Pontey 1808b).

In 1827, the first edition of *The Planter's Guide* by Sir Henry Steuart (1828) was published. This gained immediate public attention through favourable reviews by Sir Walter Scott in the *Quarterly Review* and another by James Main in the *Gardeners Magazine* (Tait 1976, 14). The book made a significant contribution to promoting good arboricultural standards, not least because of its popularity, even though some of its practices would now be questioned. As well as focusing extensively on the topic of tree transplanting, Steuart had much to say about pruning standards (Steuart 1828) (Figure 8). He was also conscious of the value of research into all aspects of arboriculture and detailed the contribution made by his predecessors and contemporaries and gave considerable praise to William Boutcher and William Marshall. However, in contrast to both these individuals

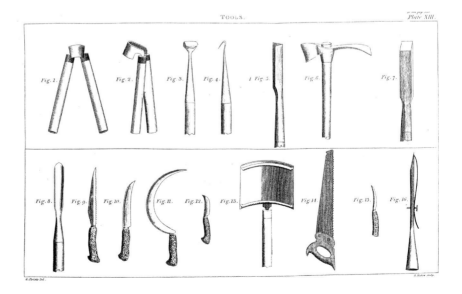

FIGURE 7. A set of hand tools for tree work from an illustration in *The Culture and Management of Fruit-Trees* by William Forsyth, published in 1802. Apart from the cavity cleaning equipment, some of the other tools would still be useful today.

FIGURE 8. In the early nineteenth century Sir Henry Steuart established a considerable reputation with his exploits in transplanting large trees. Although these were moved 'bare-rooted' despite being very large, he was satisfied with the level of success he achieved (Steuart 1828).

who favoured extensive top pruning when transplanting, Steuart preferred to encourage more root growth to achieve a root-shoot balance.

Although tree transplanting was not new, in the 1820s and 1830s it was undertaken on a grand scale using novel techniques and equipment (Elliott *et al.* 2007, 140). Much of this innovation was due to William Barron, one of the great Victorian landscape gardeners. In contrast to Steuart who transplanted with bare roots, Barron generally recommended that balls of earth remain around the roots. He was also responsible for inventing new tree-transplanting machines, the first making its appearance in 1831. Like many of his contemporaries Barron was employed by wealthy private landowners but he was also engaged in public works in parks and cemeteries. He was particularly attracted to conifers because of their cultural associations and natural characteristics, which he was able to exploit for economic and moral purposes (*ibid.*, 130). These views were expressed in his book *The British Winter Garden*, which became widely read among the middle class with an interest in gardening (Barron 1852). As a result, Barron played a significant role in fostering the mid-Victorian fashion for evergreen planting (see Chapter 4). In terms of planting conifers in towns and cities this had both advantages and disadvantages. Coniferous trees excited the imagination by providing an enormous variety of form, size, colour and texture, as well as the timeless quality of their evergreen foliage. Unfortunately, many were unsuitable for urban planting. Most pines (*Pinus*), spruces (*Picea*), silver firs (*Abies)* and similar conifers with needles found it difficult to survive the smoky and polluted atmosphere of densely urban areas (Ravenscroft 1883). Barron's arboricultural expertise was recognised by the Select Committee on Forestry which questioned him as their first witness in 1887 (Elliott *et al.* 2011, 163).

The main purpose of the Select Committee on Forestry formed in 1885 was to consider the establishment of a Forest School (James 1981, 192). Although

Parliament had been dissolved before the Committee had time to report, moves towards more formalised forestry education were already underway. At this time, there was a significant German influence on the development of British forestry, with German ideas and practice being disseminated through the translation of pioneering works, such as *A Manual of Forestry* by Dr William Schlich (1889–1896). In 1885, the first forestry courses were introduced at the Royal Indian Engineering College at Coopers Hill. However, these were directed towards colonial service and aspects of arboriculture were not included. When the college closed in 1906, the forestry section together with Dr Schlich, the senior academic, was transferred to Oxford University. The emphasis on timber production continued because the subject of amenity trees, particularly in urban areas, was not regarded as forestry.

While forestry courses were being established, horticultural education had continued to make advances. A little formal training had begun at Kew Gardens in 1859 but this only took place after the normal six-day working week (Paterson 2008, 172). Following questions in Parliament, more permanent and structured educational arrangements were instituted at Kew. The School of Horticulture was established and in 1870 Kew began it issue diplomas in horticulture. In 1866, the Royal Horticultural Society held its first examinations for gardeners (Musgrave 2007, 65). As part of these new examinations candidates would have been examined on aspects of tree planting and maintenance, although this would have been done under the auspices of horticulture as arboriculture was still not regarded as a separate subject.

FIGURE 9. Portrait of John Claudius Loudon by an unknown artist. This was the frontispiece in *Self-Instruction for Young Gardeners* published in 1845 just after his death. As well as being a giant in the world of horticulture and public parks, Loudon contributed more to the cause of trees and arboriculture than any other nineteenth century figure.

John Claudius Loudon and William Robinson

Two figures stand out as giants in terms of their influence on the development of arboriculture in the nineteenth century and for decades after. They are John Claudius Loudon and William Robinson. Loudon was active in the first half of the century, while Robinson's main efforts came towards the end of the century. Both men were hugely influential in horticulture, landscape, urban planning and other fields but we focus here on their contribution to arboriculture.

John Claudius Loudon was a Scotsman born in Lanarkshire in 1783 (Simo 1988) (Figure 9). He became a prolific writer on an enormous range of horticultural and landscape topics. Indeed, he founded a horticultural publishing empire, producing a host of gardening magazines and books designed to appeal to a greatly expanding and newly affluent readership. Through his publications, he spread his ideas on public open spaces and city planning and well as many aspects of horticulture, arboriculture, and related subjects to both amateur enthusiasts and professionals.

In 1803, Loudon wrote his first article for the *Literary Journal* entitled *Hints respecting the manner of Laying out the Public Squares in London* and this had some immediate relevance to arboriculture (Simo 1988, 291). It recommended the introduction of lighter trees rather than those with dense canopies. His first major horticultural book was published in 1822 entitled *An Encyclopaedia of Gardening, comprising the theory and practice of horticulture, floriculture, arboriculture and landscape-gardening*. In 1835, a considerably improved and enlarged edition was published (Loudon 1835). Book III in Part III of the *Encyclopaedia of Gardening* is entitled 'Arboriculture, or planting of trees'. It is mainly about trees in plantations and what is now regarded as forestry. There are some references to the ornamental uses of trees but this is mostly limited to the rural landscapes of country estates. In the Arboricultural Catalogue towards the end of the *Encyclopaedia of Gardening* Loudon describes the principal timber trees. Where he makes reference to trees in private gardens this tends to occur in the section on 'landscape-gardening'. Later, Loudon was instrumental in the adoption of the term 'landscape architecture' by the modern profession. He took up the term from its originator Gilbert Laing Meason and gave it publicity through his book *Landscape Gardening and Landscape Architecture of the Late Humphry Repton* (Loudon 1840).

In 1826, Loudon founded the *Gardener's Magazine*, described as the first periodical devoted solely to horticulture, although William Curtis had commenced *The Botanical Magazine* in 1787 and it continues to this day (Tjaden 1983). Loudon's magazine had a tremendous impact on Britain's horticultural world and did much to stimulate popular interest in trees and their cultivation (Elliott *et al.* 2007, 230). In his writing for magazines and other publications, Loudon directed his attention mainly towards the new suburban middle classes with their villas and gardens. He specifically focused on this in his book *The Suburban Gardener and Villa Companion* where he stressed the value of trees and shrubs to these gardens (Loudon 1838b).

Perhaps Loudon's most important work was *Arboretum et Fruticetum Britannicum* (often abbreviated to *Arboretum Britannicum*) first published in 1838 (Loudon 1838). Although a very costly and time-consuming project, its eventual publication had a huge impact. Its remarkable scope and detail in describing and illustrating all the trees and shrubs growing in Britain was an astonishing accomplishment. They were drawn from life, many from the grounds of Syon House, Kew or most especially from the Loddiges arboretum, located at their famous nursery in Hackney (Elliott *et al.* 2011, 97). Loudon wrote *Arboretum Britannicum* for the public good, believing it an object of national importance to give a complete portrait of trees in Britain and it remains one of the greatest works on arboriculture ever written. It not only gave further stimulation to popular interest in trees, it also encouraged the proliferation of arboretums and exotic tree collections.

In 1839, he was commissioned to design the Derby Arboretum, which inspired many more public parks (see Chapter 5). Over many years, he made a huge practical contribution to the eighteenth century development of public parks, cemeteries and the planning of public open space (Elliott *et al.* 2011). Loudon believed that all these public improvements should be undertaken in a democratic fashion, providing a facility that could be enjoyed by everyone. Furthermore, their provision in towns and cities everywhere should be undertaken in a comprehensive and inclusive way, and not dependent on the occasional benevolence of the wealthy. In his commissions, Loudon put into practice the principles that he advocated in his writings, aiming to create open spaces that would promote community pride where all classes of people could mingle easily. In the world of horticulture, Loudon will always be remembered for his 'gardenesque' style of landscaping (Hobhouse 2002, 249) (see Chapter 4). This used plenty of exotic trees and other plants to create significant impact and seemed particularly suited at the time to the relatively confined space of the suburban garden.

Unlike many of his prominent contemporaries in horticulture, Loudon was never a Head Gardener. Nevertheless, he was very conscious of the crucial role of all gardeners in delivering the improvements that he sought in horticulture and landscape design. His many books and articles became a definitive source of reference for all gardening professionals. In 1845 his *Self-instruction for Young Gardeners, Foresters, Bailiffs, Land-Stewards, and Farmers* was published posthumously and this set out his approach to professional education (Loudon 1845). As might be expected, Loudon was a firm believer in the value of books and felt these should be provided by the employer at their expense.

The second nineteenth century figure with a huge influence on the development of British arboriculture was William Robinson, an Irishman born in 1838 who spent most of his working life in England (Allan 1982). Emerging towards the end of the nineteenth century, his impact came after Loudon, a man he much admired, although not so much his 'gardenesque' style of landscaping. Indeed, although Robinson's most famous books came out in the Victorian era his influence was probably at its height in the Edwardian period (*ibid.*, 183–91). While Robinson's huge contribution to horticulture has been well-celebrated, his influence on arboriculture is less well-known and more indirect than Loudon. His vital contribution to specific elements of the urban landscape is discussed in the relevant chapters of this book.

As an Irish landscape gardener and writer Robinson laid much of the foundations of our modern British approach to horticulture and introduced many now accepted gardening practices. He recommended gardening with hardy plants in woods, at the wood's edge and in meadows (Robinson 1870). In particular, he advocated more natural and less formal-looking plantings of hardy perennials, shrubs and climbers. He railed against the High Victorian gardening practices that used tropical material and other artificial elements. His ideas about wild gardening spurred the movement that evolved into the English

THE WILD GARDEN

OR,

OUR GROVES & SHRUBBERIES

MADE BEAUTIFUL

BY THE NATURALIZATION OF HARDY EXOTIC PLANTS:

WITH A CHAPTER

ON THE GARDEN OF BRITISH WILD FLOWERS.

By W. ROBINSON,

AUTHOR OF

"ALPINE FLOWERS FOR ENGLISH GARDENS," "THE PARKS, PROMENADES,
AND GARDENS OF PARIS," ETC.

LONDON:
JOHN MURRAY, ALBEMARLE STREET.
1870.

"I wish it to be framed, as much as may be, to a naturall wildnesse."
LORD BACON.

cottage garden, a parallel to the search for honesty, simplicity and vernacular style of the Arts and Crafts movement. While Robinson was interested in the horticultural potential of native British plants, he was not an advocate of using only native tree or plant species. What was important to him was whether species were suitable to the site rather than their origin. Robinson's ideas on gardening were set out in a number of highly popular books such as *The Wild Garden* (1870) (Figure 10) and *The English Flower Garden* (1883), two of the most widely-read and influential gardening books ever written (Allan 1982).

Robinson also founded a gardening periodical, *The Garden*, which ran from 1871–1927 (Allan 1982, 99). In 1883, when Britain's first magazine on trees was launched entitled *Woods and Forests*, it struggled financially and it was decided to incorporate this into *The Garden* after only 68 weekly issues (*ibid.*, 136).

Not only was Robinson a key figure in the history of British gardening, he also had a major influence on ideas regarding the management of the urban landscape. In 1869 he published *The Parks, Promenades and Gardens of Paris*, in which he not only described and evaluated these but also considered them in relation to the wants of our own cities, especially the role of smaller parks and boulevards (Robinson 1869). In this book he had much to say about the

FIGURE 10. *The Wild Garden* by William Robinson has not just been a hugely significant book for horticulture and garden landscapes but it has also had a major impact on our use of trees in urban and amenity landscapes. Since it was first published in 1870, it has gone through several editions and facsimiles.

trees of Paris, praising the creation of the boulevards and the extensive semi-mature transplanting being undertaken, although he was also quite critical of some aspects of tree management. Robinson was never short of opinions on horticultural and arboricultural topics and having learnt from the Parisian experience he had much to say about urban greening that has considerable relevance today. He was critical of the substantial amounts of money spent on establishing and maintaining highly ornamental features with expensive bedding plants in public parks. He felt this money would be better spent on street trees and small squares using plants from temperate regions that would thrive without intensive maintenance. He also proposed that local authorities in Britain save money by operating their plant nurseries in those large parks where there was often plenty of room to establish these, rather than buying in plants at greater cost from commercial nurseries.

Robinson had a life-long love of trees and implicitly understood their importance in the landscape, both urban and rural. In 1903, he began publication of *Flora and Sylva*, described as a monthly review for lovers of garden, woodland, tree or flower (Robinson 1905). In his introduction to the first issue he clearly states his intention to give substantial coverage to trees:

> As regards the plan of *Flora and Sylva*, it struck me that periodicals of this kind had always been over much devoted to flowers as distinct from trees and shrubs, while every day of my life I see more and more the beauty and value of the tree. So I married Flora to Sylva – a pair not far apart in nature, only in books.
>
> Robinson, 1905

As well as including many of Robinson's own articles on the cultivation and uses of trees and shrubs, *Flora and Sylva* had contributions from other notable tree and shrub experts of the day, such as Augustine Henry, Maurice de Vilmorin, Ernest Wilson and William Jackson Bean. The magazine also included topical articles on current developments in horticulture, forestry, arboriculture and urban parks, including critical evaluations of government policy. Unfortunately, the substantial production costs of *Flora and Sylva* led to this sumptuous publication ceasing after only three years.

In 1906, Robinson published *The Garden Beautiful*, which in spite of its title deals mainly with trees (Robinson 1906). It contained much information, not only about a wide variety of trees, but also about methods of planting, pruning and cultivation, and the suitability of different trees to a range of locations. It has been described as a lightweight successor to Loudon's *Arboretum Britannicum* and although it cannot be seriously compared with this, its coverage of trees and shrubs, both native and exotic, is extensive (Massingham 1978). As Robinson grew older he is reported to have become full of inconsistencies, reflected in his preference or otherwise of native or exotic trees. He was also known for some quite dogmatic views such as his antipathy towards Latin names for trees and his insistence on always using 'a good English name'.

Regardless of Robinson's substantial contribution to arboriculture, he hardly uses the term himself, considering the cultivation and management of amenity trees as the province of horticulture. His frustration with the names of tree-related disciplines comes out in his book review of *English Estate Forestry* by Forbes where he complains about the "free use of such new words as 'sylviculture', 'arboriculture' and the like, leading to English which is far from pure, and ... only confuses a very simple subject" (Robinson 1905, vol. 3, 32)

The beginnings of professional representation

In the early development of arboriculture, as we now understand the term, its roots were based largely in the disciplines of horticulture and forestry. Sometimes the planting and care of trees was embraced by horticulture, particularly in the context of gardens. At the same time, especially in the context of country estates and woodlands, arboriculture or 'tree culture' was almost synonymous with forestry (James 1982, 122). Nevertheless, tree planting and care, particularly involving mature trees, was increasingly regarded as an activity requiring people with specialist skills and equipment (Steuart 1828). Despite that, finding a 'home' for these specialists in a distinct and separate profession was a long time in coming.

By the early nineteenth century, the study of horticulture was already experiencing the benefit of some professional representation. The Worshipful Company of Gardeners had been first mentioned in City of London Corporation records in 1345 and in 1605 was incorporated by Royal Charter (Steele 1964). For mainly affluent people with an interest in horticulture, there was the Royal Horticultural Society and other more local horticultural societies, some with an interest in specific plants. By the early 1850s there was still no professional representation for those engaged in forestry or with an interest in the subject.

Sir Henry Steuart was one of the first to recognise the importance of arboriculture as a distinct field of study, although his definition of this included aspects of what we now regard as forestry (Steuart 1828, 6–7). He was disappointed that it was invariably treated as just a branch of horticulture rather than a subject in its own right. To overcome this, he stressed the importance of the formation of "a Society, exclusively for the improvement of Arboriculture." Although Steuart's call for an arboricultural society had no immediate product, his views were given a sympathetic hearing among his friends and fellow landowners, particularly in Scotland. Eventually, the Scottish Arboricultural Society was founded in 1854 (Aldhous 2004). This was followed in 1882 by the founding of the English Arboricultural Society, no doubt influenced by the Scottish example (James 1982, 7).

Despite the name of these two societies, they were primarily concerned with forestry, or the planting and management of woodlands and plantations for their economic value. Nonetheless, there was still a degree of interest in what is now regarded as arboriculture. One of the two founders of the English Arboricultural Society was J. W. Robson, a nurseryman and authority on ornamental as well as forest trees (James 1982, 122). Furthermore, from an analysis of the occupations of the Society's first members taken from a list in 1884, it is probably that some 20 per cent were interested in arboriculture in terms of amenity trees.

The continuing use of the term arboriculture as almost synonymous with forestry is typified by two popular books published around this time. In 1868, John Grigor produced his first edition of *Arboriculture or a practical treatise on raising and managing forest trees* (Grigor 1881). While the book is titled 'arboriculture', it is concerned almost exclusively with forestry in a rural context. In 1880, William Ablett published *Arboriculture for Amateurs* (Ablett 1880). Although predominantly about forestry, this did take a slightly broader view of arboriculture by including some chapters on trees for ornamental use. However, urban trees were not mentioned.

In the late nineteenth century there were the beginnings of a debate about making a clear distinction between the scope of arboriculture and forestry. In the inaugural lecture of the School of Forestry at Edinburgh in 1889, Dr William Somerville defined 'forestry' as including formal management of land for sustained timber production and 'arboriculture' as relating to the more general management of individual trees (Aldhous 2004). While this may have stimulated some comment at the time, it does not appear to have any significant impact on the use of the terms.

French and American influences on British arboriculture

With the dawn of the twentieth century, there were two significant overseas influences on the development of British arboriculture. One came from France and the other from the United States of America.

In some major French cities, especially Paris, many of the tree-lined boulevards and public open spaces now contained large mature trees that required regular tree maintenance from skilled workers. This demand for skilled labour helped prompt the publication of various French works on arboriculture. One of these was published in 1864 by J.-L. Préclaire entitled *Traité Théorique et Pratique D'Arboriculture: Nouvelle Théorie* (Theoretical and practical treatise of arboriculture: new theory) (Préclaire 1864). This focused on the cultivation and pruning of trees, including fruit trees. As these works were in French, they had little direct influence on British arboriculture. Also in 1864, Count Des Cars (1881) published his book *Tree Pruning: A Treatise on Pruning Forest and Ornamental Trees* based on another great arboricultural work by M. de Courval in 1861 entitled *Taille et Conduite des Arbres Forestiers*. As Director of Parks in Paris, Des Cars held an internationally prestigious position that enabled him to influence arboricultural practices not only in France but also overseas. He recommended using coal tar as a wound dressing in preference to other preparations and this became accepted practice by American and many European arboriculturists. In 1881, the seventh edition of his *Tree Pruning* was translated into English by Charles Sargent, then Professor of Arboriculture at Harvard College (University) in the United States. As a result of this translation, the book became widely read by professionals on both sides of the Atlantic Ocean. As well as pioneering new arboricultural techniques, the French were also instrumental in developing specialist equipment for tree work. The 'City of Paris' safety-belt was a specially designed tree climbing aid, one of the first of its type, and used by pruning crews working on trees in Paris (Le Sueur 1934, 30) (Figure 11). It later became adopted by tree pruning crews in several other countries, including Britain.

The birthplace of modern arboriculture is often considered to be the United States of America around the beginning of the twentieth century. That popular view in Britain often fails to give due recognition to slightly earlier French and other European advances around that time. Developments in the United States were initially prompted by some major American works on tree pruning published towards the end of the nineteenth century, which also had a significant impact in Britain. One notable book was by Liberty Hyde Bailey, horticulturist and co-founder of the American Society of Horticultural Science. Bailey's *The Pruning-Book*, later known as *The Pruning Manual*, was first published in 1898 and went through numerous editions (Bailey 1898). Interestingly, it was largely through the efforts of an Englishman that modern commercial arboriculture became established in North America, which also later inspired similar developments in Britain.

John Davey was born in rural Somerset in 1846 and undertook an apprenticeship in horticulture before emigrating to the United States in 1873 (Pfleger 1977, 7). There he gained further experience of tree work before establishing the Davey Tree Expert Company, later to become one of the largest tree surgery companies in the world. He also wrote *The Tree Doctor*, a major work on tree care, first published at his own expense as a limited edition in 1901 (Davey 1901). Not only was this a pioneering work on the subject, it also arguably inspired the development of the arboricultural industry in Northern America. What was effectively a second expanded edition was published in 1907 and this achieved a much wider readership, including some professionals in Britain (Davey 1907).

Other American books on arboriculture and tree care followed, some of which were also published in Britain or became known there. Several of these had some relevance to urban trees and two are particularly notable. Prussian-

FIGURE 11. The 'City of Paris' safety-belt was one of the first specially designed tree climbing aids, used by tree pruning crews in Paris in the early 1900s. It was later adopted by tree workers employed by the City of London (Le Sueur 1934).

born Bernard Fernow's book *The Care of Trees in Lawn, Street and Park* had a profound influence in both the United States and Canada and also gained recognition on the other side of the Altantic (Fernow 1910). A specifically urban text by William Solotaroff (1911) entitled *Shade-Trees in Towns and Cities* was probably the first substantial modern text on urban tree management and set out some of the basic principles that over 50 years later were identified as 'urban forestry'. Of particularly significance was his idea of putting a financial value on urban trees to enable officials and politicians to more than justify the expense of tree management programmes. It is impossible to gauge the precise impact of these works on the theory and practice of urban tree management in Britain. They were certainly read by some British professionals and many of the practices were adopted in subsequent years. It is interesting to note that many British developments in arboriculture and urban tree management during the twentieth century often followed what had already happened in the United States.

British arboriculture from 1900–1945

As modern arboriculture was developing rapidly in North America from the 1900s, British arboriculture was also undergoing a period of significant transformation. The growth of public parks and street tree planting in the second half of the nineteenth century had established vast numbers of new trees in our towns and cities. By the beginning of the twentieth century, many of these were maturing and required routine tree maintenance, such as pruning, felling and remedial work. The 1900s also witnessed further programmes of street tree planting in many of our major cities.

While there were several American books of this period focusing on urban trees, there seems to be only one British author of note, Angus Webster. After Webster (1894) wrote a popular handbook on forestry that later went through five editions, he then focused on some arboricultural topics. In 1910, he produced Britain's first substantial book on urban trees entitled *Town Planting: And the trees, shrubs and other plants that are best adapted for resisting smoke* (Webster 1910). This was based on an essay for the Royal Scottish Arboricultural Society which won him their Gold Medal. It was followed by another book that looked at the care of individual trees entitled *Tree Wounds and Diseases* (Webster 1916). Two very significant general works on trees were also published around this time. Henry Elwes and Augustine Henry (1906) produced their classic text *The Trees of Great Britain and Ireland* that remains one of the world's great works on trees. It was followed shortly after by another classic from William Jackson Bean (1914) entitled *Trees and Shrubs Hardy in the British Isles*, which remains a standard textbook after five editions.

The First World War had a major impact on urban tree management in Britain. Much of this work would not have been considered essential and the men employed were desperately needed on the Western Front. While the loss of male gardeners resulted in a huge increase in female gardeners at horticultural establishments such as Kew (Paterson 2008, 172), there is no evidence that women replaced men in any significant numbers for tree work.

In the 1920s, the constantly increasing volume of tree work in Britain's towns and cities was stimulating a demand for more arboricultural expertise. Sadly, this was not being met with a sufficient supply of suitably trained and experienced personnel, particularly into municipal arboriculture, both at the level of manual worker and technician. While advances were being made in the theory and practice of arboriculture at an international level, particularly in the United States and France, the practice in Britain lagged some way behind. This situation appears to have continued throughout the 1930s. Frederick Balfour (1935) presented a paper to the Institution of Municipal and County Engineers in 1934 in which he complained about the poor standards of pruning on roadside trees undertaken by local authority staff with little or no arboricultural knowledge.

During the 1920s and '30s, the Royal Botanic Gardens at Kew became established as a 'centre of excellence' for arboriculture. Leading figures on the staff at Kew were establishing their reputations as authorities on the subject of tree care and pruning. One of the most notable was William Dallimore, who was also a world-renowned expert on conifers (Hadfield *et al.* 1980, 90). Dallimore spent most of his career at Kew, first as a student before moving to the arboretum and eventually rising to the position now known as Assistant Curator. His book *The Pruning of Trees and Shrubs* was first published in 1926 and was a description of the methods practised at Kew (Dallimore 1926). Another contribution from Kew was made by Arthur Osborn, in charge of the arboretum in the 1930s, with his book *Shrubs and Trees for the Garden* (Osborn 1933). Not to be left out, Edinburgh Botanic Gardens had its own early twentieth century expert in Professor Isaac Bayley Balfour, described by Frederick Balfour (no relation) as the best pruning authority of his time (Balfour 1935; Cotton 1945).

One individual who was not a product of either Kew or Edinburgh RBG stands out as the pre-eminent British arboriculturist of this era: Denis Le Sueur (Boulton 1969). Le Sueur began his career studying agriculture at Wye College from 1908–11. After serving in the Army during the First World War and recovering from his injuries, he studied arboriculture and forestry, later obtaining the special diploma in these subjects from the then Institution of Chartered Surveyors (Anon 1969). Le Sueur began his career as a forestry consultant in London, engaged frequently by the Corporation of the City of London where a significant portion of his work was with amenity trees. In 1925 he was appointed Head of Forestry at the Royal Agricultural College, Cirencester, and held this post until 1946. His most lasting contribution to arboriculture was his book *The Care and Repair of Ornamental Trees* (Le Sueur 1934). This was the most important work on practical tree care to be published in Britain in the first half of the twentieth century and the first to outline much of what we now understand to be modern arboricultural practice. Le Sueur was also aware of the important American texts then available and lists both

Fernow and Solotaroff in his own book, as well *Practical Tree Repair* by Elbert Peets (1915) which he considered the best work he had read.

While some of the techniques Le Sueur describes have now changed or are discouraged, there is much here that today's arboriculturist will recognise as good practice. For example, he criticised the use of metal bands in bracing as this eventually cuts into the tree and restricts the flow of sap. He also disapproved of the use of tar and concrete for wound dressing. However, he did give details of how to use concrete for cavity filling, something which had been recommended by Forsyth back in the 1800s, although he later questions the value of this in the second edition of his book (Le Sueur 1949, 86). He also recommended pruning branches to just outside the 'branch ring' rather than the common practice of 'flush cutting' (Le Sueur 1934, 18). This vital piece of pruning advice seems to have been forgotten by the arboricultural industry for nearly forty years until it was repeated as 'new' information in the 1970s (Shigo and Marx 1976).

Le Sueur was keen on promoting safety equipment and recommended the use of the 'City of Paris' safety-belt for all tree workers (Le Sueur 1934, 30) In the United States and on the Continent workman were frequently provided with such belts but in Britain they were seldom used even if provided. He introduced the belt to workers at the Corporation of the City of London in the 1930s, probably the only public authority at that time using it. Le Sueur later introduced the more advanced American Safety Sling (Le Sueur 1949, 52). He was always highly critical of tree workers who refused to use a rope and safety harness, preferring instead to 'free climb':

> There seems to be a definite streak of obstinacy in such people, who often work at a great height from which a fall may mean not only disablement but possibly a slow and ghastly death by impalement on park or other railings. Such belts need to be used at all times... No workman should have an idea that the use of such a belt is a confession of cowardice. The use of a safety-belt is a question of common sense.
>
> Le Sueur, 1934, 30

Le Sueur's book gives a good insight into the tools and equipment used by some British tree workers at this time (Figure 12). Before the development of the tree care industry in the United States, all this was relatively simple with usually just a length of rope, a hand saw and some paint. Now, new specialist equipment was being used by a few authorities such as the City of London, which in addition to safety equipment included different types of saw, including the pole saw. Interestingly, there is no mention in Le Sueur's book of any powered chainsaws, even though steam-powered saws had been used for felling in Britain as early as 1878 (Campbell-Culver 2006, 226) and petrol engine two-handed models were now available (Campana 1999, 366). In addition to a few progressive local authorities, there were also some developments in the commercial sector. During the 1930s, there emerged a few specialist companies offering tree surgery services, such as the English Tree Expert Company and the Chiltern Tree Surgeons (Bridgeman 1976a, 8).

By the 1930s, there was general agreement in most horticultural and forestry circles that arboriculture was a distinct discipline, even if it was still included under the umbrella of these two larger and more influential disciplines. Its definition had also evolved into that which we now recognise today. This distinction was then recognised officially by the both the Royal Scottish and English Arboricultural Societies which changed their names from arboriculture to forestry, in Scotland in 1930 and England in 1931 (James 1982, 49) The Royal English Forestry Society then announced that an Arboricultural Committee was being formed to ensure that this side of the Society's activities were not overlooked (*ibid.*, 123). This committee continued in operation until 1937 when it was replaced by the Arboricultural subdivision of the newly formed Technical Panel. This was not very active, especially during the war years, and was terminated in 1946.

Meanwhile, related disciplines were becoming increasingly organised in terms of professional representation. In the built

FIGURE 12. Moving a large tree in London during the 1920s in an operation requiring considerable skill and expense. The photo shows work undertaken by Barron and Company using a system of rollers (Le Sueur 1934).

environment sector the Royal Institute of British Architects had been formed as far back as 1834 (as the Institute of British Architects in London) and the Institute of Town Planning was founded 1914, becoming the Royal Town Planning Institute when its Royal Charter was granted in 1959 (RTPI 1989). In terms of the landscaped environment, in 1929 the British Association of Garden Architects became the Institute of Landscape Architects (Merriman 2006). During the early 1940s an increasing number of architects and planners were elected as members of the Institute of Landscape Architects which now sought to move away from its pre-war image as a 'domestic garden society'. While all these related professions were increasingly organised and influential, there was still no professional representation for arboriculturists.

The outbreak of the Second World War in 1939 had the effect of putting a major brake on any developments in British arboriculture. Public and private sector spending on tree work fell dramatically as did the number of people employed on planting and maintaining urban trees and woodlands. At the same time, considerable damage was inflicted on our urban forests and not just as a result of German bombing (Le Sueur 1949) (see Chapter 3).

British arboriculture comes of age

The period from the end of the Second World War in 1945 to the mid-1970s could be described as a 'coming of age' for British arboriculture. After centuries of living under the shadow of both horticulture and forestry, arboriculture finally emerged as a discipline in its own right. Along with this came huge advances in its practical development in both the public and private sectors. Furthermore, this was supported by specialist arboricultural education courses together with distinct professional representation for those employed in the emerging arboricultural industry.

The development of municipal arboriculture as a specialist service can be related to the immediate post-war period when the country was still in the grip of austerity measures (Winning 1973, 150). London was the initial pioneer in this and the first 'arboriculturally conscious' local authority. In 1953, the London County Council (LCC) appointed Ted Storey as Arboricultural Officer, the first full-time 'tree officer' post for any local authority in Britain (Bridgeman 2013, 215). The LCC (later the Greater London Council) also established the first local authority 'tree banks', extensive areas where young nursery stock could be grown on until it was a much larger size and then transplanted to various planting sites throughout the capital. With the increasing importance of tree planting in urban areas, these 'tree banks' were later replicated by other local authorities (Winning 1973, 157). During the late 1950s, semi-mature tree transplanting by local authorities became more widespread. This led to the development of new transplanting equipment that had remained much the same since the nineteenth century heydays of tree moving on private estates (Newman 1969). In 1963, Civic Trees was formed as one of the first commercial companies to specialise in this work (Mabbett 2011, 24).

Following London's lead, an increasing number of local authorities now recognised the importance of employing specialist 'tree officers' to deal with various aspects of amenity tree management within their districts. With the growth of full-time arboricultural education from the mid-1960s, an increasing number of these professionals came with arboricultural qualifications (Bridgeman 1976b) (see Chapter 2).

While there had been few specialist tree surgery companies in the 1930s, after the Second World War commercial arboriculture really took off in Britain. A number of new companies were formed, often by ex-servicemen who in trying to adjust to civilian life were looking for an outdoor occupation that involve a degree of excitement and possibly even risk. It was an era of pioneering tree surgery companies run by determined, hardworking and colourful characters. One of these, Tom Wilson, was a Canadian who had returned to England in 1947 to become manager of the English Tree Expert Company (Matthews and Draper 1971). When this company was wound up he held a similar post with the Tree Specialist Company. In 1951, Wilson and Bill Matthew formed Southern Tree Surgeons, which later became the largest tree care company in Britain.

Other companies established at this time included the wonderfully named Beeching of Ash formed by Jim Beeching in 1946, Northern Tree Surgeons formed in the mid-1950s by Conrad Jorgensen, and Honey Brothers formed by Peter and Tony Honey in 1957. This growth in commercial tree surgery companies was undoubtedly fuelled by the nation's economic recovery in the 1950s and early 60s. Not only did local and central government have more money to spend on urban and amenity trees but the increase in disposable income for many families was reflected in the booming popularity for gardening that also included spending money on garden trees (Way 2010, 162–75).

There is no doubt that these early British tree surgery companies were significantly influenced by developments in North America. Information was coming across the Atlantic in the form of books and magazines that promoted new ideas and practices. There was also personal contacts made, one of the first being when Tom Wilson attended the International Shade Tree Conference in Toronto in 1963 (Matthews and Draper 1971). As a result of overseas and also British-based contacts tree surgery companies and local authorities were introduced to new specialist equipment, such as improved types of chainsaws, winches and a wide range of tree surgery tools and fittings, all aiding the professional engaged in practical tree care (Bridgeman 1976a, 31). The use of safety equipment was now more accepted by staff, with improved safety-belts and harnesses, and climbing ropes made of nylon and polypropylene. The use of large mechanical equipment was also becoming common, with hydraulic platforms, stump-cutters and brushwood chippers proving popular among larger companies with the volume of work to justify them. In the early 1970s, Honey Brothers established the first British specialist company to retail arboricultural equipment and supplies to the industry, issuing their first catalogue of products in 1974 (Honey Brothers 1974).

The growing sophistication and potential hazards of tree surgery practices were now attracting calls for some form of regulation or control. From the mid-1960s, the British Standards Institution (BSI) issued a number of standards that were directly relevant to the arboricultural industry (Wells 1972). As with all BSI's work, these standards were intended to have a vital role in setting benchmarks for work specifications, training and as a way of 'raising the bar' for professionalism. In the arboricultural industry, the most significant of these was BS 3998: Recommendations for Tree Work published in March 1966. The Health and Safety at Work Act of 1974 was also to have major implications for the industry, although the full impact of this would be felt later.

Apart from the growing demand for practical tree care, there were also the beginnings of a small but steady demand for arboricultural consultancy services. Tree surgery companies had always given advice on trees and some had also offered consultancy services such as surveys, inspections and reports. Now some arboriculturists felt the time was right to establish companies that were exclusively focused on consultancy. Although consultancy work was undertaken back in the 1930s by a few experts such as Le Sueur, the first post-war consultancy company was probably Tree Conservation Ltd. This was formed by Dr Giles Biddle when he left Southern Tree Surgeons in the early 1970s (Jorgensen 1991, 20).

The rapid rise of professionalism in British arboriculture through the 1950s and 1960s was now prompting calls for some distinct professional representation for the arboricultural industry. The first to organise themselves were a number of tree surgery companies. Part of the inspiration for this was undoubtedly the International Shade Tree Conference (later the International Society of Arboriculture), initially formed in the United States in 1924 which by the 1960s represented professional arboriculturists in a number of other countries (Campana 1999). The Association of British Tree Surgeons and Arborists (ABTSA) was formed in 1963 after the principal members had been meeting informally for a short while (Bridgeman 2010a). Tom Wilson was the first Chairman of ABTSA and other founding members included Peter Honey, Bill Matthews, Jim Beeching and Conrad Jorgensen. In 1964, another specialist arboricultural organisation was formed, The Arboricultural Association, this time by mainly public-employed horticultural and landscape officers (Wells 1974, 217–9). Don Wells was the first Chairman and other founding members included Hubert Taylor, Derek Honour and Anthony Dunball. Both ABTSA and The Arboricultural Association aimed to raise standards in arboricultural work nationally and to promote the employment of skilled and qualified arboriculturists. The two organisations coexisted alongside each other for several years, although many arboriculturists were members of both. In 1974, it was agreed that the two organisations should merge, forming a new organisation called the Arboricultural Association (including ABTSA) that would be a unified and influential voice representing and promoting British arboriculture (Lewington 1974).

By the mid-1950s, there were still no separate qualifications in arboriculture, the subject being included as a part of some horticultural and forestry examinations. This finally changed through the initiative of the Royal Forestry Society of England, Wales and Northern Ireland (RFS) when it reformed its Arboricultural Committee in 1957 and proposed the introduction of two examinations in arboriculture, leading to a certificate and a diploma respectively (James 1982, 107). The first examination for the Certificate in Arboriculture was held in 1958 and the first examination for the Diploma in Arboriculture in 1959. The RFS received much encouragement to offer these qualifications from some prominent arboriculturists, particularly Hubert Taylor who took over as senior examiner on the death of George Taylor in 1961, a position he held for 10 years (Anon 1988). A three-week course to prepare candidates for the Certificate was offered at Cumberland and Westmoreland College of Agriculture and Horticulture at Newton Rigg (Bridgeman 1976b, 452).

In 1967, leading members of ABTSA approached Merrist Wood Agricultural College in Surrey to help organise and provide a venue for a two-day arboricultural course (Bridgeman 2010a, 25). The college was conveniently located close to the current Chair of ABTSA and some of its leading members. The new College

Principal, Tony Harris, was also very enthusiastic and supportive. The 'course' was effectively the first annual conference for ABTSA and comprised talks and demonstrations of tree surgery techniques by several of its members. What was envisaged to be a low-key one-off gathering signalled the start of a remarkable decade of growth for arboricultural education and the industry in general. The high numbers attending convinced the college that there was a demand for education and training in arboriculture. The initial step towards this was to appoint the country's first full-time Lecturer in Arboriculture, Peter Bridgeman, a Kew horticulture graduate who had previously worked as an arboriculturist at the GLC (Bridgeman 1991, 17). In September 1968, the first ten-week tree surgery course commenced, followed in 1970 by a three-week tree surgery course for foremen and a much broader and detailed one-year Certificate in Arboriculture course. In 1972, the first students embarked on a three-year course for the Ordinary National Diploma in Arboriculture. Full-time arboricultural education was now firmly established in Britain and Merrist Wood College was its national centre. There is no doubt that much of the success for this was due to the drive and ability of Peter Bridgeman, now Head of Department, who was ably assisted by a very supportive College Principal and industry organisations. Arboricultural courses were also being established at other education and training centres, often linked with the requirements of the Local Government Training Board that was emphasising the importance of arboriculture in its recommendations for parks and playing field staff (Winning 1973, 154).

As well as ABTSA's efforts, the Arboricultural Association was also taking a keen interest in developing arboricultural education. In an award-winning essay one member had stated that "the low standard of practical knowledge amongst local authority workmen is more or less universal" and he hoped training courses would soon address this (Kerr 1967, 97). In September 1969, the Association held a two-day symposium at Merrist Wood College to discuss the broad scope of arboricultural education and training and the development of appropriate examinations (Arboricultural Association, 1969). Some twenty people attended including representatives from ABTSA, Forestry Commission, Institute of Landscape Architects, Department of Education and Science, Askham Bryan College and other interested parties. The symposium appointed a Joint Working Party to consider the report of the symposium and make recommendations for the future development of arboricultural education and training. This reported in early in 1970 and its findings were then put to an open meeting arranged by the Association in conjunction with ABTSA at a three-day conference in September 1970 (Anon 1970). In 1970, the Standing Committee on Arboricultural Education was established to implement the Joint Working Party's recommendations (Bridgeman 2010b, 22). Frank Knight was appointed as Chairman of the Standing Committee with Peter Bridgeman as its Secretary (Bridgeman 1991, 18). Its main role was to promote and monitor developments in arboricultural education to ensure a consistently high standard of provision across the country.

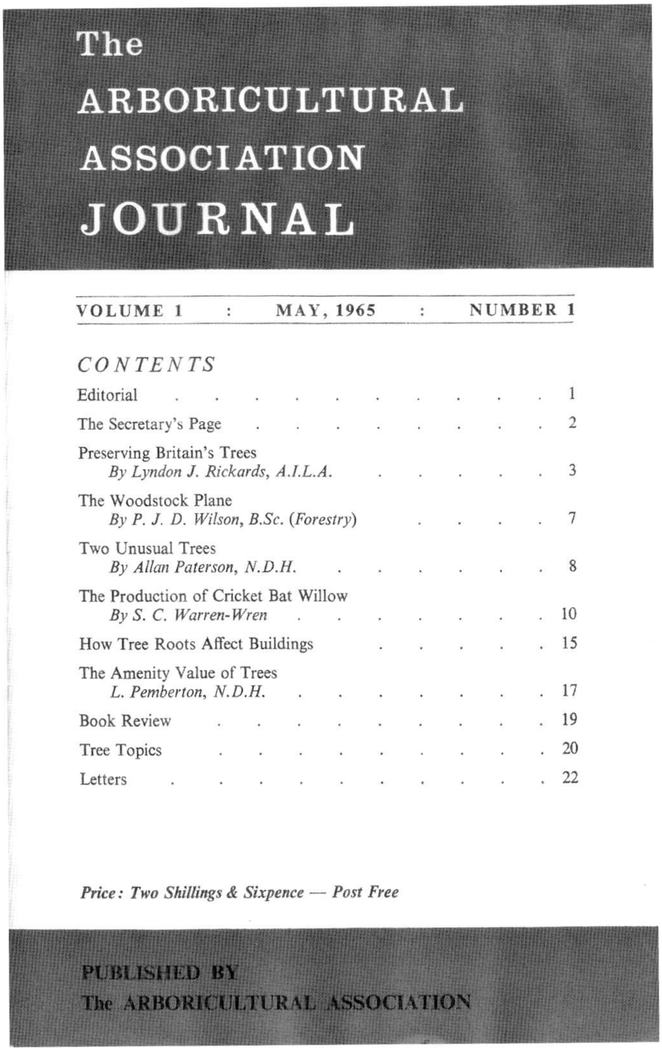

By the mid-1970s, the arboricultural industry had come a long way in a relatively short time. Since the end of the Second World War it had established itself as a distinct profession quite separate from horticulture and forestry. Furthermore, the industry now had its own professional representation in one unified organisation for British arboriculture. Arboricultural education was also firmly established with a range of full-time courses at Merrist Wood College. While these were still at the level of further education, there had been some talk of developing degrees in the subject, particularly at MSc level (Turner 1974). In a related development the Arboricultural Association's publication *The Arboricultural Journal* was also reflecting the industry's rising professionalism. In 1974, Dr Tom Hall was appointed Editor and in his twenty-four years in the post he transformed the *Journal* into an internationally-recognised academic publication and in the process did much to enhance the standing of British arboriculture (Johnston 2013) (Figure 13).

It is interesting to note the prominent role that people from RBG Kew played in this phase of development in British arboriculture. Many of the leading figures at this time had trained or were members of staff at this world famous centre for horticulture (Bridgeman 2013). These included Don Wells, Hubert Taylor, Sidney Pearce, Ted Storey, Frank Knight, Anthony Dunball and Peter Bridgeman. In 1966, seven of the thirteen members of the Arboricultural Association's Executive Committee were former staff or students from Kew. George Brown, a founder member of the Association also distinguished himself as Assistant Curator at Kew, a post he held until his retirement in 1977 (Storey 1980). In 1972, he published *The Pruning of Trees, Shrubs and Conifers* and this has remained one of the most authoritative works in arboricultural literature (Brown 1972).

The ARBORICULTURAL ASSOCIATION JOURNAL

VOLUME 1   :   MAY, 1965   :   NUMBER 1

CONTENTS

Price: Two Shillings & Sixpence — Post Free

PUBLISHED BY
The ARBORICULTURAL ASSOCIATION

FIGURE 13. The first issue of *The Arboricultural Association Journal* published in May 1965. Under the editorship of Dr Tom Hall during the 1970s-90s this became an internationally respected academic journal on arboriculture and urban forestry.

Difficult times for the arboricultural industry

The development of a unique range of arboricultural courses at Merrist Wood had established the college as the national centre for arboricultural education. In 1977, Peter Bridgeman left the college to form his own consultancy company. At the same time, he published a book entitled *Tree Surgery: A Complete Guide*, an important text that marked the remarkable progress made by British arboriculture over the past two decades (Bridgeman 1976a). However, the timing was unfortunate as new research in tree care around this time made some aspects of it rapidly out-of-date (see Chapter 3).

The success of arboricultural courses at Merrist Wood College led to other institutions starting full-time courses. By the mid-1970s, Myerscough (Lancashire), Cannington (Somerset), Reaseheath (Cheshire), Capel Manor (Enfield), Houghall (Durham) and Askham Bryan (Yorkshire) were among the colleges now offering full-time courses in arboriculture (Bridgeman 2010c, 43). Despite this progress, all these courses were still at further education (FE) level and arboricultural education remained 'grounded' at this level for many years. Attitudes within the industry were partly responsible. Many senior industry figures had never received any formal arboricultural education themselves and did not recognise the pressing need for this, particularly at management level. Furthermore, some major arboricultural contractors were stressing the shortage of skilled manual workers in the industry and believed any new courses should concentrate of teaching practical skills (Matthews 1982). It was not until 1992 that the breakthrough came when Myerscough College offered the first full-time higher education (HE) course with its Higher National Diploma in Arboriculture (Johnston and Hirons 2012, 105). This was followed in 1998 with Myerscough offering the first degree-level course with its BSc (Hons) in Arboriculture and the first MSc course in arboriculture in 2007. Although an MSc course had been offer by Middlesex University in 1998, this was actually an MSc in Resource Management with just an option in arboriculture (Johnston 2001, 163).

With the development of HE courses at Myerscough College, this institution now replaced Merrist Wood as the national centre for arboricultural education. That position was consolidated further when Myerscough became the first educational institution in the world to offer degree-level arboricultural courses through e-learning (Johnston and Hirons 2012). Students from as far away as Japan, Brazil, Australia and South Africa could now gain a degree in arboriculture at Myerscough via the internet. While these developments were major breakthroughs, the future of arboricultural education at HE level remained uncertain as it was still being taught through FE colleges. In contrast to related subjects such as forestry, horticulture and landscape architecture that had been firmly established in the university sector for many years, these FE colleges generally had a weak academic and research culture, and low salaries created difficulties in the recruitment of suitable academic staff (Johnston 2011,

34). There was also a major gender imbalance in the arboricultural industry that needed to be addressed (Britt and Johnston 2008, 319). The industry's public image of demanding practical work rather than the technical aspects of environmental management was undoubtedly a factor in ensuring very few women were pursuing a career in arboriculture.

The significant delay in the development of degree-level courses had been damaging to the professional standing of arboriculture. While related professions had produced graduate-level professionals for many decades, usually with chartered status, arboriculture had remained something of a craft-level occupation. As many tree officers were only qualified to FE level, this had limited their role in the more strategic aspects of urban tree management. The emergence of an urban forestry movement in Britain from the late 1980s also served to reinforce this. Originating in Canada in the mid-1960s, urban forestry ideas and practice represented a radical new approach to urban tree management that would have an enormous impact internationally (Johnston 1996) (see Chapter 2). While arboriculturists in North America had advanced their own professional standing by leading its development, the leadership of the Arboricultural Association in the late 1980s and 90s effectively disassociated itself from the concept and the movement in Britain. This resulted in a significant missed opportunity to promote arboriculture and arboriculturists (Johnston 1997, 109).

From the mid-1970s onwards, the arboricultural industry became increasing preoccupied with safety considerations following The Health and Safety at Work Act of 1974. In view of this, the Arboricultural Association set up a Working Party in 1986 to review all aspects of arboricultural practice (Preston 1991, 38). In an effort to establish standardised safe working practices in the industry, the Arboricultural Association initially tried to achieve this through the Forestry Safety Council (FSC). However, this was not satisfactory and after several frustrating years the FSC's remit was limited to forestry operations and the Arboricultural Safety Council (ASC) was formed. This comprised representatives from the Arboricultural Association together with some forestry, trade and professional bodies and local authority organisations. There is no doubt that the ASC filled a much needed role but a preoccupation with safety issues has continued to dominate many aspects of arboriculture over the past few decades (Eden 2007). This is undoubtedly a reflection of an increasingly risk-averse society but it has encouraged many local authority tree officers to take a more wary approach to urban tree management.

The unified voice for British arboriculture that was achieved with the 1974 merger was sadly short-lived. By the early 1990s, many Arboricultural Association members were unhappy with their leadership on several major issues. These included a lack of progress in promoting the professional status of arboriculturists and a perceived reluctance to develop overseas contacts (Johnston 2001, 154). The debate over various contentious issues was frequently played out in the trade and professional press, often in an acrimonious manner.

As these issues remained unresolved, various disillusioned groups of members decided to break away from the Arboricultural Association to form separate organisations which they hoped would better represent their interests. The first new group to be formed was the United Kingdom and Ireland Chapter of the International Society of Arboriculture (ISA). The ISA was, and still remains, the world's largest organisation for professional arborists with Chapters in many different countries. The National Association of Tree Officers and the Consulting Arborists Society were two further groups that were formed.

At the same time as this fragmentation, the Institute of Chartered Foresters (ICF) was emerging as a major player in the world of professional arboriculture. Founded in 1925 as the Society of Foresters of Great Britain (James 1981, 220), it was granted its Royal Charter in 1982 that included a definition of forestry that embraced arboriculture. Although the leadership of the Arboricultural Association at the time failed to recognise the implications of this, the Association's own efforts to become the professional body for British arboriculture were now effectively over. A watershed moment in the ICF's championing of arboriculture came in 2008 when it was granted a variation in its Royal Charter to allow its professional members working in the arboricultural industry to designate themselves 'Chartered Arboriculturist' (Ibrahim 2008). After all those years of arboriculturists trying to gain equal recognition with similar professionals with chartered status, this had finally arrived.

Despite some remarkable progress in the professional standing of British arboriculture over the past fifty years, the industry entered the twenty-first century in a somewhat fragile state. Some aspects of arboriculture's development over the previous twenty-five years had substantially weakened its initial momentum from the 1950s, '60s and early '70s. Nevertheless, there were also positive signs for the future. Efforts had begun to reverse the fragmented industry representation, while the Arboricultural Association was now embracing the concept of urban forestry and attempting to redefine its role as a trade association embracing the whole industry. Most importantly, the crucial environmental, economic and social role of urban trees was being increasingly recognised by society and government (see Chapter 2). This meant a continuing and hopefully growing demand for professional arboriculturists and urban foresters with the knowledge and experience to manage those trees.

References

Ablett, W. H. (1880) *Arboriculture for Amateurs: being instructions for the planting and cultivation of trees for ornament and use.* 'The Bazaar Office': London.

Allan, M. (1982) *William Robinson 1838–1935: Father of the English Flower Garden.* Faber and Faber: London.

Aldhous, J. R. (2004) A Short History of the Royal Scottish Forestry Society. *Scottish Forestry* 58(4), 7–13.

Amherst, A. (1896) *A History of Gardening in England.* Bernard Quaritch: London.

Anon (1969) A. D. C. Le Sueur. *Forestry* 42(2), 208.

Anon (1970) *Report on Arboricultural Training, Education and Examinations.* Joint Working Party on Arboricultural Education: Surrey.

Anon (1988) Arboricultural Association Award, 1988: Hubert Taylor MBE. *Arboricultural Journal* 12(4), 363–364.

Arboricultural Association (1969) *Symposium to discuss Arboricultural Education, Training and Examinations.* Symposium Report, October 1969. Arboricultural Association: Surrey.

Austen, R. (1653) *A Treatise of Fruit-trees.* Printed for Thomas Robinson: Oxford.

Bailey, L. H. (1898) *The Pruning-Book: A monograph of the pruning and training of plants as applied to American conditions.* The Macmillan Company: London.

Balfour, F. R. S. (1935) The Planting and After Care of Roadside Trees. *Quarterly Journal of Forestry* 29, 163–188.

Bean, W. J. (1914) *Trees and Shrubs Hardy in the British Isles.* In two volumes. John Murray: London.

Barron, W. (1852) *The British Winter Garden: Being a practical treatise on evergreens.* Bradbury and Evans: London.

Boutcher, W. (1775) *A Treatise on Forest-trees containing not only the best methods of their culture hitherto practiced, but a variety of new and useful discoveries, the result of many repeated experiments.* Printed by R. Fleming and sold by the author: Edinburgh.

Boulton, E. H. B. (1969) A. D. C. Le Sueur, OBE: An Appreciation. *The Arboricultural Association Journal* 1(9), 247–248.

Bridgeman, P. H. (1976a) *Tree Surgery: A complete guide.* David and Charles: Newton Abbot.

Bridgeman, P. H. (1976b) Arboricultural Education. *Arboricultural Journal* 2(10), 452–457.

Bridgeman, P. (1991) Twenty-five Years of Arboriculture: A personal view. In Hall, T. H. R. (ed.) *The First Twenty-five Years.* Arboricultural Association: Ampfield, Hampshire.

Bridgeman, P. (2010a) Merrist Wood 1967–1977. *Essential Arb.* Issue 31, 24–26.

Bridgeman, P. (2010b) Merrist Wood 1970–1973. *Essential Arb.* Issue 32, 22–23.

Bridgeman, P. (2010c) Merrist Wood 1974–1977. *Essential Arb.* Issue 33, 42–43.

Bridgeman, P. (2013) Kewites in Arboriculture. *The Journal of the Kew Guild* 16 (117), 215–221.

Britt, C. and Johnston, M. (2008) *Trees in Towns II: A new survey of urban trees in England and their condition and management.* Department for Communities and Local Government: London.

Brown, George E. (1972) *The Pruning of Trees, Shrubs and Conifers.* Faber and Faber: London.

Campana, R. J. (1999) *Arboriculture: History and Development in North America.* Michigan State University Press: East Lansing.

Campbell-Culver, M. (2006) *A Passion for Trees: The Legacy of John Evelyn.* Eden Project Books: London.

Chalmers, A. (1812) *The General Biographical Dictionary: containing an historical and critical account of the lives and writings of the most eminent persons in every nation, particularly the British and Irish, from the earliest accounts to the present time.* Vol. 22, p. 163. J. Nichols and Son: London.

Cook, M. (1676) *The Manner of Raising, Ordering, and Improving Forest-Trees: Also, How to Plant, Make and Keep Woods, Walks, Avenues, Lawns, Hedges, etc.* Peter Parker at the Leg and Star: London.

Cotton, A. D. (1945) Mr F. R. S. Balfour CVO, *Nature* 155, 357–358.

Dallimore, W. (1926) *The Pruning of Trees and Shrubs: Being a description of the methods practised in the Royal Botanic Gardens, Kew*. Dulau: Oxford

Davey, J. (1901) *The Tree Doctor: A Book on Tree Culture*. Published by the Author, Akron: Ohio.

Davey, J. (1907) *The Tree Doctor: The Care of Plants and Trees*. The Saalfield Publishing Company: New York, Akron and Chicago.

Des Cars, A. (1881) *Tree Pruning: A Treatise on Pruning Forest and Ornamental Trees*. Translated from the Seventh French Edition by Charles S. Sargent. A. Williams and Company: Boston.

Eden, N. (2007) Towards a National Standard for Tree Risk Inspections. *Arboricultural Journal* 30(2), 127–136.

Elwes, John H. and Henry, A. (1906) *The Trees of Great Britain and Ireland*. Printed privately: Edinburgh.

Elliott, P., Watkins, C. and Daniels, S. (2007) William Barron (1905–91) and Nineteenth Century British Arboriculture: Evergreens in Victorian Industrialising Society. In Elliott, P., Watkins, C. and Daniels, S. (eds) Cultural and Historical Geographies of the Arboretum. *Garden History*, Vol. 35: Supplement 2. 129–148.

Elliott, P., Watkins, C. and Daniels, S. (2011) *The British Arboretum: Trees, Science and Culture in the Nineteenth Century*. Pickering and Chatto: London.

Elliott, B. (2004) *The Royal Horticultural Society: A History 1804–2004*. Phillimore: Chichester.

Evelyn, J. (1664) *Sylva or a Discourse of Forest-Trees, and the propagation of timber in His Majesties Dominions*. First edition. J. Martyn and J. Allestry: London.

Evelyn, J. (1776) *Sylva or a Discourse of Forest-Trees, and the propagation of timber in His Majesties Dominions*. With notes by A. Hunter. A. Ward, etc: London.

Fairchild, T. (1722) *The City Gardener – Containing the most experienced method of cultivating and ordering such evergreens, fruit-trees, flowering shrubs, exotick plants, etc, as will be Ornamental, and thrive best in London Gardens*. Printed for T. Woodward: London.

Fernow, B. E. (1910) *The Care of Trees in Lawn, Street and Park*. Henry Holt and Company: New York.

Fitzherbert, A. (1882) *The Book of Husbandry by Master Fitzherbert*. Reprinted from the Edition of 1534 and edited with an introduction and glossarial index by the Rev. Walter W. Skeat. Published for the English Dialect Society by Trubner and Co: London.

Forsyth, W. (1802) *A Treatise on the Culture and Management of Fruit-Trees*. Published by Order of the Government by T. N. Longman, O. Rees, T. Cadell and others: London.

Gilpin, W. (1794) *Remarks on Forest Scenery and other Woodland Views*. Second edition. R. Blamire in the Strand: London.

Grigor, J. (1881) *Arboriculture or a practical treatise on raising and managing forest trees*. Second edition. Oliphant, Anderson and Ferrier: Edinburgh.

Hadfield, M. (1967) *Landscape with Trees*. Country Life: London.

Hadfield, M., Harling, R. and Highton, L. (1980) *British Gardeners: A Biographical Dictionary*. A. Zwemmer: London.

Hanbury, W. (1758) *An Essay on Planting and a Scheme for Making It Conducive to the Glory of God and the Advantage of Society*. S. Parker: Oxford.

Hanbury, W. (1770) *A Complete Body of Planting and Gardening. Containing the Natural History, Culture and Management of Deciduous and Evergreen Forest-Trees. Also Instructions for Laying-out and Disposing of Pleasure and Flower-gardens*. Volumes 1–2. Published for the author by E. and C. Dilly: London.

Hayes, S. (1794) *Practical Treatise on Planting and the Management of Woods and Coppices*. Published privately and printed by William Slater: Dundalk, Ireland.

Henrey, B. (1975) *British Botanical and Horticultural Literature before 1800. Vol. 1: Sixteenth and Seventeenth* Centuries. Oxford University Press: Oxford.

Hill, T. (1987) *The Gardener's Labyrinth*. Edited with an introduction by Richard Mabey. Oxford University Press: Oxford.

Hobhouse, P. (2002) *The Story of Gardening*. Dorling Kindersley: London.

Honey Brothers (1974) *The 1974/5 Honey Brothers Catalogue*. Honey Brothers: Peasmarsh.

Ibrahim, M. (2008) Institute creates chartered status for arboriculturists. *Horticulture Week*, 3 July. Available at: http://www.hortweek.com/Arboriculture/article/828775/Institute-creates-chartered-status-arboriculturists/ (accessed 29.7.2014).

James, N. D. G. (1981) *A History of English Forestry*. Basil Blackwell: Oxford.

James, N. D. G. (1982) *A Forest Centenary: A History of the Royal Forestry Society of England, Wales and Northern Ireland*. Basil Blackwell: Oxford.

Johnson, H. (2010) *Trees – A Lifetime's Journey through Forests, Woods and Gardens*. Mitchell Beazley: London.

Johnston, M. (1996) A Brief History of Urban Forestry in the United States. *Arboricultural Journal* 20, 257–278.

Johnston, M. (1997) The Early Development of Urban Forestry in Britain: Part I. *Arboricultural Journal* 21, 107–126.

Johnston, M. (2001) British Urban Forestry in Transition – Developments between 1993–1998, Part II. *Arboricultural Journal* 25, 153–178.

Johnston, M. (2011) The Future for the Arboricultural Industry. *Essential Arb.* Issue 38, 32–34.

Johnston, M. and Hirons, A. (2012) Going Online with Arboricultural Education. *Arboriculture and Urban Forestry* 38(3), 105–111.

Johnston, M. (2013) Dr Tom Hall – Obituary. *Arboricultural Journal* 35, 4–5.

Jorgensen, C. W. (1991) Silver Jubilee Commemorative Event 25 Years of Arboriculture. In Hall, T. H. R. (ed.) *The First Twenty-five Years*. Arboricultural Association: Ampfield.

Kerr, J. M. (1967) The problems of tree planting in streets. *The Arboricultural Association Journal* 1(4), 96–100.

Langley, B. (1728a) *New Principles of Gardening: Or the Laying out and Planting Parterres, Groves, Wildernesses, Labyrinths, Avenues, Parks, etc.* Printed for A Bettesworth and J. Batley in Peter-Noster Row: London.

Langley, B. (1728b) *A Sure Method of Improving Estates by the plantation of oak, elm, ash, beech and other timber-trees, coppice-woods, etc.* Francis Clay at the Bible, and Daniel Browne, at the Black Swan, without Temple-Bar: London.

Lawson, W. (1618) *A New Orchard and Garden, etc. With the Country-Housewifes Garden, etc.* W. Wilson, for E. Brewster and George Sawbridge: Fleetbridge.

Le Sueur, A. D. C. (1934) *The Care and Repair of Ornamental Trees*. Country Life: London.

Le Sueur, A. D. C. (1949) *The Care and Repair of Ornamental Trees*. Second edition. Country Life: London.

Lewington, W. R. (1974) The Merger with the Association of British Tree Surgeons and Arborists. *The Arboricultural Journal* 2(7), 227.

Loudon, J. C. (1835) *Encyclopaedia of Gardening, comprising the theory and practice of horticulture, floriculture, arboriculture and landscape-gardening*. A new edition. Longman, Rees, Orme, Brown, Green and Longmans: London.

Loudon, J. C. (1838a) *Arboretum et Fruticetum Britannicum or the Trees and Shrubs of Britain*. In eight volumes. Longman, Brown, Green and Longmans: London.

Loudon, J. C. (1838b) *The Suburban Gardener and Villa Companion*. Longman, Orme, Brown, Green and Longmans: London.

Loudon, J. C. (1840) *Landscape Gardening and Landscape Architecture of the Late Humphry Repton*. A new edition. Longman and Co and A. C. Black: Edinburgh.

Loudon, J. C. (1845) *Self-instruction for Young Gardeners, Foresters, Bailiffs, Land-Stewards, and Farmers*. Longmans, Green and Co: London.

Mabbett, T. (2011) Civic Trees on the Move. *Essential Arb*. Issue 38, 24–26.

Marshall, W. (1785) *Planting and Ornamental Gardening: A Practical Treatise*. J. Dodsley: London.

Mascall, L. (1569) *A Booke of the Arte and maner howe to plant and graffe all sortes of trees*, etc. Henrie Denham, for John Wight: London.

Massingham, B. (1978) William Robinson: A Portrait. *Garden History* 6(1), Spring 1978, 61–85.

Matthews, W. (1982) The Tree Scene in Great Britain. *Journal of Arboriculture* 8(7), 176–177.

Matthews, W. E. and Draper, A. G. (1971) Profile: F. T. Wilson. *The Arboricultural Association Journal* 1(12), 335–337.

Merriman, P. (2006) A New Look at the English Landscape: Landscape Architecture, Movement and the Aesthetics of Motorways in Early Postwar Britain. *Cultural Geographies* 13, 78–105.

Miller, P. (1735) *The Gardener's Dictionary: Containing the Methods of Cultivating and Improving the Kitchen, Fruit, and Flower Garden, as Also, the Physick Garden, Wilderness, Conservatory and Vineyard*. Abridged from the Folio Edition in two volumes. Printed for the Author and sold by C. Rivington: London.

Musgrave, T. (2007) *The Head Gardeners – Forgotten Heroes of Horticulture*. Aurum Press: London.

Newman, C. J. (1969) Introducing the Tree Spade. *The Arboricultural Association Journal* 1(8), 215–217.

Nicol, W. (1803) *The Practical Planter, Or, A Treatise on Forest Planting*. Second edition: corrected and improved. J. Scatcherd, Ave-Maria-Lane, and H. D. Symonds: London.

Osborn, A. (1933) *Shrubs and Trees for the Garden*. Ward, Lock: London.

Paterson, A. (2008) *The Gardens at Kew*. Frances Lincoln: London.

Peets, E. (1915) *Practical Tree Repair*. The Field and Queen (Horace Cox): London.

Pfleger, R. E. (1977) *Green Leaves: A History of The Davey Tree Expert Company*. The Pequot Press: Conneticut.

Pontey, W. (1808a) *The Forest Pruner or Timber Owner's Assistant*. Second Edition. J. Harding: London.

Pontey, W. (1808b) *The Profitable Planter: A treatise on the theory and practice of planting forest trees*. Second Edition. J. Harding: London.

Préclaire, J.-L. (1864) *Traité théorique et pratique d'arboriculture: nouvelle théorie*. Librairie Agricole De La Maison Rustique: Paris.

Preston, T. (1991) Arboricultural Safety Council. In Hall, T. H. R. (ed.) *The First Twenty-five Years*, 38–40. Arboricultural Association: Ampfield.

Quest-Ritson, C. (2001) *The English Garden: A Social History*. Penguin Group: London.

Ravenscroft, B. C. (1883) *Town Gardening*. George Routledge and Sons: London.

Robinson, W. (1869) *The Parks, Promenades and Gardens of Paris Described and*

Considered in Relation to the Wants of our Own Cities and of Public and Private Gardens. John Murray: London.

Robinson, W. (1870) *The Wild Garden or our Groves and Shrubberies made Beautiful*. John Murray: London.

Robinson, W. (1883) *The English Flower Garden*. John Murray: London.

Robinson, W. (1905) *Flora and Sylva*. Complete set published in three volumes, 1903–1905. Gardening Illustrated magazine: London.

Robinson, W. (1906) *The Garden Beautiful; Home Woods, Home landscape*. John Murray: London.

RTPI (1989) *Planning for Town and Country: Context and Achievement, 1914–1989*. 75th Anniversary brochure. Royal Town Planning Institute: London.

Schlich, W. (1889–1896) *A Manual of Forestry*. English translation in five volumes. Bradbury, Agnew and Company: London.

Shigo, A. and Marx, H. (1976) *RX for Wounded Trees*. AIB-387. United States Department of Agriculture Forest Service: Washington, DC.

Simo, M. L. (1988) *Loudon and the Landscape: From Country Seat to Metropolis*. Yale University Press: New Haven.

Society of Gardeners (1730) *Catalogus Plantarum, Tum Exoticarum tum Domesticicarum. A Catalogue of Trees, Shrubs, Plants and Flowers, both Exotic and Domestic, which are Proposed for Sale in the Gardens near London. Divided According to their Different Degrees of Hardiness, etc.* Society of Gardeners: London.

Solotaroff, W. (1911) *Shade-Trees in Towns and Cities*. John Wiley and Sons: New York.

Steele, A. F. (1964) *The Worshipful Company of Gardeners of London: A History of its Revival: 1890–1960*. Published privately: London.

Steuart, Sir H. (1828) *The Planter's Guide*. Second edition. John Murray: London

Storey, W. E. (1980) Obituary – George Brown. *Arboricultural Journal* 4(2), 177.

Strutt, J. (1830) *Sylva Britannica or Portraits of Forest Trees Distinguished for their Antiquity, Magnitude or Beauty*. Expanded edition. Longman, Rees, Orme, Brown and Green; London.

Tait, A. A. (1976) The Instant Landscape of Sir Henry Seuart. *The Burlington Magazine* 118(874), January 1976, 14–23.

Tjaden, W. (1983) The Gardeners Gazette 1837–1847and its rivals. *Garden History* 11(1), 70–78.

Trevelyan, G. M. (1951) *Illustrated English Social History. Volume Three: The Eighteenth Century*. Longmans, Green and Company: London.

Turner, A. L. (1974) Profile – Peter Wilson. *Arboricultural Journal* 2(7), 258–261.

University of Toronto (2012) *Ornamental Trees and Shrubs*. Thomas Fisher Rare Book Library. Available at: http://fisher.library.utoronto.ca/how-does-my-garden-grow/written-word/case2–4/trees-shrubs (accessed 29.7.2014).

Way, T. (2010) *A Nation of Gardeners: How the British Fell in Love with Gardening*. Prion (Carlton Publishing): London.

Webster, A. D. (1894) *Webster's Practical Forestry: A Popular Handbook on the Rearing and Growth of Trees for Profit and Ornament*. Second and enlarged edition. William Rider and Son: London.

Webster, A. D. (1910) *Town Planting: And the Trees, Shrubs, Herbaceous and Other Plants that are Best Adapted for Resisting Smoke*. George Routledge and Sons: London.

Webster, A. D. (1916) *Tree Wounds and Diseases: Their Prevention and Treatment*. Williams and Northgate: London.

Wells, D. V. (1974) The Arboricultural Association Ten Years on 1964–1974. *The Arboricultural Journal* 2(7), 217–226.

Wells, P. S. (1972) British Standards for Arboriculture. *The Arboricultural Association Journal* 2(3), 70–74.

Wilson, P. (2013) *A–Z of Tree Terms: A Companion to British Arboriculture*. Ethelburga House: Lyminge.

Winning, A. L. (1973) Arboriculture: the emerging specialism. *The Arboricultural Association Journal* 2(5), 148–160.

2

The Governance of Urban Trees

Landscape at any time and in any location is far more than just an expanse of scenery, whether this is natural or shaped by human activity. It can be 'read' as well as simply viewed and this is especially true of the urban landscape. Trees and woodlands in the landscape can be read as symbols in religious, psychological and political allegories (Mitchell 2002, 1). Furthermore, landscape can be considered not simply as an object to be seen or a text to be read, but as an instrument of cultural power or force, a central tool in the creation of various identities. Landscape is now a central theme in the study of cultural geography and the past twenty-five years have seen much research in this area (Wylie 2007).

If landscapes can be both symbols and instruments of cultural power, to understand the nature of those landscapes we must understand the social, economic and political forces at work behind this (Mitchell 2002, 1–2). For example, a purely aesthetic appreciation of the English landscape movement would be a quite limited perspective without placing this in the context of the enclosure of common fields and the dispossession of the English peasantry (Bermingham 1986). So, with our account of the history of trees in Britain's urban landscapes we must also place this in the context of the social, economic and political factors that have shape those treescapes throughout the centuries and which continue to have influence today.

Ownership, control and access to urban trees

In this chapter we examine some of the underlying forces at play in the history of trees in our urban landscapes. This will also be a feature in other chapters that look at distinct elements of these urban treescapes and the discussion here will help to give additional context to those different elements of the urban forest. Coming to a deeper understanding of the landscape is not always an easy task, particularly those landscapes that have been extensively shaped by human activity. They can often appear as 'scenery' or as 'nature' in a way that obscures and masks the social and economic conditions that go into their making (Daniels 1989). In order to go beyond the purely visual and aesthetic appreciation of historic urban treescapes in Britain, we explore some important questions, such as who owned the trees and landscape, who had access to this, who shaped those treescapes, and in whose benefit was this done?

These aspects of urban trees come within the scope of 'governance' and more specifically 'urban forest governance', a field of study that has only recently become widely recognised. Governance can be defined as the institutions, organisations, knowledge and processes involved in making policy and management decisions (Lawrence *et al.* 2011). The act of governing is closely bound up with issues of power and control and this is equally relevant in the planning and management of the urban forest (Lawrence *et al.* 2013). In the context of the ownership and management of the urban forest this has changed significantly in many different ways over the past few centuries. However, it could also be said that in some crucial respects little has actually changed.

Monarchs and aristocrats

When the Romans ended their occupation of Britain, the civil administration of their Governors was replaced by the rule of a succession of monarchs and local aristocrats. It was these individuals that were to have the power to significantly shape much of the urban landscape for several hundred years to come.

In the Medieval era, many of Britain's towns and cities were surrounded by defensive walls constructed to repel hostile forces and maintain the authority of the monarch or local aristocrat (Morris 1997, 12; Keene 2000, 83). These walls restricted urban growth which often resulted in intense competition for space and little room for public open space, except in churchyards or around the market place. Any trees were likely to be confined to the private gardens of wealthy and influential residents. The street pattern comprised mainly a complex network of irregular narrow lanes where the provision of any greenspace or trees, even if this had been possible, would have been regarded as inappropriate. Outside of these walls the public was often excluded from nearby woodland as this was frequently an exclusive hunting preserve for the monarchy and aristocracy (Young 1979).

As England became progressively more peaceful, the military need for defensive walls became less necessary and by the fourteenth century many were used mainly as customs barriers to protect the tradespeople within (Morris 1997, 12). The urban rich and powerful were also able to devote increasingly larger areas of their land to gardens. Not only were these private gardens a source of recreation and aesthetic pleasure, they also served as expressions of their owner's power and wealth to all those who visited (Quest-Ritson 2001, 4). Often, their scale and grandeur were intended to impress and please visiting monarchs, aristocrats and other influential people. In the case of Cardinal Wolsey and his magnificent gardens at Hampton Court, this had an unexpected impact on Henry VIII (MacLeod 1972, 4). As the two spent many hours strolling through the gardens discussing the important matters of state, Henry's admiration of Wolsey's magnificent landscape turned increasingly to jealousy. When Henry striped Wolsey of his power in 1529, he officially took over Hampton Court and made it his main London residence (Figure 14).

As some major cities expanded rapidly in the Elizabethan era consideration was given to controlling this sprawl. Elizabeth I introduced the first ever green belt in Britain by restricting new building construction around London to within three thousand paces of the City gates (MacLeod 1972, 291). Charles I was another monarch to have a personal interest in town planning and he prompted the development of one of the most imaginative new schemes of his age. Having been offended by the condition of the road and the houses along Long Acre, London, he resolved to change this (Sheppard 1970). In 1630, that led to the commissioning of Inigo Jones to design Covent Garden with its Italian-style piazza and associated buildings and gardens. For England, this concept of garden and city intertwined was an absolute innovation (Mowl 2010, 4) (See Chapter 4).

FIGURE 14. The beautiful and neatly manicured gardens of Cardinal Thomas Wolsey at Hampton Court near London were intended to impress and please his aristocratic and influential visitors. Henry VIII was so impressed that when he stripped Wolsey of his power in 1529 he took possession of the gardens, retained Wolsey's gardener and made the Palace his main London residence.

After the Great Fire of London in 1666, in which Covent Garden survived, John Evelyn proposed a scheme for a garden city that included a greenbelt of gardens and plantations to make London the envy of the world (Evelyn 1938). Christopher Wren and Robert Hooke also proposed equally ambitious and visionary plans. The rebuilding of London was an opportunity for new ideas in town planning but this was not taken by Charles II. Instead of seizing the moment with an imaginative redesigning of his capital that could have included many more trees and public open space, he succumbed to pressure from vested interests. Everything was put back as it was, apart from some major new buildings and broadening of selected streets. This historic lack of vision in seventeenth century London can be contrasted with the assertive approach of Napoleon III and Baron von Haussmann in rebuilding Paris in the nineteenth

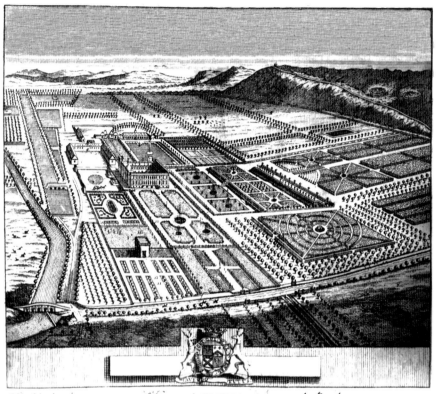

The Duke of DEVONSHIRE'S House at CHATSWORTH near the Peake DERBYSHIRE.

FIGURE 15. The Baroque gardens of the late seventeenth century were expressions of power and status, such as the gardens at Chatsworth House created for the first Duke of Devonshire between 1684–1707. The very formal and geometric arrangements of the trees were to find expression in some of the early urban landscapes. This is a view of the garden in 1699 from an engraving by the celebrated duo of Knyff and Kip (Cotton 1715).

century, now an internationally admired model of urban planning (Girouard 1985, 285–91).

While the sixteenth century gardens of the English Renaissance were often expressions of power, this feature of landscape design emphasising social and economic status was taken to an extreme in the Baroque gardens of the seventeenth century (Knyff and Kip 1984) (Figure 15). Much of the inspiration for this came from the French landscape designer André Le Nôtre and the breathtaking splendor of his gardens for Louis XIV at Versailles (Thompson 2006). Although many of the British Baroque gardens were not specifically urban, they are of significant interest here. Following the restoration of the monarchy in 1660, Charles II ordered some very impressive redevelopments at St James's Park and Hampton Court in London involving the planting of single and double avenues of trees (Mowl 2010, 49). These grand designs then influenced other redevelopments in London and on the country estates of the aristocracy. Following the new fashion set by the King the aristocracy showed its devotion to the restored monarchy by imitating that landscape style. The use of vast numbers of trees was a major part of these spectacular designs and they were arranged in grand avenues and walks radiating from the mansion and stretching out through extensive plantations into the distant countryside beyond. The scale and ambition of these landscapes was clearly meant to reflect the character of their owner. Close to the mansion in the more formal gardens, the trees were clipped into tightly regimented shapes projecting an image of order and control. The landscape created by Moses Cook for the Earl of Essex at Cassiobury in Hertfordshire was the epitome of this style and much admired (Cook 1676; Chambers 1993, 43). The considerable extravagance and expense of these formal gardens and landscapes following the Restoration gave a major boost to the horticultural industry in Britain (Mowl 2010, 48–61). While these park landscapes had beauty and style, they were enjoyed by only a small number of privileged owners and their guests. For the great majority of the population the landscapes of their neighbourhoods in both the towns and the countryside were often far from idyllic.

In the seventeenth century some provincial towns grew rapidly but the dominance of London remained. Its size then was relatively greater than it is today and surpassed its nearer rivals, Bristol and Norwich, with at least fifteen times the population (Trevelyan 1951, 43). This urban expansion had been prompted by significant commercial and industrial growth across Britain and fuelled a rising demand among middle class residents for high-status social and consumer services (Borsay 1989). This led to many towns becoming centres of fashionable society, places where the more affluent could engage in conspicuous consumption and reside in some elegance. The redevelopment of London after the Great Fire had encouraged many provincial towns in Britain to try to emulate these urban improvements. Meanwhile, the conditions for much of the working class in these urban centres were often desperate, with filthy and overcrowded housing, without sanitation and with almost no prospect of escape or respite from these seemingly endless slums. In many locations the only 'public' provision of trees and greenspace was in the local churchyard.

After the Hanoverian succession in 1714 power shifted from the crown to the landed aristocracy, which tended to spend much of its time in the country (Quest-Ritson 2001, 121). This growth in the wealth and power of the aristocracy, with its love of gracious estate living, gave another significant impetus to horticulture and landscaping. When the Hanoverians came to the throne, the popular style of garden design was to become far more simplified. This reflected the ascendency of the Whig party which tended to associate formal gardens, particularly in the French style, with royal tyranny and autocratic power (Everett 1994). As a consequence expenditure on the royal gardens dropped sharply and parterres and other formal and expensive features were less popular (Mowl 2010, 53). However, the extensive use of tree planting continued as before but now in a more informal style of landscape. Tree planting to create garden features had two advantages. By their mere size trees outgrew gardens and directed designers eventually towards the laying out of parks. The other advantage was that they were an investment. The opposite was true of parterres, which were best enjoyed on an intimate scale and were very expensive to establish and maintain and never gave a financial return.

By the late seventeenth and eighteenth century, some privileged individuals had access to urban trees and greenspace such as gardens and walks (a tree-lined promenade) belonging to some of the institutions and official bodies. For the working class in the major urban centres one of the few places where they could enjoy greenspace and trees, and also mingle with other classes, was in the pleasure gardens (Conlin, 2012). Initially emerging in the late seventeenth century and reaching their height of popularity in the eighteenth century, these forerunners of the Victorian public park were privately owned and charged for admission (see Chapter 5). During the eighteenth century, many larger towns and cities had at least one pleasure garden.

As the eighteenth century progressed the benefits of a strengthening economy were reflected in what has become known as the English Urban Renaissance (Borsay 1989). This was a period of dramatic urban improvements that transformed many urban landscapes under the influence of classical architecture and the emergent forces of planning. It also witnessed a remarkable expansion in the provision of public leisure. With the nation's growing prosperity spreading among the burgeoning urban middle class, there was a steady increase in people with the time and money to enjoy their leisure – and they often chose to do this in places planted with trees (Lawrence 2006, 61). This growth of the middle class led to tensions in the use of public space and threatened the established social hierarchies. Anyone who could now afford the right clothes could pose as a gentleman or a lady, creating confusion in the social standing of people seen in public. There was also a rapid increase in the size and political volatility of the urban working class, whose presence in streets and other public places was a concern for the upper class. These tensions were expressed in iron gates and armed guards and in greater social segregation of residential and amenity areas.

From the mid-eighteenth century, many towns and cities in Britain began to spill out over their medieval walls or long-established boundaries (Burnett 1986, 3–18). This was the beginning of what we now call the growth of suburbia. Generally, it was the more wealthy citizens who moved out to settle in these areas in what was classic greenfield development as former market gardens and fields were taken over by fashionable residential districts with large houses and gardens. In the original urban core, much of the existing structure of towns and cities remained the same. Throughout the eighteenth century, Britain did not embrace the general pattern of urban embellishment that was then flourishing on the Continent (Lawrence 2006, 76). Despite increased contact with the continent, often by members of the upper class on their 'Grand Tour', British cities maintained their own distinct green landscape forms. Walks were still being laid out, although most were relatively small compared to continental promenades, and many were in parks, gardens or outside the town. The most important forms of greenspace were private residential square gardens, small residential front gardens, and common land on the urban fringe. In the case of London, there was access to some of the Royal Parks for the general public. However, almost no consideration was given to the planting and maintenance of street trees.

In the late eighteenth and early nineteenth century large parts of Europe and North America were in the grips of revolutionary wars. Old monarchies were deposed and the political and social order changed radically (Hobsbawm 1975a). In Britain, the monarchy survived but was severely shaken by these events, particularly those in France that were close in more than just a physical sense. At the same time any agitation by working people in Britain to obtain reforms, such as extending the right to vote, was invariably met with brutal suppression, most infamously with the Peterloo Massacre of 1819 (Thompson 1963, 746–60). The upper class were determined that the 'Tree of Liberty' that had been planted by the people in the American and French revolutionary wars would never take root in British soil. Nevertheless, there were some fundamental changes in British society over this period, although the outward signs were less in politics and class relations than in culture and taste (Lawrence 2006, 145). The late Georgian and Regency periods from 1780 to 1820 witnessed a transformation from a British *ancien régime* to the beginnings of a new social order in which the middle class joined the aristocracy as the makers of urban form. The survival of the aristocracy in Britain was significant for the development of the urban landscape in three ways. First, the ownership of urban land in most cities was still firmly in the hands of a few aristocratic families. Secondly, the development of residential space in the city followed the patterns developed over the previous century. The residential square with its arboreal garden still served as the centrepiece for speculative real estate projects. And thirdly, there was a growing desire for living away from the centre of town, imbued with the symbols of an aristocratic country estate.

When the French and their allies had finally been defeated, the British economy entered a period of domestic growth. The years immediately after Waterloo saw a boom in house building and property speculation (Burnett 1986, 107). In turn, this gave a significant boost to the landscape and horticultural industries that led to an increase in the numbers of urban trees. A number of grand urban development schemes were undertaken during this period. The largest and most innovative was Regent's Park in London on land privately owned by the Prince Regent (MacLeod 1972, 250–5). The basic arrangement of the scheme was a series of large residential terraces surrounding a large private garden, not dissimilar to a classic residential square on a grand scale (Lawrence 2006, 148). The cost of the entire project was recovered by the sale of expensive leases for the residential properties, for which there was much demand because of the extensive landscape park at the centre of the development. Adjoining the project on the east side were two smaller schemes of detached and semi-detached villas with private gardens. All this was connected southwards to the palaces at Westminster by the new Regent Street. The route taken by this new thoroughfare was based on strong ideas about class segregation and privatization of open space. The new thoroughfare followed a path through the west side of London that carefully avoided the fashionable squares. In fact, it was laid out to form a class barrier. No trees were planted along the new route but were reserved instead for the Park and the private gardens of the villas. This reflected the widely-held view in British urban landscape design that trees did not really belong in the streets of commercial districts, only in residential areas. The late Sir John Summerson, the architectural historian, called Regent's Park a 'private garden city for the aristocracy' (Simo 1988, 230). This and similar smaller schemes in other cities highlighted the fact that despite the grim living conditions for much of the urban population, the rich could always buy into a comfortable and well-treed neighbourhood.

The Regency was a period of important experimentation in urban design and some of the most important innovations involved new uses of trees in the urban landscape (Lawrence 2006, 177). While the most extensive were in London, other key changes took place in provincial cities, such as Edinburgh and Bath. In the development of the new Regency towns such as Cheltenham many hundreds of forest trees were planted in the spacious streets and squares (Edwards 1962, 30). This period also saw the height of the urban enclosure movement, with at least seventeen separate acts passed for London, encompassing over thirty squares (Lawrence 2006, 146). The trend towards privatisation of the urban landscape that had become so prominent in the mid-eighteenth century became positively triumphant by the beginning of the nineteenth century. This also included the privatisation of streets as barriers were set up at the entrances to many new developments to exclude 'undesirables' and through traffic (Atkins 1993).

Although the increasing use of trees in accessible public open space was benefiting more people, the power to create such places remained in the hands of the aristocracy and upper class. The initial appearance of urban trees in malls, *cours* and promenades had strong associations with aristocratic government. Their function in these new urban landscape forms reflected their earlier role in formal gardens as structural elements in an extensive, geometrical and spatial composition that expressed the power of the landowner, and not just over the landscape. Meanwhile, in the countryside the 'improvements' to landed estates that were typified by the popularity of the English landscape designs of Bridgeman, Kent and Brown often involved the removal of these grand avenues and formal features. This move away from formal landscape design was a reflection of the underlying Whig political ideology that emphasised the market economy and the power of the individual capitalist (Everett 1994). This was in sharp contrast to the traditional Tory and more formal and aristocratic view of landscape.

The economy and the Industrial Revolution

The state of the economy has always had a major impact on urban greening and the extent of urban tree cover. When the economic climate is depressed, spending on urban trees and landscape is invariably cut back. When the economy is healthy, this is usually good news for those involved in the arboricultural, horticultural and landscape industries. Of course, the extent

FIGURE 16. 'Over London by Rail', a wood engraving by Gustave Doré in 1872, gives a grim image of typical working class housing at the height of the Industrial Revolution. There are no rear gardens, only small backyards for various household activities.

of urban tree cover is also a reflection of spending priorities. It seems that, historically, the urban forest and green infrastructure have often been relatively low priorities for central and local government, in comparison to other public services and built infrastructure.

By the late 1820s, the economic revival after Waterloo had turned into a slump reaching its height in the 1830s (Morton 1938, 377). This recession also inflicted severe economic pressures on the horticultural and landscape industries (Simo 1988, 161). Horticultural collections were dispersed, some nurserymen went bankrupt and head gardeners as well as apprentices were losing their jobs. In the view of John Claudius Loudon, the famous horticultural writer of the time, the recession challenged the very survival of landscape gardening as a profession.

The Industrial Revolution that had begun in the 1780s was now in full force across much of Britain by the 1830s and 40s (Hobsbawm 1975b). While the process of industrialisation is inevitably painful and must involve the erosion of traditional patterns of life, it was carried through with exceptional violence in Britain (Thompson 1963, 486). While it had brought unimaginable wealth to a very small number of people, the bulk of the population at the bottom of the social scale had suffered severe reductions in their living standards. Their abject poverty was detailed by Frederick Engels (1892) in his classic work *The Condition of the Working Class in England*, first published in 1844. Many of the novels of Charles Dickens written around the same time paint a similar picture of unrelenting poverty, sickness and exploitation. The desperate housing conditions for most working class families throughout this period have been very graphically described in the research of Enid Gauldie (1974) (Figure 16).

This was also a time of unprecedented population growth, particularly in England and Wales. It doubled between 1801 and 1851, due not only to an increase in the birth rate but also a fall in death rate due to medical advances (Burnett 1986, 4–7). The 1851 census showed that the population of England and Wales was for the first time mostly urban (some 54%), concentrated into a relatively small number of great cities and conurbations. This was due to vast numbers of people leaving the depressed countryside to find work in the new industrial centres, which were mainly in the north. There was a huge increase in the population of new industrial towns like Manchester, Leeds, Birmingham, Bradford, Sheffield and Nottingham. The growth of most towns was not planned; they grew by expansion outwards and by in-filling within existing boundaries. Usually, remaining pockets of spare land were built on first, rear gardens were acquired and additional rows of houses in-filled behind the earlier ones. The use of spare ground and rear gardens meant that any existing greenspace and urban trees in the locality were invariably lost. Then, the town began to move outwards, although the density of development was often similar. A typical example of this was the development of Nottingham (*ibid.*, 90). Known as the 'Fair City' in 1750, it had a population of 10,000 in 2,000 houses, many of the houses being located in gardens and orchards. By 1841, the population had exploded to 53,000, two-thirds of whom lived in back-to-back cottages, many of which were built in narrow courts on what had once been gardens and cherry-orchards.

When the Great Famine in Ireland began in 1845, the steady flow of Irish migrants into Britain over the previous decades turned dramatically into a flood. Tens of thousands of Irish men, women and children now arrived on these shores as part of over one million people who fled that terrible event (Swift 2002). Cities such as London, Liverpool, Glasgow and Manchester witnessed a huge influx of desperately poor and unhappy people further exacerbating the already difficult conditions. City centres now became the poorest areas and as poverty and crime increased they were no longer suitable environments to raise children or places where women could walk the streets without fear (Burnett 1986, 104). The worst period for sanitary conditions in the industrial regions was the middle of the nineteenth century rather than the beginning, because so many of the new houses had then had time to become slums, through initial jerry-built construction and lack of repair as the years went by (Trevelyan 1952, 13).

The Industrial Revolution was now creating sharp divisions between town and country and urban and rural life, which were becoming more marked each year (Trevelyan 1952, 3). The New Poor Law enacted by the Whig government in 1834 was an effort to address the conditions of the very poor by encouraging every able bodied person to seek some form of employment rather than face the fearful regime of the workhouse (Schama 2002, 180). Nevertheless, widespread conditions of abject poverty persisted. There was also a crucial difference now in that rural poverty in the past had usually been an individual misfortune; now in the cities it was a group grievance (Trevelyan 1952, 4). The importance of this would become apparent later when working people began to organise themselves to improve their conditions.

The rural poor who flocked to the towns had come from places where there were often plenty of trees and greenery in and around their villages (Trevelyan 1952, 13). Now they lived in extensive areas of back-to-back dwellings with no trees or greenspace around them. For their children, the only playground was usually the hard and dirty street. To millions of people their sadness at the loss of the pastoral life was vividly expressed in William Wordsworth's lyrical poem 'Poor Susan'. However, this 'divorce from nature' resulting from the Industrial Revolution was rather less significant than the violence inflicted on the 'human nature' of the working class through the factory system (Thompson 1963, 487). The mass of humanity working in the factories and mines were now in desperate conditions without any social services or public parks to compensate for the lost amenities and traditions of their former country life. At the same time, those rural conditions were also changing radically as the rural economy collapsed against a backdrop of enclosures, the Poor Laws and the decline of rural industries.

As people, traffic, dirt and disease multiplied in the towns and cities of the mid-nineteenth century, those who could afford to keep a horse and carriage moved out of the central areas to new suburban villas where the air was cleaner and the neighbourhoods safer (Burnett 1986, 13) (Figure 17). This middleclass separation of their businesses in the central areas and their homes in the suburbs allowed and encouraged the development of a new kind of social life. Invariable, it reinforced the growing separation of the sexes where, for women,

FIGURE 17. By the mid-nineteenth century, many wealthy urban residents had moved out of the increasingly dirty and overcrowded city-centres and purchased villas in the suburbs that were invariable located in pleasant and well-treed landscapes. This is Chester Terrace in Regent's Park, London, designed by John Nash and built in 1825.

the home became the centre of their existence and social life. Social interaction became increasing ordered and regulated by prearranged 'calls' for teas, dinners and parties. To ensure a degree of separation from any neighbours, detached houses with substantial gardens full of trees and shrubs became the preferred choice and terraced housing was increasingly out of favour. The semi-detached was also a popular choice in the inner suburbs where land prices were relatively high. Segregation was further enhanced if the house was situated in a private, unadopted estate which excluded undesirable visitors at the access points by gates and gatekeepers. However, such estates were not confined to the suburbs (Atkins 1993). In 1875, about 150 existed in central and western districts of London alone, and they were also well represented in other major cities. At the same time, the middle class also wanted the creation of some public places where genteel families could enjoy themselves (Lawrence 2006, 218). These spaces were usually marked by the presence of trees and the proliferation of trees in the urban landscape in the later Victorian era can be seen as marking an enlargement of the public space suitable for women and children. However, it is worth noting that very few middle class children were taken to public parks except by their nannies for short strolls.

The Industrial Revolution in the Victorian era had increased the disparity between the very rich and the very poor (Trevelyan 1952, 85). Instead of the life of the villages and market towns where there were some common features and interests, the industrial towns and cities had segregated classes geographically, divided into various social quarters. Access to trees and greenspace was often just one example of many that typified this class separation. Industrial change had also increased the numbers of the middle class of varying levels of health and comfort; and it had raised the standard of living for professional, technical and business people far above the unskilled labourer and slum-dweller.

Democracy and the rise of Local Authorities

From the 1830s onwards significant advances were made in the development of local government in Britain and some of the initial impetus for this began as a movement towards greater democracy at a national level (Morton 1938). At the beginning of the 1830s, the essential character of Parliament, the landed class that dominated it, the methods by which elections were carried out, and the very limited and unrepresentative electorate, had remained virtually unchanged from that which prevailed in the eighteenth century. However, the dramatic changes in society spawned by the Industrial Revolution ensured that the agitation of the working class for fundamental reform and democratic representation was now more widespread and more 'dangerous' than ever before. The passing of the Reform Act of 1832, proposed by the Whig government, was finally meant to address this issue. In reality, it was a fairly small step towards democracy. While the size of the electorate nearly doubled, it still only gave less than 8 per cent of the adult population (over the age of 21) the vote (Johnston 2013, 23).

Furthermore, although it abolished the 'Rotten Boroughs' and opened up the franchise to more property-owners, this succeeded in placing power more firmly in the hands of the industrialists and their middle class followers.

After the Reform Act 1832, the Whig's first task was to extend these gains into the sphere of local government (Morton 1938, 384). The Burgh Act 1833 in Scotland and the Municipal Corporations Act 1835 for England and Wales swept away a number of existing bodies and replaced them by corporations elected, in the first case, by the ten pound householders and in the second by all ratepayers. In practice, this ensured the control of most of the larger towns by the Whig middle class. After the 1832 Act the threat of 'revolution' posed by the rise of the Chartist movement that wanted a much greater measure of electoral reform was employed by the middle class to bring their own influence to bear on achieving some change. It was not until later in the century that the working class entered national and municipal politics as an independent force. In 1833, the Parliamentary Select Committee on Public Walks issued its report urging the development of urban public parks, partly motivated by a health agenda but also mindful of the potential role of these parks in pacifying the working class and heading off civil unrest (Conway 1991, 35–6) (see Chapter 5).

The Municipal Corporations Act 1835 (sometimes called the Municipal Reform Act) was notable for recognising the weakness of existing local government and marking the beginning of a formal structure for it (Conway 1991, 17). The four different types of institution responsible for local government in the 1830s were the Municipal Corporation, the Improvement Commission, which existed in most large towns, the Manorial Court and the Surveyors of Highways. The latter were to be found in every parish or town in the country, but the existence of the other three depended on local historical background. The Act gave a more liberal constitution to those boroughs where it applied, although major towns such as Manchester and Birmingham that lay outside its scope did not achieve municipal incorporation until 1838. The new Act did not automatically make the new corporations more effective as the divided responsibility between Corporations and Improvement Commissions continued. Nevertheless, the Act was an important measure that meant much to the social life of cities as the basis on which was to arise, during the next hundred years, the great structure of municipal social service for the benefit of all classes of the community, particularly the poor (Trevelyan 1952, 63–4). It was also notable in giving the local franchise to all ratepayers, ensuring the working class had a say at least in local elections and some 'official' influence over local government services.

The City of London was not included in the 1835 Act and it was twenty years later when a major breakthrough in local government occurred there (Chadwick 1966, 135). In 1855, the Metropolis Management Act set up the Metropolitan Board of Works, the first comprehensive body to be constituted for the government of London. The Board, which was appointed rather than elected, was responsible for the London-wide construction of infrastructure. This meant that the government could absolve itself completely of such irritations as the provision of public parks and street trees for London, and transfer them to the new body.

With a predominantly urban Britain, the poor sanitation and overcrowded conditions began to attract the attention of Parliament and fuel demands for a remedy (Trevelyan 1952, 65). The Public Health Act of 1848 was undoubtedly prompted by the recent cholera epidemic that had devastated the population of many urban slums. However, the main principle of the Act was permission rather than any compulsion to take action and it was not properly enacted by the municipalities for another twenty years. It was only in the 1870s, with the establishment of the Local Government Board to enforce the law and the rise of Joseph Chamberlain as the social-reforming Mayor of Birmingham, that a new age was eventually ushered in.

During the 1860s, much of the local improvement activity for housing and sanitation was an indirect result of the Local Government Act of 1858 which was a crucial step forward in formalising central and institutional control of buildings (Burnett 1986, 158–9). In 1871, the Public Parks Act allowed land to be donated for use as a public park. More importantly, the Public Health Act of 1875 gave local authorities powers to control housing conditions in their district, which also included the specifications for new streets and street improvements, thus raising the possibility of establishing street trees in the future. The Act also enabled a local authority to raise loans through government and to levy its own rate to create and manage parks (Lasdun 1991, 165).

Further steps to increase the parliamentary franchise were made in the Reform Act of 1867. For the first time, the Act enfranchised part of the male adult working class in England and Wales and a year later this led to the extension of the vote to all householders (Morton 1938, 406). This still left voteless all agricultural workers and those industrial workers, including a large proportion of miners, who did not live in Parliamentary Boroughs. Vast sections of the working class still had no right to vote for the government, both central and local, that regulated so many aspects of their lives. Indeed, universal suffrage for all men over 21 only came in 1918 and this was eventually extended to all women in 1928 (Johnston 2013, 59).

As the nineteenth century advanced, local government was gradually made to attend to its duties, by being subjected to democratic local election and to central control from Whitehall (Trevelyan 1952, 116–7). While the Municipal Reform Act of 1835 had affected only a limited number of towns, the scheme of urban self-government was made general throughout England and Wales by the Local Government Act of 1888. The Act established County Councils and County Boroughs, and the former included the creation of the London County Council in 1889, replacing the Metropolitan Board of Works. Although the government withdrew the sections of the legislation relating to the creation of District Councils, these were eventually brought into existence by the Local Government Act 1894.

Many towns and cities in the last decades of Victoria's reign had witnessed significant improvements in terms of improved living and working conditions and in the development of new infrastructure. This included the provision of public parks, street trees, and to some extent decent housing. The Housing of the Working Class Act of 1890 allowed local authorities either to buy whole areas of slums and clear them or to condemn individual buildings that detracted from their surroundings (Creese 1966, 78). While this Act had made some significant advances, it had also effectively promoted further class segregation by confining workers' housing to special areas.

An example in the improved provision of public services to address urban problems was set by Birmingham municipality in the 1870s under the enlightened Joseph Chamberlain. This was emulated by the London County Council twenty years later and was widely followed elsewhere (Trevelyan 1952, 117). These early pioneers of good local government saw the urgent need for improved public service, including trees and greenspace, against a background of severe social unrest and increasing class polarisation (Conway 1991, 35). They saw their work as part of the political process, hoping that by creating orderly urban parks and landscapes they would encourage 'orderly' people and help to avoid civil unrest (see Chapter 5).

As the nineteenth century drew to a close, the urban landscape of most towns and cities was a very extensive and complex mass of built development and infrastructure. The power to influence that landscape had moved away from the monarch and their elite circle of aristocrats. These very privileged individuals no longer had much interest in the wide aspects of urban planning, apart from the occasional pet project that was close to their heart (Lawrence 2006, 262). That power had now shifted decisively in favour of elected bodies, initially in central government but as the century progressed this was increasingly a matter for local government. Even if vast numbers of the adult population, particularly women, still did not have the vote, the working class were at last beginning to have some limited influence of the provision of public services. As the twentieth century dawned, almost every large city had its parks department and street or highways department. Although the power to influence the public urban landscape was now under the control of elected politicians and their officials, this did not mean a more democratic landscape. Decisions about what trees were planted and where they were planted more often reflected the wishes of the upper class than those of the working class. The provision of public trees and greenspace still often favoured those parts of the city where wealthy people lived, a pattern in the distribution of urban forest that largely continues today.

In terms of the privately-owned landscape, the middle and upper class could continue to buy themselves a well-treed and pleasantly green environment. Around their detached or semi-detached houses they had the gardens and the space within them to plant and enjoy their own trees. This was not surprising as the new money, the money for making gardens, was no longer in the countryside but in suburbia. The streets where they lived were often wider and more spacious enabling the growth of fine avenues of plane and lime trees. The tree-lined streets and leafy gardens gave these neighbourhoods an air of respectability and prosperity that many poorer people longed to enjoy themselves.

Development of municipal arboriculture

The Town Planning Act 1909 was a very significant piece of government legislation. It is often remembered today for preventing the building of 'back-to-back' housing, so symbolic of the poverty of the industrial towns and cities. It also gave local authorities (LAs) the power, for the first time, to plan for the future rather than just reacting to the problems of the past and trying to ameliorate them (Conway 1991, 221). This marked the date when the parks and open spaces movement became absorbed into town planning. LAs were now able to make far-reaching decisions about how to provide urban trees and greenspace for their residents.

With the development of LAs in Britain, urban tree management became essentially an LA function. Of course, central government has always set the legislative framework for LA tree management and influenced the overall funding of LA services. Nevertheless, what spending was actually allocated to tree management and how that was spent was generally a matter for the individual LA. In the early years of the twentieth century, some LAs gained a national reputation for promoting urban greening and tree planting in their districts. A notable example was the London Metropolitan Borough of Bermondsey which became a model for socialist reforms and social welfare programmes (Lebas 1999). Part of that involved municipal arboriculture and horticulture projects that were viewed as central to promoting a healthy and beautiful environment for all its citizens. For example, in 1919 the borough had 376 street trees but by 1927 this had increased dramatically to 6,101.

The Association of Municipal Engineers (subsequently called the Institution of Municipal Engineers) was formed in 1874, initially to address issues of public sanitation (Buchanan 1985). By the early twentieth century municipal engineering had become a very broad discipline embracing many of the responsibilities now entrusted to LAs. These included town planning, roads, parks, public housing and other areas of direct relevance to urban trees. Many of these areas were subsequently embraced by specialist individuals with their own professional bodies or associations but nevertheless still came under the overall responsibility of an individual whose job title was 'Borough Engineer' or similar. Another group of professionals in LAs that often had some responsibility for trees were the Borough Surveyors, who were qualified and experienced property professionals. Unfortunately, those LA officers with engineering and surveying backgrounds who had some responsibility for the planting and management of trees in streets, on LA land and other properties were unlikely to have any specialist expertise in this subject area. This was because there was no formal training or qualification yet available in arboriculture. However, that did not preclude them from making a valuable contribution to the planting and care of publicly owned trees in their district. It should be remembered it was these professionals who undertook the extensive planting of trees in parks and streets throughout the Victorian era and we still benefit from that legacy today. Some of these LA officers could also be proactive in encouraging more tree planting in privately owned gardens for public benefit. For example, in Birmingham in 1854, the Borough Surveyor persuaded certain property owners on the A38 Bristol Road to plant trees in their front gardens, thus making a valuable contribution to the streetscape that everyone could enjoy (Brown 1975, 302–3).

In contrast to those LA officers with engineering and surveying background, officers employed in parks departments with some responsibilities for trees probably had some limited arboricultural training. This was because they would have come from a horticultural background or, to a lesser extent, from landscape architecture, where some aspects of arboriculture were now being embraced as part of that training.

The situation where Borough Engineers, Borough Surveyors and Parks Superintendents and their staff were largely responsible for the planting and management of urban trees continued through the first half of the twentieth century. In most of the County Councils that lay outside major urban areas, responsibility for trees and woodlands rested with Forestry Officers who were invariably forestry-trained (Winning 1973, 152). That situation only changed from the 1950s onwards, with the development of arboricultural education and the appointment of the first tree officers in mainly urban LAs. Part of the pressure for that change came from some prominent individuals in the forestry sector with a good knowledge of urban trees. They were particularly critical of LAs in general for their lack of arboricultural expertise and poor standard of tree work (Balfour 1935). There was also awareness that since the 1930s many LAs in the United States now employed somebody with the title of 'Tree Warden', who had specialist arboricultural training. Furthermore, there was clearly a growing need among British LAs for this specialist expertise. With the development of public parks and the extensive planting of street trees over the past several decades, many LAs were now responsible for the management of literally tens of thousands of mature trees in their district.

The flowering of municipal arboriculture in Britain began in the immediate post-war period. London was the initial centre for this and the first 'arboriculturally conscious' local authority. In 1946, the London County Council (LCC) Parks Department created a new division to look after all its trees (Leathart 1973, 103). The person appointed to organise and run this division was Hubert Taylor, a Kew-trained horticulturist. With a team of 85 tree pruners, Taylor set about rectifying the lopping and topping that had disfigured so many of London's trees in the war years and before. In 1953, he appointed Ted Storey as Arboricultural Officer to take charge of these teams, the first full-time 'tree officer' post for any local authority in Britain (Bridgeman

2013, 215). Another team was established to take responsibility for the new Tree Preservation Orders that were being made in London (Leathart 1973, 104). In 1965, Peter Bridgeman was appointed Arboricultural Technical Officer to the now Greater London Council (GLC) under Hubert Taylor and Ted Storey (Bridgeman 1991, 17).

Other LAs outside of London were also beginning to recognise the importance of having specialist arboricultural staff and sections to deal with the planting, maintenance and management of their trees and woodlands. One of these was Sheffield City Council, due largely due to the efforts of Arroll Winning who became the city's Director of Recreation in 1969 (Jorgensen 1991, 20). Winning's time at Sheffield was notable for the development of an integrated and specialist arboricultural service across the whole LA (Winning 1973, 158). In the first instance, many of the new tree officer posts in LAs were titled 'arboricultural officer' and the Arboricultural Association (1971) produced a public leaflet with that title that set out the duties of such a post. It rapidly became apparent that the word 'arboriculture' meant little or nothing to most members of the public (Johnston and Rushton 1999, 3). Soon, an increasing number of LAs were using job titles such as 'Trees and Woodlands Officer', 'Tree Protection Officer' or just 'Tree Officer'. It is now common practice to refer to all these tree-related LA posts as 'tree officers'.

Despite the employment of more arboriculturists, some in the arboricultural industry felt that in many LAs' arboricultural operations were still being approached from a horticultural viewpoint which they considered was less proficient than this specialist work demanded (Winning 1973, 159). It should be noted that at that time, many LA parks managers were themselves concerned at a steady reduction of horticultural expertise among their staff, both officers and manual workers. This trend away from horticulture was reinforced by the Baines Report (1972) which merged LA Parks Departments with Recreation Services, Swimming Pools and the Arts (Conway 1991, 8). As a result, there was no separate budget for parks managers who now had to compete with these other areas, often resulting in a shortage of funds with reduced staff and maintenance levels. This inevitably had an impact on arboricultural operations that came under the responsibility of the parks departments. Despite the difficult times for many LA tree sections the need for specialist training was recognised by the Local Government Training Board in 1973 with the introduction of arboricultural courses for parks and playing field operatives (Bridgeman 1976, 455).

The reorganisation of local government for England and Wales in 1974 and for Scotland in 1975 had a huge impact on the structure and function of LAs across Britain. The changes were generally viewed as a significant opportunity for the advancement of municipal arboriculture (Winning 1973, 153). It was hoped that the radical reduction in the number of LAs would give opportunities for the adequate staffing of arboricultural specialists and funding for arboricultural services. There is no doubt that the number of LA tree officers across Britain increased in the wake of the reorganisation. However, the reorganisation did little to halt the growing fragmentation of LA tree management services, with responsibility for trees split across a number of different LA departments and sections. This had been exacerbated by the common problem of departmentalism where major sections within an organisation work to their own policies and agenda with minimal integration with the rest of the organisation.

Departmentalism in LAs has its roots in the nineteenth century origins of modern local government in Britain when the expansion of functions was undertaken through the establishment of single-purpose Boards (Cole and Fenwick 2003). When these Boards were abolished and their powers transferred to multi-purpose LAs, the separate functions retained substantial independence. With the emergence of new professions to administer these functions, 'departmentalist' attitudes among LA officers were encouraged rather than discouraged. LA tree management has traditionally been split between different departments because LA responsibilities for trees and woodlands cut across departmental boundaries (Britt and Johnston 2008, 545). A wide range of traditional LA departments, such as Parks, Housing, Highways, Education and Social Services invariable have some major responsibilities for trees, in many cases because they have trees growing on their land. Following the reorganisation of LAs in 1974, there was a further fragmentation of LA tree management services. Many more LAs now sought to create specialist tree officer posts in their Planning Department, to manage increasing responsibilities for trees through the implementation of planning legislation. Previously, the Planning Department might have sought this specialist arboricultural advice from a tree officer located in the Parks Department. This was all happening at a time when central government was becoming more proactive in urban tree management with the publication of its *Trees and Forestry* circular giving guidance to LAs (DoE 1978).

The election of a Conservative government in 1979, led by Margaret Thatcher, marked a radical change in the relationship between central and local government in Britain (Travers 2013). In the immediate post-war period, government in Britain had been characterised by a considerable amount of state intervention and socialist ideals. This was particularly evident in strategies relating to industry and town planning. The new Thatcher government would dramatically reverse many of those policies, while at the same time reasserting the power of central government. From the start, in 1979–80, there were cuts in government funding for LAs. The Local Government, Planning and Land Act 1980 introduced a new 'block grant' and compulsory competitive tendering (CCT) for direct labour organisations. The block grant allowed the government to impose grant penalties on councils which exceeded expenditure targets and CCT exposed many LA services, including grounds maintenance and tree work operations, to external competition (Ball 1995). CCT further fragmented LA tree services into 'the client' and 'the contractor' split and raised concerns in the industry about LAs' ability to maintain high standards in arboricultural work.

In 1999, CCT was replaced in England and Wales by the Labour government with a system known as Best Value.

In order to impose a legally enforceable ceiling on the rating power of LAs, Thatcher's government introduced 'rate-capping', which aimed to penalise high-spending authorities (Travers 2013). This led to many LAs making substantial cuts in their services in order to reduce their rates. Tree management was an obvious target for cuts in many LAs, being a relatively low priority in comparison to some other services. Some LAs suspended or seriously limited their tree planting programmes, perhaps hoping this would not be noticed immediately by the public. In other LAs the frequency of street tree pruning regimes were extended, although after a few years this led to many complaints from residents about trees blocking light to residential properties (Anon 1980). In a few LAs dead or dangerous street trees that had to be felled were left with their stumps at waist-height to save money on having to immediately remove this and reinstate the pavement. The stump was then perceived to be like a bollard and not a hazard to pedestrians. In some city streets these stumps remained for a number of years until the financial climate improved (Figure 18).

FIGURE 18. In the early 1980s some tree management programmes came under severe pressure due to restrictions on local authority spending introduced by the Thatcher government. Dead or dangerous street trees that had to be felled were often left with their stumps at waist-height to save money on immediately removing these. The stump was then perceived to be like a bollard and not a hazard to pedestrians. The condition of this stump in south London suggests it had been left for some time.

The 1980s and 1990s was a period of great change and uncertainty in municipal arboriculture with many LA tree management services under severe pressure from lack of funding and frequent restructuring. Nevertheless, as the twentieth century ended, major advances had been made over the past 50 years. For example, 69 per cent of LAs in Britain now had a least one specialist tree officer with most having an arboricultural qualification (Johnston and Rushton 1999, 3). Some of the larger urban LAs in major cities had specialist tree sections comprising several tree officers. Meanwhile there had been some less positive developments generally with local government's relationship with central government. Public parks and extensive street tree planting had developed in the Victorian era as a result of changing economic and social factors and a legislative framework that gradually gave LAs powers to confront some of the problems of urban living (Conway 1991, 7). By the end of the twentieth century that situation had been largely reversed with LA powers becoming increasingly restricted and more power centralised.

Statute law on tree protection

It seems there have always been some laws that relate to trees and woodlands and these have affected people's relationship with them. Here, we give a brief historical outline that focuses specifically on measures to promote tree protection and which generally have some urban perspective.

Urban trees, particularly those standing near the boundaries of properties, have always had the potential to cause 'nuisance' or be a potential hazard. This will have inevitably given rise to conflict between neighbouring owners in a variety of circumstances. This might include situations where trees fall over, branches encroach and roots cause subsidence. Much of this is regulated by common law that is derived from custom and precedents set in the courts and often built up over many centuries rather than by statutes passed by Parliament. Common law is outside the scope of this study.

Laws made in the medieval era that related to trees were generally part of 'forest law', initiated by William the Conqueror after 1066 and concerned with protecting game animals for hunting (Young 1979). Forest law was a complex system of rules and harsh penalties that included the protection of the 'vert' – the trees – and was a very early example of tree protection law. These laws applied almost entire to rural trees and woodland and were initiated by monarchs in their own interest. Of relevance to urban areas, a statute had to be passed in 1307 to prevent rectors from felling trees in church graveyards (Mynors 2002, 404). At that time, churchyards were probably one of the very few public places in towns and villages where ordinary people could enjoy trees and greenspace. By Tudor times the relentless felling and destruction of forests and woodlands in England was causing alarm and various acts of parliament were passed to try and regulate felling and planting (Lasdun 1991, 37). The Statute of Woods of 1544, which was a form of management plan for coppices, is notable as effectively the first legal formalisation of silviculture. Over 100 years later, John Evelyn (1664) gives an account 'Of the Laws and Statutes for the Preservation, and Improvement of Woods' in his classic book *Sylva* but there is no specific mention of urban trees.

While penalties for breaking forest law was usually very harsh (Young 1979, 11), the common inhabitants of these forests and other expanses of woodland often had rights and privileges that enabled them to graze animals and collect firewood (*ibid.*, 67–9). Outside of royal forests, many rural woodlands were historically regarded as common property (Lefevre 1894). However, in towns and cities residents would be conscious that trees and the land they stand on had recognised owners. This was particularly true before the advent of trees in public parks and streets. Trees would have stood in private property such as residential and institutional gardens and clearly not available to ordinary people as a source of timber, fuel or fruit.

Throughout the seventeenth and eighteenth centuries, severe punishments for destroying or damaging trees were aimed primarily at discouraging such action by ordinary people and to protect the property of the landed and upper class. In 1723, for example, Walpole's parliament put no fewer than fifty capital offences on the statute book and while most of them dealt with poaching, this included the felling of trees and even cutting tree limbs (Schama 2001, 361). Further protection for trees, which specifically included trees in urban locations, was incorporated into legislation enacted in the nineteenth century. The Malicious Injuries to Property Act 1827 was replaced with a revised version in the form of the Malicious Damage Act 1861 which specifically referred to unlawful and malicious damage to trees. This was spelt out in Section 20 and 21 of the Act, with the two sections defining different punishments for different costs of the damage (HM Government 1876). Section 20 stated:

> Whosoever shall unlawfully and maliciously cut, break, bark, root up, or otherwise destroy or damage the whole or any Part of any Tree, Sapling, or Shrub, or any Underwood, growing in any Park, Pleasure Ground, Garden, Orchard, or Avenue, or in any Ground adjoining or belonging to any Dwelling House, (in case the Amount of the Injury done shall exceed the Sum of One Pound) shall be guilty of Felony, and being convicted thereof shall be liable, at the Discretion of the Court, to be kept in Penal Servitude for the Term of Three Years, – or to be imprisoned for any Term not exceeding Two Years, with or without Hard Labour, and with or without Solitary Confinement, and, if a Male under the Age of Sixteen Years, with or without Whipping.

The Malicious Damage Act 1861 remained in force largely unchanged until it was mostly replaced by the Criminal Damage Act 1971. Another nineteenth century act to be passed included among its provision the protection of street trees. The Public Health Act 1875 ensured that responsibility not only for the street but also for the trees growing in the street was vested in the urban authority. However, it was not until the passing of the Public Health Amendment Act in 1890 that urban authorities were given powers specifically to plant and protect trees in any highway which was repairable by the inhabitants (Pettigrew 1937, 182). Any person who injured the trees was liable to a penalty and pay compensation to the LA as set by a court. A poster produced around that time for the Cardiff Local Board of Health (Figure 19) encourages the public to report any criminal behaviour by giving notice that:

> Any person destroying or damaging any tree or shrub planted by the Local Board in any of the streets or thoroughfares within the district, will be prosecuted, and that upon the conviction of the offender the sum of ten shillings will be paid to the person giving such information as shall lead thereto.
>
> Salmon *c.*1879

All Planning Acts since 1909 have made provision for the securing of amenity, and since the Town and Country Planning Act 1932 this has explicitly included the protection of trees (James 1972, 200). This and subsequent legislation has enabled a local planning authority to make Tree Preservation Orders (TPOs) 'in the interests of amenity' to ensure that important trees are protected for the public benefit (Mynors 2002, 408). The owner of the tree then has to apply

CARDIFF
Local Board of Health.

Destroying or Damaging
TREES!
TEN SHILLINGS REWARD.

NOTICE IS HEREBY GIVEN, that any Person DESTROYING or DAMAGING any TREE or SHRUB planted by the Local Board in any of the Streets or thoroughfares within the District, will be Prosecuted, and that upon the Conviction of any Offender, the sum of TEN SHILLINGS will be paid the Person giving such Information as shall lead thereto.

BY ORDER,
GEO. SALMON,
CLERK TO THE LOCAL BOARD OF HEALTH.

PRINTED AT THE WESTERN MAIL OFFICES, CARDIFF.

FIGURE 19. This poster from the Cardiff Health Board around 1879 is a warning to people not to destroy or damage trees. It offers a reward of ten shillings, a considerable sum then, to anyone giving information about such an offence that leads to a conviction.

to the authority for permission to carry out authorised works, unless under exceptional circumstances, for example, when the tree is posing an immediate danger. In the 1960s, when TPO legislation was relatively new, there was some concern that LAs were not making sufficient use of those powers, that they were failing to appreciate the value of established trees and recognise the frequent need for protection (Riseley 1969). Nowadays, the reverse is the case where some authorities have literally hundreds of TPOs but often without the resources to regularly monitor them (Britt and Johnston 2009, 233). Since 1967, some areas of special architectural or historic interest have been designated as a Conservation Area. Here, trees generally cannot be pruned or felled without giving six weeks prior notice to the authority, enabling it to issue a TPO if desired (Mynors 2002, 391).

Over the past 60 years LAs have also been able to protect privately-owned trees through a system of planning permissions and planning conditions required for development proposals. This arose with the Town and Country Planning Act 1947 that required all planning proposals, with only a few exceptions, to gain planning permission from the LA in order to proceed (Morris 1997, 89–91). Ownership by itself no longer conferred the right to develop the land. Permission to proceed could be granted with certain planning conditions that had to be met. These could include the protection and retention of trees already on the site or the planting of new trees in specified numbers and locations. The 1947 Act also introduced a requirement on LAs to produce Local Plans and Unitary Development Plans that outline what types of development in different districts and to indicate special areas on Local Plan Maps. These plans must include policies that promote the conservation and the natural beauty and amenity of the land. Consequently, most include policies for the protection and planting of trees. The planning system has subsequently undergone various revisions and is now consolidated in the Town and Country Planning Act 1990 for England and Wales and similar legislation for Scotland.

Another form of tree protection over the past several decades has been the system of felling licences, administered by the Forestry Commission, where a licence is required to fell trees over a specified volume of timber (James 1981,

226). These were initially introduced during the Second World War but retained afterwards as a useful conservation measure to conserve the nation's timber resources. The term 'felling' includes the wilful destruction of trees by any other means (Mynors 2002), 340). Although the measure applies to both urban and rural areas, a licence is not needed for the felling of fruit trees or trees growing in an orchard, garden, churchyard, or public open space.

The enactment of planning legislation that regulates what happens to privately owned trees, particularly TPO legislation, has always been controversial. The idea that an LA has the right to tell tree owners what they can or cannot do with their own trees has not been universally popular and frequently a source of annoyance to those subject to these orders. The argument that TPOs are sometimes necessary to ensure important trees are protected from their owners 'in the interests of public amenity' has left many people feeling that this is another example of the 'nanny state' where government is interfering unnecessarily with personal choice. This impression if often strengthened in situations where the tree owners themselves are recognised by their neighbours as tree enthusiasts or where the tree being protected is not regarded as an outstanding specimen or in clear public view. The argument has often been made that the time and money spent on administering TPOs would be better spent on publicly owned trees in streets and parks.

In Britain today we now have a considerable body of statute law relating to the governance of the urban forest. As with all legislation about local government, it takes two forms (Welch 1991, 35). It may permit LAs to take action if they want to, or compel them to do something whether they like it or not. Much of the legislation that relates to the latter concerns the LA's 'duty of care' to try to ensure 'so far as is reasonably practical' that its trees or tree work operations do not injure or cause damage to people or property. In an increasingly 'risk-averse' society and with many LAs suffering financial pressures and shortage of staff it is understandable that these aspects of governance have often dominated LA tree management in recent decades.

Community involvement and the voluntary sector

Before the mid-nineteenth century and the emergence of the Victorian parks movement, working class people and even those from the middle class generally had no say in the creation and management of public open space. It was a matter for the monarchy or landed aristocracy, who might, as a benevolent gesture, allow common people to have occasional access to some Royal Parks or privately owned gardens. The idea that they should be involved in the creation and management of any publicly-owned greenspace was unthinkable.

The story of how the first public parks were created with the support of middle and working class people is covered in Chapter 5. It is an inspiring tale that we will not cover here. Around the same time as these first parks, the enclosure of open fields was continuing apace, stimulated by the General

Enclosure Act of 1845 (Trevelyan 1952, 76). The movement for the enclosure of common land was halted at last in the decade 1865–75, by the protest not of the rural population but of the urban population, who objected to exclusion from its holiday playgrounds and rural breathing spaces. The Commons Preservation Society (CPS), a voluntary organisation founded in 1865, played a leading role in protecting this common land, much of it adjacent to urban areas and much of it with extensive woodland (Lefevre 1894) (see Chapter 5). It is now known as the Open Space Society and is Britain's oldest national conservation body.

Another early voluntary organisation with an interest in urban trees and greenspace was the Metropolitan Public Gardens Association (MPGA). This was founded in London in 1882 under the Chairmanship of Lord Brabazon and it continues to operate today (Malchow 1988, 109). Its main aim was the protection, preservation and acquiring of open space in London for public use. An additional aim was, and still is, the planting of trees. In support of its general interest in trees, the MPGA was also involved in promoting street tree planting in various parts of London in the years before and after First World War (Lebas 1999, 230).

Towards the end of the nineteenth century various civic societies were formed with an interest in the enhancement and protection of the urban environment, usually with a local focus (Hewitt 2012, 596). A civic society might be involved in campaigning for the conservation of historic buildings, higher standards in new buildings and improved traffic schemes to ease congestion. Many were also active in promoting tree protection and tree planting in their towns and cities, recognising trees as an important amenity for their area. In 1957, the civic movement was given a major boost when the government established the Civic Trust as an umbrella organisation for the different societies and to give a national voice to the movement (*ibid.*, 591). This has now been replaced by Civic Voice.

Some civic societies were formed that focused specifically on trees and woodlands in their respective town and cities. An early example was the Glasgow Tree Lovers Society, established in 1933 and which continues to operate today (GTLS 2013).The catalyst for this was correspondence in the *Glasgow Herald* about the cutting down of trees in University Avenue by the city authorities. It drew together like-minded people who collaborated with the local Civic Society as its Tree Planting Committee in an effort to make Glasgow more beautiful though planting and protecting trees and woodland. This soon evolved into a separate grouping calling itself the Glasgow Tree Lovers Society (GTLS) and within a year this had 300 members. The GTLS continues to organise a yearly programme of tree planting schemes and tree-related educational activities.

By the 1950s, a significant number of civic societies and similar organisations were involved in tree planting and tree-related activities in their districts. However, they often had quite limited influence over the tree management policies and practice of their own LAs. The selection, planting and management of the trees was undertaken by LA staff that provided a service on behalf of the public (Johnston 1985). The prevailing attitude among both the public and the

LA was that professional trained staff were employed for this work and therefore there was little point in questioning any decisions as they were 'the experts'. If the LA received few complaints it was generally assumed that the service was admired and appreciated. This detached approach is epitomised by the story of a women coming home to her council house after work to find that the Parks Department has planted a tree in her garden. When she contacts the LA to ask for an explanation she was told, "(Yours) just happened to be the every-other-house that gets a tree in the garden" (Ward 1974, 25).

The development of high-rise public housing from the 1950s to the late 1970s only served to exacerbate this gulf between LA tenants and trees. The demand on urban space had created vast areas of high density housing with no individual gardens (Burnett 1986, 301). As a result, these tenants were now out of touch with trees; quite literally, they did not come into contact with them (Johnston 1985, 122). For these less fortunate urban residents, the private ownership of trees and gardens was replaced by the provision of publicly-owned trees in communal open space. In reality this was often little more than a barren stretch of mown grass many floors below with hardly a tree in sight. Where there were trees, the LA continued to plant, maintain and manage these without any reference to the tenants. Understandably, this detached approach simply reinforced a sense of alienation from the trees. The phrase 'the council's trees' was not just a term of convenience but accurately described the tenants' perception of the trees (Figure 20).

By the 1980s and '90s, that detached approach to tree management was being widely criticised and discouraged (Johnston 1985). It was increasingly recognised that the provision of publicly-owned urban trees should not be regarded as just another public service to be operated with the same degree of detachment as the provision of street lighting. There were two major reasons for this shift in approach that largely prevail today. The first was a fundamental change in public attitudes that demanded it. The rapid growth of the voluntary sector over the past few decades has resulted in large numbers of locally-based environmental and conservation organisations, amenity societies and other community groups all wanting to be consulted and involved in the management of trees in their district. This has undoubtedly been a reflection of a general rise in environmental concerns across Britain through the 1960s to 80s that expressed itself nationally in 1989 when the Green Party gained 15 per cent of the vote in the European elections (Curtice 1989). The second factor was a significant shift in central and local government policy to reflect the public's growing interest in the environment and its desire to get involved with the decision-making process that affected this. The environment was now of considerable importance politically and the ever-expanding Department of the Environment had assumed far-reaching responsibilities for the quality of life in which trees played an appreciable part (Winning 1973, 148). The need to involve or at least consult with the public in the planning process was formally enshrined in the Town and Country Planning Act 1968. In 1969, the principle of consulting the public was elaborated in the Skeffington Report entitled *People and Planning* (Skeffington 1969). This report also led to the growth in number of

FIGURE 20. A small ornamental tree in communal open space on a GLC housing estate in Battersea in the 1970s. The local authority planted, maintained and removed these trees without any reference to the tenants. The phrase 'the council's trees' was not just a term of convenience but accurately described the tenants' perception of the trees.

amenity and conservation societies and an increase in their influence (Winning 1973, 151). Many of these newer conservation organisations, both at a national and local level, recognised the importance of trees, although that was more often expressed in a rural rather than an urban context.

In 1974, the government helped to set up The Tree Council, a voluntary sector umbrella body for UK organisations involved in tree planting, care and conservation. The idea was to keep up the momentum of the National Tree Planting Year, held the previous year. In 1975, one of its first actions was to organise National Tree Week which is now an annual event. In 1990, to support tree-related community involvement activities, The Tree Council launched a national network of volunteer Tree Wardens (Anon 1990). Tree Warden Schemes now operated in many towns and cities and well as rural districts, with assistance from their LA or local conservation organisation.

This is no doubt that the latter part of the twentieth century witnessed a steady increase in community involvement in LA tree management, largely prompted by urban forestry ideas and practice. However, this has not always led to increased involvement among disadvantaged and 'difficult to reach' groups within our urban communities (Johnston and Shimada 2004). In terms of deciding what happens to trees within their district, LAs sometimes seem to be unduly influenced by vocal and high-profile local groups rather than by the wishes of the broader community.

National urban tree planting initiatives

National tree planting initiatives have been a feature of British life since early times. In 1457, the English Parliament passed an Act to encourage more tree planting, followed in 1503 by a similar Act passed by the Scottish Parliament (Forestry Commission 2013). In the 1660s, John Evelyn's book *Sylva* inspired a national tree planting campaign to replant our much depleted traditional forests. In the eighteenth century other writers appealed to the patriotism of landowners and urged them to plant trees, especially oak, for the sake of the nation's wealth and Navy (James 1981). These initiatives met with varying degrees of success. By the end of the Napoleonic Wars, Britain's forest cover was at an all-time low. The government of the day became so alarmed by the situation that in 1815 it called for a national tree planting campaign, although again this focused on rural trees and forests (Forestry Commission 2013). In 1919, the Forestry Commission was established with its brief to plant extensive new forests across the country, particularly in upland areas. This was intended to ensure that Britain would always have a strategic reserve of timber in times of war and national crisis.

There was no clearly defined national tree planting initiative in Britain before 1900 that included a significant focus on urban trees. Of course, the Victorian parks movement was hugely important in establishing many urban trees but it was not just focused on the trees. By contrast, the first 'Arbor Day' to be held in the USA was in Nebraska in 1872 and within a few years this was being observed in many other states (Egleston 1896). This American national day of celebration for trees and tree planting, with a definite emphasis of trees in cities, towns and villages, has subsequently been adopted as an annual event in many other countries around the world. It took almost exactly another 100 years for something similar to be established in Britain. The 1920s saw the first significant national initiative to plant trees in and around urban areas. This was the work of the wonderfully named Roads Beautifying Association, a voluntary organisation formed in 1928 to promote roadside planting throughout Britain (Wells 1970) (see Chapter 6).

Royalist celebrations such as the coronation of a new monarch, the birth of a royal heir or the jubilee celebrations of a reigning monarch have often been the occasion for the creation of new parks and open spaces or a tree planting initiative (Lambert 2012). Possibly the most notable initiative for its tree planting component was held in 1936–37 to celebrate of the coronation of King George VI. The details are recorded in *The Royal Record of Tree Planting,* a publication that lists all the trees planted and the open spaces and recreation grounds created as part of this national effort (Coronation Planting Committee 1939).

In the 1960s, the Civic Trust launched its 'Plant More Trees' campaign, a government inspired national scheme to repopulate urban areas with large trees (Mabbett 2011). As part of this initiative, semi-mature tree transplanting by LAs became more widespread, often undertaken with the assistance of Civic Trees, a privately owned company specialising in this work that was founded in 1963 by Chris Newman. European Conservation Year, held in 1970, prompted many tree planting initiatives throughout Britain to mark the occasion (Winning 1973).

'Plant a Tree in '73' was a national tree planting campaign that is probably the most memorable of such initiatives in living memory. The campaign focused mainly on non-woodland trees in urban and suburban districts and was instigated by Sydney Chapman MP, who gained government backing for his idea. Many organisations, including LAs, schools, businesses and communities supported the campaign by planting or donating trees, or making land available. The campaign captured the public imagination, not least because of the concern

2. The Governance of Urban Trees

at that time about the loss of trees through Dutch elm disease. Despite the considerable public enthusiasm for the campaign and many thousands of trees planted, there was much criticism of this later, particularly in terms of the lack of planning for post-planting maintenance to ensure the trees survived (Rackham 1976, 178). There is a popular rhyme that sums up some of the cynicism that still surrounds this initiative and those held a few years later. It goes: "*Plant a tree in 73, plant some more in 74, see them die in 75, dead as sticks in 76.*" National Tree Week still continues as an annual event but now with greater attention to planting techniques and tree survival.

The principles and practice of urban forestry

The development of urban forestry over the past 50 years has had an enormous impact internationally on the management of urban trees, particularly in the area of governance. While the concept has its origins in Canada in the mid-1960s, urban forestry ideas and practice have now radically changed the whole approach to the management of urban trees and woodland in many other countries, including Britain (Jorgensen 1986; Johnston 1996). Urban forestry emphasises the importance of a planned, systematic and integrated approach to the management of the 'urban forest', the collective term for all the trees in and around a town or city (Johnston and Hirons 2014, 693–711). It also brings together in a multidiscipline approach all the relevant professionals from both the natural and social sciences, including arboriculturists, horticulturists, landscape architects, planners, sociologists and ecologists. With the development of urban forestry has come a growing recognition of the many environmental, economic and social benefits of urban trees. Urban forestry also focuses on the use of computerised management technology and the development of long-term tree management strategies, partnership working and community involvement. This approach is in contrast to the mainly unplanned, unsystematic and fragmented approach that has characterised urban tree 'management' since trees were first planted in our towns and cities. Sadly, this continues in many LAs in Britain, largely due to lack of funding and staff.

When the British urban forestry movement emerged in the late 1980s, there was some resistance to the concept among many arboriculturists (Johnston 1997a). While the reasons behind this are complex, they relate to a mistaken believe that it was a threat to the professional standing of arboriculturists and an attempt by foresters to 'take over' urban tree management. In reality, urban forestry is a multi-discipline approach that involves not only arboriculturists but also landscape architects, ecologists, foresters, horticulturists, planners and many others. Some of the negative reaction from arboriculturists also stemmed from a basic misunderstanding of the concept.

The British urban forestry movement had its origins in three separate initiatives (Johnston 1997a and 1997b). The first was the work of Northern Planners, a planning and landscape consultancy based in Scotland that incorporated the underlying principles into some of their projects in the early 1980s. The second was the 'Forest of London' Project, a tree planting and education initiative that was Britain's first city-wide urban forestry project. Work on this began in 1984 and when it was launched in 1987 it involved all of London's LAs, relevant voluntary organisations and hundreds of local community groups. It later inspired or influenced a number of similar 'Forest of...' projects in other cities. The third initiative arose in the Black Country in 1986 among a small group of planners and other professionals who were particularly interested in restoring the derelict and degraded land in the region. All three of these early urban forestry initiatives came together to help organise the First UK Conference on Urban Forestry, held in 1988 (Johnston 1997b). Called appropriately 'A Seed in Time', this was held in Wolverhampton and with 310 delegates was one of the largest tree conferences ever held in Britain.

Following the First UK Conference, many new projects and initiatives were launched and further national urban forestry conferences were held in 1991 and 1993 (Johnston 1999 and 2000). New initiatives included the launch of a quarterly magazine called *Urban Forests* and the establishment of the Black Country Urban Forestry Unit (BCUFU), which then became the National Urban Forestry Unit until this closed ten years later in 2005. The most high-profile initiative was the government's 'Forest for the Community' programme launched in 1989 by the Forestry Commission and the Countryside Commission. This aimed to create 12 new 'community forests' on the edge of major cities in England, each with the involvement of LAs in the region, major voluntary organisations and some private sector sponsorship (Johnston 1989). It was significant that this government-inspired initiative incorporated many urban forestry ideas and practice.

The urban forestry movement in Britain faded in the 1990s as its ideas and practice became accepted into the mainstream of urban tree management (Johnston 2007). Urban forestry was no longer a 'buzzword' but now accepted as just another name for modern urban tree management.

References

Anon (1980) They Can't See the Wood for the Trees. *Balham and Tooting News*, Friday 27 June, 1.

Anon (1990) National Tree Warden Network is Lunched. *Urban Forests* Magazine. Autumn 1990, Issue 5, 1. A Seed in Time: Hoddesdon, Hertfordshire.

Arboricultural Association (1971) *The Arboricultural Officer*. Leaflet published by the Arboricultural Association: Stansted.

Atkins. P. J. (1993) How the West End was Won: the Struggle to Remove Street Barriers in Victorian London. *Journal of Historical Geography* 19(3), 265–277.

Baines Report (1972) *The New Local Authorities; Management and Structures*. HMSO: London.

Balfour, F. R. S. (1935) The Planting and After Care of Roadside Trees. *Quarterly Journal of Forestry* 29, 163–188.

Ball, R. (1995) White Collar Compulsory Competitive Tendering (CCT): the

Death Knell for Arboricultural Officers and the End of Professional Street Tree Management. *Arboricultural Journal* 19(3), 285–293.

Bermingham, A. (1986) *Landscape and Ideology: The English Rustic Tradition, 1740–1860.* University of California Press: Berkeley and Los Angeles.

Borsay, P. (1989) *The English Urban Renaissance: Culture and Society in The Provincial Town 1660–1770.* Oxford University Press: Oxford.

Bridgeman, P. H. (1976) Arboricultural Education. *Arboricultural Journal* 2(10), 452–457.

Bridgeman, P. (1991) Twenty-five Years of Arboriculture: A personal view. In Hall, T. H. R. (ed.) *The First Twenty-five Years.* Arboricultural Association: Ampfield.

Bridgeman, P. (2013) Kewites in Arboriculture. *The Journal of the Kew Guild* 16 (117), 215–221.

Britt, C. and Johnston, M. (2008) *Trees in Towns II: A new survey of urban trees in England and their condition and management.* Department for Communities and Local Government: London.

Brown, D. (1975) Trees in Cities 2: Birmingham – City of a Million Trees. *Arboricultural Journal* 2(8), 302–306.

Buchanan, R. A. (1985) Institutional proliferation in the British Engineering Profession, 1847–1914. *The Economic History Review* 38(1), 42–60.

Burnett, J. (1986) *A Social History of Housing 1815–1985.* Second edition. Routledge: London and New York.

Chadwick, G. F. (1966) *The Park and the Town: Public landscape in the 19th and 20th centuries.* Frederick A. Praeger: New York and Washington.

Chambers, D. (1993) *The Planters of the English Landscape Garden: Botany, Trees, and the Georgics.* Yale University Press: New Haven and London.

Cole, M. and Fenwick, J. (2003) UK local government: the impact of modernization on departmentalism. *International Review of Administrative Sciences* 69(2), 259–270.

Conlin, J. (ed.) (2012) *The Pleasure Garden, from Vauxhall to Coney Island.* University of Pennsylvania Press: Philadelphia.

Conway, H. (1991) *People's Parks: The Design and Development of Victorian Parks in Britain.* Cambridge University Press: Cambridge.

Cook, M. (1676) *The Manner of Raising, Ordering, and Improving Forest-Trees: Also, How to Plant, Make and Keep Woods, Walks, Avenues, Lawns, Hedges, etc.* Peter Parker at the Leg and Star: London.

Coronation Planting Committee (1939) *The Royal Record of Tree Planting, The Provision of Open Spaces, Recreation Grounds and Other Schemes in Honour of the Coronation of His Majesty King George VI.* Cambridge University Press Cambridge.

Creese, W. (1966) *The Search for Environment: The Garden City: Before and After.* Yale University Press: New Haven and London.

Curtice, J. (1989) The 1989 European Election: protest or green tide? *Electoral Studies* 8(3), 217–230.

Daniels, S. (1989) Marxism, culture and the duplicity of landscape. In Peet, R. And Thrift, N. (eds) *New Models in Geography* Vol. 2. Unwin Hyman: London.

DoE (1978) *Trees and Forestry.* Circular 36/78. Joint Circular from the Department of the Environment and Welsh Office. HMSO: London.

Edwards, P. (1962) *Trees and the English Landscape.* G. Bell and Sons: London.

Egleston, N. H. (1896) *Arbor Day: Its History and Observance.* US Department of Agriculture: Washington.

Engels, F. (1892) *The Condition of the Working Class in England in 1844.* Swan Sonnenschein and Company: London.

Evelyn, J. (1641) *The Diary of John Evelyn*. Edited in 1901 from the original manuscript by William Bray in two volumes. Volume 1. M. Walter Dunne: New York and London.

Evelyn, J. (1664) *Sylva or a Discourse of Forest-Trees, and the Propagation of Timber in His Majesties Dominions*. First edition. J. Martyn and J. Allestry: London.

Evelyn, J. (1938) *London Revived, Consideration for its Rebuilding in 1666*. De Beer, E. S. (ed.). Oxford at the Clarendon Press: London.

Everett, N. (1994) *The Tory View of Landscape*. Yale University Press: New Haven and London.

Forestry Commission (2013) Sheep, Archers and Books. Timeline text version. Available at: http://www.forestry.gov.uk/forestry/infd-5rjk68 (accessed 2.8.2014)

Gauldie, E. (1974) *Cruel Habitations: History of Working Class Housing, 1780–1918*. Allen and Unwin: London.

Girouard, M. (1985) *Cities and People: A Social and Architectural History*. Yale University Press: New Haven and London.

GTLS (2013) *Chronological History*. Five-page factsheet issued by the Glasgow Tree Lovers Society: Glasgow.

Hewitt, L. E. (2012) Associational Culture and the Shaping of Urban Space: Civic Societies in Britain before 1960. *Urban History* 39(4), 590–606.

HM Government (1876) *Malicious Damage Act 1861*. Printed by George Edward Eyre and William Spottzswoode. Printers to the Queen's most Excellent Majesty: London.

Hobsbawm, E. (1975a) *The Age of Revolution: Europe 1789–1848*. Weidenfeld and Nicolson: London.

Hobsbawm, E. (1975b) *The Age of Capital 1848–1875*. Weidenfeld and Nicolson: London.

James, N. D. G. (1972) *The Arboriculturalist's Companion*. Basil Blackwell: Oxford.

James, N. D. G. (1981) *A History of English Forestry*. Basil Blackwell: Oxford.

Johnston, M. (1985) Community Forestry: a Sociological Approach to Urban Forestry *Arboricultural Journal* 9, 121–126.

Johnston, M. (1989) *Forests for the Community*. CCP No.270. Forestry Commission and Countryside Commission: Cheltenham.

Johnston, M. (1996) A Brief History of Urban Forestry in the United States. *Arboricultural Journal* 20, 257–278.

Johnston, M. (1997a) The Early Development of Urban Forestry in Britain: Part I. *Arboricultural Journal* 21, 107–126.

Johnston, M. (1997b) The Early Development of Urban Forestry in Britain: Part II.*Arboricultural Journal* 21, 317–330.

Johnston, M. (1999) The Springtime of Urban Forestry in Britain – Developments Between the 1st and 3rd Conferences, 1988–1993, Part I. *Arboricultural Journal* 23, 233–260.

Johnston, M. (2000) The Springtime of Urban Forestry in Britain – Developments Between the 1st and 3rd Conferences, 1988–1993, Part II. *Arboricultural Journal* 23, 313–341.

Johnston, M. (2009) Trees in Towns II: Government Recognition of Urban Forest Needs. In *Trees and Urban Climate Adaptation: An Agenda for Liveable Cities*. Proceedings on a Treework Environmental Practice (TEP) Seminar at The Royal Geographical Society, London. TEP: Bristol.

Johnston, M. and Hirons, A. (2014) Urban Trees. In Dixon, G. and Aldous, D. (eds) *Horticulture: Plants for People and Place, Volume 2 – Environmental Horticulture*. Springer: Heildelberg.

Johnston, M. and Rushton, B. S. (1999) *A Survey of Urban Forestry in Britain*. University of Ulster: Coleraine.

Johnston, M. and Shimada, L. D. (2004) Urban Forestry in a Multicultural Society. *Journal of Arboriculture* 185–192.

Johnston, N. (2013) *The History of the Parliamentary Franchise*. Research Paper 13/14, March 1, 2013. House of Commons Library: London.

Jorgensen, E. (1986) Urban Forestry in the Rearview Mirror. *Arboricultural Journal* 10, 177–190.

Jorgensen, C. W. (1991) Silver Jubilee Commemorative Event 25 Years of Arboriculture. In Hall, T. H. R. (ed.) *The First Twenty-five Years*. Arboricultural Association: Ampfield.

Keene, D. (2000) The Medieval Urban Landscape, AD 900–1540. In Waller, P. (ed.) *The English Urban Landscape*. Oxford University Press: Oxford.

Knyff, L. and Kip, J. (1984) *Britannia Illustrata*. J. Harris, and G. Jackson-Stops (eds). Published privately for the members of The National Trust by Paradigm Press: Bungay.

Lambert, D. (2012) *Jubilee-ation! A History of Royal Jubilees in Public Parks*. English Heritage: Swindon.

Lasdun, S. (1991) *The English Park: Royal, Private and Public*. Andre Deutsch: London.

Lawrence, A., Johnston, M., Konijnendijk, C. and De Vreese, R. (2011) *The Governance of (Peri-)urban Forestry in Europe, Briefing Paper 3. Workshop on Sharing Experiences on Urban and Peri-urban Forestry. 28 January 2011*. European Commission, Brussels. Available at: http://ec.europa.eu/agriculture/fore/events/28–01–2011/lawrence_en.pdf (accessed 2.8.2014)

Lawrence, A., De Vreese, R., Johnston, M., Konijnendijk, C. and Sanesi, G. (2013) Urban Forest Governance: Towards a Framework for Comparing Approaches. *Urban Forestry and Urban Greening* 12, 464–473.

Lawrence, H. W. (2006) *City Trees: A Historical Geography from the Renaissance Through the Nineteenth Century*. University of Virginia Press: Charlottesville and London.

Leathart, P. S. (1973) Profile: Hubert Taylor. *The Arboricultural Association Journal* 2(4), 101–105.

Lebas, E. (1999) The Making of a Socialist Arcadia: Arboriculture and Horticulture in the London Borough of Bermondsey after the Great War. *Garden History* 27(2), 219–237.

Lefevre, G. S. (1894) *English Commons and Forests*. Cassell and Company: London.

Longstaffe-Gowan, T. (2012) *The London Square: Gardens in the Midst of Town*. Yale University Press: New Haven and London.

Mabbett, T. (2011) Civic Trees on the move. *Essential Arb*. Issue 38, Autumn, 24–26.

MacLeod, D. (1972) *The Gardener's London*. Gerald Duckworth: London.

Malchow, H. L. (1985) Public Gardens and Social Action in Late Victorian London. *Victorian studies*, 97–124.

Mitchell, W. J. T. (ed.) (2002) *Landscape and Power*. Second edition. University of Chicago Press: Chicago.

Morris, E. S. (1997) *British Town Planning and Urban Design: Principles and Policies*. Addison Wesley Longmans: Harlow.

Morton, A. L. (1938) *A People's History of England*. Victor Gollancz: London.

Mowl, T. (2010) *Gentlemen Gardeners: The men who Created the English Landscape Garden*. The History Press; Gloucestershire.

Mynors, C. (2002) *The Law of Trees, Forests and Hedgerows*. Sweet and Maxwell: London.

Pettigrew, W. W. (1937) *Municipal Parks: Layout, Management and Administration*. The Journal of Park Administration: London.

Quest-Ritson, C. (2001) *The English Garden: A Social History*. Penguin Group: London.

Rackham, O. (1976) *Trees and Woodland in the British Landscape*. Archaeology in the Field Series. J. M. Dent and Sons: London.

Riseley, T. F. (1969) Street Trees – Liabilities or Assets? *The Arboricultural Association Journal* 1 (8), 194–198.

Salmon, G. (c.1879) *Destroying or Damaging Trees! Ten Shilling Reward*. Poster detailing the reward for information securing a conviction. Cardiff Local Board of Health: Cardiff.

Schama, S. (2002) *A History of Britain; Volume 3: The Fate of the Empire 1776–2000*. BBC Worldwide: London.

Sheppard, F. H. W. (1970). *Survey of London: volume 36: Covent Garden*. Institute of Historical Research, 25–34.

Skeffington, A. (1969) *People and Planning*. Report of the Committee on Public Participation in Planning ('Skeffington Report'). HMSO: London.

Simo, M. L. (1988) *Loudon and the Landscape: From Country Seat to Metropolis*. Yale University Press: New Haven and London.

Swift, R. (2002) *Irish Migrants in Britain 1815–1914: A Documentary History*. Cork University Press: Cork.

Thompson, E. P. (1963) *The Making of the English Working Class*. Victor Gollancz: London.

Thompson, I. (2006) *The Sun King's Garden: Louis XIV, André Le Nôtre And the Creation of the Gardens of Versailles*. Bloomsbury Publishing: London.

Travers, T. (2013) Local Government: Margaret Thatcher's 11-year war. *The Guardian – Professional*, Tuesday 9 April. Available at: http://www.guardian.co.uk/local-government-network/2013/apr/09/local-government-margaret-thatcher-war-politics (accessed 2.8.2014)

Trevelyan, G. M. (1951) *Illustrated English Social History. Volume Three: The Eighteenth Century*. Longmans, Green and Co: London.

Trevelyan, G. M. (1952) *Illustrated English Social History. Volume Four: The Nineteenth Century*. Longmans, Green and Co: London.

Ward, C. (1974) *Tenants Take Over*. Architectural Press: London.

Welch, D. (1991) *The Management of Urban Parks*. Longman Group UK Limited: Harlow.

Wells, D. V. (1970) History of the Roads Beautifying Association. *Arboricultural Association Journal* 1(11), 295–306.

Winning, Arroll L. (1973) Arboriculture – the Emerging Specialism. *Arboricultural Journal* 2(5), 148–160.

Young, C. R. (1979) *The Royal Forests of Mediaeval England*. Leicester University Press: Leicester.

Wylie, J. (2007) *Landscape*. Key Ideas in Geography series. Routledge: Oxford.

3

Threats to Urban Trees

Ever since the first human settlements were carved out of the ancient wildwood there have been threats to the health and survival of trees in the built environment. Our towns and cities are essentially human habitats not natural ones and many of the features of the built environment that make our lives comfortable, convenient and safe can also have a detrimental impact on trees.

Even at the best of times, the urban environment has been a tough habitat for trees. Lack of space and light, compacted and contaminated soil, suffocated roots and air pollution have taken their toll on the urban forest over the centuries. Then, either through lack of funding or just sheer neglect, there is often the absence of essential maintenance to ensure the trees, once planted, actually survive and flourish. Unlike trees in their natural habitat, urban trees invariably need significant and regular attention, particularly when young. Without this, many of those harmful agencies in the urban environment begin to attack the already weakened tree. The first symptoms of ill-health are often shown by the leaves. These turn yellow and then brown and fall prematurely. Dead twigs become dead branches as the tree steadily dies back. When death eventually comes, or even before this, the tree has to be removed for safety reasons. Many street trees and those planted in hard surfaces in built surroundings have a particularly difficult time. Even where these trees manage to survive, the slow reduction in crown size through die-back and the pruning of deadwood can give the appearance that the trees are steadily shrinking.

The threats to urban trees can come from many different sources. In this chapter we look at the numerous pressures on trees that have arisen over recent centuries as the physical structure of our towns and cities has become more dense and complex. We also focus on how 'forces of nature', such as wind, snow and drought, have periodically wrought havoc on urban tree populations during extreme weather conditions. While trees in any situation can be subject to attack from pests and diseases, some of these pathogens also have special significance in urban areas. Lastly, we give an outline of the historical development of research into trees and tree pathology, with the emphasis on urban trees.

Pressures from urban expansion and industrial development

There is little evidence from the Roman era of any conflict between trees and built development. The Romans did plant trees in British towns but these tended to be located in villa gardens (Jennings 2006) where they probably had sufficient space to grow without causing significant problems.

The expansion of British towns and cities over the centuries since Roman times has had a detrimental impact on the planting or retention of urban trees. As urban areas expanded and became denser, the existing tree cover generally suffered and declined. However, one hugely significant event in the fourteenth century saw that process thrown into reverse across much of Britain. The Black Death of 1348–49 affected both Britain and Ireland and resulted in the loss from plague of possibly half of the population of England (Trevelyan 1949, 8). While the social, political and economic consequences of this disaster were to herald enormous transformations in British society, the decimation of the urban population had a positive impact on the urban tree population that was to endure for many decades. As extensive areas of towns and cities were now devoid of people and falling into disrepair and decay, numerous gaps appeared in the urban fabric (Stott 1990, 44). Abandoned and derelict house sites became yards, gardens or more often just scrubland following natural colonisation by trees. In many towns and cities it took nearly 150 years for the population to recover and urban expansion, at least in England, to once again become the general pattern (Keene 2000, 75–8).

One of the common threats to urban trees to receive early attention was air pollution. This started to be a problem in the late sixteenth century, when numerous industrial and domestic properties in London and other major cities burned what was known as sea coal, brought by ship from Newcastle and other north-eastern ports (Willes 2014, 141). In 1661, John Evelyn published a pamphlet entitled *Fumifugium, or, The inconveniencie of the aer and smoak of London dissipated* (Evelyn, 1661). Although one of the earliest works on air pollution it made only limited reference to trees. In 1722, Thomas Fairchild went into the subject in far more detail in his influential book *The City Gardener*. He wrote:

> Now we must consider, that in places in London, where every part is encompassed with smoke, and the air is suffocated, or wants its true freedom; plants, which are generally used to the open air, will not always be healthful: and therefore I have now made it my business to consult what plants will live even in the worst air of chimneys, and the most pent up air that I know.
>
> Fairchild, 1722, 45

Much of Fairchild's book was devoted to a description of the trees, shrubs and flowers which would thrive best in London's polluted air. He was a London nurseryman and from his own experience recommended planting the plane tree in towns and cities for its resistance to pollution. When the Swedish botanist Pehr Kalm visited London in 1748 he noted that the numerous small gardens were commonly planted with trees and other plants that could withstand the coal-smoke (Longstaffe-Gowan 2001, 23–4).

With the coming of the Industrial Revolution and stream power, cities became even dirtier (Trinder 1982). Those residents that could afford it ensured their homes were at a safe distance away from the polluting factories. The wealthier suburbs were generally to the west of towns and cities, to avoid the air pollution that prevailing winds carried (Lawrence 2006, 224). As the problem of air pollution became more apparent, understanding of it also increased. The Victorians identified two types of air pollution, particulate and gaseous, and the different sources of each (Ravenscroft 1883, 6; Hartig 1894, 301). They also realised that very few conifers succeeded in or near industrial towns because when the dust and dirt clogged the stomata in the conifer needles, these remained on the tree for a few years, unlike deciduous trees that got fresh leaves every year. Fortunately, conifers with cypress-like foliage did fare a little better.

In early Victorian times, the view was held that air pollution damage was due to metallic poisons (arsenic, zinc and lead) present in the smoke, or in the soot deposited on the leaves. In the 1870s, investigations by researchers in Germany had shown that this damage is due entirely to the sulphurous acid present in the smoke, which was absorbed by the leaf surface (Hartig 1894, 301). It was also found, not unexpectedly, that the health of the foliage increased the greater the distance from the source of the smoke. Furthermore, in towns where it was only in winter that large quantities of coal were used as fuel, conifers alone suffered. Some industrial processes were also responsible for the emission of acid, the most notable being alkaline manufacture, the largest branch of the heavy chemical industry in nineteenth century Britain (Clapp 1994, 24). Towns such as Runcorn, Widnes and St Helens where this manufacture was located were notorious for the impurity of their air and trees would be killed for several miles to the leeward side of the alkaline works.

One of the main problems of Victorian park maintenance in industrial cities related to the effects of air pollution (Conway 1991, 180). Trees provided the main structure for any park planting but were unlikely to survive to maturity. Park superintendents were faced with the problem of creating a landscape in which trees had only a short lifespan instead of providing the permanent framework of the design (see Chapter 5). In Manchester in the mid-1850s, trees and other plants were carefully selected to withstand the conditions. A few decades later the problem had, if anything, become worse, and even plane trees could not withstand the Manchester atmosphere. One of the few trees to cope with the extensive pollution was the native black poplar (*Populus nigra* subsp *betulifolia*), which became known as the Manchester Poplar as it was much planted in the city's parks and streets and around industrial sites (Cooper 2006, 48–52). For about 100 years, these majestic trees graced the Greater Manchester skyline and brought much needed greenery to the drab and dirty urban fabric. Sadly, this fascinating population of trees is almost certainly now going to be lost as the result of the rapid spread of poplar scab, caused by a pathogenic fungus (*Venturia populina*), and first identified in the area in 2000. This unique and historic industrial treescape is disappearing fast and it seems nothing can be done to prevent it. The fate of the Manchester poplar highlights the danger of an over-reliance on a single species within a relatively small geographical area. Furthermore, these poplars were especially vulnerable as the vast majority had been raised through vegetative propagation and were generically identical clones, reducing significantly the resilience of the tree population.

As if to emphasise the importance attached to the threat of air pollution, Britain's first book specifically about urban trees focused on this topic. *Town Planting* was published in 1910 by Angus Webster and subtitled *The trees, shrubs and other plants that are best adapted for resisting smoke* (Webster 1910). Concerns about the problem continued into the 1920s and 30s. William Pettigrew (1928), an authority on parks management, highlighted the damage being inflicted on many urban trees in a report presented to the Smoke Abatement League of Great Britain in 1928, which was reported in both the *Gardeners Chronicle* and the *British Medical Journal*. This highlighted how impossible it was to grow pines trees within three miles of Manchester Town Hall.

The levels of air pollution in some major cities remained high until the late 1950s and trees, particularly conifers, continued to suffer. In London, the continual loss and damage to conifers and some evergreens in the pinetum at Kew Gardens led to the establishment of a separate National Pinetum in 1924 on land owned by the Forestry Commission at Bedgebury in Kent (Morgan 2003). It was not until the introduction of the Clean Air Act of 1956 and other antipollution legislation that the situation in some of our larger cities began to improve (Beckett *et al.* 1998).

It was not just pollution from the air that was a threat to urban trees; the harmful effects of various types of soil pollution were also being recognised in the late Victorian era (Hartig 1894, 281). Research, again in Germany, had shown that the roots of trees were injured by coal gas when large quantities escaped from pipes into the soil. Coal gas was now used throughout Victorian towns and cities in Britain for street and domestic lighting. Other substances poisonous to tree roots were also sometimes conveyed to the soil in large quantities in the impure water that flowed from factories. However, it was realised that the unhealthy condition or death of street trees was not always a result of air or soil pollution. The cause could often be found in the close paving of the streets and footpaths, which severely restricted the movement of water and air to tree-roots.

The Industrial Revolution transformed vast areas of the British urban landscape, not just in existing towns and cities but also in previously rural areas now engulfed by the rapid growth of industry and housing (Trinder 1982). Some parts of Britain became particularly notorious as industrial 'black spots'. The Black Country, an aptly named area of South Staffordshire and North Worcestershire, was one of the most heavily industrialised areas in late Victorian times. In 1851, the writer and traveller Samuel Sidney (1851) described the Black Country as an exceedingly bleak landscape, "where the pleasant green of pastures is almost unknown and ... the few trees are stunted and blasted."

Many historians have considered the early Industrial Revolution to have had a negative impact on the overall woodland cover of Britain. While not specifically effecting trees and woodlands located within our towns and cities, the influence of industry on woodland cover adjacent to major urban areas should be considered. According to the woodland historian Oliver Rackham (1976, 91–2), there has been an almost universal but mistaken belief among historians that the iron industry was responsible for the widespread destruction of English woodlands to provide fuel in the form of charcoal. He regards this as inherently implausible since through coppice management it was possible to achieve a sustainable supply of charcoal wood without the necessity and ever greater expenses of going further afield every year for supplies from virgin woodlands. To do otherwise would have been 'economic suicide' for the ironmasters. Most wanted to protect their investment and maintain their profits and that needed fuel for the future as well as the present (Hammersley 1973). Rackham mentions the opposite thesis, that iron and other industries preserved and even created woodland. Why, then, were the ironmasters persistently accused of the wholesale destruction of woodlands by politicians and the public at the time? Perhaps the answer lies partly in the over-reaction of the public which (then as now) thought all trees were irreplaceable. There were also genuine conflicts of interest when industrialists took over woods that were already being used for other purposes. Later in the Industrial Revolution, coal was substituted for wood in different industries, not because wood was scarce but because coal was cheap and falling in price, its labour costs being less (Rackham 2003, 153).

There is evidence of quite early efforts to use forestry as a way of restoring land devastated by the Industrial Revolution and one significant initiative was the Midlands Reafforesting Association (MRA), formed in 1903 (Webber 2008). As a result of industrial contraction in the latter part of the nineteenth century, vast swathes of derelict land had emerged within the Black Country. Although the MRA planted up sites totalling 83 acres (33 ha) before dissolving in 1925, it failed in its mission of reafforesting the Black Country. Nevertheless, its main legacy was in literally 'preparing the ground' for other local organisations and government agencies that emerged some 60 years later, which were able to have a much greater success in greening those blighted landscapes.

While the Industrial Revolution had a very negative impact on the Britain's urban tree cover, the latter part of the Victorian era witnessed a remarkable renaissance in urban greenery in many of our towns and cities. New public parks were created and many street trees planted, developments covered in other chapters of this book. However, as Britain became an increasingly urban and industrial country the pressures on the growing numbers of trees in our towns and cities also increased, both in their range and extent.

Trees in any situation require adequate space for their roots and crown to grow if they are to flourish and reach maturity. Sufficient growing space, both above and below ground, has always been at a premium in towns and cities, particularly since the Industrial Revolution. In the built-up portions of London, Edinburgh, Bristol and other cities it was the residential squares that provided the superior places for planting trees. However, as the trees grew to maturity in some of the older squares, there were complaints about the dank shade they produced, and they were redesigned to make them more open (Lawrence 2006, 77). A positive change in the urban landscapes of Britain came with improvements in infrastructure. The Westminster Paving Act of 1762 pioneered the way for separate pedestrian zones on either side of our streets. While this had no immediate impact on the planting of trees, it would provide a protected place in the urban landscape for trees in the nineteenth century (see Chapter 6).

The polluted and confined urban environment has always limited the range of tree species that could be grown in our towns and cities. Nevertheless, the range was greatly extended in the eighteenth and nineteenth centuries following the intrepid exploits of the plant hunters in faraway lands and the introduction of new species (Mitchell 1989). By 1820, exotic species of trees were becoming common in private gardens, and by 1870 some of them became popular as street trees. Parks generally contained a much greater range of species than streets, where the physical conditions were more demanding. From early times it is likely that the value of fastigiate urban trees was appreciated, with their compact crowns of upswept branches making them ideally suited to confined urban spaces. One of the first fastigiate trees to be planted in Britain was the Lombardy poplar (*Populus nigra* 'Italica'), of Italian origin and introduced in 1758 (Mitchell 1996, 281). It soon became one of the most common trees in our towns and cities, noted for its tolerance of coal-smoke and chemical fumes (Webster 1910, 62). As the nineteenth century ended and arboricultural knowledge expanded, it was then recognised that its advantages for urban planting were often outweighed by less attractive characteristics, such as its brittle branches and invasive root system.

Conflicts above and below ground

A history of urban trees in twentieth century Britain could read like an extensive catalogue of conflicts between the trees and urban development and infrastructure. In this epic saga of endless battles between trees and the forces of development, the trees invariably lost. But such an account would make this chapter unbalanced and, besides, much of it would be less about history and more of our current preoccupations. Nevertheless, some mention of these conflicts is necessary. For convenience they can be classified as those appearing above ground and those below ground – with some having an impact on both.

The obstruction of light to residential property caused by urban trees has a long history. In English law, the 'doctrine of ancient lights' refers to the right of householder to the light received through their windows (Kerr 1865). Originating in 1663, this rule of law stated that the windows used for light by an owner for 20 years or more could not be obstructed by the erection of an edifice or by any other act by an adjacent landowner. There are several caveats

FIGURE 21. Many large forest-type trees that were planted in the pavement (sidewalk) several decades ago are now causing problems by lifting pavement surfaces and disrupting surrounding brickwork. Unless the overall tree has outgrown its situation, the surface problems can be remedied and the tree retained.

to this and there remains much public misunderstanding of the issue. Local authorities, the owners of most street trees, receive many requests for pruning to facilitate more light. However, individual requests are invariably declined as these trees are generally pruned systematically, street by street, every few years. The reverse situation is also common where tree selection is limited by shade from buildings creating a lack of light at street level. Even in the late nineteenth century when London was a relatively low-rise city, Ravenscroft (1883, 2) wrote in his book *Town Gardening* about how the lack of light from tall buildings restricted tree selection and tree growth.

Other above-ground conflicts with trees that have grown in prominence include leaves blocking guttering and interference with overhead services such a telephone and electricity cables (Biddle 1981). With the growth in television (TV) ownership since the 1950s, it has been noticed that trees can have a negative effect on TV reception (AAIS 1998). Interference to signals tends to be worse when trees are in full leaf and during bad weather conditions. Another threat has resulted from the installation of thousands of CCTV cameras in urban areas. This has led to many trees being removed or drastically pruned to facilitate improved surveillance (Body 2011). At ground level, tree roots can disrupt and lift pavement surfaces causing a hazard to pedestrians who may trip over the uneven surface (Figure 21).

A recent above-ground conflict with trees and urban infrastructure relates, ironically, to the use of 'green' energy. The number of British households with solar panels increases every year and this has led to conflicts between solar access and the urban forest, particularly with trees in streets and residential gardens

(Thayer 1983). Requests for local authorities or neighbours to prune offending trees have often led to disputes between the parties that have generated more heat than light. A local authority that recently installed Britain's first solar-powered parking meters found significant problems with low levels of light (Bitten 2001). While the gloomy British weather was mainly responsible, some machines had been drained of power even in the finest weather because they were situated beneath trees.

While above-ground conflicts with trees receive much attention, there are also many below-ground issues that have resulted in thousands of urban trees being removed and drastically pruned over the past two hundred years. During Victorian times, the construction works associated with the installation of extensive underground sewerage systems in our major cities undoubtedly led to the removal of many trees in their vicinity. As other new underground services were installed in Victorian times, such as water and gas, these invariable ran underneath pavements at the side of the road. The construction work had a detrimental impact on many street trees in their path. Similar problems again came to prominence in the 1990s (Johnston 2000, 76–8). The introduction of cable television in Britain required a vast programme of civil engineering that involved excavating service trenches along the length of almost every street in the country. In the early stages of this work, little consideration was given to tree roots and this led to the loss of many mature street trees. The loss of roots resulted in trees becoming unstable and falling over in high winds or being felled as a safety precaution. Some trees just suffered a slow death as the loss of vital roots critically reduced their ability to take up water and nutrients. Even when the utility industry adopted a voluntary code of practice to try to prevent this, the guidelines were often broken and many street trees continued to be lost. There is no accurate record of the number of street trees that were lost but it must have run to many thousands.

Another below-ground conflict that has led to the removal of many mature urban trees relates to tree roots and structural damage to building foundations. This can occur in shrinkable clay soils, particularly in periods of drought when tree roots remove significant amounts of soil moisture causing the soil to shrink and building foundations to subside. Some species of tree with a high water demand and extensive root systems, such as willows and poplars, are often involved when in close proximity to buildings. These problems first attracted significant attention in the very dry summer of 1947 (Biddle 1981, 17) and an indication of the importance given to this was the inclusion of an article on the subject in the very first issue of *The Arboricultural Association Journal* (Webb 1965). It was particularly a problem with the extensive shrinkable clay soils in urban areas in the south east of England. The seasonal changes in moisture content that caused the soils to swell and shrink were exaggerated by the effects of tree roots resulting in subsidence and sometimes heave to the building foundations. In the very severe drought of 1976 extensive damage was caused leading to expensive insurance claims and the removal of large number of mature trees, particularly local authority street trees. This experience also had an impact on street tree policy in many at-risk areas with tree officers becoming reluctant to planting large-growing species to avoid any potential problems in the future (Britt and Johnston 2008, 214). Faced with expensive insurance claims, many local authorities have often been quick to remove street trees without an extensive site investigation. In many cases this might have revealed that defective foundations had played the most significant role (ISE 2000).

Other threats to urban trees can occur both above and below ground. When motorised vehicles first appeared in numbers on British roads from the beginning of the twentieth century, this heralded the arrival of another major conflict with trees. Apart from the regular removal of existing trees to facilitate new roads or road widening schemes, urban trees have suffered in other ways. Since the Second World War, rock salt (sodium chloride) has been used in increasing quantities to minimise the danger to motorists and pedestrians from icy roads (Dobson 1991). The effect of salt damage on trees was first recognised in the USA in 1944 and soon became noticeable on roadside trees in Britain. Damage occurs through salt-contaminated water from melting snow and ice entering the soil and being taken up by tree roots, or by salt spray created by fast-moving traffic being deposited on leaves. There is no doubt that over the past 50 years many thousands of trees in our towns and cities have either died or been severely debilitated as a result of salt application to roads. It is impossible to be precise because trees weakened in this way often subsequently die through other agencies. Fortunately, salt usage has been reduced in recent years and alternative de-icing materials used, such as urea and CMA (calcium magnesium acetate) (Rose and Webber 2011).

Over the past two hundred years, countless thousands of trees have been lost as a result of new built development. In many cases, they simply stood in the way and were removed. Poor site management also led to many dying which were actually intended to be retained. Changes in grade around the rooting area can suffocate roots; spillage of toxic substances can contaminate the rooting area; materials stacked against the trunk can remove the bark and encourage decay. It is probably only in the past 30 years with the rise of arboricultural education and research that the subject has received the attention it deserves. Since 1980 there have been strict guidelines in place to protect trees in the form of a British Standard.

The dramatic growth of car ownership since the Second Wold War has led to intense competition for parking space in many residential streets. Continual parking underneath trees on grass verges has caused compaction in the rooting zone and many trees have suffered. Competition for parking has also prompted numerous homeowners to pave or concrete over their front gardens to provide personal car parking spaces (RHS 2006). Countless garden trees have been felled to facilitate this and it has also meant the loss of potential tree planting sites in the future. In the worst affected areas, 47 per cent of front gardens in North-east England and 31 per cent in Scotland are now more than three-quarters paved.

Other garden trees are continually being removed due to neighbours claiming they are causing a nuisance. Most instances of this now appear to be related to high hedges of Leyland cypress (×*Cupressocyparis leylandii*) where the trees are blocking light or the size is creating an overpowering presence close to the house (Richardson 2002). This problem has now abated to a certain extent with legislation to regulate high hedges having been introduced across Britain.

Risk adverse society

In texts from the nineteenth century by Loudon and other leading authors on horticulture and arboriculture, there is little reference to the potential conflict between trees and urban development. Instead, they focus on making recommendations on the appropriate trees to plant in different situations. By contrast, modern arboricultural texts can often sound very cautious or even alarmist about the potential problems of urban trees. This has been reflected in an increasingly wary approach to tree selection in built environments over the past few decades. Rather than plant forest-type trees even where there is the space, the tendency is often to favour small ornamental species. This has prompted fears that the trend will lead to a proliferation of 'lollipop landscapes' (Johnston 2010, 33).

In Britain over the past 50 years there appears to have been a growing focus on urban trees as liabilities rather than assets (Johnston 2010, 33). This has led to a shift in resources for urban tree programmes by local authorities towards more risk management, often in the form of extensive regimes for monitoring risk. There has been concern that this has often been at the expense of the more creative aspects of arboriculture, such as more tree planting, community involvement and public education. In an increasingly risk-averse society those responsible for planning and managing our urban forests are often pessimistic that tree programmes in the future will get sufficient public and political support (Britt and Johnston 2008, 303). They fear that because of all their perceived problems, urban trees are now getting a bad name, despite their enormous benefits. While most members of the public may still claim to 'love trees' this often does not apply to the tree outside their house or in their child's playground.

War and vandalism

Vandalism of urban trees may sometime be regarded as a feature of our modern society but this has always occurred to some extent (Figure 22). From earliest times, branches were removed and whole trees felled without the consent of their owners, usually for fuel wood or for construction timber. Some trees were undoubtedly killed or heavily pruned to give more light or a better view for adjacent properties, again without the consent of their owners. This unfortunate behaviour continues to this day with local authority tree officers

FIGURE 22. Vandalism to trees may not always be malicious and can just be the result of thoughtless actions. The fragile bark of this young tree in London's East End in the late-1970s was damaged by people using its protective guard as a litter bin. The picture seems to epitomise the 'throw-away' society of that time.

regularly reporting incidents of unauthorised and unsightly 'hacking back' of street trees, almost certainly by adjacent residents.

Some urban trees have always been prone to vandalism because of the nature of their bark. Beech trees have consistently been subjected to people inscribing words into their smooth bark, most often in the more secluded areas of parks and woodlands where the perpetrators are less easily observed. On some trees the inscriptions can last for decades before they eventually disappear, giving the trees an appearance of a living history book. Fortunately, the damage to the tree's health is usually minimal (Edlin and Nimmo 1956, 33). The birch is another tree to have suffered over the centuries as some children and even adults find it difficult to resist peeling off the bark.

Animals belonging to humans have also been known to damage urban trees. In the 1930s, it was recommended that all pavement trees must have tree-guards of woven galvanised wire because milkmen on their rounds often left their ponies untended and these were attacking the bark and young shoots (Balfour 1935, 179). Ever since it became fashionable for urban residents to keep dogs as pets, their faeces and urine in the rooting area of young trees has had a toxic affect on soil and tree health. It would appear that dogs are inexorably attracted to trees. In recent years hundreds of parkland trees across the country have been mauled and destroyed by pitbulls, bull terriers and other 'weapon dogs' (Barkham 2009). These are goaded by their owners to attack trunks, hang from branches and bite off tree bark, as part of a training regime.

Fire has occasionally been responsible for the destruction of urban trees. The Fire of London in 1666 that destroyed most of the old City of London was especially devastating (Trevelyan 1950, 146). While London was then not a green city, it still killed all the trees in residential gardens, churchyards and open spaces that lay in its path. While this historic tragedy was the result of an accident, deliberate vandalism to trees using fire has featured much in recent years. For example, during The Great Drought of 1975–76 many fires in urban heaths and urban woodlands were almost certainly started by human hands (Cox 1978).

The wars and violent civil disturbances that have periodically engulfed our towns and cities over the centuries have also had a detrimental impact on urban trees. In military sieges, particularly during the Medieval Era and the English Civil War, it was inevitable that some trees within the defensive walls were sacrificed for fuel and construction materials by the defenders. During civil disturbances, where trees were available they would have been ideal material for building barricades. During the First World War, German forces targeted some British urban residential districts, mainly by Zeppelin airships, resulting in some collateral damage and destruction to urban trees, particularly from incendiary bombs. However, far more damage was done to the urban forest by the felling of many large mature trees in urban parks to help overcome the chronic shortage of timber that was the result of the German naval blockade.

It was the Second World War that had a much greater impact on urban trees and woodlands (Le Sueur 1949, 96). Public parks had an important defensive role to play in our major cities (Conway 2000, 123). Much of the anti-aircraft artillery for urban areas was positioned in parks where gun crews could get a wide and largely unobstructed view of the skies. Consequently, they were also a target for bombs themselves with nearby trees suffering collateral damage. Many of the mature trees in the parks of cities such as London, Cardiff and Coventry have shrapnel imbedded in the trunks and major branches. Large numbers of other trees were damaged or destroyed by the heat and fire from incendiary bombs. The revised edition of *The Care and Repair of Ornamental Trees* by Le Sueur (1949, 96) has a short chapter devoted to war and bomb damage. Nevertheless, in contrast to all this destruction, the numbers of trees actually increased in some urban areas as a result of the conflict. As the war continued and the aerial bombardment intensified, increasingly larger areas of some major cities were reduced to wastelands that quickly became colonised by herbaceous weeds. By the end of the war and for several years after before the sites were redeveloped, the process of plant succession ensured that natural regeneration of woodland appeared on many of these undisturbed bomb sites. Despite this, the overall condition of the tree cover in our towns and cities suffered greatly as a result of neglect during the Second World War. After the war, the newly-established tree division of the London County Council spend much of its time rectifying the lopping and topping that had disfigured many of the capital's trees during the war years (Leathart 1973, 104).

Forces of nature

The trees and woodlands of Britain have always been ravaged periodically by extreme weather events in the form of high winds, drought, snow and ice. While it may be true that urban trees are often less exposed than their rural counterparts and urban climate less extreme than the open countryside, these trees have nevertheless suffered much over the centuries.

Storm-force winds were identified as the cause of major damage to trees in Britain as early as the seventeenth century by John Evelyn and he noted that some species were particularly susceptible to windthrow (Evelyn 1679, 145). The Great Storm of 1703 remains one of the most severe ever to hit Britain and was particularly damaging across much of England (Risk Management Solutions,

2003). It uprooted countless thousands of trees as well as causing extensive structural damage to numerous buildings. Thousands of people also lost their lives, many of them seaman (Wheeler 2003). In 1704, Daniel Dafoe wrote his book *The Storm* in response to the tragedy, calling it "the tempest that destroyed woods and forests all over England" (Dafoe 1704).

It was not until recently that a storm of similar ferocity hit Britain and, again, the southern part of England was worst affected (Ogley 1988). In the early hours of the October 16, 1987, hurricane-force winds swept across England resulting in some 15 million trees being blown down in rural and urban areas. This included the loss of some famous urban trees, such as six of the seven oaks at Sevenoaks in Kent (Ogley 1988, 17), some grand old trees among nearly 500 lost at Kew Gardens (Flanagan 1988) and countless others in historic urban gardens and parks. The urban residents of towns and cities across the south of England were faced with scenes of major devastation – and particularly noticeable were the numerous trees lying across roads, railway lines, houses and parked cars. A huge 'clear-up' operation was undertaken by local authorities to remove the tree debris that lasted for months (Johnston 1991, 136). It was not until early 1988 that tree officers and parks managers could give any thought to replanting. Total insurance losses for the storm in Britain were £1.4 billion (Risk Management Solutions 2007). One beneficial outcome of this storm was the opportunity it provided scientists to study the rooting habits of a wide range of tree species (Cutler *et al.* 1990).

The story behind the naming of the 1987 storm has significance in cultural history. On BBC television the previous evening, the weather presenter Michael Fish had announced that earlier that day a woman had phoned asking if a hurricane was on the way (Houghton, 1988, 68). He reassured millions of viewers that there was not. In the days and weeks that followed this devastating event it became known among the public and the media as 'The Hurricane'. However, a group of conservationists and other professionals decided that, as technically it was not a hurricane, it should be known as 'The Great Storm', presumably unaware that this was already the name of the 1703 event. Although this is the name often given in official texts, members of the public still refer to the event as 'The Hurricane'. It is unfortunate that some professionals saw fit to try and rename something that was part of popular culture. Although the 1987 storm was supposed to be a 'once in a lifetime' meteorological event, similar hurricane-force winds struck again in January 1990 (Anon 1990). As well as covering similar ground, the damage also extended into parts of Wales and the Midlands. Some four million trees were lost, again including many urban trees.

Freezing weather bringing frost, ice and snow has always been a threat to susceptible trees. While not really a problem with native trees this does affect introduced species from milder climates, where damage and death can often result from lack of knowledge about their hardiness. An early example of this was the Mediterranean cypress (*Cupressus sempervirens*) that became fashionable during John Evelyn's time and was widely planted (Evelyn, 1679, 119). In the very harsh winter of 1683–84, nearly every cypress tree in England was killed (MacLeod 1972, 123). With the dramatic increase in new introductions during the eighteenth and nineteenth centuries, death and damage to tender tree species as a result of icy weather became ever more noticeable. After a particularly harsh winter in 1739–40, the great horticulturist Peter Collinson was delighted to record that all the plants at Lord Petre's estate at Thorndon had survived in good condition (Wulf 2008, 89). This was a significant achievement since Lord Petre had planted thousands of the recently introduced trees from North America, many of which were initially feared to be quite tender.

Since the Industrial Revolution the temperatures in our towns and cities have generally been a few degrees warmer than those in the surrounding countryside (Lamb 1995). This has been to the benefit of tender tree species as the higher temperatures limit the severity of frost, ice and snow in winter times and promote more favourable growing conditions. From at least the beginning of the nineteenth century it was noticeable that newly introduced tree species from mild overseas climates had fared much better in urban gardens than in the exposed countryside (Loudon 1838). However, it would appear that just as arboriculturists become confident of the hardiness of some newly introduced species, a very severe frost proves them wrong. In recent times, the harsh winters of 1946–47 and 1962–63 were particularly damaging for many tender urban trees.

Trees in the built environment invariably suffer from insufficient water resulting in severe drought stress, especially in long, hot and very dry summers. The need to irrigate frequently some urban trees and shrubs was recognised in early British works on urban horticulture (Fairchild 1722, 57). As our towns and cities have become more densely developed with hard surfaces and buildings the amount of open ground has been much reduced. When rain falls on roofs or on paved and tarmaced surfaces it quickly disappears down drains and sewers before it has a chance to percolate into the rooting area of urban trees. When there is little rain, the problem is greatly exacerbated.

Severe drought periodically affects parts of Britain and in the first half of the twentieth century major events featured in 1909, 1911 and 1947 (Seifert 1948). The most memorable drought in terms of its impact on urban trees occurred quite recently. The Great Drought of 1976 was the driest summer for two hundred years and followed an unusually dry summer and winter the previous year (Cox 1978). Newly-planted trees, in streets and other areas with hard surfaces, were some of the more immediate casualties, particularly where they had received no watering by the local authorities in the springtime. As the summer became even hotter, the drought problem began to embrace other trees. In an effort to conserve water supplies, the authorities issued restrictions on the use of water for what were considered 'non-essential' purposes, which included watering in gardens, parks and golf courses. Again, young trees were hit particularly hard by this lack of water. As the grass in parks and gardens turned yellow and then brown, the young trees wilted and died. Many local authorities issued a call to residents to help by watering young street trees with waste water from domestic baths and washing, provided this was not too contaminated. The public responded in great numbers and this was undoubted an outstanding example in Britain of mass community involvement with urban trees.

The real extent of the damage did not show up until the spring of 1977 (Cox 1978, 146). As the grass came back underfoot, many thousands of mature trees struggled into leaf for what was their last season. Having severely weakened them, the drought then made them susceptible to various pests and diseases in a manner that the Forestry Commission likened to a flu epidemic among older people. Beech and sycamore were particularly badly affected with high incidences of beech bark disease and sooty bark disease respectively.

Pest and diseases

In the early literature on the threats to trees there are plenty of references to abiotic problems, such as wind, drought and even the consequence of poor maintenance. There is also some reference to biotic problems in the form of pests, for example, insects that can have a damaging impact on the health of trees. However, it is not until the early 1800s that there is any substantial reference to the diseases of trees. Although the term 'diseases' does appear in earlier texts, it was used in a much broader context than is recognised today.

The early literature uses a variety of terms to refer to all the various threats to trees. In *Sylva* by John Evelyn (1664) there is a chapter on the 'Infirmities' of trees, which includes all the known problems, including weeds, small mammals and ivy. Insects 'pests' such as caterpillars, snails and wasps are also mentioned. While the word 'disease' appears, this is used to embrace all the 'infirmities' of trees. Cankers and 'hollowness', which we would now regard as aspects of disease, are mentioned but not with any reference to biological processes. The only cure proposed for this was to cut out the 'bad bits'. Around the same time as Evelyn, Moses Cook (1676) has a chapter 'Of the Diseases of Trees' in his seminal work entitled *The Manner of Raising, Ordering and Improving Forrest-Trees*. This covers similar ground to Evelyn's *Sylva*, which is not surprising since the two knew and influenced each other. Richard Bradley writing some fifty years later does not offer much more. In his book *New Improvements of Planting and Gardening* he also has a chapter devoted to what he calls the 'Blights' of trees. He stated, "Plants of all Degrees are subject to Blights, which as so variously communicated to them, that sometimes a whole tree will perish by that Distemper" (Bradley 1718, 53). Included within his category of Blights are all the known agents harmful to trees. Samuel Hayes writing much later in the eighteenth century also has little to add on this subject, although he does mention Dutch Wax and Mr Forsyth's composition as two substances that can be used as wound dressings which, he claims, can actually cure some injuries to trees (Hayes 1794, 99–104). William Forsyth, the Scottish horticulturist, gives further details of these compositions in his book *A Treatise on the Culture and Management of Fruit-Trees* in a chapter entitled 'Observations on the Diseases, Defects, and Injuries, in all kinds of Fruit and Forest Trees' (Forsyth 1802, 287–326). Again, the term 'disease' is mentioned without much apparent understanding of the biological processes involved.

British forestry books from the eighteenth and nineteenth century generally confine themselves to the problems of forest trees, with almost no reference to trees in urban situations. Towards the end of the nineteenth century there appeared an English translation of the classic German work entitled *Text-book of the Diseases of Trees* by Professor Robert Hartig (1894). This is discussed in more detail later. It is not until the early twentieth century that pests and diseases of urban trees get a significant mention in any original British text. One of the most important was by Angus Webster (1916) entitled *Tree Wounds and Diseases*. While Webster was essentially a forester, he recognised the gap in the literature about pests and diseases of amenity and urban trees. His text mentions a wide range of pests and diseases and various measures for prevention and treatment. The classic text by Denis Le Sueur (1934) entitled *The Care and Repair of Ornamental Trees* has a chapter focusing on 'Fungal Diseases' and another on 'Insect Pests'. Both Webster and Le Sueur mention the disease known as honey fungus (*Armillaria* spp.) as a potential killer of all woody plants and especially of trees in domestic gardens.

Today, when many older people think of tree diseases, Dutch elm disease immediately comes to mind. The devastating outbreak of the virulent form of this disease from the late 1960s onwards remains a painful memory for those who witnessed its destructive transformation of the landscape in both rural and urban areas. By 1985, it was estimated that 30 million elms had died in Britain and trees continue to be lost as fresh outbreaks flare up periodically (Webber 2010). However, it seems that less destructive forms of the disease may have been with us many years before. Oliver Rackham (2003, 262) believes that evidence from staining of the annual rings of some very old elms confirms that the disease was present in England as early as 1867. In Richard Jefferies' (1883) book *Nature Near London*, the English nature writer remarked, "There is something wrong with elm trees. In the early part of this summer, not long after the leaves were fairly out upon them, here and there a branch appeared as if it had been touched with red-hot iron and burnt up, all the leaves withered and browned on the boughs. First one tree was thus affected, then another, then a third." He describes symptoms remarkably similar to the modern disease and comments that the problem was quite widespread and capable of killing entire avenues of elm trees.

In the twentieth century, Le Sueur (1934) mentions Dutch elm disease as a significant problem for elms of all ages and types, having been first recorded in England in 1927. As the disease was widespread in southern England in the late 1920s it was assumed it must have become established much earlier in that decade. It reached its peak in 1936 and 1937, whereupon it declined and by 1960 it was thought that the worst was over (Peace 1962, 422). Sadly, that was not the case. In the late 1960s a very aggressive strain was imported on logs at Southampton. Although initially thought to be just a flare up of the old disease, it was soon recognised that this was a far more virulent form of Dutch elm disease. As people became alarmed at its rapid spread, Peter Scott, the well-known naturalist, requested that the Army be used for control. Although this did not happen, there was a significant shift in responsibility for the disease from central government to the local authorities. Despite the alarm and the control measures, the disease spread rapidly to hitherto unaffected parts of northern England and Wales through the movement of diseased elm timber from the south (Gibbs 1977).

One of the most distinctive trees of the English countryside, the English elm (*Ulmus procera*) was particularly susceptible. It was also believed that this was a native tree and the sense of loss was heightened because of this. In his timely book *Epitaph for the Elm* Gerald Wilkinson (1978, 53) quotes the work of Melville (1948) at RBG Kew, stating that there are six native elms, including the English elm. It is now known that this tree is actually a 2000-year old Roman clone (Gil *et al.* 2004). One definitely native elm, the wych elm (*Ulmus glabra*), is particularly common in Scotland and this seems to be the least preferred elm for the disease (Webber 2010). This may have helped slow the spread of the disease north of the border.

As well as being a dominant tree in many rural areas, the elm was also an important urban tree and once constituted a significant proportion of the tree population in many towns and cities in northern England (Gibbs 1977, 110). The largest concentration of mature elms in Scotland remains in Edinburgh, where in 2009 an estimated 5000 still survived out of a population of 35,000 in 1976 (Coleman 2009). A strict policy of sanitary felling now keeps losses to an average of 1000 a year. The estimated 17,000 elms of Brighton and Hove constitute probably the most varied and important urban elm population in southern Britain, several of which are estimated to be over 400 years old (BHCC 2013). Their survival is due to the isolation of the area between the English Channel and the South Downs, and the stringent sanitation efforts of the local authority to identify and remove infected trees and branches (Figure 23).

The Dutch elm disease crisis had a profound impact on how the British public viewed not only their trees but the wider natural environment. The idea that such a well-loved and iconic tree could just disappear from our rural and urban landscapes was difficult for many people to grasp. While there were recriminations about a lack of government action to prevent this, for most of the public there was just a feeling of sadness and helplessness at the enormity of this disaster for Britain's treescape. There is no doubt the incident prompted wider concerns about the vulnerability not just of trees but also of the environment in general. As the full impact of the disease was becoming apparent, these concerns were articulated in a book by Robert Lamb (1979) entitled *World Without Trees*.

The book's subtitle *Dutch elm disease and other human errors* leaves little doubt that the author holds people largely responsible for what happened.

There have been other tree diseases in the second half of the twentieth century that have been particularly noticeable in urban areas. Fireblight is caused by the bacterium *Erwinia amylovora* and is a serious disease of trees and shrubs in the family Rosaceae, sub-family Maloideae (Pome fruits) (Strouts and Winter 2000, 124). This includes many ornamental tree species that are common in our towns and cities, such as apple (*Malus*), hawthorn (*Crataegus*), pear (*Pyrus*), mountain ash and whitebeams (*Sorbus*), *Cotoneaster*, *Pyracantha* and *Amelanchier*. Not only are many of these species very popular in urban residential gardens, they can also form a large proportion of the street tree population, particularly in the suburbs. The disease affects all the aerial parts of the host plant, with withering and death of young shoots and flowers, and infected fruit turning brown or black. The first British finding of fireblight was in a pear orchard in Kent in 1957. It is now widespread in south and central England and also in Wales. The control is to fell and burn infected plants and not to plant susceptible species in affected areas.

Sooty bark disease of sycamore was initially noticed in London following the hot summers of 1947 and 1959 (Anon 1977). Possibly introduced from North America, it was first described appearing on maple logs in Ontario in 1889

FIGURE 23. Some of the majestic elm trees in Brighton that have so far survived the ravages of Dutch elm disease. Thanks to a vigorous disease control programme by the local authority these remarkable trees continue to make a magnificent contribution to the town's Regency landscape.

(Strouts and Winter 2000, 257). During the drought of 1976 it became very noticeable, killing many sycamore trees, particularly in London parks but also elsewhere in the southern part of England. It is caused by a fungus *Cryptostroma corticale* and symptoms include the wilting of leaves followed by death of branches and then the whole tree. At a later stage, the bark loosens and falls away revealing a sooty layer of blackish spores. Its incidence is linked to hot dry summers and these climatic conditions tend to be even more pronounced in urban areas. It continues to be a problem and its incidence will probably increase with urban climate change.

In the past few years, a major threat to the London plane tree (*Plantanus x hispanica*) has emerged in our capital city (Tubby and Rose 2009). London's most iconic tree is threatened by a fungal menace known as massaria (*Splanchnonema platani*), previously unknown in Britain. The disease is particularly disturbing because London plane has been renowned for being tolerant to most pests and diseases and resilient to changes in environmental conditions, factors which have made it an ideal urban tree and widespread in many British towns and cities (Milmo 2010). Although the disease is not known to kill trees, the Forestry Commission has warned that its ability to kill individual branches has created a risk to public safety requiring increased monitoring. Finally, ash dieback has just arrived in Britain and is threatening to decimate our ash trees (*Fraxinus excelsior*) (Derbyshire 2013). While much concern has so far focused on rural areas, it should be remembered that various ash species and their cultivars form a major proportion of our urban forests.

Apart from new diseases threatening urban trees, there are also deadly insect pests recently arrived in our towns and cities or likely to do so soon (O'Callaghan 2012). It appears that with this recent wave of new pests and diseases our urban trees now face an unprecedented threat. This only serves to emphasise the vital need to plant a wide range of species or genotypes to promote biodiversity in our urban tree populations that will improve their resilience against attack from deadly pathogens.

Research in arboriculture and tree pathology

In the next part of this chapter we examine the history of research into urban arboriculture and tree pathology. It is a story that has its origins many centuries ago, although only in relatively recent times has major progress been made. During the Medieval era and even into the eighteenth century, many of the accepted practices in arboriculture and horticulture were based on myth and the flawed advice of the ancient Greeks and Romans (Wulf 2008, 11). Scientific enquiry as we understand it today was virtually nonexistent in most disciplines. One of the earliest contributions to arboricultural knowledge was made by Moses Cook in his seminal work *The Manner of Raising, Ordering and Improving Forrest-Trees*, published in 1676. Of particular interest here is his introduction 'To the Reader' where he exposes a number of 'errors' in tree cultivation, based on his own practical experience and research (Cook 1676). These include boring a hole in a tree and pouring in honey to make its fruit sweet, and watering seeds with coloured water so that they would produce flowers of that colour. However, some popular misconceptions of that time continued for many years and were repeated in some quite learned works.

During the eighteenth century, advances in tree biology and pathology were often achieved more by chance than scientific means. For example, *The Retir'd Gard'ner* by George London and Henry Wise (1706) contained a description of the origin of sap, and although this was fairly accurate it was probably achieved mostly by guesswork (Musgrave 2007, 21). A huge advance in horticultural science came in 1716 when Thomas Fairchild (author of *The City Gardener*) conducted the first successful experiment in plant breeding (Wulf 2008, 7). By the simple act of taking pollen from a carnation and inserted it into a sweet william in his Hoxton nursery, Fairchild produced an entirely new variety that became known as 'Fairchild's Mule'. A year or so later, some significant advances in the science of woody plants were recorded by Richard Bradley, a friend of Fairchild, in his book *New Improvements of Planting and Gardening* (Bradley 1718). He attempted to underpin his horticultural and arboricultural advice with sound scientific knowledge. In 1724, this was recognised in his appointment as the first Professor of Botany at Cambridge University (Hadfield *et al.* 1980, 43).

The foundation of the Royal Society in 1660 gave major impetus to scientific enquiry in horticulture, arboriculture and related fields (Wulf 2008, 13). In its early days, many of its 'leading lights' were not only passionately interested in plants but also dedicated to its aim of working 'for the improvement of natural knowledge by experiment'. Part of this included encouraging research into the many agencies that were a threat to the health and survival of trees. Members of other learned societies played an important role. William Forsyth, the Scottish horticulturist, was a founding member of the Royal Horticultural Society and very keen on research into tree pathology (Forsyth 1802). In recognition of his important contribution, the government made a grant of £3000 to Forsyth on condition he made public the secret of his composition for 'repairing' the injuries to the stems of trees (Webster 1916, viii). In the early nineteenth century, Sir Henry Steuart (1828, 5) was another arboriculturist who was conscious of the value of research into all aspects of arboriculture and recognised the valuable contribution made by his predecessors and contemporaries.

The British literature on tree pathology was quite limited until the end of the nineteenth century. Then, the most significant contribution came from the English translation of a German text. Just as German ideas and practice had such a profound impact on the development of modern British forestry in the late nineteenth century, so it was a German scientist of that time who, in the words of the eminent British scientist Marshall Ward, "succeeded in founding a plant pathology really worthy of the name" and established himself as the 'Father of Tree Pathology' (Ward 1894, v) (Figure 24). *Text-book of the Diseases of Trees* by Professor Robert Hartig (1894) remains one of the great works of science

FIGURE 24 *(opposite)*. The British literature on tree pathology was quite limited until the end of the nineteenth century. Then, the most significant contribution came from the English translation of a German text. *Text-book of the Diseases of Trees* by Professor Robert Hartig (1894) remains one of the great works of science in any field. In the words of the eminent British scientist Marshall Ward, Hartig "succeeded in founding a plant pathology really worthy of the name" and established himself as the 'Father of Tree Pathology'.

The "Country Life" Library.

TEXT-BOOK

OF THE

DISEASES OF TREES

BY

PROFESSOR R. HARTIG

OF THE UNIVERSITY OF MUNICH

TRANSLATED BY

WILLIAM SOMERVILLE, D.Œc., B.Sc., F.R.S.E., F.L.S.

PROFESSOR OF AGRICULTURE AND FORESTRY
DURHAM COLLEGE OF SCIENCE, NEWCASTLE-ON-TYNE

REVISED AND EDITED, WITH A PREFACE, BY

H. MARSHALL WARD, D.Sc., F.R.S., F.L.S., F.R.H.S.

LATE FELLOW OF CHRIST'S COLLEGE, CAMBRIDGE
PROFESSOR OF BOTANY AT THE ROYAL INDIAN ENGINEERING COLLEGE, COOPER'S HILL

London

PUBLISHED AT THE OFFICES OF
"COUNTRY LIFE," 20, TAVISTOCK STREET, W.C.
AND BY
GEO. NEWNES, Ltd., 7-12, SOUTHAMPTON ST., COVENT GARDEN, W.C.

in any field. His advances reached across a wide spectrum of tree pathology and were particularly groundbreaking in our understanding of tree decay. In accordance with the principles of abiogensis, scientists had traditionally believed that tree decay led to fungal growth. Hartig stated that the reverse was the case and developed an entirely new model where trees were wounded, fungi infected the wounds and this led to tree decay (Hubert 1931). Hartig's tree pathology work is also notable for its attention to specifically urban problems. In his classic textbook he discusses the death of urban trees caused by atmospheric pollution, the toxic effect on tree roots of coal gas escaping from underground pipes, the harmful impact on tree growth of some hard surfaces for pavements and streets, and other typically urban problems.

The early twentieth century saw one of the first British books to focus on tree pathology with a distinctly arboricultural perspective. As mentioned above, Webster's (1916) book on *Tree Wounds and Diseases* was a major contribution to our literature on tree pathology with a significant urban focus. In the 1950s, another major British work on tree pathology was *Tree Injuries: Their Cause and Prevention* by Edlin and Nimmo (1956). This groundbreaking work contained 125 photographs to illustrate many of the 77 different causes of injury described in its authoritative text.

Possibly the most significant British book ever written on tree pathology appeared in the 1960s. The seminal work by Tom Peace (1962) entitled *Pathology of Trees and Shrubs* was the first comprehensive account of the pest, diseases and other agencies that were damaging to woody plants in Britain. The scope, detail and academic rigour of this 750-page book is quite remarkable. At the time of publication Peace was Chief Research Officer for the Forestry Commission and the whole project was only made possible by the Commission which allowed him to use official time to deliver it. Although there have undoubtedly been some advances in our knowledge of tree pathology since Peace's book and some nomenclature has changed, it is still being recommended as a major source of further information by current authoritative texts (Strouts and Winter 2000).

Throughout the twentieth century, British arboricultural research and especially tree pathology research have always been intimately bound up with the whole topic of forest research. Furthermore, forest research itself has been dominated by the activities, capabilities and requirements of the Forestry Commission since its formation. In 1974, the Forestry Commission published a review of the forest research that it had supported from 1920 to 1970 (Wood 1974). In a publication of 134 pages, less than one page deals with arboriculture and most of that focuses on its two arboreta at Westonbirt and Bedgebury. Interestingly, the text reveals the Forestry Commission's approach to arboriculture at that time. It states that, "as the forest authority, the Commission retains more than a marginal interest in arboriculture..." However, it goes on to say that, "There is no central body for arboricultural research; nor could there be; the interests being far too varied" (*ibid.*, 60). In recent years, the Forestry Commission has become far more active in arboriculture and urban forestry research and has supported a wide range of initiatives.

The North American influence

In the final part of this chapter we describe two major influences on the development of British arboricultural research that emerged from North America in the 1970s. One of these was specifically focused on tree pathology, although it had huge implications for many aspects of practical arboriculture. The other influence was to change fundamentally the way not only arboriculturists viewed urban trees and woodland but also those in related professions involved with urban greening.

While Robert Hartig had revolutionised our understanding of tree decay processes in the late nineteenth century, many aspects of arboricultural practice had remained much the same as it had done over the past few centuries. Tree care was based largely on an anthropomorphic approach where treatments were administered to 'the patient' in much the same ways as a doctor or dentist would work. Limbs were amputated, wounds were dressed and cavities were filled (Figure 25). Indeed, the popular name of 'tree surgery' for this work seems to encapsulate this approach. That was to all change in the late 1970s as a result of new research in the USA. Dr Alex Shigo of the USDA Forest Service developed a new model for tree decay that has become known by its acronym CODIT (Compartmentalization of Decay in Trees). According to the CODIT model, when a tree is wounded its cells undergo changes to form 'walls' around the wound, slowing or preventing the spread of disease and decay to the rest of the tree (Shigo 1977). The implications for tree care practice at the time were enormous. Flush cutting (pruning), traditional wound sealants, cavity draining and filling, along with other traditional practices were all questioned and no longer regarded as good practice. However, not all of this was entirely new. For example, in Le Sueur's classic work published in 1934 he urges against flush cutting and advocates pruning to the furthest extent of the 'branch ring' (now called the branch collar in Shigo's work) (Le Sueur 1934, 18). Although it took a while for Shigo's ideas

FIGURE 25. For many hundreds of years people tried to cut out the decay in tree trunks and fill the cavity with all sorts of materials, just as a dentist would fill a cavity in a tooth. This tree in Cambridge Botanic Garden has brickwork that is probably around one hundred years old. Following research by Alex Shigo in the United States in the 1970s, this anthropomorphic approach to cavity treatment is no longer practiced.

to become accepted, once he had made a few personal appearances in Britain and his work became widely read, all this fundamentally changed the arboricultural industry forever (Bridgeman 2007). Unfortunately, many of today's arboriculturists seem to believe that everything Shigo said was 'gospel' and entirely original. While he was undoubtedly a 'giant' of modern arboriculture, this unquestioning approach does not do him justice.

Shigo's pioneering research was one of a number of factors to prompt a fresh look at arboricultural research and encourage this to become more distinct from general forest research. Following the ravages of Dutch elm disease there was also an understandable acceleration of interest in the need for wide-ranging research on trees that were not just of silivicultural importance (Winning 1973, 160). Not least was a feeling that the emerging arboricultural industry needed to be serviced by a research initiative that understood its particular needs and circumstances, and there was a lack of confidence that the Forestry Commission on its own could do this.

In September 1972, the Sixth Annual Conference of ABSTA unanimously passed a motion calling for the formation of an arboricultural research working party (Insley 1976, 54). This was formed under the chairmanship of Professor Fred Last with representatives from all the main arboricultural organisations, plus consultants and the Forestry Commission. It produced a report entitled *Arboricultural Research and Advisory Needs* in November 1973. By October 1974, The Forestry Commission had appointed an arboriculturist to begin to develop work in this field and further staff were to follow with funds from the Department of the Environment. The initial objectives of the research were to improve techniques of tree production and establishment, knowledge and control of decay in amenity trees, and the provision of an arboricultural information and advisory service. At last, arboricultural research was beginning to get the recognition it deserved. Later, from the early 1990s through to 2008, the Department of the Environment (succeeded by the Department for Communities and Local Government) produced a series of major publications on urban tree research. The series was entitled 'Research for Amenity Trees' and nine titles were published on a range of subjects, including tree pathology, tree risk assessment and management, urban woodlands and air quality, and tree roots in the built environment.

From the 1980s, as well as actively engaging in arboricultural research, the Forestry Commission was also involved in 'showcasing' the latest research in this field through a series of Arboricultural Research Conferences, organised jointly with the Arboricultural Association. These were held in 1980, 1985 and 1990. A similar conference was held in 1995, with the support of the Department of the Environment, Transport and the Regions. The papers presented at all four of the research conferences were published in individual volumes (Anon 1980; Patch 1987; Hodge 1991; Claridge 1997). Much British arboricultural research was also being published in the *Arboricultural Journal*.

The second major North American influence on the development of British arboricultural research also came in the 1970s with the emergence of the urban forestry movement (see Chapter 2). The impact of this was felt not just in arboriculture but across all the professions involved with urban trees and urban greening. Of particular importance here, it marked a shift in research away from concentrating mainly on the 'problems' of individual trees to a far more proactive emphasis on the benefits and management of the urban forest. In previous centuries our recognition of the benefits of urban trees and woodland was confined largely to the aesthetic and spiritual. Put quite simply, trees looked good and they made us feel good. Now, with new research from the USA there was many more reason to plant urban trees and to resist the various pressures that threatened them. The findings of this new research were brought together for the first time by Gary Robinette (1972), an American landscape architect, in his groundbreaking book *People, Plants and Environmental Quality*. This outlined for the first time the many environmental, economic and social benefits of urban trees and established the very *raison d'être* for urban forest management. The body of research on the benefits of urban trees and what is often referred to as 'green infrastructure' continues to grow and the Forestry Commission has recently published a compilation of this (Forest Research 2010).

The growing focus on urban forestry in the early 1990s prompted a groundbreaking government-commissioned research study on the urban forest in England. *Trees in Towns: A Survey of Trees in 66 Towns and Villages in England* was actually the first publication in the Research for Amenity Trees series (DoE 1993). The survey itself was the first to be conducted that gave a picture of the urban forest across England. Some aspects of tree management were also included. In 1999, independent researchers at the University of Ulster produced a report entitled *A Survey of Urban Forestry in Britain* that focused on how British local authorities were performing in various aspects of planned, systematic and integrated management (Johnston and Rushton 1999). This was the first such survey to cover the whole of Britain. In 2008, a far more detail survey of England was published entitled *Trees in Towns II* (Britt and Johnston 2008). This not only gave a very detailed picture of the nature and extent of the urban forest, it also provided a wealth of information about how those trees were being managed, particularly by local authorities.

Inspired by the Arboricultural Research Conferences held in the 1980s and 90s, a small group of urban forestry professionals got together in early 2010 to propose a major research conference, specifically on urban trees and urban forests. In April 2011 in Birmingham, the 'Trees, People and the Built Environment' research conference attracted some 400 delegates, not only from Britain but also many from overseas. All the papers presented at the conference were then included in the proceedings published by the Forestry Commission (Johnston and Percival 2012). Another hugely successful conference, 'Trees, People and the Built Environment II' was held, again in Birmingham, in April 2014. Of particular significance, these conferences were supported by a wide range of professional and trade bodies not only associated with trees but also with the built environment. The Trees and Design Action Group (TDAG) has been performing a similar role in uniting natural and built environment professionals and promoting research. Now that tree professionals had finally reached out and embraced architects, engineers, surveyor and others, urban forestry and arboricultural research had come of age in Britain.

References

AAIS (1998) *The Effect of Trees on Television Reception.* Arboriculture Research Note, ref 146/98/TV. Arboricultural Advisory and Information Service. Tree Advice Trust: Farnham.

Anon (1977) *Sooty Bark Disease of Sycamore.* Forestry Commission Press Notice No. 26/76. *Arboricultural Journal* 3 (2), 130.

Anon (1980) *Research for Practical Arboriculture.* Occasional paper No. 10. Forestry Commission: Edinburgh.

Anon (1990) Severe Storms Strike Again. *Urban Forests* Magazine. Spring 1990, Issue 3, 1. A Seed in Time: Hoddesdon.

Balfour, F. R. S. (1935) The Planting and After Care of Roadside Trees. *Quarterly Journal of Forestry* 29, 163–188.

Barkham, P. (2009) Thousands of Urban Trees Mauled and Destroyed as 'Weapon Dog' Owners Train Animal for Fighting. *The Guardian*, Tuesday 11 August. Available at: http://www.guardian.co.uk/world/2009/aug/11/urban-trees-destroyed-fighting-dogs (accessed 2.8.2014).

Beckett, K. P., Freer-Smith, P. H. and Taylor, G. (1998) Urban Woodlands: their Role in Reducing the Effects of Particulate Pollution. *Environmental Pollution* 99, 347–360.

BHCC (2013) National Elm Collection. Brighton and Hove City Council website. Available at: http://www.brighton-hove.gov.uk/content/leisure-and-libraries/parks-and-green-spaces/national-elm-collection (accessed 25.06.2013).

Biddle, G. (1981) Physical Problems Caused by Trees to Buildings and Services. In Clouston, B. and Stansfield, K. (eds) *Trees in Towns: Maintenance and management.* The Architectural Press: London.

Bitten, N. (2001) Cloud over Solar Parking Meters. *The Telegraph*, 6 September 2001. Available at: http://www.telegraph.co.uk/news/uknews/1339645/Cloud-over-solar-parking-meters.html (accessed 2.8.2014).

Body, S. (2011) Investigation into the Interactions Between Closed Circuit Television and Urban Forest Vegetation in Wales. In Johnston, M. and Percival, G. (eds) *Trees, People and the Built Environment.* Forestry Commission Research Report. Forestry Commission: Edinburgh.

Bradley, R. (1718) *New Improvements of Planting and Gardening, both Philosophical and Practical.* In Three Parts. Printed for W. Mears: London.

Bridgeman, P. (2007) Alex Lloyd Shigo: 1930–2006, A Personal Tribute. *Arboricultural Journal*, 30(1), 5–6.

Britt, C. and Johnston, M. (2008) *Trees in Towns II: A New Survey of Urban Trees in England and their Condition and Management.* Department for Communities and Local Government: London.

Clapp, B. W. (1994) *An Environmental History of Britain since the Industrial Revolution.* Longman: London.

Claridge, J. (ed.) (1997) *Arboricultural Practice: Present and Future.* Research for Amenity Trees No. 6. Department of the Environment, Transport and the Regions: London.

Coleman, M. (2009) *Wych Elm.* Royal Botanic Gardens Edinburgh: Edinburgh.

Conway, H. (1991) *People's Parks: The Design and Development of Victorian Parks in Britain.* Cambridge University Press: Cambridge.

Conway, H. (2000) Everyday Landscapes: Public Parks from 1930 to 2000. *Garden History*, 117–134.

Cook, M. (1676) *The Manner of Raising, Ordering, and Improving Forest and Fruit- Trees* and *How to Plant, Make and Keep Woods, Walks, Avenues, Lawns, Hedges, etc.* Peter Parker at the Leg and Star: London.

Cooper, F. (2006) *The Black Poplar: History, Ecology and Conservation.* Windgather Press: Macclesfield.

Cox, E. (1978) *The Great Drought of 1976.* Hutchinson: London.

Cutler, D. F., Gasson, P. E. and Farmer, M. C. (1990) The Wind Blow Tree Survey: Analysis of Results. *Arboricultural Journal* 14 (3), 265–286.

Defoe, D. (1704) *The Storm: or, A Collection of the Most Remarkable Casualties and Disasters which Happen'd in the Late Dreadful Tempest, both by Sea and Land.* G. Sawbridge: London

Derbyshire, D. (2013) Thought the Threat to our Noble Ash Trees was Over? They Could ALL be Lost in Ten Years. *Daily Mail*, 14 May 2013. Available at: http://www.dailymail.co.uk/news/article-2324089/Ash-dieback-Thought-threat-noble-ash-trees-They-ALL-lost-10–years.html (accessed 2.8.2014).

DoE (1993) *Trees in Towns: A Survey of Trees in 66 Towns and Villages in England.* Research for Amenity Trees No. 1. Prepared for the Department of the Environment by Land Use Consultants. HMSO: London.

Dobson, M. C. (1991) *De-icing Salt Damage to Trees and Shrubs.* Forestry Commission Bulletin 101. HMSO: London.

Edlin, H. L. and Nimmo, M. (1956) *Tree Injuries: Their Causes and Prevention.* Thames and Hudson: London.

Evelyn, J. (1661) *Fumifugium, or, The inconveniencie of the aer and smoak of London dissipated together with some remedies humbly proposed by J. E. esq. to His Sacred Majestie, and to the Parliament.* Now assembled as a pamphlet published in London.

Evelyn, J. (1664) *Sylva or a Discourse of Forest-Trees, and the Propagation of Timber in His Majesties Dominions.* First edition. J. Martyn and J. Allestry: London.

Evelyn, J. (1679) *Sylva or a Discourse of Forest-Trees, and the Propagation of Timber in His Majesties Dominions.* Third edition. Printed for John Martyn: London.

Fairchild, T. (1722) *The City Gardener.* T. Woodward and J. Peele: London.

Flanagan, M. (1988) The Damage Caused by Hurricane Force Winds to the Trees at the Royal Botanic Gardens, Kew. *Arboricultural Journal* 12, 181–188.

Forest Research (2010) *Benefits of Green Infrastructure*. Report to Defra and CLG. Forest Research: Farnham.

Forsyth, W. (1802) *A Treatise on the Culture and Management of Fruit-Trees*. Published by Order of the Government by T. N. Longman, O. Rees, T. Cadell and others: London.

Gibbs, J. N. (1977) A Review of Dutch Elm Disease Control Programmes in England, Wales and the Channel Islands – Autumn 1976. *Arboricultural Journal* 3 (2), 110–114.

Gil, L., Fuentes-Utrilla, P., Soto, A., Cervera, M. T. and Collada, C. (2004) English Elm is a 2000–year old Roman Clone. *Nature* 431, 1053.

Hadfield, M., Harling, R. and Highton, L. (1980) *British Gardeners: A Biographical Dictionary*. A. Zwemmer: London.

Hammersley, G. (1973) The Charcoal Iron Industry and its Fuel. *The Economic History Review* New Series 26(4), 593–613

Hartig, R. (1894) *Textbook of the Diseases of Trees*. Translated by William Somerville and revised and edited, with a preface, by H. Marshall Ward. Country Life: London.

Hayes, S. (1794) *Practical Treatise on Planting and the Management of Woods and Coppices*. Published privately and printed by William Slater: Dundalk, Ireland.

Hodge, S. J. (ed.) (1991) *Research for Practical Arboriculture*. Forestry Commission Bulletin 97. HMSO: London.

Houghton, J. T. (1988) The Storm, The Media and the Enquiry. *Weather* 43, 67–70.

Hubert, E. E. (1931) *An Outline of Forest Pathology*. Wiley and Sons: London.

Insley, H. (1976) Amenity Tree Research: a New Move in the Forestry Commission to Extend Research on Arboriculture. *Arboricultural Journal* 3(1), 54–57.

ISE (2000) *Subsidence of Low Rise Buildings*. Second edition. The Institution of Structural Engineers: London.

Jefferies, R. (1883) *Nature Near London*. Chatto and Windus: London.

Jennings, A. (2006) *Roman Gardens*. English Heritage: London.

Johnston, M. (1991) The Forest of London: I – Planting an Idea. *Arboricultural Journal* 15, 127–143.

Johnston, M. (2000) British Urban Forestry in Transition: Developments Between 1993–1998, Part I. *Arboricultural Journal* 25, 59–92.

Johnston, M. (2010) Trees in Towns II and the Contribution of Arboriculture. *Arboricultural Journal* 33, 27–41.

Johnston, M. and Rushton, B. S. (1999) *A Survey of Urban Forestry in Britain*. University of Ulster: Coleraine.

Johnston, M. and Percival, G. (eds) (2012) *Trees, People and the Built Environment*. Forestry Commission Research Report. Forestry Commission: Edinburgh. Available at: http://www.forestry.gov.uk/pdf/FCRP017.pdf/$FILE/FCRP017.pdf (accessed 28.7.2014).

Keene, D. (2000) The Medieval Urban Landscape AD 900–1540. In Waller, P. (ed.) *The English Urban Landscape*. Oxford University Press: Oxford.

Kerr, R. (1865) *On Ancient Lights, and the Evidence of Surveyors Thereon*. John Murray: London.

Lamb, H. H. (1995) *Climate, History and the Modern World*. Routledge: London.

Lamb, R. (1979) *World Without Trees: Dutch Elm Disease and other Human Errors*. Wildwood House: London.

Lawrence, H. W. (2006) *City Trees: A Historical Geography from the Renaissance through the Nineteenth Century*. University of Virginia Press: Charlottesville and London.

Leathart, P. S. (1973) Profile: Hubert Taylor. *The Arboricultural Association Journal* 2(4), 101–105.

Le Sueur, A. D. C. (1934) *The Care and Repair of Ornamental Trees*. Country Life: London.

Le Sueur, A. D. C. (1949) *The Care and Repair of Ornamental Trees*. Second edition. Country Life: London.

Longstaffe-Gowan, T. (2001) *The London Town Garden 1700–1840*. Yale University Press: New Haven and London.

London, Ge. and Wise, H. (1706) *The Retir'd Gard'ner*. Printed for J. Tonson: London.

Loudon, J. C. (1838) *The Suburban Gardener and Villa Companion*. Longman, Orme, Brown, Green and Longmans: London.

MacLeod, D. (1972) *The Gardener's London*. Gerald Duckworth: London.

Melville, R. (1948) The British Elms. *The New Naturalist: A Journal of British Natural History*. Collins. 36–41.

Milmo, C. (2010) Fast-spreading New Disease Threatens Plane Trees. *The Independent*, Monday, 11 October 2010. Available at: http://www.independent.co.uk/environment/nature/fastspreading-new-disease-threatens-plane-trees-2103182.html (accessed 2.8.2014).

Mitchell, A. (1989) The Plant Hunters and their Effect on the Introduction of Exotic Species to the Urban Environment. In Chaplin, J. (ed.) *Celebration of Trees: Silver Jubilee Conference Proceedings*. Arboricultural Association: Ampfield

Mitchell, A. (1996) *Alan Mitchell's Trees of Britain*. Harper-Collins: London.

Morgan, C. (2003) The National Pinetum, Bedgebury: Its history and collections. *Acta Hort.* (ISHS) 615, 269–272.

Musgrave, T, (2007) *The Head Gardeners – Forgotten Heroes of Horticulture*. Aurum Press: London.

O'Callaghan, D. P. (2012) Tree Pest and Diseases – Wake up and Smell the Coffee. *Arb. Magazine*, Issue 159, 28–30.

Ogley, B. (1988) *In the Wake of the Hurricane*. National Edition. Froglets Publications: Westerham.

Patch, D. (ed.) (1987) *Advances in Practical Arboriculture*. Forestry Commission Bulletin 65. HMSO: London.

Peace, T. R. (1962) *Pathology of Trees and Shrubs with Special Reference to Britain*. Oxford University Press: Oxford.

Pettigrew, W. W. (1928) The influence of air pollution on vegetation. *The Gardeners' Chronicle* 84(292), 308–309.

Rackham, O. (1976) *Trees and Woodland in the British Landscape*. Archaeology in the Field Series. J. M. Dent and Sons: London.

Rackham, O. (2003) *Ancient Woodland: Its History, Vegetation and Uses in England*. New edition. Castlepoint Press: Dalbeattie.

Ravenscroft, B. C. (1883) *Town Gardening*. George Routledge and Sons: London.

RHS (2006) *Front Gardens*. Gardening Matters Urban Series. Royal Horticultural Society: London.

Richardson, J. (2002) High Hedges – new laws. *Arboricultural Journal* 26 (1), 55–64.

Risk Management Solutions (2003) *December 1703 Windstorm – 300-year retrospective*. Risk Management Solutions: London.

Risk Management Solutions (2007) *The Great Storm of 1987: 20-year retrospective*. Risk Management Solutions: London.

Robinette, G. O. (1972) *People, Plants and Environmental Quality*. United States Department of the Interior in collaboration with the American Society of Landscape Architects Foundation.

Rose, D. and Webber, J. (2011) *De-icing Salt Damage to Trees*. Pathology Advisory Note No. 11. Forest Research. Forestry Commission: Edinburgh.

Seifert, A. (1948) What Means this Drought? *Journal of Ecology* 36(1), 174–179.

Shigo, A. L. (1977) *Compartmentalization of Decay in Trees*. Agriculture Information Bulletin No. 405. United States Department of Agriculture, Forest Service: Washington, DC.

Sidney, S. (1851) *Rides on Railways*. Reprinted 1973 by Phillimore: London.

Stott, P. (1990) The Medieval Garden. In: Galinou, M., *London's Pride: The Glorious History of the Capital's Gardens*: Anaya Publishers: London.

Strouts, R. G. and Winter, T. G. (2000) *Diagnosis on Ill-health in Trees*. Research for Amenity Trees No. 2. Second edition. Department of the Environment, Transport and the Regions. The Stationary Office: London.

Steuart, Sir H. (1828) *The Planter's Guide*. Second edition. John Murray: London

Thayer, R.t L. (1983) Solar Access and the Urban Forest. *Arboricultural Journal* 7, 179–190.

Trevelyan, G. M. (1949) *Illustrated English Social History. Volume One: Chaucers's England and the Early* Tudors. Longmans, Green and Co: London.

Trevelyan, G. M. (1950) *Illustrated English Social History. Volume Two: The Age of Shakespeare and the Stuart Period*. Longmans, Green and Co: London.

Trinder, B. (1982) *The Making of the Industrial Landscape*. J. M. Dent and Sons Ltd: London.

Tubby, K. V. and Rose, D. R. (2009) Problems facing plane trees. *Arboriculture Association Newsletter* 144, Spring. 18–19.

Ward, H. M. (1894) Preface to the English Edition. In: Hartig, R. *Textbook of the Diseases of Trees*. Translated by William Somerville and revised and edited by H. Marshall Ward. Country Life: London.

Webb, J. (1965) How Tree Roots Affect Buildings. *The Arboricultural Association Journal* 1 (1), 15–17.

Webber, J. (2008) Greening the Black Country: The Work of the Midland Reafforesting Association in the Early Twentieth Century. *Arboricultural Journal* 31(1), 45–62.

Webber, J. (2010) *Dutch Elm Disease – Q&A*. Pathology Advisory Note No 10, Forest Research.

Webster, A. D. (1910) *Town Planting: And the Trees, Shrubs, Herbaceous and other Plants that are Best Adapted for Resisting Smoke*. George Routledge and Sons: London.

Webster, A. D. (1916) *Tree Wounds and Diseases: Their Prevention and Cure*. Williams and Northgate: London.

Wheeler, D. (2003) The Great Storm of November 1703: A New Look at the Seamen's Records. *Weather* 58(11), 419–427.

Wilkinson, G. (1978) *Epitaph for the Elm*. Hutchinson: London.

Willes, M. (2014) *The Gardens of the British Working Class*. Yale University Press: New Haven and London.

Winning, A. L. (1973) Arboriculture: the Emerging Specialism. *The Arboricultural Association Journal* 2(5), 148–160.

Wood, R. F. (1974) *Fifty Years of Forestry Research: A Review of Work Conducted and Supported by the Forestry Commission, 1920–1970*. Forestry Commission Bulletin No. 50. HMSO: London.

Wulf, A. (2008) *The Brother Gardeners: Botany, Empire and the Birth of an Obsession*. William Heinemann: London.

4

Trees in Private Gardens

Trees and shrubs in the gardens of residential properties have always formed part of our urban forests, a part that has grown in significance with the passing centuries. Even from earliest times, they have served a variety of functions ranging from the purely economic to the delightfully aesthetic. Trees bearing fruit and nuts have been a source of food for their owners and have also provided fuel and timber. Trees in residential gardens have also been used to mark the boundary of the property, to create a sense of intimate enclosure in the garden or to obscure unsightly views of the city beyond. As an integral part of the overall design of urban gardens, they have performed tasks ranging from essential structural elements to providing beautiful harmonies or striking contrasts of size, form and texture.

While we may admire the aesthetic qualities of trees, their social and psychological benefits are not simply experienced through casual observation (Johnston 1985, 121). Urban residents with their own trees and gardens are able to experience the benefits of involvement in the *process* of arboriculture. In selecting and cultivating trees in their gardens, urban residents can creatively express their personalities and gain the satisfaction of influencing their surroundings. As a personal imprint on the landscape trees can strengthen a sense of territoriality and promote social identity. Planting and caring for trees can also be a form of recreation, arousing feelings of pride and self-esteem and can assist in relieving the stress of an urban existence.

This chapter explores the history of garden trees through the ages, and to some extent this includes shrubs. Its focus in not on the great gardens of the aristocracy on their landed estates; it is about the residential gardens of all types that have graced our town and cities through the centuries. Garden and landscape historians have for so long focused on the monumental rather than the commonplace, on the unusual rather than the ongoing (Bell 1990, 481). While some grander gardens of the urban elite may have accommodated many trees, working class gardens were invariably quite small and with scarcely any room for trees. However, it has generally been the private gardens of the aristocracy that have set the fashion for the gardens of their time and led the way in innovative developments – and these were invariably located on country estates. Of course, some fashions such as the English landscape style of the eighteenth century could only realistically be followed by those wealthy urban residents who had extensive grounds. Nevertheless, there were still plenty of earlier and later landscape styles or features, even those usually displayed in a much grander context, which could have been reproduced in miniature or in part by urban residents with relatively small gardens.

Roman and Medieval gardens

Much of our information about Roman gardens comes from Italian remains and literary and artistic references, although there is some evidence of these early gardens in Britain (Farrar 1998; Jennings 2006). It seems reasonable to assume that Romano-British gardens were similar to those on the Continent, although probably not as fine (Amherst 1896, 2). Much of our archaeological evidence in Britain comes from the discovery of a Roman settlement at Fishbourne in the 1960s that unearthed a royal palace and garden dating back to AD 75. While the Fishbourne garden would not have been typical of Roman garden-making in Britain, it does give some idea of how their horticultural ideas and styles were adapted here. In Roman Silchester there were plenty of detached houses each with their own gardens that had orchards as well as vegetable and herb gardens (Berrall 1978, 227) (Figure 26). There appears to have been little compromise between utilitarianism and aestheticism; herbs and fruit trees became incidental to the overall plan and the garden for food crops was usually a separate entity. Roman gardens were arranged formally, often with paths lined with hedges and intricately patterned box hedging. A major contribution of Roman gardens was the recognition of the beauty and worth of ornamental plants and that the garden was an inseparable extension of the house. The Romans were also responsible for introducing several trees into Britain, many of which still make

FIGURE 26. In Roman towns in Britain there were usually plenty of detached houses each with their own garden that often contained an orchard. However, there tended to be few trees in most public open spaces within the town walls. This reconstruction drawing of the Roman town of Silchester is by Ivan Lapper (Copyright: English Heritage).

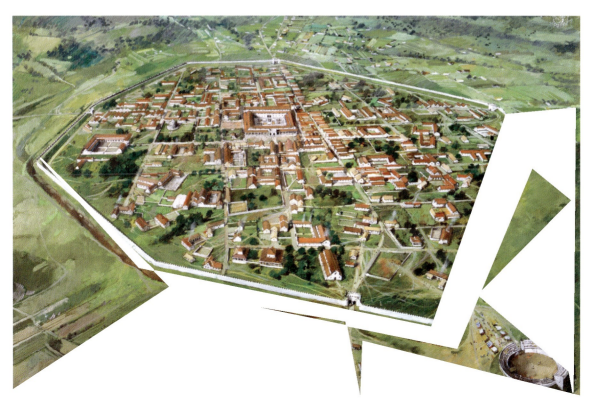

a contribution to our gardens (Mitchell 1981). These include walnut, sweet chestnut, Swedish whitebeam and possibly sycamore.

When the Roman occupation of Britain ended in 410, their gardens and horticulture generally went into decline. Indeed, it has been said that the art of horticulture in the Anglo-Saxon period was really only preserved behind the walls of monasteries (Barker 2012, 170). Unfortunately, our knowledge of medieval gardens in Britain is fairly limited and much of the evidence that exists has been pieced together from records of contemporary writing, art, cookery, medicine and social life (Landsberg 1995, 5). Were it not for John Harvey's (1981) classic work *Mediaeval Gardens*, the by-product of over forty years of reading building documents, we would not have our current understanding of the various trees, shrubs and other plants cultivated in these gardens. Most authorities on this era of horticultural history agree that there was a general trend where subsistence gardening largely replaced ornamental gardening. When London began to be reoccupied in the ninth century, the whole area within the walls was largely open space dotted among the ruins of the larger Roman buildings, and much of this was probably cultivated for fruit and vegetables (Schofield 1999, 73). By the fourteenth century, for the ordinary citizens of London, gardens were separate assets in the area immediately around the city. There were also orchards within the city walls, and individual trees mentioned in records include ash and elm. Where there were gardens within the walls of medieval towns, these were only ornamental for those wealthy citizens who could afford to treat their gardens as luxury items (Stott 1990, 41). For the rest of the population the common presence of pigsties and hens coop in their gardens meant these invariably had the character of smallholdings.

When we think of medieval gardens it is the monastic garden that usually comes to mind, with its physic garden of medicinal herbs as well as vegetable plots, vineyards and orchards (Berrall 1978, 91). After the Plague, as gaps appeared in the urban fabric, abandoned and derelict house-sites became yards and gardens or part of the common street, even in the centre of towns (Stott 1990, 44). It was then increasingly common to have private gardens adjacent to the homes of people of all classes and these invariably contained some small fruit trees such as apples, pears and pomegranates (Berrall 1978, 95). The edible cherry tree, thought to be introduced by the Romans, was also popular and frequently found in monastic gardens (Amherst 1896, 20). Trees also featured in the more formal ornamental gardens with small clipped evergreens such as yew or box, trained into tiers; and in more urban setting, larger versions became wonderful dining pavilions. Despite this, the art of topiary, which had initially been developed by the Romans, was not generally revived and certainly not in any complicated forms. Within the garden area there was often a variety of other features for entertainment. Grass-covered mounds offered vantage points for viewing the garden as a whole or the landscape beyond.

Ruralia commoda by Petrus de Crescentius from Bologna, written between 1304 and 1309, is often regarded as the most important medieval work on agriculture and horticulture (Smith 2005). The work has a section on 'arboriculture' that features trees useful for food and medicine. Another section gives descriptions of ideal pleasure gardens of the medieval era where three sorts of gardens are described, for common people, for the middle class, and for noblemen and kings (Berrall 1978, 96). Crescentius believed all should be created on flat ground and have sections for fragrant herbs as well as for flowers. The garden should be enclosed by hedges, walls or moat and within the garden turf was laid between the beds. He was also quite specific about the place of trees in the garden. He recommended that a few shade trees should be planted 'in the sun's path', but not so densely as to kill the grass, and not manured because that could also damage it. Trees were to be set widely enough apart to prevent spiders from stretching their webs from one tree to another and from catching in the faces of those who walked beneath.

Gardens of the Tudor and Stuart era

With increased population pressure in the Tudor era the spaciousness in the urban fabric following the Plague began to disappear, as gardens and yards were built over to provide new accommodation (Stott 1990, 45). This random 'infilling' of open space not only removed any existing trees in the way, it also meant that the smaller houses in London and other major settlements often had to make do with urban gardens of equally small size and often awkward shape (Schofield 1999, 81). Although the dissolution of the religious houses in the 1530s had released some open spaces in towns and cities, these were usually snapped up by the rich and powerful (Willes 2014, 18). By the end of the Tudor period, the small and constricted gardens of many Londoners were at least complemented by some public greenspace, such as public tree-lined walks in Moorfields. This pattern of urban open space in London is confirmed by the Copperplate Map of the late 1550s, the earliest known map of the capital (Stott 1990, 41). This shows some large gardens in the centre of the City but little in the way of smaller gardens that were likely to be hidden from the view of the draughtsman. During the Stuart period in the seventeenth century this pattern of garden ownership continued. The large gardens in London were owned by the most influential individuals in the country, or by institutions or corporate bodies that chose to keep them as gardens and could afford to forgo the profits of development (Harding 1990, 53). Maps of the time show that Londoners who had individual houses or cottages did not usually have gardens of any scale and consequently few garden trees (Halliwell 1990, 66).

For the wealthy Tudor and Stuart citizens of London and other cities, their larger gardens gave scope for extensive designs and numerous garden features. Nevertheless, these were normally quite intricate, artificial and confined as they served as outdoor rooms to be lived in and enjoyed in the same way as the indoor ones (Berrall 1978, 228). While less wealthy citizens and those with smaller urban gardens could not compete with these, much of the basic style of those gardens and many of their more popular features were still reproduced on a limited scale. 'Alyes' of arched trees and shrubs together with rose and jasmine-covered wooden arbours were very popular. With their paths underneath for promenading these provided shade in the summer and some shelter in poor weather. Knot gardens, with their intricate designs often formed by a low-growing box hedge, appeared as a garden feature at the beginning of the sixteenth century. Hedges of various species were also planted around the knot garden and because of their convenient height they were often used for spreading out and drying laundry, a use of hedges also found in the much smaller gardens of common people. The larger formal gardens of this period were best viewed from a high vantage point to show off their intricate patterns and overall design (Strong 1979). To help facilitate this, the 'mount' became a much more important garden accessory than formerly, often located in the corner of the orchard (Amherst 1896, 79). While they were usually covered in trees, they also had views out across the broad expanse of the garden and the landscape beyond.

While hedges helped create the overall design of these gardens, various tree and shrub species also had a role in creating other significant garden features. No garden of any size was complete without topiary or 'antike worke', an art brought back into Britain in the sixteenth century from Italy via France (Berrall 1978, 237). Although juniper was sometimes used, the favourite plant for topiary was yew because it grew slowly, lived long, and could be trained into delicate shapes. Not everyone was enthusiastic about the fashion for topiary and there were probably quite a few who shared Francis Bacon's view that "images cut out in juniper or other garden stuff, be for children." The maze was also now a well-established feature in the larger gardens of the most impressive urban residencies and was generally formed out of clipped yew hedges (Matthews 1922, 110–27).

As a consequence of these popular features in the Tudor and Stuart garden, many of the regular horticultural tasks involved working with tree and shrub species, such as trimming the hedges, clipping the arbours and mazes, shaping the topiary, and shearing the knots (Berrall 1978, 237). Another major source of tree work during this time involved orchards and fruit trees in general, often a feature of both urban and rural gardens. The popularity of fruit trees was reflected in contemporary horticultural texts. Gervase Markham (1613) and William Lawson (1618) were authorities on estate and garden management who discussed at length the design and management of orchards, which they both saw as the prime area in which pleasure and profit combine (Roberts 1999, 95). Indeed, for Lawson, the orchard *was* the garden. In his book *A New Orchard and Garden* there is a plan for an ideal garden that has ordered rows of fruit trees as well as topiary, knots and garden ornaments (Lawson 1618, 10) (Figure 27).

The Tudor and Stuart period saw a steady expansion in the range of different trees planted in urban gardens. John Evelyn was prominent in encouraging people to plant a much wider variety of trees in their gardens, particularly

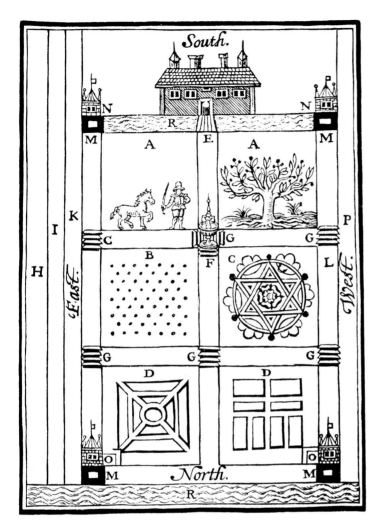

some of the recent introductions such as tulip tree and cedar (Amherst 1896, 192). The efforts of James I to encourage the cultivation of mulberry trees to establish a silk industry resulted in many being planted. For many decades after, the presence of solitary mulberry trees in town or city gardens probably dated from that time. For most urban gardens small trees were favoured, such Judas tree or laburnum, as it was not suitable to allow untrained trees to develop naturally as they were generally too large when mature. Sometimes larger-growing species of tree were used but these would be regularly clipped to keep them within bounds and to produce a formal shape that could be incorporated into the pattern of the garden (Halliwell 1990, 68).

Georgian gardens

Early in the Georgian era most urban residents continued to be deprived of their own private gardens (Brown 1999, 151). As before, there were also some wealthy individuals who could retain substantial urban properties

FIGURE 27. William Lawson's ideal plan for a garden from his *New Orchard and Garden*, first published in 1612. The parts where he makes specific reference to tree species include (A) all these squares must be set with trees, (B) trees 20 yards asunder, (C) garden knots, (H) walks set with great wood thick, (I) walks set with great wood round about your orchard.

with large gardens. While maps of London at that time may give the impression it was a city with plenty of garden spaces, their accuracy on that aspect is disputed. With John Rocque's map of 1746 the precise extent of any greenspace or tree cover is difficult to determine.

In the early 1700s front gardens for urban properties in most town and cities were largely nonexistent, or greatly restricted in size by the pressures of road use (Longstaffe-Gowan 2001, 58). Any space to the rear of houses was usually a yard reserved for privies and clotheslines. The most common urban dwelling was the terraced house, and small front and back gardens were not common to these types of property before 1775. Most residential property was also rented, leased or shared. For the working class this would have been tenements, lodging housing and cellars that were adapted from their original use as family dwellings for better-off urban residents and never intended for multi-occupation (Burnett 1986, 70). Even where these properties had a garden and space for one or more trees, restrictions of the tenancy agreement or lack of security in their tenure meant that tenants were probably prohibited or discouraged from planting any trees. While the upper class from the country rented town houses for the Season that often had a quite spacious curtilage, they probably had little interest in the gardens during their limited stays (Longstaffe-Gowan 2001, 38).

In Georgian towns and cities the relentless commercial development, increases in population, road building and road improvements all imposed restrictions on the creation and extension of residential gardens (Harding and Taigel 1996, 237). The use of ground for gardens on the outskirts of town was in many cases an economic necessity since land in commercial centres commanded a high rental and was invariably densely developed. As land for new housing became increasingly scarce within the existing urban core, orchards, gardens, yards and any patch of waste ground was swallowed up (Burnett 1986, 10). As a consequence, the vast majority of British families remained without a private garden and with no opportunity to plant and enjoy their own trees.

As the eighteenth century progressed, the ownership or use of a small private town garden became, for the first time, a common expectation for many middle class people as these slowly became available (Longstaffe-Gowan 1990, 122). This was reflected in the emergence of town gardening as a commercialised leisure activity and one of the products of a wider consumer revolution that was taking place at this time. The services of jobbing gardeners were frequently employed by wealthier householders for cheap, quick and practical garden work. These self-employed, itinerant garden operatives or tradesmen gardeners would solicit work by calling door-to-door or advertising in local papers. Thomas Fairchild's (1722) *The City Gardener* marked an important early point in these developments as this popular little book was the first published work to make recommendations on beautifying city gardens. It contained astute observations on practical urban gardening that included recommending those trees and shrubs more resistant to the smoke that hung in the London air. Fairchild's advice on this topic might have had some impact. When Swedish botanist Pehr Kalm visited London in 1748, he noticed many small gardens and yards where trees and other plants which could withstand the coal-smoke were commonly planted, sometimes in the ground and sometimes in containers (Kalm 1892, 85). The presence of these plants and gardens indicated to Kalm that Londoners "sought to have some of the pleasant enjoyment of country life in the midst of the hubbub of the town." However, Kalm's assertion that there were plenty of small gardens in London at that time is in contrast to other contemporary evidence (Longstaffe-Gowan 2001, 23).

The growing popularity of small gardens and the involvement in gardening by a broader section of urban society has been ascribed to the opportunities this offered for social emulation (Ellis 2000, 40). Fashions in gardens changed almost as often as those with clothes and architecture and it provided a means of classifying the wealth, taste and aspirations of friends and rivals. The growing wealth and scale of the Georgian middle class allowed this section of urban society to indulge in gardening as an enjoyable hobby and to use this to enhance their status. Fashion thus reinforced the growing appreciation of the natural world in Georgian towns and made a private garden into a status symbol. The cultivation of garden trees and shrubs, especially rare or recently introduced species, was part of that trend.

It was now becoming increasingly common for middle class houses to have rear gardens. For example, every house in London's Grosvenor Square that was completed in the 1720s had a small rear garden, a landscape amenity that had not been provided in the older squares. Since the middle of the eighteenth century, much of the new housing for the middle and upper class in London and elsewhere had included the provision of small backyards that were often turned into gardens by the residents (Lawrence 1993, 108). In the older residential areas, waste ground or orchards could sometimes be purchased by those with sufficient money and converted into gardens (Ellis 2000, 41). Others simply used their wealth to reverse the usual infill development, buying up and demolishing existing properties to obtain a plot with a suitably pleasant look. For example, East Hill House in Colchester acquired a garden at the expense of nine cottages. If all else failed, a 'detached' garden in the suburbs was better than no garden at all, and these were frequently advertised in local newspapers.

Research into the design and appearance of small Georgian urban gardens is difficult because the planting and layout was regularly modified to keep pace with changing tastes (Ellis 2000, 41). Furthermore, there is hardly any record of these gardens as individually they were of little significance to anyone but their owners. Therefore, the nature and extent of any tree planting is almost impossible to ascertain. The detailed plan that we have of Francis Douce's garden in London's Gower Street in the 1790s, which did contain plenty of trees, is probably far from typical (Longstaffe-Gowan 1987). It is also likely that all the attention paid by historians to the great landscape gardens of the aristocracy has obscured the extent to which towns shared in the 'garden revolution' of this period.

Like the architecture of this time, gardening was an art riddled with classical values. In the early Georgian period, town gardens were laid out in strict formality with straight lines of box hedges surrounding small flower beds (Ellis 2000, 42) (Figure 28). In larger gardens, the knot garden of Tudor times had now been largely superseded by the more embroidered and grander parterre of the French. Flowering shrubs and fruit trees, carefully clipped and trained, were placed amid straight gravel paths. However, the winds of change were starting to blow. In the wider landscape on country estates, Batty Langley (1728) led the way against all this formality with the publication of his *New Principles of Gardening* in which he was critical of other garden designers for their stiff and regular plans of knots, parterres and extensive use of evergreens. Topiary also came in for much criticism from other landscape and garden enthusiasts, particularly after a memorable article in 1712 by Joseph Addison in *The Spectator*. Addison declared:

Our British gardeners, instead of honouring nature, love to deviate from it as much as possible. Our trees rise in Cones, Globes and Pyramids. We see the marks of the scissors upon every plant and bush. ...for my own part, I would rather look upon a tree in all its Luxuriancy and Diffusion of Bough and Branches, than when it is thus cut and trimmed into a Mechanical figure.

Addison, 1712, 101–2

FIGURE 28. The Privy Garden at Hampton Court Palace, London, was original laid out in 1702 and epitomises the formal style of gardening that was fashionable among the ruling class in the early Georgian period. Small trees were carefully clipped and trained and placed at regular intervals among straight lines of box hedges.

As the century progressed, the popularity of the more informal and picturesque styles of rural landscapes began to influence some urban gardeners, just as they were to influence the layout of town squares. Not everyone favoured the new approach and Thomas Fairchild (1722) was notable in deploring the fashionable preference for luxuriant greenery at the expense of flower growing. Despite these opposing voices, enthusiasm for the new approach spread quickly from the great country estates to the larger provincial gardens. Serpentine paths, wilderness shrubberies, unclipped trees and sloping lawns right up to the house marked out the new style of gardens 'planted with tasteful economy', in contrast to the 'childishly laid out' flowerbeds of earlier years. Yet these natural styles never came to dominate private town gardens, which seem to have remained remarkably faithful to the classical tradition, even in the heart of fashionable Bath (Ellis 2000, 42). This resilience owed much to the essential 'urbanity' of formal gardens but even more to the practical constraint within which urban gardeners had to operate. Foremost among these were the limitations of size and the uncompromisingly regular shape of most town gardens, which simply did not lend themselves to the expansive curves of natural landscaping. Even where there was space for a few garden trees, it was unlikely these were the forest-type trees favoured by the great landscape improvers. Furthermore, the multitude of uses for urban gardens also played an important part in determining their layout, which required considerable ingenuity to accommodate all these in such a small space. Privet hedging was then among the more common means of dividing up small gardens for shelter or ornament, particularly favoured for its smoke-tolerance and evergreen quality (Longstaffe-Gowan 2001, 133).

As Britain's commercial and industrial growth gathered pace in the late eighteenth century, so did the wealth and scale of its urban middle class (Borsay 1989). This was followed by an increasing desire among the middle class to separate their business activities and their home life in separate premises, a trend that was to prompt the development of suburban homes (Burnett 1986, 105). This middle class separation of business and living encouraged the development of a new kind of social life that favoured the house itself being as separate as possible from its neighbours and, at all costs, from neighbouring areas of an inferior social status. For these reasons, terraces became increasingly out of favour as the century progressed, and the suburban detached house increasingly the ideal. The semi-detached house was also popular as a compromise solution typically employed in the inner suburbs where land costs were relatively high. All these developments in residential housing offered new and exciting opportunities for urban horticulture and arboriculture.

Where town gardens and particularly suburban gardens contained some mature trees, this tended to add to the desirability of the property. This is evidenced by the fact that ornamental trees and specimen fruit trees featured prominently in the sale particulars for suburban properties from the early eighteenth century (Longstaffe-Gowan 2001, 86). Nevertheless, trees only appear to have been a valuable commodity if the garden was relatively large, the fruit trees in a 'bearing state', and the ornamental trees were 'of sufficient size to produce considerable effect'. The value of established trees in residential properties was reflected in some of the new suburban developments where it became the practice to plant trees in advance of the main building work. For example, the architect John Nash had initiated the tree planting for his private housing development at Regent's Park as early as 1811, at which time it lay mostly in pasture. According to the contemporary author James Elmes (1827, 20) this gave "the advantage of so many years growth while the buildings were in progress". By 1816 over 14,500 trees were planted by three firms of nurserymen. This ensured the park had an air of cultivated amenity before a single villa or terrace was built. The trees were planted in two distinct patterns: the first was in regular plantations of forest trees such as plane, sweet chestnut and larch on sites designated for future building. These trees could be felled and sold as timber when the plots were selectively cleared for building. The second involved a series of naturalistic thickets of more ornamental trees, most of which would remain undisturbed. As the landscape of Regent's Park matured the various individual villas designed by Nash were surrounded by trees and shrubs so that they would not be visible to each other and the whole park appeared to 'belong' to each villa (Conway 1991, 12). Around much of the Outer Circle of the park several elegant terraces of houses were built, also designed by Nash, with views across the extensive treescape (Williams 1978, 208).

By the 1790s, concern over the lack of garden ground, particularly for the poor, was widespread (Harding and Taigel 1996, 238). Philanthropic attempts were made by some concerned middle class citizens to provide small plots of land for the poor. There were instances of the division and lease of the paddocks and garden ground attached to major town houses of the period, particularly where the owner also leased out the house. These were generally used for growing vegetables and were unlikely to have resulted in trees being planted, with the possible exception of small fruit trees grown in containers.

Even towards the end of the Georgian era when the popularity of town gardening was well-established, few members of the urban working class were fortunate enough to have their own gardens (Ellis 2000, 44). This was particularly the case in fast-growing towns like Birmingham where land was too expensive for commercial developers to provide their cheaper houses with gardens. The building boom that followed the Napoleonic Wars was also encroaching steadily on existing open spaces and while speculative schemes for the middle class made some provision for parkland and gardens, this was very seldom accessible to non-residents (Elliott 1986, 52). Nonetheless, it was still possible for working class families to rent allotments on the edge of town, which as well as providing a source of vegetables also gave some escape from the dirty and confined urban conditions. Meanwhile, the high prices paid for building land in the fastest growing towns created a continual tension between the inhabitants' love of greenery and the profits to be made from industrial and residential development. The poorest sections of society had very little to protect them from the environmental blight that followed from intensive urban development (Ellis 2000, 45). By the end of the Georgian period, the landscape of the larger English towns had become sharply divided between relatively small wealthy areas where trees and greenery softened the hard outlines of development and the much larger areas of unrelenting urban blight. This period also saw the beginnings of neighbourhoods of detached and semi-detached houses surrounded by garden space, one of the main ways that trees entered the urban environment later in the nineteenth century.

Seventeenth century and Georgian residential squares

The residential squares of London, Edinburgh, Bath and other cities that developed in the seventeenth and eighteenth century became a uniquely British urban landscape form (Lawrence 1993, 90). It introduced rural landscape values into the urban fabric in ways that continue today. While the origin of these squares can be traced back to the public plazas of the seventeenth century, most were initially created as private gardens for the residents of the surrounding houses. (See Chapter 5 for the later history of squares as public open spaces).

The first London residential square was Covent Garden, begun in 1630 with designs by Inigo Jones on land owned by the Earl of Bedford (Longstaffe-Gowan 2012, 26). The space at the centre was paved and completely open, which allowed public use that grew in importance over the years. It was an exclusively hard landscape without trees or any horticultural features of note. Another square emerged at the same period around fields adjacent to Lincoln's Inn, one of the City's Inns of Court. Lincoln's Inn Fields lay just west of the City and had been open to common use for many years (Lawrence 1993, 94). In the 1630s investors brought up the property surrounding the three sides of the field away from Lincoln's Inn and begun to build houses. Three other squares, Bloomsbury, St James's and Leicester, were established just before the Great Fire. The residential square was the centrepiece of a larger development that often included a separate market square, shops, a parish church, residential housing for the major tenants of the square and lesser accommodation for servants and artisans.

These seventeenth century squares were socially ambiguous landscapes (Lawrence 1993, 97). The land was usually the property of aristocratic landowners, as were the surrounding houses that were leased to tenants, while residents leased a right to use the land and the houses. Some of the squares were in effect commons to which prior residents had old rights of access for productive activities like drying and bleaching of cloth, or non-productive activities such as military training and recreation. These were not entirely private places under the control of the landlord or of the estate residents who resided in them. Exclusion of the public was difficult and, until 1720s, not clearly legal.

The open spaces of the squares changed from open plazas in the seventeenth century to enclosed private parks at the end of the eighteenth century, a trend based on the social values of the aristocracy, later adopted by the middle class (Lawrence 1993, 90). Public rights of access were steadily extinguished through parliamentary enclosure acts similar to those used at the same time on rural estates. The first was passed in 1726 to enable the residents of St James's Square to restrict access to the square and to levy a rate on themselves for its improvement and maintenance. In 1735, Lincoln's Inn Fields were enclosed and following a precedent there, Parliament allowed squares to be enclosed with an iron fence to which the surrounding residents had keys. From the late 1720s onwards, squares were consistently regarded as the most fashionable urban districts and their continuing respectability depended largely on the exclusion of 'undesirables'. The squares and their surrounding residential districts represented some of the first expressions of the desire for class segregation, domestic isolation and privatised open space that later were to form the basis of suburban living. They were also a major arena for playing out the tension between classes over access to open space and they were to influence the development of early public parks.

The residential square and its garden formed the central elements in the landscape of elite districts of London and many provincial towns from the late seventeenth century to the mid-nineteenth century (Lawrence 1993, 90). They played a pivotal role in introducing trees and gardens into the urban landscape and in shaping subsequent ideals of urban life. The aesthetics of these gardens in the residential squares were also quite varied throughout most of the eighteenth century. Contemporary views show a wide range of conditions, from open pavement to grass plots to tree-lined walks. In the early part of the eighteenth century the landscape of the gardens was usually quite formal. In Queen's Square in fashionable Bath the horticultural arrangements were particularly elaborate with the four quarters of the square enclosed with espaliers of elm and lime trees and planted with flowering shrubs, while the intersecting footpaths were arranged in a striking geometric pattern (Borsay 1989, 77).

Thomas Fairchild's (1722, 43) *The City Gardener* included a section on the landscape design of squares in what he termed 'the rural manner'. Despite this term, the actual designs proposed were quite formal with regular segments bounded by hedges and intersected by straight paths (Figure 29). The height of the trees within these segments were to be kept to within a few feet above the top of the hedges so as not to 'incumber the prospect'. However, the middle walk could be planted with horse-chestnuts, which would be allowed to grow naturally and above the rest of the tree and shrub planting. There would then be a mound at the centre of the garden, covered with trees planted quite closely together. There should be no planting of trees on the outside of the square that would rise higher than the wall or palisade surrounding the garden as this might "rob the Gentleman of that View which they have by their Expense endeavour'd to gain" (*ibid.*, 42). This regular layout of squares remained popular for some time as it was inexpensive to maintain and easy to guard.

As the eighteenth century progressed, there was a noticeable trend in the design of these gardens from open to closed landscapes and from grass and gravel to trees and shrubs (Figure 30). Trees and shrubs became an increasingly dominant feature of these squares and initially they were kept far enough apart and sufficiently low to allow views across and through the open space. Small trees such as laburnum were frequently planted and when larger ones such as limes and hornbeams were used they were usually tightly pruned and pleached. By the third quarter of the eighteenth century, there was a noticeable increase in the density of vegetation. While the basic pattern of gravel paths and grass plots remained unchanged, squares were increasingly dominated by 'natural' shrubberies and mature deciduous trees, especially elms (Ellis 2000, 39). Other larger tree species such as London plane and sycamore were also planted and allowed to grow to their full height (Lawrence 1993, 101). Many of the older trees that had previously been pruned were now allowed to grow freely. As a result of these management changes the larger squares in particular began to look like little English landscape parks. There was a clear desire on the part of the local residents, who paid for the upkeep of the gardens, to create an

FIGURE 29. *(right)* Leicester Square in London around 1750, with the view looking north. This engraving shows the very formal arrangement of the trees and other horticultural features. The large house set behind a forecourt in the northeast corner is Leicester House, then the residence of Frederick, Prince of Wales (Sexby 1898).

FIGURE 30. *(below)* Red Lion Square in London was originally laid out in 1684, taking its name from the nearby Red Lion Inn. This engraving shows the square around 1800, not long before its landscape was to become 'picturesque' (Sexby 1898).

imitation of the country estate, something that posed quite a challenge to the skill of garden designers.

John Claudius Loudon, the great horticultural writer, published his first article in the *Literary Journal* in 1803 on his plans to plant the residential squares of London with trees and shrubs (Loudon 1803). Loudon criticised the gardens for their overuse of evergreen trees and shrubs and lack of 'picturesque beauty'. At that time there were still many squares with just grass and very few trees. Loudon demanded this be remedied with more planting and a much wider selection of species, although contrary to popular believe he did not recommended the planting of plane trees in these squares (Simo 1988, 322).

The private pleasure grounds of Edinburgh's New Town deserve a special mention. In comparison to many London squares and those of other provincial cities, these were on a lavish scale (Byrom 1995, 68). The New Town was built in stages between 1765 and around 1850 and is now regarded as a masterpiece of urban planning. Around 10 per cent of the area was devoted to private communal gardens formed over a period of about 100 years, mostly following the completion of the surrounding houses. Evidence from early garden minute books shows that the gardens were generally planted first with trees and shrubs, with flowers and smaller decorative planting later. Most trees were deciduous, with lime the most popular choice to line the edges and grander walks along with other trees such as elm, sycamore, oak, ash, plane and beech. While smaller ornamental species such as cherry, lilac and laburnum did appear later, these were not in great numbers. Willow and poplar were commonly planted at the start to provide quick growth and shelter, to be thinned out when the larger forest trees were established. The outer edges of the gardens were usually planted with shrubs to provide increased shelter and privacy. When Loudon, who had studied at Edinburgh University, published his critique of London squares in 1803, only one of the New Town gardens had been completed. His cautionary comments about layout and management came at an opportune time for the gardens' management committees, although their subsequent choice of species suggests some independent views on this aspect.

One feature of squares that Loudon was determined to change related to public access to their gardens (Figure 31). By 1800, Lincoln's Inn Fields was the only one of the great city squares that was open regularly to the public (Longstaffe-Gowan 2001, 224). Later, non-residents were allowed access to the gardens in a few squares in other cities but usually at an annual fee that precluded the working class. In a letter to the editor of the *Literary Journal* in 1803, Loudon claimed the squares could contribute greatly to the beauty of the metropolis, to the health and well-being of its inhabitants, and even to some extent that of national honour. Nevertheless, such a role was dependent on some public access to the gardens. While this did not necessarily involve allowing access to the central areas of the major squares, Loudon did urge the residents of all private squares to plant these gardens to the 'utmost picturesque advantage' so that everyone could get some benefit of the view, if only from a distance. Ideally, he envisaged that garden squares might one day be open to everyone and provide a structured natural setting for passive public recreation and public instruction, particularly the pursuit of botany.

The appeal of living in a residential square lay not just in the prestige of the estate or in the amenity of the garden in the square (Lawrence 1993, 108). It also lay in the location of the neighbourhood at the edge of the town. Most had been built on previously open ground in the urban fringe. In their early years, the relatively slow rate of urban growth meant that they remained for many years in relatively suburban locations. As the eighteenth century progressed and urban expansion gathered pace, what had previously been rather quiet and picturesque locations were now in the middle of increasingly frenetic and dense urban development. Furthermore, by the late eighteenth century, just having a pleasant 'prospect' through the visual appropriation of nature was no longer sufficiently satisfying (Longstaffe-Gowan 1990, 132). Actual ownership or 'property' was becoming more important than 'prospect'. Wealthy urban residents who had previously condescended to share their garden amenity with other keyholders now found the notion unattractive. They preferred their own small private garden enclosures and were significantly less interested in the shared gardens of squares.

Victorian gardens

The Victorian garden arose out of a rebellion against the eighteenth century landscape park as a conscious move away from 'nature' (Elliott 1986, 7). In 1808, the great landscape gardener Humphry Repton had declared that "gardens are works of art rather than of nature" (Repton 1840, 374). The component parts of the landscape began to be freed from subordination to the overall scheme. The values of the garden were no longer dependent on the values of landscape painting and Repton ensured that his gardens were laid out for their uses, not as a picture. Once again, this trend started in the great country gardens but then spread to urban areas.

During the 1820s large garden landscapes were still mainly characterised by a 'free and easy' style poised somewhere between 'nature' and 'art' (Elliott 1986, 59). The style was dominated by the flowering shrubbery, a group of shrubs designed for display, which had long been a feature of many gardens but now promoted even more with the publication of the first work on the subject, *Sylva Florifera* by Henry Phillips (1823). Flower gardens of increasing formality were also to be found in many larger private gardens and once again close to the house itself. By the 1830s, it was increasingly appropriate for the garden to display the unmistakable signs of artifice. Furthermore, it was widely accepted that there was no constant in terms of taste as everyone could have their own view and even this could change over time. Some horticultural writers such as Loudon were adamant that no attempt should be made to replicate the English landscape style in urban and suburban gardens. In one of his earlier texts

FIGURE 31. St George's Square in London, laid out in 1839, is typical of the late-Georgian residential squares and gardens in London, Edinburgh, Bath and other cities. Originally, access to this garden was limited to the surrounding residents who were given keys. St George's Square is now managed by the City of Westminster Council as a public open space.

entitled *Hints on the Formation of Gardens and Pleasure Grounds*, Loudon (1812) highlighted the absurdity of trying to make small villa gardens in the landscape style with miniature lawns and little clumps of trees. Instead, he recommends more formal designs.

The revival of formal and architectural styles was the most obvious way of making the garden as a whole into a work of art (Elliott 1986, 33). In order to achieve this, Loudon in particular was keen on the use of exotics in landscape planting (Loudon 1838). Indeed, exotic planting was to become one of the major determinants of Victorian gardening as it so clearly demonstrated that 'Nature must acknowledge the supremacy of Art'. However, the use of exotics raised questions about the classification of trees that were originally exotic but had since become commonplace, such as larch and horse chestnut. Associationism provided the answer (Elliott 1986, 33). Plants that lacked 'associations of culture and keeping' should be treated as indigenous, whether they were native or not. Similarly, trees of unusual shape or habit became immediate signals of art when planted so as to attract attention. Many of the well-known weeping tree cultivars, such as those of elm and beech, initially appeared in the first quarter of the nineteenth century. The fastigiate Lombardy poplar was also a much planted tree at this time.

By the 1830s, the isolation of trees as individual specimens was a major feature of gardens (Elliott 1986, 34). This involved not merely separation, but allowing each tree to 'arrive at perfection' by displaying to the maximum its most aesthetically pleasing characteristics. Loudon and others before him had long complained that trees were invariable planted so that their main surface roots were concealed. In Loudon's view, they should be planted on mounds, the width of the base being three times the height of the hill, to expose the main roots at the junction with the trunk. The practice of planting trees on mounds was adopted by other landscape gardeners and became a feature of mid-nineteenth century gardens. Robert Marnock, another landscape designer, recommended the mound to be a foot higher than the surrounding surface with a slight rim to hold the rain. While Loudon could not claim to be the originator of specimen planting, he deserves recognition as the man who introduced the concept of artistic grouping of trees into nineteenth century British landscapes. He frequently protested in his own *Gardener's Magazine* against the 'meaningless dotting' of single trees in places such as Regent's Park.

At the start of the Victorian era, Loudon had coined a term for his own distinctive approach to landscape design: the 'gardenesque' style. In his classic text *The Suburban Gardener and Villa Companion*, first published in 1838, Loudon makes clear the distinction between the picturesque and the gardenesque (Loudon 1838, 164). The picturesque was "the imitation of nature in a wild state, such as the painter delights to copy", while the gardenesque was "the imitation of nature subjected to a certain degree of cultivation and improvement, suitable to the wants and wishes of man". *The Suburban Gardener* was one of Loudon's last works and it gives us some remarkable insights into many aspects of early Victorian gardening. He was very conscious of the growing desire of many middle class families to relocate to the suburbs and enjoy a more relaxed and 'greener' home life. So, he published a book which would provide them with all the information they needed for their new suburban homes (Simo 1988, 257). Indeed, Loudon's own villa in Bayswater, which he constructed in 1823, became a prototype for his idealised middle class villa. In his book Loudon sets out a hierarchy of four types of suburban garden that he considered may be classed in the same manner as their houses (Figure 32). These ranged from 'first-rate' gardens, with not less than 50–100 acres (20.2–40.5 ha) and usually a park and a farm, to 'fourth-rate' gardens in which the house formed part of a street or a row and the extent of the garden was no more than one acre. Loudon planned the garden to illustrate the social position of the landowner. Even for a small villa plantations of trees and shrubs were as important as the house architecture in achieving general effects and in demonstrating the 'means and taste' of the owner. Loudon classified his own garden at Bayswater as 'fourth rate' and he devotes more space in his book to this class of garden than any other (Figure 33). It is also clear from the illustrations of the houses that these are still middle class dwellings far beyond the purse of working class families. Considering the limited size of these 'fourth rate' gardens, it is remarkable how many different features and how much variety of planting are included in the proposed designs, a reflection of what Loudon managed to achieve over the years with different designs in his own garden.

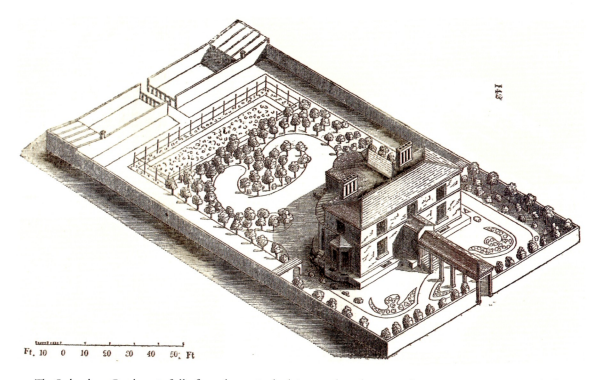

Ft. 10 0   10   20   30   40   50 Ft

The Suburban Gardener is full of good practical advice on the selection, planting and maintenance of garden trees (Loudon 1838). Trees should be procured at 6 or 8 feet in height so that when planted their tops would be out of the reach of children. While the choice of trees could be left to the taste of the owners, the finest species of trees (and Loudon had firm opinions on this) should be planted nearer the house so that they would be more noticeable. Loudon's preoccupation throughout his career with the concept of the arboretum extended to his plans for suburban gardens. Those with larger gardens might chose to establish a 'complete arboretum', while those with less space in their garden could focus on a selection of 'showy trees and shrubs'. The planting of low-growing trees near paths should be avoided as this will necessitate the expense of frequent pruning for clearance. For the same reason, no tree or shrub should be planted against the house because this will incur the expense of training and pruning to keep them clear of windows and doors. Even allowing for the restrictions on planting too close to the house or paths, the density of planting in Loudon's designs for villa gardens is quite considerable. In his own garden, the vast number of trees that were initially planted ensured that he was eventually forced to remove many larger specimens. In order to slow the rapid growth of the more vigorous trees and shrubs, these were often dug up and their roots pruned annually.

Loudon was conscious of the combined effect of trees in neighbouring gardens and suggested that a degree of symmetry might be achieved. He was also aware of an opportunity to promote the planting of arboretums in even the most unlikely situations. He declared:

FIGURE 32. Loudon's *Suburban Gardener and Villa Companion* set out a hierarchy of four types of suburban garden and he planned them to illustrate the social position of the landowner. The 'third-rate' garden that is pictured here still covers a sizable area and has plenty of space for trees (Loudon 1838).

FIGURE 33. Loudon classified his own garden at 3–5 Porchester Terrace, Bayswater, as a 'fourth rate' garden. Over the years the design of this changed frequently as he sought to display the range of trees and shrubs and the variety of designs that could be accommodated in a relatively small space.

> With respect to the trees along the front of these gardens next the road or street, which, if the street was long enough, may include the whole of the popular series from the British arboretum. Were this mode adopted in any long street, with front gardens on both sides of it, the same series ought to be adopted on both sides of the road, for the sake of preserving symmetry to the public in walking or driving along the street.
>
> Loudon 1838, 278

What is especially striking about Loudon's work on trees, gardens and the landscape is his understanding of the many different benefits of urban trees. While he emphasises the aesthetic value of trees and shrubs in suburban gardens, he is also conscious of their wider contribution to urban life for all classes of residents and to the welfare of the human race in general. While this broader perspective is not evident in many of his horticultural contemporaries, Loudon states:

> Trees are not only, in appearance, the most striking and grand objects of the vegetable creation; but, in reality, they are those which contribute most to human comfort and improvement.
>
> Loudon, 1838, 1

While Loudon had a major impact on the suburban gardens of the middle class, the vast majority of urban working class families in the Victorian era continued to live in dwellings that had no gardens. The pressure on urban land was now even more intense due to the urban population explosion and spiralling land values. For many working class families the only prospect for having their own garden was to try to secure a small plot of land at the edge of the city. Some of these detached urban gardens were originally established as 'guinea gardens', which were usually allotment-sized plots rented on a commercial basis by landholders and developers (Way 2010, 115). Unfortunately for the working class, the high rents meant these gardens were invariably taken by middle class shopkeepers and tradesmen who were denied gardens because they lived over their shops or used their small yards for business. In the early nineteenth century Birmingham had a population of 80,000, out of which only 1. per cent was able to afford to lease one of these gardens (Willes 2014, 151). The working class people of Nottingham seemed to have fared much better. The author William Howitt, writing in 1844, claimed there were upwards of 5000 gardens on the outskirts of Nottingham, the bulk of which were occupied by the working class (Howitt 1844, 550–1). Many of these gardens also had trees, since Howitt describes the scene in spring where tree pruning was undertaken and the gardens form "one wide expanse of blossomed fruit trees and flowering fragrance."

The Victorian era witnessed considerable innovation and experimentation in horticultural techniques and practice. The drive behind this lay partly in that desire for garden owners and their staff to make an unmistakable human and artistic imprint on their landscapes (Elliott 1986, 79). By the 1840s, the doctrine of the creative imagination was taking root in the gardening world. The informing spirit of the garden was increasingly seen as emanating from man's mind rather than from nature; the 'genius of the place' was giving way to the 'inventive genius of man'. Grafting was one technique whereby gardeners could demonstrate their mastery over nature (*ibid.*, 32). The exploits of William Barron at Elvaston Castle became legendary as he steadily turned the Earl of Hartington's grounds into a grafter's playground, with rows of grafted cedars in avenues and specimens of weeping beech grafted onto mature trees to produce cascades of branches from great heights. Training shrubs into standards was another popular technique, although some regarded this particular distortion of the natural habit to be unsightly. Of all the technical improvements of the time the one that had the most obvious impact on garden design was the art of transplanting, with Barron pioneering the novel idea of transplanting root-balled trees. His book *The British Winter Garden* gives a detailed account of his techniques to successfully transplant a great many trees, some of substantial size and over considerable distances (Barron 1852). It was reported that the trees were often so large that as they passed through the streets of Derby windows were frequently broken in houses on both sides of the street (Elliott 1986, 84). While much of this transplanting involved moving trees on country estates, there is evidence that it also occurred to a significant extent in urban areas.

In common with many horticulturists of that time, both Barron and Loudon favoured evergreen species of trees and shrubs. Indeed, coniferous trees have a close association with the Victorian garden. This fashion for conifers began, as did many garden trends of the time, in the landscape gardens of the upper class on their country estates. Within a few years of the revelations from Elvaston Castle, the popularity of the pinetum was reaching its peak. Thomas Appleby, touring the north in 1852, reported that many prominent industrialists' estates were being planted with conifers, often in arboretums or in newly designed pinetums (Elliott, 1986, 115). Barron's book *The British Winter Garden,* published that same year, did much to further promote the advantages of coniferous planting at the expense of many native deciduous species. He states emphatically:

> What is so common as to see, even at the present time, close to our mansions, such common-place things as elms, ashes, sycamores, poplars, or any other rubbish that the nearest provincial nursery may happen to be over-stocked with; all stuck in to produce either immediate, or lasting effect!
>
> Barron, 1852, 11

The introduction of exotic conifers had initially peaked in the 1820s following the heroic expeditions of David Douglas and other plant collectors (Elliot 1986, 116). Douglas Fir (*Pseudotsuga menziesii*), Deodar cedar (*Cedrus deodara*) and Sitka spruce (*Picea sitchensis*) were just a few of many notable introductions. Others trees such as the monkey puzzle or Chile pine (*Araucaria araucana*) had arrived earlier in the 1790s but now became more popular (Figure 34). In the 1840s came exciting new conifers from California, South America and Asia, particularly the Japanese red cedar (*Cryptomeria japonica*). What really caused a stir in Britain was the discovery in the 1840s and 1850s of the coast redwood (*Sequoia sempervirens*) and giant sequoia (*Sequoiadendron giganteum*) (called Wellingtonia by the Victorians). These huge trees were clearly unsuitable for anything but the largest gardens but the enormous publicity they generated boosted interest in many other exotic conifers. There were conflicting views about the best way to arrange conifers and other evergreens in the landscape, largely between the older followers of the picturesque and those with a different approach (Elliott 1986, 117). Throughout the 1850s and '60s, avenues enjoyed great popularity as a method of arranging conifers in the landscape, although this was mostly on country estates where the favoured long and straight lines of these imposing trees could be more easily accommodated. Some conifers also became firm favourites in Victorian villa gardens, particularly the monkey puzzle and cedars. Edward Kemp (1851, 6) remarked that Cedars of Lebanon were such a feature in the landscape of the London suburbs that "the traveller could scarcely pass a hundred yards down portions of the western roads without coming upon fresh specimens or groups of them."

Another development of the time using coniferous trees was the rival of interest in topiary. Barron's exploits at Elvaston Castle had included a substantial amount of topiary work and the favourable publicity for those gardens prompted a sudden rush of interest in this ancient horticultural technique (Elliott 1986, 118). Until then, despite Loudon and some revivalists, efforts at the reintroduction of topiary had been an uphill struggle. Mazes also became popular again with the surviving example at Hampton Court getting much attention. They also became popular settings in which to attempt the more elaborate forms of architectural topiary.

Despite the growing popularity of evergreens and conifers, the landscape of many gardens was also becoming more colourful. Little attention was paid to colour in gardening literature before the Victorian era, although this cannot have been because there was a monotony of colour in the landscape garden (Elliott 1986, 48). The innovative landscape at Painshill was already famous for its many colourful exotics and trees like purple beech were being offered by nurserymen in the 1770s. Colour experiments in the garden mainly involve flowers and trees and although most attention at the time was given to the flower garden, we are concerned here with trees, some of which do have attractive flowers.

Interest in the contribution of trees and shrubs to colour in the garden took a variety of forms. Planting for autumn colour began to attract more attention, stimulated in part when Uvedale Price's *Essay on the Picturesque* was reissued in the 1840s. Colour groupings in the garden depended on flowering shrubs, especially rhododendrons and azaleas. The nurseryman, William Paul, attempted to take this matter a step further

FIGURE 34. Although the Chile pine or monkey puzzle was introduced into Britain in 1795, it was the Victorians who made it one of their most popular conifers. It became a firm favourite for urban and suburban villa gardens, often at the front of the property (Mongredien 1870).

(Elliott 1986, 182). In a series of articles in the *Gardener's Chronicle* in 1864 he urged gardeners to cast their eyes beyond just flower colour to the use of trees with purple, golden or silver leaves or with coloured bark for winter effect. Along with trees of pyramidal or weeping effect, he labelled these together as 'pictorial trees'. The excitement generated by Paul's ideas can be measured by the eruption in the gardening literature over the next decade of various proposals for landscape colour. For much of the Victorian era there had been little interest in flowering trees and shrubs (Ottewill 1989, 41). Now, the overwhelming trend was the rejection of conifers as the basis of planting, and a revival of interest in deciduous trees, especially with the new introductions of Japanese maples and *Prunus x pissardii* (Elliott 1986, 183). Variegated foliage became particularly popular with many late Victorian gardeners, although this trend towards 'colourful trees' did meet with some significant opposition. Probably the most influential critic of arboricultural colour was Alexander Dean, who at the turn of the century launched an attack on positive colour in trees, in favour of green (*ibid.*, 184). Dean had powerful opponents but he also had much support. As a result of this controversy the planting of purple beech nearly came to a halt in the 1890s.

The Victorian fashion for various styles of garden and different garden features gave a variety of opportunities to include trees and shrubs in the garden. A return to historic styles of gardens proceeded hand in hand with similar revivals in architecture and the Elizabethan and Jacobean revivals during the 1830s prompted the revival in gardens of these styles attached to the buildings (Elliott 1986, 71). William Andrews Nesfield became associated with these styles with his enthusiasm for the box parterre, particularly the *parterre de broderie* using box and gravel alone, which had been a major device in the late seventeenth century. However, his repertoire was not limited to the box parterre, for he also designed mazes, bowling greens and arboreta. As well as returning to architectural and garden styles of the past, there were also interest in designs that reflected the traditions of some other countries and cultures. The Italianate villa, through the work of Loudon and Nash, became a dominant style for the suburban villa. These gardens had an emphasis on cypresses, parterres, the use of gravel instead of grass, terracing and the addition of statues (Elliot 1986, 74). Considerable importance was accorded to evergreen trees. The popularity of the Italian style also prompted a demand for fastigiate trees to produce the effect of the Mediterranean cypresses. Japanese gardens

FIGURE 35. Biddulph Grange, the creation of James Bateman, is regarded as an important precursor to the High Victorian style of gardening. Many aspects of this garden, such as the formal elements of this Dahlia Walk with its clipped hedges and beds of flowers, were influential in the design of Victorian public parks.

also became fashionable, especially after a miniature Japanese village became a permanent feature in the grounds of Alexander Palace (*ibid.*, 200). Naturally, Japanese trees and shrubs were a requirement of the planting design of these gardens. As part of this focus on different styles, much emphasis was given to harmonising the garden with the house and planting choice was an important way to achieve that (*ibid.*, 112). Different selections accompanied different styles, but no longer on Repton's basis of overall form, which had stipulated conical for Grecian, and round-headed for gothic. Edward Kemp, a leading Victorian landscape gardener, recommended association by virtue of leaf patterns and concluded that trees could be planted nearer to Gothic houses than to Grecian (Kemp 1858, 220).

By the 1860s, rock gardens were becoming increasingly fashionable, even on a small scale in urban gardens. The choice of trees and shrubs for these included broom, gorse, rhododendrons, hollies, silver birch, mountain ash and pyramidal conifers (Elliot 1986, 176). Another garden feature popular in the later Victorian era was the 'medley garden' where fruit trees were mixed with flowers. Reginald Blomfield had criticised what he considered an artificial distinction between use and embellishment and urged the greater use of fruit for ornament (Blomfield 1892, 228–30). Two further garden features to emerge in the Victorian era involving trees, if somewhat unusually, were the stumpery and the rootery (Elliott 1986, 103). The stumpery was a garden feature made up of an assembly of the stumps of dead trees, usually hardwoods for durability, with plants such as ferns, mosses and lichens encouraged to grow in and around them. The first stumpery was created at Biddulph Grange and it soon became a popular feature of Victorian gardens, although it required considerable maintenance to keep it in good shape. The rootery was an area studded with the stems of old trees, inserted roots upwards in the ground, to be draped with ivy and other trailing plants.

Another feature of much larger Victorian gardens involving trees was the trend towards woodland embellishment. Although this had some impact on public parks and open spaces in and around urban areas, it was only significant in private urban gardens that were sufficiently extensive to accommodate any woodland. As early as 1830, in gardens such Bagshot Park and Caen Wood, exotic collections of trees and shrubs were being introduced into the woodland that surrounded the pleasure grounds (Elliott 1986, 93). According to Loudon, the plan was to distribute exotic trees over the margins of the woodland to enrich them. Probably the most significant and widespread example of this practice was the use of rhododendrons as underwood, to replace the laurels so frequently used for that purpose. Some of these rhododendrons, particularly *Rhododendron ponticum*, became self-seeding. As the 1840s advanced, the mixing of exotics with native woodland trees steadily became more common. In 1870, William Robinson gave the tradition of woodland embellishment its textbook with the publication of *The Wild Garden, or Our Groves and Shrubberies Made Beautiful* (Robinson 1870). However, Robinson's message about the need to match hardy plants to the site is still often misunderstood as a call to plant native rather than exotic species. The subtitle of his book clearly states the effects are achieved 'by the naturalisation of hardy exotic plants'. In Scotland, Robinson's ideas were echoed in the writings of Frances Jane Hope (1881) whose many articles in *The Gardeners' Chronicle* were later published posthumously in a book entitled *Notes and Thoughts on Gardens and Woodlands*.

Robinson's more naturalistic approach to planting and garden design was significantly at odds with many other garden writers and designers of the late Victorian era. The general philosophy of High Victorian landscaping was that a garden was essentially an artificial contrivance, a creation of art and not a patch of wild nature that had been 'scooped out of a wood' (Hibberd 1857, 330). This was epitomised at Biddulph Grange, the creation of James Bateman and regarded as an important precursor to the High Victorian style of gardening (Elliot 1986, 102) (Figure 35). In contrast to these exotic creations, Robinson's approach derived much of its aesthetic effect from a series of exclusions: the elimination of formal beds, of recognisable pattern, and the avoidance of plants most associated with the bedding system, which was now very popular. Carpet bedding was a variation of the bedding system that appeared like groundcover with a very uniform surface, achieved through careful clipping, and giving a 'carpet-like' appearance. The majority of country houses during the 1870s boasted some carpet beds and the fashion later spread into suburban villas and town gardens (*ibid.*, 155).

From the 1850s, due largely to the efforts of Shirley Hibberd, amateur gardening steadily became established as a popular pursuit among the British middle class. Hibberd has been described as the 'Father of Amateur Gardening' and he was arguably the first person to promote this nationally when it was reviled by the horticultural establishment (Wilkinson, 2012). Hibberd's (1855) first major book *The Town Garden* was a manual for city and suburban gardens and described his own garden in Pentonville. He was also a prolific writer for magazines and along with his most famous book, *Rustic Adornments for Homes of Taste*, he had great influence on garden fashions of the time, although he had surprisingly little to say about garden trees (Hibberd 1856). Despite the popularity of gardening among the middle class, as the Victorian era ended this was not an option for most urban working class families. Millions were living in housing that had just a little back yard and no garden (Burnett 1986, 74).

Edwardian gardens

The Edwardian garden, with its formal enclosures and exuberant informal plantings, was one of the cultural highlights of that era (Ottewill 1989). Staid and geometric Victorian landscapes gave way to picturesque gardens laid out architecturally but that also contained imaginative touches such as pergolas, trellised roses, herbaceous borders, water gardens and exotic species from the Far East. It can be difficult to make clear distinctions between the Victorian and the Edwardian garden as many aspects of the latter have their roots in the previous century. The development of the Edwardian garden is more a case of steady evolution than any dramatic revolution in style and design. The era is often considered to be a golden age in British gardening, particularly in terms of the gardens of the rich and famous (Jennings 2005, 1). Before the outbreak of the First World War, labour was cheap and plentiful and the wealthy enjoyed a luxurious standard of living. Meanwhile, in the fast-growing suburbs, the middle class were enjoying what for many was the first experience of home and garden ownership.

In 1892, even before the start of the era, a battle raged that was to have a profound effect on the Edwardian garden (Ottewill 1989, 5). It was about whether a garden should be 'natural' or 'formal' and who should be primarily responsible for its design, the gardener or the architect. The chief protagonists were the gardener William Robinson and the architect Reginald Blomfield. Blomfield's (1892) influential book, *The Formal Garden in England*, had been written quite deliberately as the 'formal' response to Robinson and a direct challenge to his naturalistic approach. His ideas struck a chord with many wealthy Edwardian garden owners since their affluence could accommodate the expense of the formal garden with its long herbaceous borders, many yards of clipped hedges, extensive kitchen gardens and the large teams of gardeners this required (Jennings 2005, 3). The popularity of the formal garden also reflected a general revival of Classicism that had been prevailing in all aspects of the arts since the late Victorian period (Ottewill, 1989, 10). Somewhere between the directly opposing views of Robinson and Blomfield was the contribution of John Dando Sedding (1891) with his influential book entitled *Garden-Craft Old and New*. Like Blomfield, Sedding had trained as an architect, but later developed an interest in garden design. He resisted Blomfield's formal architectural features and substituted clipped hedges, shrubs and topiary to achieve more variety of height and form to soften the overall geometry (Ottewill 1989, 27). While Sedding agreed with many of Robinson's views, he was still firmly on the formalist side of the fence and the two exchanged some strongly worded rebukes of each other's approach to garden design.

In contrast to the formal garden, Robinson and his allies also favoured the somewhat mythical image of the English cottage garden, with its roses, honeysuckle, foxgloves, hollyhocks, marigolds and primroses (Ottewill 1989, 52). Regardless of the actual style, there has always been much debate regarding the extent to which the cottage garden was a genuine feature of the ancestral English past, and to what extent it was a nineteenth century invention (Elliott 1986, 63). Nevertheless, it was championed by Robinson (1883) most famously in is celebrated book *The English Flower Garden*.

During the last years of the nineteenth century, the central theme in historical garden revival was the attempt to identify and promote the English vernacular – the truly English style (Elliott 1986, 221). The most common vernacular style, because it was widely used in smaller urban and suburban gardens, was that known as 'arts and crafts'. This artistic and design movement stood for traditional

FIGURE 36. The revival of interest in figurative topiary in the Edwardian era was partly driven by the public's fascination with the remarkable work at Levens Hall in the Lake District. In response to popular demand, more figurative topiary began to appear in the formal gardens of public parks. This photograph from around 1900 shows how the Levens Hall gardens looked at the time (Mawson 1926).

craftsmanship using simple forms and often applied medieval, romantic or folk styles of decoration. It also advocated economic and social reform and has been said to be essentially anti-industrial (Blakesley 2006). In the garden, the first sign of the movement's influence was the revival of interest in rustic work, with rustic bridges and arbours becoming increasing common in the late Victorian era. In the Edwardian era its emphasis on combining both hard and soft landscaping became particularly evident with plants becoming the softening 'flesh' around the 'bones' of the garden that was the hard landscaping, which often included terraces, paths, pools, summerhouses and pergolas (Jennings 2005, 10). Planting often came right up to the house with wisteria, roses, clematis, honeysuckle and jasmine trained up walls, around windows and over doors. Notable proponents of the arts and crafts style of garden design included Gertrude Jekyll and Edwin Lutyens, a partnership of self-taught gardener and professional architect that was responsible for several great gardens of the period. Jekyll was also a prolific author on garden topics and for trees and the woodland garden her book *Wood and Garden* remains a classic (Jekyll 1899). Perhaps the leading professional exponent of the arts and crafts garden style was Thomas Mawson who set out his ideas on garden design in *The Art and Craft of Garden Making*, a sumptuously book that makes extensive reference to trees (Mawson 1900).

A classic feature of larger Edwardian gardens was to divide the outdoor space into smaller rooms. This was generally achieved with yew hedges with the classic example being Lawrence Johnston's garden at Hidcote Manor in Gloucestershire. This maintained the revival of interest in topiary, which also now involved the popularisation of figurative topiary, encouraged by texts such as *The Book of Topiary* (Curtis and Gibson 1905) (Figure 36). Other dividing or defining features of the Edwardian garden involving trees included low box hedges to delineate beds, and beech, lime and hornbeam trained into 'pleached' screens. Nut walks became increasingly popular and many of the garden enclosures functioned as orchards (Blomfield 1892, 228).

In the cities and their suburbs, far from the world of Blomfield, Robinson, Sedding and Jekyll, gardening was becoming an ever more fashionable pastime (Jennings 2005, 43). This had its own horticultural style and culture that was significantly different from the large gardens of the rich and famous. The demand for housing continued in the first decade of the twentieth century and new extensive middle class suburban estates appeared on the outskirts of many towns and cities. These now came with back gardens as standard and significant front gardens for the larger properties. Just as the width of the road, types of street trees, street names and other features were used to draw social distinctions between localities, the status of an area was further confirmed by the extent and style of the garden space provided at the back and front of the house (Long 1993, 40). As the numbers of small private gardens and new amateur gardeners increased dramatically, a horticultural retail industry grew to cater for these selling gardening products, equipment, plants and literature.

Most middle and working class families could not hope to create gardens of similar style and scale to those fashioned for wealthy clients by the leading garden designers of the day. However, thanks to the growth of horticultural literature full of imaginative garden designs and ideas, together with the greater availability of plants and equipment, limited or miniature versions of some of these garden features could be attempted. So, the flower garden, the herbaceous border, the rock garden and the water garden, along with the pergolas and trellised roses, could all find homes in Edwardian town gardens, if not all in the same garden.

The prevailing gardening trends were taken up in cheap books of basic instruction specifically designed to give advice to those new homeowners with small urban and suburban gardens. These tended to promote more formal designs rather than a 'wild gardening' approach. *The Small Garden Beautiful* by A. C. Curtis in 1906 proved popular with its range of different designs and encouragement to readers to create distinct features such as small rock gardens and herbaceous borders (Curtis 1906). *The Back Garden Beautiful* by Harry Havart was aimed at the lower-middle class and also included simple designs to copy (Havart 1912). Both these books focused far more on shrubs than trees, although understandable given the size of the gardens they were aimed at. While Curtis frequently included various small fruit trees in his designs, Havart was cautious about planting any sort of trees (Figure 37).

The interwar years and the suburban gardens

Immediately after the First World War there was an enormous increase in local authority house building throughout Britain and huge further expansion of the suburbs (Conway 2000, 118). In England, over four million new suburban homes were built between 1919 and 1939, making what had been the most

FIGURE 37. This is one of several designs for small urban and suburban gardens in *The Small Garden Beautiful* by A. C. Curtis, a popular book in Edwardian times. While this design does make provision for some fruit trees at the side and the rear, many garden books of this time were cautious about planting any trees in small urban gardens (Curtis 1906).

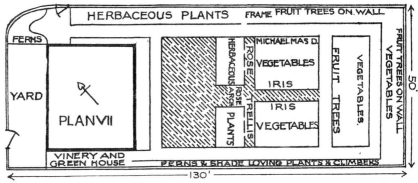

SMALL GARDEN DESIGN VII.

urbanised country in the world at the end of the First World War the most suburbanised by the beginning of Second World War (Hollow 2011, 2). Local authorities built over one million of all suburban homes in this period. With all the new suburban gardens there was great expectation that this would usher in a new horticultural era. The provision of gardens varied enormously in both scale and quality, as did the wider landscapes on these new suburban estates. New private estates in suburbia were generally planned at a low density of 12 houses an acre, which gave room for gardens of moderate size (Fox 1990, 185).

For many new suburban homes the garden was just a bare patch of ground at their front and rear. Neither speculative nor municipal developers extended their activities to garden preparation other than the basic provision of paths, boundary fences and walls (Scott 2013, 182). For the new homeowners this was DIY gardening from scratch and it was often back-breaking work to get the garden into shape. Many had come from old terraced housing without gardens and had no idea about ornamental gardening. The building firm Costain often pointed to attractive gardens already established on their estates as examples of what might be achieved by new owners. Another builder, John Laing, was quite unusual in giving a fruit tree to every householder who bought a new house from his firm (Fox 1990, 185). Any estate landscaping undertaken before the new owners arrived was often rather limited. Sometime contractors were engaged to plant a few trees but this was hardly imaginative planting and often poorly executed (Scott 2013, 182). Again, John Laing was usual in being one of the few builders to carefully plan their estates to include the preservation of existing trees and some of these were incorporated into private gardens. Laing also provided privet hedges and leaflets for homeowners on how to take care of them.

The gardening boom led to a demand for magazines dealing with the design, planting and maintenance of small urban and suburban gardens. Many popular books were also published, such as Norman Humphrey's (1922) *Planning the Suburban Garden*, Solly's (1934) *Gardens for Town and Suburb* and Henslow's (1934) *Suburban Gardens*. Generally, these interwar suburban gardens were conservative and drew almost exclusively on an established approach to garden and landscape design. The dominant design influence was the English cottage garden tradition of Gertrude Jekyll's 'arts and crafts' gardening philosophy, which involved a combination of formal layouts and informal planting arrangements within them (Scott 2013, 189). Many also drew inspiration from the late nineteenth century reinterpretation of the gardening traditions of the Tudor and Stuart periods (Roberts 1996). Some even included elaborate bedding displays reminiscent of public parks. While discussions in gardening magazines appeared on the surface to be purely about a design approach, there was often a distinct undercurrent of discourse about how gardens should promote social identity and instil a sense of order, taste and decorum.

While trees do feature to some extent in the popular gardening literature on the interwar suburban garden, this is often in the context of one small ornamental or fruit tree forming a focal point rather than any group planting. This period did see an explosion of interest in Chinese flowering shrubs such as rhododendrons, azaleas, camellias and the smaller magnolias (Richardson 2005, 87). The planting of these species was undoubtedly encouraged by their popularity in more famous gardens, with Bodnant being particularly influential.

Although many local authority tenants developed a keen interest in gardening, large numbers of them undoubtedly held back on any major work such as hard landscaping or tree planting as they were not the actual owners of their garden. For both the tenant and the landlord, tensions often seemed to exist between knowing whether to treat the local authority estate garden as a private or public space (Hollow 2011, 13). In Manchester, the tenancy agreement stipulated that any tenant wishing to make 'significant alterations' to their garden, which included planting a new tree or chopping down an existing one, had first to gain written permission from the Council.

Some mention should be made here of the influence of the Modernism movement on residential gardens of the inter-war period. Although focusing on architecture and never translated satisfactorily to gardens, many designs of this period were inspired or informed by the Modernist creed (Richardson 2005, 121). The style was most frequently found in the very fashionable private gardens of rich and famous but also impacted on gardens of smaller size and ambition. In most cases, there was very little 'garden' to speak of with lawn right up to the front of the house. However, a woodland setting for the house was a key feature of the Modernist approach. Favoured trees were pines and birches, typical of Scandinavia and Germany where Modernism came from, with the stark trunks of the nearby trees echoing the characteristic 'politis' or stilt legs that supported the elevated sections of the house.

Post-war gardens

As with the First Wold War, much ornamental gardening was put on hold for the duration of the Second World War (Richardson 2005, 144). When peace finally arrived, there was an extensive need for new housing across much of Britain

(Harwood 2000, 102). In England some 200,000 homes had been destroyed by bombing and vast numbers of houses were in poor repair. While the drive for new housing in the post-war period was led by local authorities, many schemes were built by private developers. It also seems that many of the landscape schemes, particularly for individual public housing schemes, were the work of the architects who designed the buildings rather than landscape architects.

The style and quality of the landscapes among both public and private housing schemes varied considerably (Harwood 2000, 106). For example, on the private sector Span Developments many landscapes were attractively paved or laid out with lawns and planted with shrubs, while existing trees were often carefully preserved. This careful approach was in stark contrast to some other schemes, including some that won awards, where only the hard elements and most robust trees survived. Some of the contrasts in style and quality of landscapes were most noticeable in London. The Golden Lane Estate of local authority housing in City of London, first phase opened in 1957, was described as a model for social housing and urban living (*ibid.*, 109). This had quite formal communal landscapes that included trees planted in complementary ranks, which was repeated on the nearby Barbican estate. While the Golden Lane and Barbican estates replaced mainly treeless swathes of bombed-out warehousing, the lands for the Roehampton housing projects were plum sites for public housing because of their remarkable existing landscapes. One part was built on richly planted Victorian gardens with beautiful mature trees, while on another site the landscape was made up of the surviving grounds from three eighteenth century mansions that included those of Mount Clare, designed by 'Capability' Brown. While some housing developments were fortunate in inheriting a fine treescape, most were not. For those, there was often little new tree planting in either individual or communal gardens and frequently not to a

FIGURE 38. The neatly-clipped privet hedge marking the division between two properties is particularly associated with post-war suburban housing. In recent years the Leyland cypress (×*Cupressocyparis leylandii*) has become a popular choice for dividing hedges and their unchecked growth has often led to disputes between neighbours.

standard were many trees survived. Some years later, with the building of Byker estate in Newcastle from 1970, the importance of extensive tree planting in new landscapes was recognised in the establishment of a tree bank to supply trees for the scheme (*ibid.*, 113). The use of more mature nursery stock from the tree bank rather than buying in saplings helped ensure good tree survival rates.

Although hedges had been a feature of private gardens for centuries, they are particularly associated with those manicured post-war suburban gardens with their neatly clipped privet hedges to the front and rear of countless semi-detached houses (Barker 2012) (Figure 38). Various species of trees and shrubs, particularly evergreen species, ensured garden hedges performed a variety of functions, such as acting as a barrier, marking boundaries and providing some sense of seclusion and privacy. Deciduous hedging species were popular for creating ornamental effects with their flowers, fruit and autumn colour.

For those families who moved into one of numerous post-war high-rise housing developments there were no private gardens and no hedges over which they could chat to their neighbours. While high-rise flats were seen as a way of introducing more space around buildings for attractive landscaping, this rarely happened. For these residents there was often just sparsely planted 'communal open space' some floors below with only the occasional tree among acres of mown grass (Johnston 1985, 112). Fortunately, the reversal in housing policy following the high-rise housing fiasco has meant the building of many more low-rise homes most of which have had some private garden space. However, that has not necessarily led to more trees being planted in these gardens. In the past few decades, space for tree planting in many front and rear urban gardens has disappeared at an alarming rate. This has been partly due to the phenomenon of 'garden grabbing' where new houses are built in the large back gardens of existing houses (Jones 2012). Also, covering front gardens with hard surfaces to facilitate off-road car parking and the popularity of paving and decking in rear gardens has further reduced space for any garden trees (see Chapter 3).

For those urban residents fortunate to have gardens and with the space to plant at least one tree, there was plenty of advice available on what trees to select from a number of popular books on town gardening (Brown 1999, 165). Among the most influential were books by Margot Eates (1955) *Gardening in Cities* and Lanning Roper (1957) *Successful Town Gardening*. Sylvia Crowe's (1958) *Garden Design* was equally directed at a professional audience and continues to be regarded as one of the best books ever written on the subject (Brown 1999, 166). Its impact can be seen in the popular garden book of the 1970s by John Brookes (1969) entitled *Room Outside*, described as 'a new approach to garden design'. One the most noticeable post-war garden fashions that directly involved tree species was the explosion in popularity of dwarf conifers. These were promoted in a book by Adrian Bloom (1979) entitled *The Year Round Garden* where he recommended a wide range of dwarf conifers underplanted with heathers in 'island beds'.

While many residents were exploring the joys of gardening with a wide range of plants, some horticultural writers were urging a different approach. They promoted the planting of 'native' rather than 'exotic' species in the belief this would encourage wildlife in our towns and cities. One of the early British pioneers of the wildlife garden was Robert Gathorne-Hardy (1961) with his book *The Native Garden*. The person who really popularised wildlife gardening was a landscape architect, Chris Baines, firstly with a BBC-TV film *Bluetits and Bumblebees* shown in 1984, followed with a book entitled *How to Make a Wildlife Garden* (Baines 1985). While promoting urban wildlife is a worthy aim, this is just one aim of urban gardening and the typical wildlife garden is not what most urban gardeners want to create at the expense of other more horticultural features. Furthermore, many of our 'native' trees are either too large-growing for small urban gardens or do not thrive in polluted urban environments (Johnston *et al.* 2011). TV gardener Monty Don recently took these 'conservation' views to an extreme when he said British gardeners should stick to native British planting and give up growing foreign plants (Appleby 2008). He was widely criticised for effectively calling for an end to over 1,000 years of British gardening tradition

In recent years, trees in urban residential gardens have been the subject of much adverse publicity, especially through quite alarmist media stories. Concerns about potential damage to people and property have prompted many wary urban residents to remove trees from their gardens or think twice about planting any new trees (see Chapter 3). Where these fears are genuine, the problems have invariable been caused by home-owners planting or retaining unsuitable trees in their gardens, unaware of the problems this can create in years to come. In these environmentally-conscious times when more urban residents than ever would claim to love trees, this does not necessarily include those trees growing in their neighbour's garden or wanting to have trees in their own garden! We should always remember that trees in residential gardens can contribute enormously to a green and pleasant neighbourhood and those in front gardens are especially valuable when there are no street trees.

References

Addison, J. (1712) Article on Gardening. *The Spectator* 414 (25 June 1712), 98–102 (101–2).

Amherst, A. (1896) *A History of Gardening in England*. Bernard Quaritch: London.

Appleby, M. (2008) Stick to Native Plants, says Don. *Horticulture Week*, 17 April, 9. Available at: http://m.hortweek.com/stick-native-plants-says-don/article/803335 (accessed 27.3.2014).

Baines, C. (1985) *How to Make a Wildlife Garden*. Elm Tree Books: London.

Barker, H. (2012) *Hedge Britannia: A Curious History of a British Obsession*. Bloomsbury: London.

Barron, W. (1852) *The British Winter Garden: Being a Practical Treatise on Evergreens*. Bradbury and Evans: London.

Bell, S. G. (1990) Women Create Gardens in Male Landscapes: A Revisionist Approach to Eighteenth-Century English Garden History. *Feminist Studies*, 471–491.

Berrell, J. (1978) *The Garden: An Illustrated History*. Penguin Books: Harmondsworth.

Blakesley, R. P. (2006) *The Arts and Crafts Movement*. Phaidon Press: London.

Blomfield, R. (1892) *The Formal Garden in England*. Macmillan and Company: London.

Bloom, A. (1979) *The Year Round Garden*. Floraprint: Nottingham.

Borsay, P. (1989) *The English Urban Renaissance: Culture and Society in the Provincial Town 1660–1770*. Oxford University Press: Oxford.

Brookes, J. (1969) *Room Outside*. Thames and Hudson: London.

Brown, J. (1999) *The Pursuit of Paradise: A Social History of Gardens and Gardening*. Harper Collins: London.

Burnett, J. (1986) *A Social History of Housing 1815–1985*. Second edition. Routledge: London and New York.

Byrom, C. (1995) The Pleasure Grounds of Edinburgh New Town. *Garden History*, 67–90.

Conway, H. (1991) *People's Parks: The Design and Development of Victorian Parks in Britain*. Cambridge University Press: Cambridge.

Conway, H. (2000) Everyday Landscapes: Public Parks from 1930 to 2000. *Garden History*, 117–134.

Crowe, S. (1958) *Garden Design*. Country Life: London.

Curtis, A. C. (1906) *The Small Garden Beautiful – and How to Make it so*. Smith, Elder and Co: London.

Curtis, C. H. and Gibson, W. (1905) *The Book of Topiary*. John Lane – The Bodley Head: London and New York.

Eates, M. (1955) *Gardening in Cities*. Peter Owen: London.

Elliott, B. (1986) *Victorian Gardens*. B. T. Batsford: London.

Elliott, P., Watkins, C. and Daniels, S. (2007) William Barron (1805–91) and Nineteenth-Century British Arboriculture: Evergreens in Victorian Industrializing Society. *Garden History*, 129–148.

Ellis, J. (2000) Georgian Town Gardens (British Horticulture). *History Today* 50(1), 38–45.

Elmes, J. (1827) *Metropolitan Improvements; or, London in the Nineteenth Century*. Jones and Company: London.

Fairchild, T. (1722) *The City Gardener*. T. Woodward and J. Peele: London.

Farrar, L. (1998) *Ancient Roman Gardens*. Sutton Publishing: Stroud.

Fox, C. (1990) Garden Suburb, Green Belt and Windowbox. In Galinou, M., *London's Pride: The Glorious History of the Capital's Gardens*: Anaya Publishers: London.

Gathorne-Hardy, R. (1961) *The Native Garden*. Nelson: London.

Halliwell, B. (1990) Flowers and Plants in the Seventeenth Century. In Galinou, M., *London's Pride: The Glorious History of the Capital's Gardens*: Anaya Publishers: London.

Harding, V. (1990) Gardens and Open Space in Tudor and Early Stuart London. In: Galinou, M., *London's Pride: The Glorious History of the Capital's Gardens*: Anaya Publishers: London.

Harding, J. and Taigel, A. (1996) An Air of Detachment: Town Gardens in the Eighteenth and Nineteenth Centuries. *Garden History*, 237–254.

Harwood, E. (2000) Post-War Landscape and Public Housing. *Garden History*, 102–116.

Harvey, J. (1981) *Medieval Gardens*. B. T. Batsford: London.

Havart, H. (1912) *The Back Garden Beautiful*. The Amalgamated Press: London.

Henslow, T. G. W. (1934) *Suburban Gardens*. Rich and Gowan: London.

Hibberd, S. (1855) *The Town Garden: The Management of City and Suburban Gardens*. Groombridge and Sons: London.

Hibberd, S. (1857) *Rustic Adornments for Homes of Taste*. Second edition. Groombridge and Sons: London.

Hollow, M. (2011) Suburban Ideals on England's Interwar Council Estates. *Journal of the Garden History Society* 39(2), 203–217.

Hope, F. J. (1881) *Notes and Thoughts on Gardens and Woodlands.* Macmillan and Co: London.

Howitt, W. (1844) *Rural Life in England.* Longman, Brown, Green, and Longmans: London.

Humphrey, H. (1922) *Planning the Suburban Garden.* St Clements Press: London.

Jackson, A. (1991) *Semi-detached London: Suburban Development, Life and Transport, 1900–3.* Second edition. Wild Swan Publications.

Jekyll, G. (1899) *Wood and Garden.* Longman, Green and Co: London.

Jennings, A. (2005) *Edwardian Gardens.* English Heritage: London.

Jennings, Anne (2006) *Roman Gardens.* English Heritage: London.

Johnston, M. (1985) Community Forestry: a Sociological Approach to Urban Forestry *Arboricultural Journal* 9, 121–126.

Johnston, M., Nail, S. and James, S. (2011) 'Natives Versus Aliens': the Relevance of the Debate to Urban Forest Management in Britain. In Johnston, M. and Percival, G (eds) *Trees, People and the Built Environment.* Forestry Commission Research Report. Forestry Commission: Edinburgh. Available at: http://www.forestry.gov.uk/pdf/Trees-people-and-the-buit-environment_Johnston.pdf/$FILE/Trees-people-and-the-buit-environment_Johnston.pdf (accessed 15.6.2014).

Jones, J. (2012) Government's Planning Pickle will Lead to 'Garden Grabbing'. *The Guardian*, Professional Section, Thursday 25 October. Available at:http://www.theguardian.com/local-government-network/2012/oct/25/london-planning-boris-johnson-garden-grabbing (accessed 3.3.2014).

Kalm, P. (1892) *Kalm's Account of his Visit to England on his Way to America in 1748.* Translated by Joseph Lucas. Macmillan and Co: London.

Kemp, E. (1851) *The Parks, Gardens, Etc., of London and its Suburbs, Described and Illustrated for the Guidance of Strangers.* John Weale: London.

Kemp, E. (1858) *How to Lay Out a Garden.* Second edition. Bradbury and Evans: London.

Landsberg, S. (1995) *The Medieval Garden.* British Museum Press: London.

Langley, B. (1728) *New Principles of Gardening: Or the Laying out and Planting Parterres, Groves, Wildernesses, Labyrinths, Avenues, Parks, etc.* Printed for A Bettesworth and J. Batley in Peter-Noster Row: London.

Lawrence, H. W. (1993) The Greening of the Squares of London: Transformation of Urban Landscapes and Ideals. *Annals of the Association of American Geographers* 83(1), 90–118.

Lawson, W. (1618) *A New Orchard and Garden, etc. With the Country-Housewifes Garden, etc.* W. Wilson, for E. Brewster and George Sawbridge: Fleetbridge.

Long, H. (1993) *The Edwardian House: The Middleclass Home in Britain 1880–1914.* Manchester University Press. Manchester and New York.

Longstaffe-Gowan, R. T. (1987) Proposal for a Georgian Town Garden in Gower Street: The Francis Douce Garden. *Garden History*, 136–144.

Longstaffe-Gowan, T. (1990) Gardening and the Middle Classes. In Galinou, M., *London's Pride: The Glorious History of the Capital's Gardens*: Anaya Publishers: London.

Longstaffe-Gowan, T. (2001) *The London Town Garden 1700–1840.* Yale University Press: New Haven and London.

Longstaffe-Gowan, T. (2012) *The London Square.* Yale University Press: New Haven and London.

Loudon, J. C. (1803) Letter to the Editor dated 22 December 1803. *Literary Journal*, December 31, 1803, cols 739–42.

Loudon, J. C. (1812) *Hints on the Formation of Gardens and Pleasure Grounds*. Harding and Wright for J. Harding: London.

Loudon, J. C. (1838) *The Suburban Gardener and Villa Companion*. Longman, Orme, Brown, Green and Longmans: London.

Markham, G. (1613) *The English Husbandman, The First Part: Contayning the Knowledge of the true Nature of euery Soyle within this Kingdome, etc.* Printed by T. S. for John Browne: London.

Matthews, W. H. (1922) *Mazes and Labyrinths: A General Account of Their History and Developments*. Longmans, Green and Co: London.

Mawson, T. H. (1900) *The Art and Craft of Garden Making*. B. T. Batsford: London.

Mitchell, A. F. (1981) *The Native and Exotic Trees in Britain*. Arboriculture Research Note 29 81 SILS. Issued by the Arboricultural Advisory Service of the Department for the Environment: Wrecclesham.

Ottewill, D. (1989) *The Edwardian Garden*. Yale University Press: New Haven and London.

Phillips, H. (1823) *Sylva Florifera: The Shrubbery Historically and Botanically Treated*. In two volumes. Longman, Hurst, Rees, Orme and Brown: London.

Repton, H. (1840) *The Landscape Gardening and Landscape Architecture of the Late Humphry Repton, Esq., Being his Entire Works on These Subjects*. A new edition by J. C. Loudon. Longman and Co: London, and A. and C. Black: Edinburgh.

Richardson, T. (2005) *English Gardens in the Twentieth Century. From the Archives of Country Life*. Aurum Press: London.

Roberts, J. (1996) The Gardens of Dunroamin: History and Cultural Values with Specific Reference to the Gardens of the Inter-war Semi. *International Journal of Heritage Studies* 1(4), 229–237.

Roberts, J. (1999) The Gardens of the Gentry in the Late Tudor Period. *Garden History*, 89–108.

Robinson, W. (1870) *The Wild Garden, or Our Groves and Shrubberies Made Beautiful*. John Murray: London.

Robinson, W. (1883) *The English Flower Garden*. John Murray: London.

Roper, L. (1957) *Successful Town Gardening*. Country Life: London.

Schofield, J. (1999) City of London Gardens, 1500–c.1620. *Garden History*, 73–88.

Scott, P. (2013) *The Making of the Modern British Home: The Suburban Semi and Family Life Between the Wars*. Oxford University Press: Oxford.

Sedding, J. D. (1891) *Garden-Craft Old and New*. Kegan Paul, Trench, Trübner and Co: London.

Simo, M. L. (1988) *Loudon and the Landscape: From Country Seat to Metropolis*. Yale University Press: New Haven and London.

Smith, M. (2005) Petrus de Crescentius, *Ruralia commoda*, 1471. Special Collections featured item for April 2005. Library of the University of Reading: Reading.

Solly, V. N. (1926) *Gardens for Town and Suburb*. Ernest Benn: London.

Steuart, Sir H. (1828) *The Planter's Guide*. Second edition. John Murray: London

Stott, P. (1990) The Medieval Garden. In Galinou, M., *London's Pride: The Glorious History of the Capital's Gardens*: Anaya Publishers: London.

Strong, R. (1979) *The Renaissance Garden in England*. Thames and Hudson: London.

Way, T. (2010) *A Nation of Gardeners: How the British Fell in Love with Gardening*. Prion: London.

Wilkinson, A. (2012) *Shirley Hibberd – the Father of Amateur Gardening. His Life and Works 1825–1890*. Cortex Design: Birmingham.

Willes, M. (2014) *The Gardens of the British Working Class*. Yale University Press: New Haven and London.

Trees in Public Parks and Open Spaces

Many of us today might take for granted those urban parks close to home, which were often the backdrop for childhood memories of summer days and carefree times with family and friends. It can seem as if those municipal parks were always part of the fabric of our towns and cities. However, while some greenspace with public access has always been present in urban areas, the provision of public parks and open spaces by local authorities only dates back about 170 years.

The word 'park' referred initially to an area of land, often with woodland, that had been enclosed for deer hunting (Lasdun 1991, 5). This definition was later expanded in the eighteenth century to describe a landscape park that was an open expanse of land with occasional clumps or belts of trees, beyond the formal gardens of a house. The aim of this landscape was to demonstrate the wealth and power of the owner and to create a space that appeared 'naturally occurring' to the spectator. Nowadays, thanks to pioneers of public greenspaces like John Claudius Loudon, a 'park' for most people is not the private estate of an aristocrat but a public place where there are no barriers of class or property.

In this chapter we define public parks as those parks that were accessible to the public on a regular basis, although they might be privately owned, such as the pleasure gardens and Royal Parks. Of course, being 'open to the public' did not mean everyone was able to gain access as this was often quite rigorously controlled to exclude those considered as 'undesirables'.

Commons and Royal Parks

For many hundreds of years before the development of municipal parks, the most accessible open spaces near many towns and cities were tracts of common land (Shaw-Lefevre 1894, 1–26). These were essentially working landscapes where the public could exercise their ancient rights dating back to medieval times, such as those for pasture (grazing cattle), pannage (allowing pigs to eat beech mast and acorns) and estovers (collecting wood from small trees or fallen branches). These common lands, whether open or wooded, also had a recreational role as public greenspaces, acting as the setting for traditional games, festivals and celebrations as well as informal recreation. This situation continued up until the latter part of the nineteenth century by which time most of the commons had been enclosed as privately-owned land by Acts of Parliament, and only a few had been saved for the nation as public open spaces.

Perhaps the best-known examples of public parks in Britain today are the Royal Parks of London. While some of these have been in existence for many hundreds of years, for most of their time they have been very exclusive landscapes. Queen Elizabeth I was thought to have begun the gradual admittance of the public to the Royal Parks (Lasdun 1991, 42). She had set a precedent by occasionally holding military reviews in Hyde Park to which public spectators were admitted. However, in Charles I's reign any access to Royal Parks was still a limited privilege, as clearly shown in a Proclamation of 1637 that restricted the making or possession of keys to royal houses, gardens and parks, without a special warrant. Hyde Park was opened to the public by Charles I around 1635, although still with some restrictions on access. The Royal Parks of London continued to be the focus of grandiose public celebrations instigated by the monarchy to mark events of national significance. One of these was held in Green Park in 1749 to mark the end of the War of Austrian Succession that involved displays, processions, fireworks, illuminations and the construction of temporary buildings and platforms (Chadwick 1966, 37). A similar event took place in St James's Park in 1814, in celebration on the centenary of the House of Brunswick, the General Peace and the sixteenth anniversary of the Battle of the Nile. Hyde Park and Green Park were also open to the public for this occasion.

In 1810, the Royal Parks became the responsibility of the Commissioners of Woods, Forest and Land Revenues, a new body that was hoped would bring a more consistent approach to their management (Anderson 1999, 23). However, public access to these parks remained restricted. The Parliamentary Select Committee on Public Walks (SCPW), convened to examine the provision of public open space, reported in 1833 that in the entire metropolis, the only open spaces available to all classes of society were Hyde Park and the Green Park, both at the far western edge of London (Lawrence 1993, 111). Three other Royal Parks, also on the western edge, were open only to 'persons well-behaved and properly dressed.' Following the SCPW report, with the mood of the government and the country changing decisively in favour of more public parks, steady progress was now made in opening up the majority of Royal Parks to general public access. They soon became popular not only with fashionable society but also with working people when they had time to relax with their families (Larwood 1880).

It is difficult to be precise about the nature of the tree cover that existed in these Royal Parks over three hundred years ago or even earlier. Nevertheless, some evidence can be obtained from early maps, artistic depictions and written descriptions. This suggests that with the decline in their use as hunting parks the tree cover of those smaller parks nearer to the centre of London evolved from a naturalistic to a more formal appearance (Williams 1978) (Figure 39). Meanwhile, those larger parks located further from the capital, such as Richmond Park and

FIGURE 39. As public access to the Royal Parks in central London increased, so parts of their landscape became more ornamental. This beautiful corner of Hyde Park is now much loved by nearby residents and workers as well as millions of tourists.

Bushy Park, continued to have the typical appearance of deer parks, much as they do today. Richmond Park has long been renowned for its many ancient trees, particularly oaks, which have great historical and ecological significance. In those parks close to the centre of power and government, such as Hyde Park, Kensington Gardens and St James's Park, the tree cover would have evolved from almost exclusively native or indigenous tree species to accommodating an ever increasing range of exotics. Throughout the seventeenth century the landscape of these Royal Parks would probably have been quite similar to those around other royal London residences and the country seats of the aristocracy, reflecting the landscape fashions of the time with typical French and Dutch influences (Knyff and Kip 1984). The first coherent landscaping in Hyde Park and Kensington Gardens was initiated by Queen Caroline and undertaken by Charles Bridgeman and completed in the 1730s (Williams 1978, 83). These improvements included a series of magnificent avenues in the parkland outside the gardens at Kensington Palace. As the Royal Parks became regarded more as semi-public and essentially aesthetic landscapes, the extent of their tree collections increased greatly. Evidence of this is provided by Alicia Amherst, the notable garden historian, who gives a list of the trees and shrubs growing in Hyde Park and Kensington Gardens in the Edwardian era (Amherst 1907, 368). There are nearly 600 different species and cultivars, although a small percentage are indicated as 'not in existence at present', having been removed as unsuitable for London. While there is a huge variety of broadleaved species, what is noticeable is the lack of conifers, particularly of *Abies*, *Picea* and *Pinus*. As well as listing the different species, Amherst also comments favourably on the formal planting arrangements, such as the "most prosperous" ailanthus avenue from Serpentine Bridge towards Rotten Row and the general grouping of trees according to species (*ibid.*, 51–52). She also records that the trees in Walnut Avenue, once a prominent feature of Hyde Park near Grosvenor Gate, had become decayed and were cut down in 1811, the best of the wood being used as gunstocks for the army. Amherst bemoans the fact that the avenue was not replanted.

The Royal Parks today come under the responsibility of The Crown Estate, although the public still does not have any legal right of access as this depends on the 'grace and favour' of The Crown (Williams 1978, 12). They attract million of visitors each year from both home and abroad and are rightly famous throughout the world as outstanding examples of urban parks. The Royal Parks probably contributed more than any other of London's green spaces to ensuring its reputation as one of the world's greenest capitals.

Public walks

A new form of British urban landscape that arose in the seventeenth century was 'the walk' or tree-lined promenade (Borsay 1986) (see Chapter 6). These were essentially garden allées outside the garden, many of which were used for promenading rather than for games. Although privately owned, these walks could be made available to members of the public, usually on request. Seeing the fashionable world let loose in these places, visitors from abroad sometimes mistook them for public parks (MacLeod 1972, 106). In some respects these early seventeenth century walks marked the transition from the introspective and essentially non-public enclosed garden of medieval times to the relatively public one which was conceived as integral to later town planning.

As early as 1597, a walk or promenade was laid out by the Benchers of Gray's Inn, then as now a centre for the legal profession (MacLeod 1972, 105). The Benchers paid Francis Bacon, later Lord Chancellor and an authority on gardens, for planting the trees that comprised mainly elms. Known as the 'Walkes', this remained a fashionable London promenade for over two hundred years. One of the most influential public walks was on Moorfields in London, a connected series of fields just beyond the old city walls that the Corporation of the City of London leased from St Paul's Cathedral (Harding 2006, 51). In the sixteenth century this undeveloped piece of land was subject to common rights and was the nearest open space to the city centre. It was used for a variety of activities but was in danger of encroachment and abuse as a dumping ground. In 1593, the City ordered that it be inspected and subsequently kept clean and tidy. In 1605–7, two gardeners were contracted to drain and level the ground and plant elm trees along new paths. The result was a transformation of this marshy and neglected area into what the contemporary writer Richard Johnson (1607, 3) described as: "Those sweet and delightfull walkes of More fields as it seems a garden in this Citty, and a pleasurable place of sweet ayres for Cittizens to walke in…" Provincial towns followed London's lead by creating their own walks. In 1638 in Tunbridge Wells, the Walks (later called the Pantiles) were laid out and planted with a double row of trees (Borsay 1986, 126).

The main period for laying out new walks came with the Restoration, although the true rise of the provincial promenade dates from the 1680s to 1690s (Borsay 1986, 126). Most of these walks were separate from gardens, although some were in parkland. However, many were isolated in the urban landscape, usually near a city wall or river, almost always with a view of the surrounding countryside. Many of these promenades were paved or laid with gravel, and lined with hedges or trees, such as limes, sycamores, elms and firs. The trees generally required frequent maintenance due to aging or weather damage. During the winters of 1739 and 1740, 143 trees were planted on new walks at Cheltenham, although by the following two summers 76 had died due to drought and had to be replaced (*ibid.*, 129).

As well as somewhere to take exercise these walks and promenades were also fashionable places where people came to observe the social scene and be noticed. By the eighteenth century, many towns and cities had some provision for their citizens to delight in the 'Walking Exercise' (Longstaffe-Gowan 2001, 196). However, they were not equally accessible to everyone. In London, the walks at Moorfields, Charterhouse, Drapers' Hall, Somerset House, St James's Park, the Temple and several Inns of Court were generally open 'to every person above inferior rank'. By contrast, the fine walks of the Royal Gardens of Kensington were open 'only for persons of distinction'. New walks and promenades continued to be laid out in town and cities throughout the eighteenth century, although now mainly in parks, gardens or outside the municipal boundaries (Figure 40). In York, the centre of fashionable leisure in the north, the earliest formal promenade was the Lord Mayor's Walk, which in 1718 was planted extensively with trees to give an ornamental effect (Borsay 1986, 126). In the early 1700s in Bath, the leading resort in Britain, the Gravel Walks became a major social attraction. In 1734, the original trees along the side of the walk were felled and replaced with new trees. A particularly fine example was created in Leicester where in 1785 the Corporation resolved to form a tree-lined promenade for the recreation of the local residents (Chadwick 1966, 44). Known as the New Walk, this still remains as a pleasant urban footway from Victoria Park down to the city centre. In an important paper on this topic, the historian Peter Borsay (1986) gives an extensive list of walks and gardens in provincial towns and spa created from 1639–1770.

Pleasure gardens

After the restoration of the monarchy in 1660, pleasure gardens emerged as a uniquely British form of public open space in many towns and cities. A 'pleasure garden' can be defined as a privately owned enclosed ornamental ground or piece of land, open to the public as a resort or amusement area and operated as a business (Conlin 2013, 5). Trees, shrubs and other horticultural features were invariably a prominent part of a pleasure garden (Figure 41). The term should not be confused with a 'pleasure ground', a feature of the English landscape garden close to the house that was more intensively maintained and included a wide range of trees and shrubs. While the private pleasure ground of the eighteenth century aristocrat has been described as a 'landscape of exclusion', the pleasure garden was definitely a landscape of inclusion (Williamson 1995, 107). Anyone who could afford the price of admission and whose behaviour was unlikely to upset other customers was welcome to enter. There was much to enjoy and experience in the varied and sometime bizarre attractions in the magical world of the pleasure garden. While these became a feature of town and cities throughout Britain, our knowledge of the gardens is largely restricted to the London resorts. Also, much of what we know about even these is derived from works by Warwick Wroth, now more than a century old (Wroth 1896 and 1907). Throughout their 200-year history, pleasure gardens were celebrated by visitors and promoters alike as new Edens and as an escape from the crowded and care-worn city (Conlin 2013, 17–8). However, pleasure gardens have often been left out of accounts of garden history and it is

FIGURE 40. Throughout the eighteenth century in Britain public walks were still being laid out. One of the more impressive walks in London was at The Royal Palace of St James's next to the park. This hand-coloured engraving of the walk, originally printed for Bowles and Carver, was produced around 1800 (Larwood 1880).

FIGURE 41. A general prospect of Vauxhall Gardens in 1751, then Britain's premier pleasure garden. It shows the extent to which trees, planted in blocks, avenues or individually, were the major landscape elements for both the structural planting and individual features (Wroth 1896).

significant that they were not mentioned in the nineteenth century encyclopaedias or histories of gardening by John Claudius Loudon or Alicia Amherst.

Even before the Restoration, there were forerunners of the pleasure gardens in London. When the Spring Gardens in Charring Cross opened in the 1630s it offered little more than bowls but soon became very popular. It was closed down in May 1654 but reopened the next month. Cromwell's London was willing to go without its theatres and fairs but they were not going to let the Puritans rob them of their Spring Gardens (Conlin 2013, 5). New Spring Gardens was opened in 1661 on the Lambeth side of the River Thames and was described by John Evelyn (1901, 348) as a "prettily contrived plantation," implying a pleasantly organised ground of trees and shrubs. Mulberry Garden near the present Buckingham Palace became a place of recreation and refreshment after the failure of the silkworm industry and in summer its trees provided welcome shade (MacLeod 1972, 265).

According to the historian Jonathan Conlin (2013, 18–21) pleasure garden design between 1660 and 1860 seems to have moved through three phases. The first, a market garden *ornée*, lasted from 1660 to around 1730. Its layout consisted of one or more squares with grass walks edged by shrubbery, containing beds of flowers and fruit, the produce of which might be consumed in the garden itself or sold in the city's markets.

The second phase is most commonly associated with the pleasure gardens and closely modelled on Jonathan Tyers's improvements at Vauxhall Gardens in the 1730s and 1740s. Walks were now categorised into main *allées* – wide, gravelled, processional routes – and subsidiary routes. Walks and spaces for performance were framed with isolated lime or elm trees at regular intervals. At Vauxhall the original plots seem to have been filled in with such trees, except for one corner, the so-called 'Rural Downs'. Bushes and low trellises beneath the trees were intended to keep visitors from straying off the walks. Boxes for supper parties were arranged along the walks in curving lines so that those dinning and those promenading could admire each other. There was often an orchestral pavilion and various follies, while massive false perspectives were placed at the end of the walks to create an impression of distance. From the 1750s, new shrubberies appeared along serpentine rather than straight walks.

The third and final phase of design began around 1820 and continued to the end (Conlin 2013, 21–2). While Vauxhall Gardens remained stuck in the second phase, Cremorne Gardens set the trend. This phase placed great emphasis on bedding plants which were probably 'plunged' into beds. Brighton's Promenade Grove (1793–1802) had rows of elms planted on either side of a path but also had coloured bedding plants and shrubs. Along with exotic trees in pots, the emphasis was on creating bright patches of colour that could be changed relatively easily.

Vauxhall Gardens (1728–1859) held an unrivalled position as London's premier pleasure garden for most of the first part of the eighteenth century. Then, with the opening of Ranelagh Gardens (1742–1803) it had some serious competition. Indeed, Ranelagh soon came to be regarded as more fashionable than its older rival and more innovative in its range of attractions (Figure 42). Marylebone Gardens (1738–76) was another popular venue, even though its quite rural location presented a security risk to visitors in its early days as they might be preyed upon on during their journey by highwayman and footpads (Downing 2009, 25). Also popular in the eighteenth century was Cuper's Garden (1691–1759) that had begun life as early as 1691 when it offered agreeable walks and arbours and some good bowling greens (Wroth 1896, 247). In 1736, an orchestra was included among its attractions and it also became known for firework displays. However, it lost its license in 1753 due to the loose morals of its visitors, although some limited entertainment continued as late as 1759.

While Vauxhall was the only one of the original eighteenth century gardens to survive for very long in the new century, there were several new gardens which opened in London around 1830 (Chadwick 1966, 40). The more significant of these were the Royal Surrey Gardens at Walworth (1831–77), Cremorne Gardens (1843–77) and the Eagle Tavern Gardens (1825–82).

Trees, shrubs and other forms of greenery were a universal feature of the pleasure gardens and had both aesthetic and functional roles. The larger pleasure gardens usually had extensive plantings of trees that were established in quite formal arrangements. There were avenue plantings along the main and often crowded walks that were set out in straight lines or gently curving to ensure plenty of visibility for those promenading. At the main entrance to Vauxhall, the Grand Walk lined with elm trees led away for more that 300 yards to a gilded statue of Aurora and the eastern perimeter of the gardens (Downing 2009, 23). These open avenues contrasted with the dark walks of denser tree planting that led off the main thoroughfares where couples could find some seclusion and privacy. Trees along the main paths were used for the attachment of lamps that not only illuminated the way at night but also lit up the trees and highlighted their natural beauty, shape and texture in an atmospheric glow (Conlin 2013, 23). Horace

Walpole remarked that he "used formerly to think no trees beautiful without lamps on them, like those at Vauxhall" but now found "trees beautiful without them." Larger forest-type trees such as plane, lime and elm were used to mark entrances to the gardens, such as at Vauxhall where the main entrance was said in 1767 to be "planted on each side with very lofty trees" (Anon 1767, 177). Trees also provided the framework and backdrop to the clearings where open-air displays and entertainments took place, such as for fireworks, music, dancing, theatre and the occasional ascents in a hot-air balloon. The larger gardens were keen to promote their collections of trees, shrubs and other plants as a main attraction in their own right. The Royal Surrey Gardens in Kensington was renowned for its horticultural excellence and as well as colourful shrubberies and bedding displays it had a large conservatory used for flower shows. It was particularly proud of its 200 varieties of trees from many different countries that Loudon considered to be its greatest attraction, although he was characteristically quick to point out that some were misnamed (Chadwick 1966, 41).

Because the trees and shrubs in the pleasure gardens were mostly laid out in formal arrangements their designs were largely resistant to the English landscape style of naturalism that was popular on country estates. To provide a contrast to this, some larger gardens created wilderness areas to give an impression of the countryside. However, it was not the prospect of a 'countryside' experience that attracted most people to a pleasure garden, even though they appreciated the contact with nature. If there was a common factor that defines its special position in the pleasure system, it was probably the *garden* element in its makeup (Borsay 2013, 51). This has tended to be neglected, as the focus in horticultural history has been on the rural and particularly country-house garden, and urban historians have concentrated on the non-green built environment. At the time, town dwellers were more interested in the *cultural* phenomenon of greenspace, as their access to this became more difficult with urbanisation. As well as providing some contact with plants and nature, the pleasure gardens also packaged the most exciting aspects of city living, such as encounters with the elite and the latest music, fashions and novelties.

The pleasure gardens were mainly a summer phenomenon, usually open for business between April/May to August/September (Borsay 2013, 72–4). This was understandable given their outdoor operation and their dependence on displays of trees and shrubs as main attractions. Most gardens operated to a daily and weekly schedule of events and activities and most were places of daylight pleasure with only the major gardens also operating at night. This meant that people were generally doing the same things at the same place at the same time, which encouraged social integration. However, time and space could also engineer social segregation as attendance at many events and activities depended on free-time during the weekdays, something that was impossible for most of the working population. Indeed, while it is true that the pleasure gardens were generally open to people from all classes, we should be careful not to overstate the degree of social interaction. Wroth (1896, 8) identified a hierarchy of gardens comprising three 'divisions' and this gives us some insight into this topic. While his study included more than sixty establishments, he placed only four of these in the top division – Cuper's, Marylebone, Ranelagh and Vauxhall – and these attracted many people of 'rank and fashion' (Figure 43). The bulk of establishments had more of a mix of clientele. There are a number of other factors involved in this, apart from the conflict with the working day (Borsay 2013, 65–8). While admission charges might be reasonably priced in comparison to the working man's wages, there were associated costs in visiting the pleasure gardens, such as travel (often considerable when including tolls) and the cost of leisure clothing to ensure your appearance was appropriate. Food and drink in the gardens could also be expensive. It is therefore understandable that in the four major gardens working people would often appear to be in the minority. Nevertheless, the working class were never entirely absent from even the more exclusive and polite pleasure gardens. There were the service workers such as cooks, waiters, musicians and gardeners. There were also the servants of the rich clientele, although domestic servants in livery were banned from the walks at Vauxhall and segregated in a 'coop' outside the gardens.

The majority of the larger pleasure gardens in London and in the provinces were initially located in the urban periphery, many along the line of the city walls or along main rivers (Borsay 2013, 55). John Rocque's map of London in the 1740s shows the edges of the city merging with fields and meadows and Vauxhall, Ranelagh and Marylebone are embedded within this marginal zone, surrounded by a working agricultural and horticultural landscape. Where visiting a garden involved a journey of some distance, this was often part of the attraction, especially when this was by boat across a river, arriving by night at a well-light jetty and main entrance. As urban populations increased and towns and cities expanded, many of these larger gardens became surrounded on all sides by built development and fully absorbed into the new suburban areas.

While pleasure gardens were much visited by the public during the eighteenth century, they represented only a small proportion of the greenspace or tree cover that was accessible to the public in most towns and cities. Even in London, John Rocque's map of the 1740s shows that pleasure gardens were simply one fragment in the capital's greenspace along with various other pockets of vegetation. Many of the smaller towns could not support a commercially viable pleasure garden and people there had to rely on other public or semi-public planted greenspaces (Borsay 2013, 54). These ranged from the many simple tree-lined corridors to arbours and groves (such as the Queen's Grove at Tunbridge Wells), planted squares (as in Queen's Squares, Bristol and Bath), churchyards laid out with walks (as at Painswick and St Philip's Birmingham), institution-based gardens (such as those attached to the Infirmary at Manchester), and those private gardens open to the public.

With the advent of the nineteenth century, pressures were mounting on pleasure gardens and many had already closed. Their popularity was waning across all classes and the social elite stopped attending London's pleasure gardens by

FIGURE 42. Ranelagh Gardens in the 1754, showing the Rotunda, the Chinese House and a fine avenue of trees along one of the main walks. Much of the 'company' are dressed for the masquerade ball. Ranelagh was soon to overtake Vauxhall as London's most fashionable pleasure garden. The hand-coloured engraving is by Thomas Bowles (Wroth 1896).

FIGURE 43. An entertainment in Vauxhall Gardens around 1779 with the 'company' gathered in their dining boxes and under the trees. The two women in the centre are Georgiana, Duchess of Devonshire, and her sister Lady Duncannon. The man seated at the table on the left is Samuel Johnson, with James Boswell to his left and Oliver Goldsmith to his right. To the right the actress and author Mary Darby Robinson stands next to the Prince of Wales, later George IV. The hand-coloured engraving is by Thomas Rowlandson (Wroth 1896).

the 1820s. There were a number of factors involved (Chadwick 1966, 42). Urban expansion had created ever increasing economic pressure to sell the sites for new built development. Changing views among the establishment were challenging the public benefit of the gardens and how they operated, which had prompted an increasingly tedious system of licences for music, dancing and drinking. There was also changing public attitudes regarding the nature of amusements and what had previously been the main attractions of the gardens were now available elsewhere. From the 1840s, their role as an 'oasis' of greenspace and horticultural splendour in the grey and depressing urban fabric was being superseded by the growth of the new municipal parks, which were open all year and did not charge for admission. The expanding network of canals and railways meant that travel to greenspace outside the city was increasingly possible. If the real attraction of the pleasure gardens was to experience the bright lights and glamorous life, this was now available on a grand scale at seaside resorts (see Chapter 8). While music and performing arts had been nurtured in the pleasure gardens, this was now available in a host of theatres, music halls and assembly rooms. By the 1860s, the age of the pleasure gardens had drawn to a close.

The origin of municipal parks

By the nineteenth century access to common land on the outskirts of major cities had become severely limited (Johnson 1990, 16). Successive enclosures, purchases and gifts of land for services rendered increasingly restricted the citizens' freedom of movement and exercise of rights. However, it was with the massive expansion of towns and cities in the wake of the Industrial Revolution that the urban park and private garden-space acquired their acute significance as substitutes for the unobtainable countryside. By the 1830s the need for public open space was becoming severe in some of the older parts of London and the private residential squares were eyed longingly by nearby residents who were denied access to them (Lawrence 1993, 109) (see Chapter 4). The cholera epidemic of 1832 was devastating in the crowded slums of the capital and tens of thousands of people died. One of the cures recommended was the provision of much more public open spaces that would open up the urban fabric to let in light and air. With pressure mounting on the government it established the Parliamentary Select Committee on Public Walks (SCPW) in 1833 with its members "appointed to consider the best means of securing Open Spaces in the Vicinity of populous Towns, as Public Walks and Places of Exercise calculated to promote the Health and Comfort of the Inhabitants" (Hansard 1833, 1049–59). As well as establishing what open space was already available for public use, the SCPW was asked to make recommendations for future provision. When it presented its report to Parliament this contained the first official recognition of the need for public walks or parks (Conway 1991, 2). The term 'public walk' was synonymous with 'public park' until as late as 1875, indicating that these facilities were primarily intended for walking and not for any other recreation

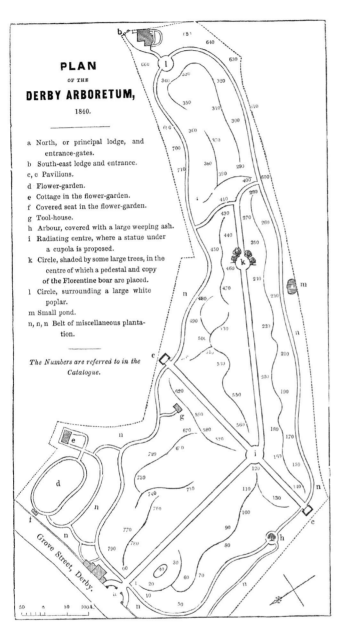

PLAN

OF THE

DERBY ARBORETUM,

1840.

a North, or principal lodge, and
    entrance-gates.
b South-east lodge and entrance.
c, c Pavilions.
d Flower-garden.
e Cottage in the flower-garden.
f Covered seat in the flower-garden.
g Tool-house.
h Arbour, covered with a large weeping ash.
i Radiating centre, where a statue under
    a cupola is proposed.
k Circle, shaded by some large trees, in the
    centre of which a pedestal and copy
    of the Florentine boar are placed.
l Circle, surrounding a large white
    poplar.
m Small pond.
n, n, n Belt of miscellaneous planta-
    tion.

*The Numbers are referred to in the
Catalogue.*

FIGURE 44. The original
plan for the Derby
Arboretum drawn up by
John Claudius Loudon
that was published in
1840 along with the
management plans and
catalogue of trees and
shrubs (Loudon 1840).
The main features of the
arboretum are clearly
indicated.

or games (Chadwick 1966, 99). As well as promoting public parks the SCPW recommended that when turnpike roads or canals were built near towns, there should be clauses in the relevant Acts to ensure that land up to a breadth of 100 yards on either side was not built on (Conway 1991, 37). This area could provide walks, with trees and seats, and would have the advantage of increasing the value of the adjacent land.

The motivation behind the promotion of new parks was not driven entirely by the altruism of the public health agenda. The need for parks in the 1830s was also identified against a background of severe social unrest and increasing class polarisation (Conway 1991, 35–6). The park promoters saw the creation of parks as part of the political process; otherwise 'great mischief must arise'. It was thought that the increased contact between classes in public parks would promote understanding, reduce class conflict and encourage moral behaviour and appearance. The SCPW members were convinced that "some places reserved for the amusement of the humbler classes would assist to wean them from low and debasing pleasures".

In 1833, the year of the SCPW, Moor Park in Preston became the first municipal park freely open to the public in an industrial town (Conway 1991, 18). It was created by enclosing 100 acres of common land on Preston Moor that was in 'a neglected and unprofitable condition'. A series of walks and carriage drives were created including an avenue of lime trees known for many years as The Ladies Walk. Although the Royal Victoria Park in Bath had opened as a public park in 1830, a few years earlier than Moor Park, this was not a municipal park as the Corporation only leased the land and did not own it (*ibid.*, 15).

John Claudius Loudon was among the earliest and most insistent advocates of the environmental and educational benefits of public parks (Elliott *et al.* 2011). In 1822, in his *An Encyclopaedia of Gardening*, he had talked of their 'improving' qualities and later urged their creation in an article entitled *Remarks on laying out Public Gardens and Promenades* (Loudon 1835). In 1839, Loudon began his involvement in the creation of Derby Arboretum, a pioneering public arboretum and park in the Rose Hill district of Derby (Elliott *et al.* 2011, 135–54). This was established on 11 acres (4.5 ha) of land donated to the town for this purpose by Joseph Strutt, a former Mayor and wealthy local industrialist. Loudon approached the planting at Derby Arboretum with considerable care (Loudon 1840, 71–82) (Figure 44). The site was relatively small and the plan shows he took great pains to lay out a sequence of serpentine paths, framed by high mounds, which effectively prohibited a simple grasp of the park's limited dimensions. However, these mounds not only enlarged the impact of the park, they also served another purpose (Figure 45). On them were planted the specimen trees which constituted Loudon's arboretum of just over 800 species, the mound planting used to display the trees and their main roots to best effect. All the trees were carefully labelled and further information was available for the enquiring visitor. Because of the large number of specimens in a relatively small area, Loudon instituted a strict policy of removing trees when they reached a height greater than 40–50 feet. He believed that this height was still sufficient to show the form and character of the tree. Pruning was forbidden, unless under exceptional circumstances, because it could distort the natural shape of the trees and shrubs. For Loudon, Derby Arboretum was a wonderful opportunity to showcase his gardenesque principles and create a living embodiment of his classic book *Arboretum Britannicum.*

FIGURE 45. Relief plan of Loudon's Derby Arboretum that shows the 'undulations to the surface' and the mounds on which many of the trees were planted (Loudon 1840).

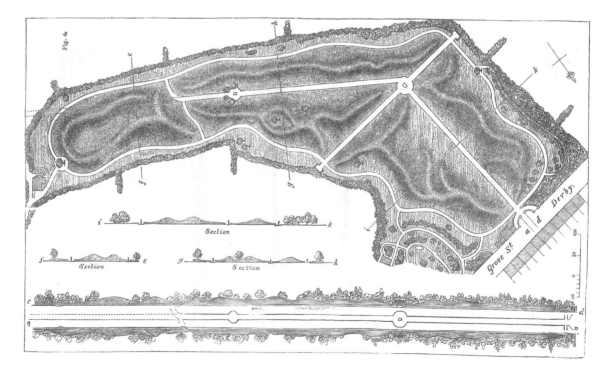

Some historians have claimed Derby Arboretum as the first specifically designed municipal park in Britain (Elliott 2001, 144). However, Moor Park in Preston does have an earlier claim, even though it was not fully landscaped until the early 1860s (Conway 1991, 18). The success of the Derby Arboretum encouraged the development of a number of other public arboretums during the Victorian era. The Nottingham Arboretum, established in 1852, was primarily an urban park laid out as a tree collection (Elliott *et al.* 2008). It also functioned as the centrepiece of one of the most ambitious schemes of urban enclosure and improvement in mid-Victorian Britain. Ipswich Arboretum, both Upper and Lower sections, were established in 1853 on land leased to the Corporation by the Fonnereau family (Conway 1991, 229). Lincoln Arboretum was designed and laid out between 1870 and 1872 by the celebrated Victorian gardener Edward Milner. While it was always intended as a public park its finest feature remains its excellent tree collection. Walsall Arboretum in the West Midlands was opened in 1874 and although it operated more as a pleasure garden, low visitor numbers could not sustain it. The Town Council took over the arboretum in 1881 and it reopened in 1884 as the town's first municipal park. There was also free admission, which was unusual for a public urban arboretum at that time as most made some small charge.

It is notable that many of these early public parks were titled 'arboretum'. This reflected their emphasis on trees, not just for their beauty and stature, but also as living botanical specimens to be studied as part of a programme of educational and moral improvement (Elliott *et al.* 2007a). They were likened to 'living museums', with the trees and shrubs clearly labelled, numbered plans, displays and guides. While many landscape gardeners such as Loudon advocated public urban arboretums as alternatives to exclusively aristocratic gardens, others such as Joseph Paxton argued that public arboretums were not usually suitable as public parks.

After 1837, largely due to Joseph Hume in the House of Commons, although initially proposed by Loudon, all parliamentary enclosure acts were required to contain provision for some public open space, representing a significant step forward in park promotion (Simo 1988, 194). Around 1845, the Victorian parks movement became recognisable as such due to the growing number of initiatives that had been undertaken or were in the planning stage (Conway 1991, 39). One of these was in direct response to the SCPW of 1833 which placed special emphasis on the crowded East End of London where there was almost no public open space. It prompted the creation of Victoria Park between 1842–6, initially as a royal park since the land was purchased by The Crown Estate (Elliott 1990, 152). The East End's first major public park rapidly became a very popular venue, particularly at weekends, as tens of thousands of working class people flocked to enjoy its attractions that included an arboretum (Conway 1991, 165). The park was laid out by Sir James Pennethorne, a protégé of John Nash, in a design reminiscent of Nash's Regent's Park. Another new royal park created in London was Battersea Park on the south side of the river Thames (*ibid.*, 40). In 1846, an Act of Parliament was passed to form this royal park with the purchase of land at Battersea Fields, the majority of which became Battersea Park with the remainder let on building leases. This park was also laid out by Pennethorne, although when it opened in 1858 it varied somewhat from his original vision. Nevertheless, the tree cover was extensive with 40,000 trees planted, 5,000 of them from Kew (Chadwick 1966, 129). The park's success owed much to the completion of Chelsea Bridge in 1858, which allowed easy public access to the park from north of the river.

The pioneering period of park development in the 1830s and 40s was marked with various initiatives from central and local government, from benefactors and from the community. Park and garden design was no longer an affair for the wealthy alone; its impact was now extending to the working class and was becoming a matter of public policy (Elliott 1986, 54). However, even the most prosperous municipal corporations were not yet empowered by a general act of Parliament to raise their own funds in order to create and maintain public walks and parks. Progress towards that goal was made with the development of Birkenhead Park on the Wirral Peninsula. In 1841, a part of Birkenhead's local government known as an Improvement Commission proposed the idea of a municipal park. A Private Act of Parliament passed in 1843 allowed it to use public money to buy 226 acres (91.5 ha) of marshy grazing land on the edge of Birkenhead. Plots of land on the edge of the proposed park were then sold off in order to finance its construction. Although some large houses and private villas were initially built by local merchants and wealthier business people, the depressed economic conditions in the latter part of the nineteenth century would mean that many plots remained undeveloped for decades.

Birkenhead Park opened in 1847 with the distinction of being the first municipal park in Britain established as a result of an application to Parliament for powers to use public funds for that purpose (Conway 1991, 49) (Figure 46). It was also an expressly designed municipal park whose 45 acres (18 ha) was dedicated to the free recreation of local residents. It became known as 'the people's park' and there is evidence that local residents had a clear sense of ownership of it (Elliott 1986, 53–4). Birkenhead's Improvement Commission had chosen Joseph Paxton to design the park and Edward Kemp as the works supervisor because both had previously worked on the successful redesigning of the gardens at Chatsworth House. The excavation of the lake created a mass of rocks and soil which was formed into mounds used in the manner of Loudon's gardenesque planting principles and later adopted by other public parks (Figure 47). The overall design of Birkenhead Park was not only imported into many new municipal parks in Britain but it famously influenced the design of Central Park in New York, following a visit to Birkenhead by Frederick Law Olmstead.

Many of the early public parks resulted from a combination of wealthy benefactors and private commercial interest, supported by determined council leaders motivated by civic pride (Taylor 1995; Layton-Jones and Lee 2008). By contrast, the parks movement in Manchester was a rare example of working people taking an active part in park development as the whole community was involved in fundraising (Conway 1991, 49). Land for parks was acquired in 1845 and Philips Park and Queen's Park in Manchester, and Peel Park in Salford, were officially opened to the public in 1846. All three were designed by Joshua Major, a landscape designer from Yorkshire, whose public parks were notable for having specific areas for sport and recreation. To Major's disappointment, his designs to facilitate this attracted some criticism and a correspondent in the *Gardeners' Chronicle* itemised a series of faults that included an absence of curving walks, a profusion of straight walks with acute angles and diminutive lakes (Elliott 1986, 100). Major defended the straight walks as appropriate for areas set aside for games. He was finally forced to abandon his aesthetic arguments in favour of his design and to claim that the park could not have been made more artistic without sacrificing the sports facilities.

The growth of the Victorian parks movement

One of the most influential public parks of the mid-Victorian era was the Crystal Palace Park, designed by Joseph Paxton (Elliott 1986, 107–10). After the 1851 Great Exhibition in Hyde Park, Paxton appealed for the retention of his Crystal Palace, a huge and remarkable glass structure that had formed the centrepiece of the exhibition. Its great height was partly to facilitate the need to retain under glass the large mature elm trees on the site. However, the government decreed that the whole structure should move to a new site at Sydenham, then in Kent. As part of this proposal, a park would be created around the Crystal Palace that would include a wide range of landscape features, such as an Italian Garden, an English landscape garden and a great maze. The park covering 200 acres (81 ha) was opened in 1854 and cost far more to create than the rebuilding of the Crystal Palace. Inspired by the Crystal Palace, public winter gardens began to appear in many towns and cities in the 1860s, and the process continued until the 1890s. Crystal Palace Park also differed from previous public parks with its inclusion of a wide range of educational features, such as the depiction of an open-cast mine, an aquarium and models of prehistoric animals grouped around the lake (*ibid.*, 121). The influence of this park on the provision of educational features in other public parks was immense. In almost every city in Britain from the 1860s onwards, aviaries, zoos and conservatories full of exotic vegetation appeared, making the aim of botanical and arboricultural education underlying such early parks as the Derby Arboretum only one strand in a broader programme of public education.

When Joseph Paxton died in 1865, his landscaping tradition and garden design principles were carried on by two of his protégés, Edward Kemp and Edward Milner (Elliott 1986, 171). Kemp's chief works included Newsham Park, Liverpool (1868), Hesketh Park, Southport (1868) and Stanley Park, Liverpool (1870). Milner's chief works included the People's Park in Halifax with Joseph Paxton (1857), Moor Park, Miller Park and Avenham Park in Preston (all 1867), The Pavilion Gardens, Buxton (1871) (Figures 48 and 49) and the Lincoln Arboretum (1872) (Conway 1991). During his last years, Milner directed the Crystal Palace School of Landscape Gardening (*ibid.*, 173). When he died in 1884, he was Robert Marnock's main

FIGURE 46. The Grand Entrance to Birkenhead Park, which opened in 1847 as Britain's first municipal park established as a result of an application to Parliament for powers to use public funding for this purpose. The scale of this magnificent entrance announced to world that this park was something special.

FIGURE 47. Joseph Paxton's design for Birkenhead Park was informal and reflected the 'picturesque' approach of the classic English landscape park, as well as elements of Loudon and his own individual style. There are winding paths offering a variety of views, two lakes, dramatic rocky outcrops and mounds that were raised using the spoil from the lakes and planted extensively with trees and shrubs. This is a view of the Boathouse with the Swiss Bridge in the background and the lower lake surrounded by dense ornamental planting.

rival and the country's most celebrated landscape gardener. His son, Henry Ernest Milner, later published *The Art and Practice of Landscape Gardening*, based on his father's work (Milner 1890). This was unusual for landscape design books of the time in having a chapter devoted to public parks and cemeteries. Another figure who was influential in later Victorian park design was William Barron who had made his mark with his innovative use of conifers at Elvaston Castle and his skill in moving large trees (Elliott *et al.* 2007b). By the 1870s, Barron was well advanced in his second career as a professional landscape gardener and recognised as an

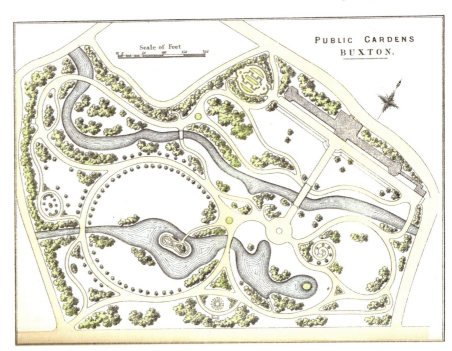

FIGURE 48. Edward Milner's plan for The Pavilion Gardens at Buxton, Derbyshire, which opened in 1871 (Milner 1890). Although the plan is titled 'Public Gardens', this was not actually the case. While the public previously had access to the area, when the gardens and associated entertainments opened they were charged a considerable sum for admission, more than most of the locals could afford.

FIGURE 49. The Pavilion Gardens, Buxton, remains the 'jewel in the crown' of this spa town in Derbyshire. In 1927, the Buxton Corporation acquired the buildings, gardens and pleasure grounds and the site has been managed ever since as a public park.

innovator in municipal park design, mainly through two projects at Locke Park, Barnsley (1877) and Abbey Park, Leicester (1882) (Elliott 1986, 171). Barron died in 1891, but his firm went on to a prolific career in park and garden design well into the twentieth century.

As part of the Victorian municipal park's moral agenda, the public were closely regulated to ensure 'proper' behaviour. This was in contrast to the commercial pleasure gardens, although these were now in terminal decline. Sunday was the day when most people had the opportunity of visiting parks, but it was also the day when use was restricted by religious concerns (Conway 1991, 200). Many parks were closed on Sunday mornings to encourage people to attend church services. The range of sports and arts activities permitted in the parks was rigidly controlled (*ibid.*, 186–207). Only those more 'gentlemanly' sports were allowed that the authorities believed would promote a good social and moral character. Football, a favourite sport of the male working class, was among the last sports to be allowed. Sporting opportunities for women in parks were strictly limited and usually segregated from male sports. It was only towards the end of the nineteenth century that restrictions on sporting activities began to be relaxed. The range of arts activities allowed in parks was particularly limited. One notable exception was the bandstand, a characteristic feature of Victorian parks. There was also some segregation of the sexes in public parks, although this was often self-segregation as women tended to avoid certain areas, such as those with dense tree and shrub cover. These areas could provide opportunities for concealment and thieves took advantage of this. Clumps of dense undergrowth also provided cover for casual sex and prostitution. Prostitutes often chose to frequent the footpath of roads going through parks, near to dense tree and shrub cover, to conduct their business discretely or hide when police were spotted. Recent research into the history of crime and policing in Birkenhead Park has revealed some fascinating insights into these topics (Lee 2013). Children were often the targets of criminals in public parks, which made the middle class wary of visiting them. Instead of being a 'safe haven', these urban parks were often rife with crime and anti-social behaviour, which contrasted sharply with the moral intentions behind their establishment – 'the moral therapy of the landscape'.

By the 1880s most towns had at least one public park or recreation ground, often on the town's outskirts or a short distance from it (Jordan 1994, 65). At the time, William Robinson was one of the few prominent voices to express concern that many of the new public parks were not where they were most needed and that efforts should be focused more on the poorer and densely-populated parts of cities (Robinson 1869, xviii). Some modern historians have cautioned against overstating the contribution of many of these new 'people's parks' to improving the lives of the working class precisely because they were often on the periphery of urban areas (O'Reilly 2013a). For working class families in the heart of the city, visiting their public park could involve travelling some distance and at some expense by tram.

There were a number of voluntary societies that played a leading role in the promotion of public open space during the Victorian era. The Manchester and Salford Sanitary Association (MSSA) was founded in 1852 and while its focus was initially on sanitation, it broadened its interest into housing and open spaces (Conway 1991, 213). In 1880, a separate organisation was formed called the Committee for Securing Open Spaces, which was closely associated with the MSSA. The Kyrle Society was founded in 1875 by Miranda Hill, a prominent social reformer, and this established numerous branches around the country. In 1879, it set up a sub-committee to work for the increased provision of open spaces and to protect those that were threatened. The Metropolitan Public Gardens Association (MPGA) was formed in London in 1882 to protect and acquire for permanent public use various gardens, disused burial grounds, churchyards, open spaces and areas of land within the metropolitan district (MPGA 2014). The first Chairman and moving spirit behind the MPGA was Lord Brabazon, later the Earl of Meath. This organisation always had a specific focus on trees and made a significant contribution to the greening of London, particularly during its early years, and continues to be active today (MacLeod 1972, 297–302). The major contribution of the Commons Preservation Society is discussed below in the section on 'Commons'.

Trees and design in Victorian parks and open spaces

Although Victorian public parks varied in size from tiny patches of greenspace to extensive landscapes of over 100 ha, they were usually quite similar in design (Conway 1991). These rather formal landscapes comprised a network of paths through closely mown lawns with some built features interspersed among groups of ornamental specimen trees and islands of flowerbeds (Figure 50). Often the first building to greet the park visitor was the lodge by the main gates, with the park regulations displayed prominently nearby. Other typical buildings included bandstands, palm houses and shelters. Statues, drinking fountains and commemorative monuments were also popular.

Most Victorian parks were extensively planted with trees, with plenty of individual specimens, avenues, belts and woodlands (Conway 1991). In some cases trees were labelled with their name and some basic information, much as in the manner of an arboretum, to promote the park's educational role. Planting around the periphery of the park could be particularly dense. When visiting Dulwich Park, J. J. Sexby, the first Superintendent of Parks for the London County Council (LCC), remarked, "We pass around the park and are so shut in by a wall of trees as to forget the outside world" (Sexby 1898, 88). The Victorian's tastes in trees for parks tended to be quite distinctive. They had a penchant for the exotic conifers, such as *Cupressus*, *Thuja*, *Cedrus*, and the redwoods. Consequently, the trees gave an overall appearance to the park landscape that was quite dark and heavy. There were also some widely accepted design principles that regulated how and where trees were planted. One important consideration related to the problem of accommodating variety while not conflicting with the need for unity of expression (Conway 1991, 80). Loudon believed that to keep interest alive there should be variety and one type of scene must succeed another. However, to give the coherent effect necessary for unity of expression and avoid stark contrasts, these scenes should be related according to some principle recognisable by the visitor.

FIGURE 50. A typical Victorian park landscape with a hard surfaced path winding through closely mown lawn among groups of ornamental trees and islands of flowerbeds. The Victorian penchant for exotic conifers, such as *Cupressus, Thuja* and *Cedrus*, often gave the overall landscape quite a dark and heavy appearance.

Park design and the selection of tree species was heavily influenced by the horticultural and arboricultural fashions of the time that featured in the major private gardens, such as Biddulph Grange, Chatsworth and Elvaston Castle (Elliott 1986) (see Chapter 4). Chinese and Japanese gardens were very popular and trees and shrubs from those counties were an essential part of the planting schemes. Rock gardens were also popular in parks, along with their typical tree and shrub species.

The act of tree planting can have symbolic significance and this has been expressed in many different cultures throughout history (Rival 1998). The Victorians were conscious of this and planting ceremonies were occasionally organised by the park authorities to commemorate important events. These could include state occasions such as a birth, wedding or death of a member of the royal family, or a crucial military victory. Sometimes, the occasion for the tree planting might have purely local relevance, such as the visit to the city by an overseas monarch or national leader. A tree planting ceremony might also be organised to celebrate the opening of the park, with the tree being planted by the main benefactor or civic dignitary. Regardless of any tree planting ceremonies, parks were used as convenient venues for general public celebrations. For example, in 1897 when Keighley, West Yorkshire, celebrated Queen Victoria's Diamond Jubilee the main event was focused on Victoria Park but entertainments were held in all the town's parks (MacGill 2007, 155).

One of the main problems of park maintenance in industrial cities was the effect of air pollution on trees and shrubs (Conway 1991, 180–1) (see Chapter 3). In Manchester in the mid-1850s, trees were carefully selected to withstand the conditions. Twenty years later the effects of air pollution had become so severe, particularly in Philips Park, that a special sub-committee was set up to inspect nearby industrial works and make recommendations. Ten years after that, the problem seemed to have deteriorated further and even plane trees could not withstand the Manchester atmosphere. Common elder, privet and Japanese knot weed proved to be the best in these conditions. Apart from the expense of trying to contain this situation, it presented a major dilemma for park management. Trees provided the main structure for any park planting but because of air pollution were unlikely to survive to maturity. Park superintendents were faced with the problem of creating a landscape in which trees had only a short lifespan instead of providing the basic permanent framework of the design.

Regardless of the importance of trees and shrubs to the overall park design, for many visitors it was flowers that were the main attraction and park superintendents strove to satisfy this (Conway 1991, 164). They usually did this by providing vast expanses of colour in the form of bedding displays over as long a period as possible. An additional advantage of bedding was also found to be its tolerance of a polluted atmosphere (Elliott 1986, 135). Where conifers and many other trees were usually failures, bedding plants that were placed out for a season were the most secure means of ensuring some horticultural colour and interest.

The taste in landscape gardening in Britain at the beginning of the 1850s was moving away from the landscaped pleasure ground of the previous century (Elliott 1986, 110). This transformation was epitomised by the new Crystal Palace Park at Sydenham. Twenty years before, the formal element of the design would have been limited to the immediate vicinity of the glasshouse, not extending beyond the terrace on which it stood. By contrast, Paxton's design extended the system of terracing as a central axis down the hillside, around which all other ornamental features were focused. A typical 'English landscape' only occupied the outer and lower fringes of the park. In its overall appearance and one overriding axis of unity, Crystal Palace Park could be compared to a baroque garden. Its use and choice of trees and shrubs, which were planted in tens of thousands, reflected this. Undoubtedly, much of the inspiration for the design of the park came from Paxton's visit to Versailles and other Le Nôtre gardens in 1834.

During the 1860s, however, a reaction was gradually building up against the character of artistic treatment assumed necessary in the previous decade, and the debate directly impacted on the public park (Elliott 1986, 166–8). While some wished for designs similar to Versailles, of broad allées, grand avenues, shrubberies and woods with straight walks, a further model for landscape gardening emerged in the work of Alexander McKenzie (*ibid.*, 174). He had laid out Alexander Palace in 1863 and his stated aim was non-interference with the natural landscape. When McKenzie laid out the gardens on the new Victoria Embankment in 1870, this immediately led to a public debate over the propriety of informal design in an urban setting (Elliott 1990, 160). The architectural press were unhappy with his more natural approach to landscaping and tree planting with the *Building News* complaining that:

All attempts at rural landscape should have been avoided, and the whole attention of the designer directed to urban embellishment. Rural landscape gardening and urban embellishment are very different things. A central avenue of plane trees, the only trees which thoroughly withstand the London smoke, terminated at the Charing Cross end by a handsome architectural entrance ... would be infinitely preferable to the meaningless paths ... which at present puzzle the public.

quoted in Elliott, 1990, 160

McKenzie later published proposals for a vast increase in parks as well as the creation of a network of major tree-lined avenues through London (Elliott 1990, 161). He also became the first Superintendent of Epping Forest where has was able to give full expression to his passion for naturalistic landscapes.

The Victorian passion for public landscaping extended beyond creating new parks to the provision of other open space as part of wider civic built developments. New municipal buildings such as Town and City Halls, museums and public libraries often had small areas of associated greenspace where people could walk, sit and relax (Hunt 2004). The landscape design and tree planting around many of these civic buildings tended to reflect the style of the more formal elements of the public parks.

Commons and squares for public use

By the mid-nineteenth century, vast areas of common land on the edge of many towns and cities had fallen victim to the enclosures. Along with concern for the need to provide public parks stimulated by the SCPW, a growing body of influential campaigners were now focusing on the need to protect this remaining common land to ensure its future enjoyment by working class people (Shaw-Lefevre 1894). While much of the campaigning focused on some high-profile locations in and around London, other areas of common land in the urban fringe around Britain featured in less celebrated campaigns. Much of this common land was well-wooded and sometimes represented the last remaining fragments of ancient forests.

The Commons Preservation Society (CPS) (now the Open Spaces Society) was founded in 1865 (Conway, 1991 70). Its founders and early members included John Stuart Mill, Lord Eversley (formerly George Lefevre MP), William Morris, Sir Robert Hunter, and Octavia Hill (Williams 1965). The last two founded the National Trust in 1895 along with Canon Rawnsley. After its initial focus on London's commons and open spaces, the CPS subsequently broadened its aims to include all commons near large towns in England and Wales. Its early successes included saving Hampstead Heath, Epping Forest, Wimbledon Common, Ashdown Forest and the Malvern Hills (Shaw-Lefevre 1894).

Many of London's commons had fine expanses of tree cover in Victorian times, often with trees that had important historical connections. Tooting Common in South London was typical with many old and fine avenues stretching across its wide expanse (Sexby 1898, 220–4). One of them was said to have stretched to London and been the favourite drive of Elizabeth I. Tooting Common, like many other places, possessed woodland with plenty of fine old oaks. Sadly, many of these trees were sacrificed in late-Victorian times with the formation of the two arms of the London, Brighton and South Coast Railway across the common. Nevertheless, some extensive tree planting was subsequently undertaken in an effort to screen the railways. These and other commons are now the major areas of public greenspace in South London.

Some of the common land saved for the nation was threatened with radical change to its tree cover both before and after it had been 'protected'. The growing taste for mixing exotics with native woodland trees that was popular on many country estates was reflected in proposals presented in 1853 for turning Hampstead Heath into a municipal park, with part of this planted as an arboretum (Elliott 1986, 93). The proposals received enthusiastic support from the *Gardener's Chronicle* but the plan was not carried out. William Paul's 1880 proposals for Epping Forest, recently saved for public use by the City of London, were slightly less radical, although again involving the use of exotics (*ibid.*, 183). While Paul stressed it would be inappropriate to turn the forest into a landscape garden or an arboretum, he nevertheless envisaged single trees, avenues and groves interspersed with open glades and wide stretches of pasture, using exotics that he claimed would still maintain Epping in the character of an English forest. The trees he suggested for this purpose included scarlet oaks, Norway maples, Douglas firs, cypresses, cedars, and giant sequoia, together with abundant plantings of *Rhododendron ponticum*. Fortunately, his extensive plans for Epping Forest were never accepted.

Other significant areas of urban greenspace that were under threat towards the end of the Victorian era were the communal gardens of the privately-owned Georgian residential squares that graced London and other major cities such as Bath and Edinburgh. These delightful ornamental gardens usually had large numbers of fine mature trees, particularly planes. The relentless pace of urban development and the demand for building land was now putting ever greater pressure on any existing greenspace that was not already protected or in public ownership. In 1890, the London and North Western Railway Company proposed to cover a quarter of Euston Square with new station premises (Longstaffe-Gowan 2012, 194–5). The company put forward the proposals as the freeholder of the square, having earlier bought the rights from all the occupants. Fortunately, recent parliamentary legislation had strengthened the powers of local government and the newly-created LCC had just formed its Parks and Open Spaces Committee to promote and protect these areas in the capital. The LCC opposed the planning application and the square's gardens were saved, to be enjoyed later as a public open space. A similar case arose in 1896 when Albert Square in Stepney was advertised for sale. Here, the LCC obtained powers of compulsory purchase in order to preserve it as an open space.

While these two cases were significant victories in efforts to protect London's squares as open spaces, neither was to have the long-term impact or be as controversial as the proposed redevelopment of Edwardes Square in Kensington (Longstaffe-Gowan 2012, 195–6). The gardens of this 'socially select and largely

FIGURE 51. Princes Street Gardens in Edinburgh were originally associated with the New Town private residential development begun in the late eighteenth century. In 1876, after some opposition from the residents, the council acquired the ground as a public park. This shows part of the very popular East Princes Street Gardens with the Scott Monument in the background, dedicated to the writer Sir Walter Scott.

self-governing enclave' were put up for sale in 1903. So great was the public disquiet that the Parks and Open Spaces Committee of Kensington Borough Council applied to Parliament for powers to prevent the square from being covered in buildings. After much debate and some initial disappointment, the LCC itself obtained its London Squares and Enclosures (Preservation) Act (1906) and while this did not specifically protect Edwardes Square, it did lead eventually to greater protection of the London squares generally.

The transfer in ownership of many London squares from private to public open space in the early years of the twentieth century is a complex story. Similar transfers of ownership took place in other towns and cities, although Edinburgh remains notable in still having most of its New Town gardens in private hands (Byrom 1995) (Figure 51). The transfer of ownership of these squares took many years to accomplish. Alicia Amherst noted in 1907 that while many in London were now open to the public, "by far the greater number of squares are maintained by the residents in their neighbourhood, who have keys to the gardens" (Amherst 1907, 218). Fortunately, thanks to the actions of some far-sighted local authorities and the efforts of public-spirited citizens many of these fine gardens in Georgian residential squares have been saved for the public. Now, we can all enjoy to the full those wonderful mature landscapes of planes, limes, ailanthus and other beautiful trees in this uniquely British form of urban greenspace.

Parks in the early twentieth century

With the increasing pace of urban expansion in the early years of the twentieth century, built development encroached upon the nearby country estates of wealthy landowners (Jordan 1994, 90). These were frequently sold to property developers and builders, often because of a dramatic loss of income or the need to pay crippling death duties (Robinson 2012). In some cases the house and its immediate grounds were secured for use as a public park. Many of these new urban fringe parks inherited landscaped parkland of high amenity value, often including gardens and pleasure grounds containing many fine mature trees, particularly exotic conifers. Acquiring these existing estates for conversion to public parks meant that the scope available to the landscape designer for originality varied considerable. In South London, for instance, J. J. Sexby made almost no changes of design in converting the Brockwell estate into a municipal park (Elliott 1986, 213–4). When he was asked to combine three separate gardens to make Ruskin Park, he had a greater opportunity to display his skills.

Despite the many public parks established in the late nineteenth and early twentieth century, remarkably little was written on their design (Jordan 1994, 91). The *Gardeners' Chronicle*, the leading horticultural magazine, focused on private estates and published little on the public sector, as did other horticultural magazines. Regardless of this lack of interest from the horticultural establishment, a number of individuals and firms specialised in the layout of public parks. Competitions were often staged by local authorities to select their preferred design among those submitted by landscape designers and architects (Cherry *et al.* 1993, 313). The most notable of these was Thomas Mawson, who has been described as probably the most successful designer of parks in the first quarter of the twentieth century (Chadwick 1966, 221; Cherry *et al.* 1993). Mawson published *The Art and Craft of Garden Making* and while this did include not public parks, it set out design principles and had a number of chapters focusing on trees (Mawson 1900). His other influential work, *Civic Art: Studies in town planning, parks, boulevards and open spaces*, has much to say on parks, as the title indicates (Mawson, 1911). Mawson was highly critical of the standard of park design at that time, stating that: "In no department of municipal enterprise is there such a lamentable absence of artistic expression, or even reasonably convenient planning, as in our public parks." (*ibid.*, 161–2). For Mawson, it seemed that anyone was regarded as capable of successfully directing landscape gardening, from the Borough Engineer down to the Chairman of the Parks Committee. He believed the 'artistic gardener' with a wide knowledge of trees and shrubs should be employed for this work. However, rather than employ such a man, the work was frequently left to the practical gardener who loved rarity, variety and novelty. The outcome was "the huddled masses of sickly, half-starved arboricultural curiosities, which so often do duty for park plantations."

Another influential figure in municipal parks in the early part of the twentieth century was William Wallace Pettigrew. He trained at Kew Gardens in the 1880s and served as Cardiff Corporation's first head gardener from 1891 (Cardiff City Council 2014). His father and brother, both called Andrew, also served in senior positions at Cardiff Parks Department. In 1913, Pettigrew was appointed superintendent of the Manchester parks where he served with distinction until his retirement in 1932. In the late-1920s, Pettigrew published statistics on Philips Park, one of Joshua Major's creations, then in the most polluted district of the city (Pettigrew 1928). The average life span of rhododendrons was three years, and flowering was only reliable the first year; poplars lasted somewhat longer. Each year some 7000 trees and shrubs had to be planted to replace the annual losses. These statistics demonstrated very forcibly that the problem of air pollution was still a headache for parks managers. In 1937, Pettigrew published the first substantial British textbook on public park management entitled *Municipal Parks: Layout, Management and Administration* (Pettigrew 1937). What is surprising about this influential book is how little it contains about trees in parks, although there is a chapter specifically on street trees.

During the 1920s and '30s the pace of new park-making by local authorities slowed considerable. Where new landscapes were acquired by local authorities, they were often not as carefully designed and planned as the early public parks. There were a number of reasons for this but they mostly concerned factors relating to style and expense (O'Reilly 2013b, 124). For example, Cardiff Corporation was given the 42 acres (17 ha) of Plymouth Wood by the Earl of Plymouth in 1923, which was kept as woodland with the addition of a few paths. These wilder landscapes were identified as more 'natural' than the planned and designed parks. They were also less expensive to establish and maintain and their wild nature was believed to be an attraction for visitors.

Recreation grounds and playing fields

Towards the end of the nineteenth century it was increasingly recognised that large parks did not solve the problems of access to open space for those living in the densest urban areas. There was a need for smaller, more local recreation grounds devoted to playgrounds and sports to provide people with opportunities for more active recreation (Conway 1991, 209). Concern about the health and physique of young people had been highlighted by the publication of the Report on Physical Deterioration in 1904 and medical reports of the poor fitness of army recruits (*ibid.*, 221). The resulting pressure led to the successful development of some small parks and recreation grounds, often by converting disused burial grounds and churchyards into open spaces for recreation (*ibid.*, 212). The movement was given further momentum by the Public Health Act of 1925 that stressed the need to reserve land for recreation. In the same year, the National Playing Fields Association (NPFA) was set up and this had a considerable impact on the creation of recreational open space throughout Britain. Its slogan was 'More Playing Fields for the People' and it promoted its 'Six Acre Standard' that recommended local authorities provide a minimum of area of recreational open space of 6 acres (2.43 ha) per 1,000 head of population (Conway 2000). On the death of George V in 1936, the King George V Memorial Fund for the provision of open space was founded. This acquired land for recreation which it then passed to the NPFA 'to preserve and safeguard for public benefit'. When the King George's Fields

Foundation was dissolved in 1965 there were 471 King George Playing Fields located throughout Britain (KGFF 1965, 14). In 1937, the Physical Training and Recreation Act gave a further boost to the movement by enabling grants to be made for the purchase and development of land for playing fields, parks and recreation grounds (Conway 2000, 118). That year also saw the launch of the National Fitness Campaign, which was endorsed by King George VI. Of all the influences on park development in the 1930s the link between public health and recreation was the most significant.

This movement toward the provision of more active recreation facilities also impacted on the established municipal parks, where large expanses of existing landscape, often ornamental areas, were redeveloped to accommodate this (O'Reilly 2013b, 112–3). Much of this new provision was aimed at the population's growing demand for more recreation and sports facilities, partly fuelled by the increase in workers' leisure time with more holidays. The result was the emergence of a tension between competing interests in the municipal park as they struggled to redefine themselves in the inter-war period as multi-functional open spaces. Leading figures in park administration grew alarmed at the consequences of this with Pettigrew (1937, 4) expressing concern that ornamental horticultural features were being viewed as 'unwanted extravagances'.

The conversion of established municipal parks to accommodate more recreation and sports facilities, and the creation of recreation grounds specifically for this, undoubtedly had a negative impact on the tree cover of these public open spaces. Sports pitches required large expanses of mown grass, which conflicted directly with the provision of extensive tree cover. With the new recreation grounds and playing fields, there was a tendency to think of them as just that without any attempt to introduce ornamental horticultural features (Conway 2000, 119). As a result, these areas usually had very few trees. Where planting did occur this was likely to be limited to single rows or narrow shelterbelts of trees around the perimeter and at strategic points between sports pitches to provide players and spectators with some protection from inclement weather.

Post-war public parks

The second part of the twentieth century witnessed a slow decline in the fortunes of the British municipal park. This began with the damage inflicted on many parks during the Second World War (see Chapter 3). The situation continued post-war as a result of a wide range of political, economic and social factors (see Lasdun 1991, 187–202; Conway 2000; O'Reilly 2013b). We consider briefly here the implications of this on the trees and landscape of public parks.

After the Second World War the influence of modernism, suspended during the war, extended not only to architecture and town planning but also to parks (Conway 1991, 8). It signalled a further movement away from the ornamental horticulture of the Victorian and Edwardian era as massed displays of flowers and ornate planting were replaced by the equivalent of 'clean-sweep' planning, bold sweeps of grass. This had the added advantage of being cheaper and easier to maintain, but was much less interesting to most visitors. This trend away from horticulture was reinforced by the Baines Report in 1972 which merged local authority Parks Departments with Recreation Services, Swimming Pools and the Arts. As a result, there was no separate budget for parks managers who now had to compete with these other areas. This was reflected later at a professional level in 1983 when the Institute of Park and Recreation Administration (formed in the 1920s as the Institute of Park Administration) transformed into the Institute of Leisure and Amenity Management (Lasdun 1991, 190).

Other developments ensured the focus of park management was being further deflected from its traditional role in managing and maintaining existing municipal parks. During the 1960s and 1970s, a significant area of park development concerned what is now recognised as the post-industrial landscape: the transformation of derelict industrial wastelands into parks and gardens (Conway 2000, 130). Many of these projects involved vast amounts of tree planting as part of the restoration effort, particularly on former industrial sites. In recognition that the large municipal parks were not always located to provide convenient access for everyone, there was also a move towards creating much smaller greenspaces more closely integrated into the urban fabric and designed to serve specific neighbourhoods. Other new forms of urban park appearing in Britain were linear parks created across redundant railway lines in towns and cities, courtesy of drastic cuts in the rail network following the Beeching Report in 1963. Of all the various factors impacting on park development it was the financial constraints on local government during the 1980s and 1990s that played a key role in the decline of many traditional urban parks and influenced some of the more negative aspects of park policy.

From the 1970s onwards, park management seemed to follow arboriculture in becoming preoccupied with risk management. Park managers were worried at the prospect of expensive insurance claims when budgets were being squeezed and tried to pre-empt these. In some parks and open spaces the lower limbs of trees were removed so that children could not climb them (Taggart 2004). Trees with tempting fruit or horse chestnuts with conkers were particular targets for this pruning. Another example of nervousness about health and safety was the removal of unofficial swings or ropes that children or their parents had attached to park trees (Mouland 2003).

With the rising 'green' awareness of the 1980s and '90s when ideas about nature were more associated with notions of 'environment' and 'ecology', the neatly managed nature of the Victorians seemed out of place to many people (Figure 52). This led to semi-natural areas appearing in many urban parks, particularly wildflower meadows and semi-natural woodland. However, these efforts at habitat creation and the promotion of 'ecological landscapes' were also viewed as a convenient excuse to save money by letting these sites 'manage' themselves (Johnston 1983, 279). Furthermore, public reaction was often

FIGURE 52. The William Curtis Ecological Park was Britain's first urban ecology park. This small park of just two acres (0.8 ha) opened near Tower Bridge in London in 1976 on what was previously a derelict lorry park. It soon became a popular attraction and study venue, especially for parties of school children undertaking nature studies. In 1985 it was returned to its owner London Docklands Development Corporation who provided the Stave Hill Ecological Park in Rotherhithe as a replacement.

negative amid fears about dense undergrowth providing convenient cover for muggers and anti-social behaviour.

Many historic urban parks that had suffered decades of neglect and decline finally found a much-needed source of new finance when the Heritage Lottery Fund (HLF) was established in 1993. This uses money raised from the National Lottery to support projects related to our national heritage, including the restoration of historic parks. Many have undergone major restoration works and there has been much research on the regeneration of public parks (Woudstra and Fieldhouse 2012). Paxton's masterpiece, Birkenhead Park, had been in a dilapidated state for years with crumbling buildings and its belts of trees and shrubs decimated by disease or over-maturity (Lasdun 1991, 187–8). Thankfully, a major restoration was completed in 2008 with funding of £11.3m, largely from the HLF. Around the same time, the decline at Derby Arboretum was finally reversed, mainly with funding of £5m from the HLF (Oakes 2011, 9). Ironically, the restoration of historic urban parks can involve not only new tree planting but also a considerable amount of tree felling. This is often necessary to remove inappropriate species and open up vistas that have become obscured, thus restoring the character of the former landscape.

It does seem remarkable that historic urban parks, such as Derby Arboretum and Birkenhead Park, could ever have been allowed to reach such a dilapidated state. The achievement of Britain's public park movement in the nineteenth century not only has huge national but also international significance – something we should all be proud to celebrate. It bodes well for the future that these two 'jewels' of the Victorian park movement, along with many other historic urban landscapes, have now been restored for the enjoyment of the next generation.

References

Amherst, A. (1907) *London Parks and Gardens*. Writing as the Hon. Mrs Evelyn Cecil. A. Constable and Co: London.

Anderson, J. (1999) Urban Development as a Component of Government Policy in the Aftermath of the Napoleonic War. *Construction History* 15, 23–37.

Anon (1767) *A Companion to Every Place of Curiosity and Entertainment in and about London and Westminster*. Printed for J. Lawrence: London.

Borsay, P. (1986) The Rise of the Promenade: the Social and Cultural Use of Space in the English Provincial Town *c.* 1660–1800. *Journal for Eighteenth-Century Studies* 9(2), 125–140.

Borsay, P. (2013) Pleasure Gardens and Urban Culture in the Long Eighteenth Century. In Conlin, J. (ed.) *The Pleasure Garden, from Vauxhall to Coney Island*. University of Pennsylvania Press: Philadelphia.

Byrom, C. (1995) The Pleasure Grounds of Edinburgh New Town. *Garden History*, 67–90.

Cardiff City Council (2014) Cardiff Parks. Text from Cardiff City Council website. Available at: http://www.cardiffparks.org.uk/ (accessed 30 May 2014).

Chadwick, G. F. (1966) *The Park and the Town: Public landscape in the 19th and 20th Centuries*. Frederick A. Praeger: New York and Washington.

Cherry, G. E., Jordan, H. and Kafkoula, K. (1993) Gardens, Civic Art and Town Planning: The Work of Thomas H. Mawson (1861–1933). *Planning Perspective* 8(3), 307–332.

Conlin, J. (ed.) (2012) *The Pleasure Garden, from Vauxhall to Coney Island*. University of Pennsylvania Press: Philadelphia.

Conway, H. (1991) *People's Parks: The Design and Development of Victorian Parks in Britain*. Cambridge University Press: Cambridge.

Conway, H.(2000) Everyday Landscapes: Public Parks from 1930 to 2000. *Garden History*, 117–134.

Downing, S. J. (2009) *The English Pleasure Garden 1660–1860*. Shire Publications: Oxford.

Elliott, B. (1986) *Victorian Gardens*. B. T. Batsford: London.

Elliott, B. (1990) Victorian Parks. In Galinou, M., *London's Pride: The Glorious History of the Capital's Gardens*: Anaya Publishers: London.

Elliott, P. A. (2001) The Derby Arboretum (1840): The First Specially Designed Municipal Public Park In Britain. *Midland History* 26(1), 144–176.

Elliott, P., Watkins, C. and Daniels, S. (2007a) Combining Science with Recreation and Pleasure: Cultural Geographies of Nineteenth-Century Arboretums. *Garden History*, 6–27.

Elliott, P., Watkins, C. and Daniels, S. (2007b) William Barron (1805–91) and Nineteenth-Century British Arboriculture: Evergreens in Victorian Industrializing Society. *Garden History*, 129–148.

Elliott, P. A., Daniels, S. and Watkins, C. (2008) The Nottingham Arboretum (1852): Natural History, Leisure and Public Culture in a Victorian Regional Centre. *Urban History* 35(1), 48.

Elliott, P. A., Watkins, C. and Daniels, S. (2011) *The British Arboretum: Trees, Science and Culture in the Nineteenth Century.* Pickering and Chatto: London.

Evelyn, J. (1901) *The Diary of John Evelyn.* Edited in 1901 from the original manuscript by William Bray in two volumes. Volume 1. M. Walter Dunne: New York and London.

Hansard (1833) *Public Health.* HC Deb 21 February 1833 Vol. 15, 1049–59.Available at: http://hansard.millbanksystems.com/commons/1833/feb/21/public-health (accessed 2.5.2014).

Harding, V. (1990) Gardens and Open Space in Tudor and Early Stuart London. In Galinou, M., *London's Pride: The Glorious History of the Capital's Gardens*: Anaya Publishers: London.

Hunt, T. (2004) *Building Jerusalem: The Rise and Fall of the Victorian City.* Weidenfeld and Nicolson: London.

Johnson, N. (1990) Citizens, Gardens and Meanings. In Galinou, M., *London's Pride: The Glorious History of the Capital's Gardens.* Anaya Publishers: London.

Johnson, R. (1607) *The Pleasant Walkes of Moore-fields, etc.* Henry Goffon: London

Johnston, M. (1983) Urban Trees and an Ecological Approach to Urban Landscape Design. *Arboricultural Journal* 7(4), 275–282.

Jordan, H. (1994) Public Parks, 1885–1914. *Garden History*, 85–113.

KGFF (1965) *Final Report of the King George's Fields Foundation.* King George's Fields Foundation: London.

Knyff, L. and Kip, J. (1984) *Britannia Illustrata.* J. Harris, and G. Jackson-Stops (eds). Published privately for the members of The National Trust by Paradigm Press: Bungay.

Larwood, J. (1880) *The Story of London Parks.* Chatto and Windus: London.

Lasdun, S. (1991) *The English Park: Royal, Private and Public.* Andre Deutsch: London.

Lawrence, H. W. (1993) The Greening of the Squares of London: Transformation of Urban Landscapes and Ideals. *Annals of the Association of American Geographers* 83(1), 90–118.

Layton-Jones, K. and Lee, R. (2008) *Places of Health and Amusement: Liverpool's Historic Parks and Gardens.* English Heritage: Swindon

Lee, R. (2013) *The People's Garden? A History of Crime and Policing in Birkenhead Park.* The Friends of Birkenhead Park.

Longstaff-Gowan, T. (2001) *The London Town Gardens 1740–1840.* Yale University Press: New Haven and London.

Longstaff-Gowan, T. (2012) *The London Square: Gardens in the Midst of Town.* Yale University Press: New Haven and London.

Loudon, J. C. (1835) Remarks on Laying out Public Gardens and Promenades. *Gardener's Magazine* 11, 644–59.

Loudon, J. C. (1840) *The Derby Arboretum: A Catalogue of the Trees and Shrubs, etc.* Longman, Orme, Brown, Green and Longmans: London.

MacGill, L. (2007) The Emergence of Public Parks in Keighley, West Yorkshire, 1887–93: Leisure, Pleasure or Reform? *Garden History*, 146–159.

MacLeod, D (1972) *The Gardener's London.* Gerald Duckworth: London.

Mawson, T. H. (1900) *The Art and Craft of Garden Making.* B. T. Batsford: London.

Mawson, T. H. (1911) *Civic Art: Studies in Town Planning, Parks, Boulevards and Open Spaces.* B. T. Batsford: London.

Milner, H. E. (1890) *The Art and Practice of Landscape Gardening.* Published by The Author and Simpkin, Marshall, Hamilton, Kent and Co: London.

MPGA (2014) *History of the Metropolitan Public Gardens Association.* Text from the MPGA website. Available at: http://www.mpga.org.uk/history.php (accessed 30 May 2014).

Mouland, B. (2003) Danger! Children having too much fun. *Daily Mail*, 22 May, 19.

Pettigrew, W. W. (1928). The Influence of Air Pollution on Vegetation. *The Gardeners' Chronicle* 84(292), 308–9.

Pettigrew, W. W. (1937) *Municipal Parks: Layout, Management and Administration.* The Journal of Park Administration: London.

Oakes, J. (2011) Arboretum's 10–year Restoration. *The Arb Magazine* Issue 154, 7–9.

O'Reilly, C. (2013a) From 'the People' to 'the Citizen': the Emergence of the Edwardian Municipal Park in Manchester, 1902–1912. *Urban History* 40(01), 136–155.

O'Reilly, C. (2013b) "We Have Gone Recreation Mad": The Consumption of Leisure and Popular Entertainment in Municipal Public Parks in Early Twentieth Century Britain. *International Journal of Regional and Local History* 8(2), 112–128.

Rival, L. (ed.) (1998) *The Social Life of Trees: Anthropological Perspectives on Tree Symbolism.* Berg: Oxford and New York.

Robinson, J. M. (2012) *Felling the Ancient Oaks: How England Lost its Great Country Estates.* Aurum Press: London.

Robinson, W. (1869) *The Parks, Promenades and Gardens of Paris Described and Considered in Relation to the Wants of our Own Cities and of Public and Private Gardens.* John Murray: London.

Sexby, J. J. (1898) *The Municipal Parks, Gardens and Open Spaces of London.* Elliot Stock: London.

Shaw-Lefevre, G. (1894) *English Commons and Forests.* Cassell and Company: London.

Simo, M. L. (1988) *Loudon and the Landscape: From Country Seat to Metropolis.* Yale University Press: New Haven and London.

Taggart, M. (2004) Trees are Axed over 'Conkers Anger'. *Daily Mail*, 22 September, 19.

Taylor, H. A. (1995) Urban Public Parks, 1840–1900: Design and Meaning. *Garden History*, 201–221.

Williams, G. (1978) *The Royal Parks of London.* Constable: London.

Williams, W. H. (1965) *The Commons, Open Spaces and Footpaths Preservation Society, 1865–1965: A Short History of its Work.* Commons, Open Spaces and Footpaths Preservation Society: London.

Williamson, T. (1995) *Polite Landscapes: Gardens and Society in Eighteenth Century England.* John Hopkins University Press: Baltimore.

Woudstra, J. and Fieldhouse, K. (eds) (2012) *The Regeneration of Public Parks.* Taylor and Francis: Abingdon, Oxon.

Wroth, W. (1896) *The London Pleasure Gardens of the Eighteenth Century.* Macmillan and Co. Ltd: London and New York.

Wroth, W. (1907) *Cremorne and the Later London Gardens.* Elliot Stock: London.

6

Street and Highway Trees

The trees in our streets are often the most noticeable in the urban forest and given the space to grow they can have an immediate and very beneficial impact on our urban lives. In the summer they provide welcome shade in hot streets while their leaves soak up some of the harmful pollution generated by motor vehicles. Throughout the year the sequence of emerging leaves, flowers, fruit, autumn colour and leaf fall mark the passage of nature's seasons on our doorstep. The stature and age of the trees in some of our most famous boulevards, such as The Mall and Park Lane in London, make these arboreal landmarks part of our national heritage (Figure 53).

A network of tree-lined streets throughout the town or city can help provide the essential framework for a green and pleasant urban environment in which to live and work. Lines of large mature trees on the main arterial routes through the city act as 'green corridors', linking other greenspaces and bring fresh air and wildlife into the heart of the metropolis. Some of our towns and cities are fortunate in having many large street trees, often a legacy from Victorian

FIGURE 53. Park Lane is a famous tree-lined thoroughfare in London that runs along the eastern boundary of Hyde Park. From the eighteenth century its views over the park on the fashionable western edge of London made it a popular location for some of the city's largest privately owned mansions. In the 1960s, Park Lane was widened into a multilane carriageway either side of a central reservation by taking land previously in Hyde Park. Although this has reduced its appeal as a residential address, the majestic plane trees remain to ensure its reputation as an arboreal landmark.

or Edwardian times. However, before the mid-nineteenth century, many urban areas, even the city centres, were virtually devoid of street trees. This chapter charts the history of our street trees and shows how they have become increasingly regarded as a vital part of urban infrastructure, despite some of their potential conflicts with urban life.

A range of terms describe the hard surfaces in British towns and cities used to convey modes of transport, such as 'street', 'road' and 'highway' (Fry 2003, 1–15). Other terms make specific reference to trees along the route, such as 'avenue' and 'boulevard'. Some of these definitions can be confusing and overlapping. This chapter uses most of these terms and also some that are historical and no longer in common use.

Roads in early British towns and cities

Ever since the development of the first settlements in Britain there had been some network of paths or tracks within and between the settlements (Lay 1992, 7–9). Little is known about the condition of pathways in pre-Roman towns but the widespread use of chariots in some major settlements suggests that the main thoroughfares would have possessed quite hard and stable surfaces (Newcomen 1951).

The Roman occupation of much of Britain began effectively in AD 43 and lasted until 410. Its enormous impact on all aspects of life and the landscape included the streets of Roman towns and cities. At that time, their high standards in design and construction were without parallel in the world, with the possible exception of the Chinese (Lay 1992, 52). While there is no evidence of any systematic planting of trees in the streets of Roman towns, this did occur along some roads through the countryside. When the Roman occupation ended, their extensive network of high quality roads steadily deteriorated along with many other aspects of the urban fabric (Lay 1992, 57). Throughout the medieval period urban roads were generally of poor quality and their condition depended largely on the underlying soils. At this time, planting any sort of trees by the side of town roads would have been most unlikely. It was only with the advent of the Elizabethan Era that any noticeable improvement occurred with Britain's roads both within and between urban areas. The English Highway Act of 1555 placed the obligation for road maintenance on the parishes and also provided them with support by requiring parishioners to devote four days a year to road work. This was the first act to apply generally to English roads rather than to specific locations and the law remained in force for over two hundred years.

In 1706, the first of a series of acts was introduced giving toll powers for roads to independent bodies of trustees, rather than to local justices (Lay 1992, 105). In effect, the system moved from public to private enterprise with the establishment of 'turnpikes' or toll roads. The toll-collecting agency was required to maintain the road from the tolls collected but that did not include the provision of any landscaping unless this was specifically for the improvement of the road itself. While this resulted in some road improvements, it was not until the eighteenth and nineteenth centuries that much change occurred. It needed the expertise of road construction pioneers such as John Metcalf and later John Loudon McAdam and Thomas Telford to restore road surfacing and reliability to something like the standard they had attained centuries previously under the Romans (*ibid.*, 72–8). Even then, the improvements were quite patchy.

Walks and promenades

A new form of British urban landscape that arose in the seventeenth century was 'the walk' or tree-lined promenade (Borsay 1986) (see Chapter 5). These were essentially garden allées outside the garden, used mainly for promenading rather than for games. Although privately owned, these walks could be made available to members of the public, usually on request. The most important and influential of the early walks was at Moorfields, just north of the wall around the City of London. The provincial towns soon followed this example when The Walks (later the Pantiles) at Tunbridge Wells was laid out in 1638 with a double row of trees and later there were tree-lined walks at The Marsh in Bristol (*ibid.*, 126).

Although these early walks were a welcome addition to the urban scene in a few towns and cities, there was still no real attempt to plant street trees. Any existing trees would have been widely regarded as an obstruction and the street as an inappropriate location for tree planting. Despite these attitudes, both Moses Cook and John Evelyn were full of admiration for the street trees of some cities in Holland, particularly Amsterdam. Cook (1676, no page number) remarked that the street plantings of lime-trees "...in the cities in Holland adde much to the Health of the Inhabitants". Evelyn was even more enthusiastic when he visited Amsterdam and saw plenty of lime trees lining many streets in the Dutch Capital:

> ...and yet their streets even, straight, and well paved, the houses so uniform and planted with lime trees, as nothing can be more beautiful. ... The Kaiser's or Emperor's Graft, which is an ample and long street, appearing like a city in a forest; the lime trees planted just before each house.
>
> Evelyn, 1901, 23

Despite this fulsome praise from both Moses Cook and John Evelyn, other horticultural writers of that era gave no consideration to street trees. For example, Thomas Fairchild's (1722) influential book entitled *The City Gardener* goes to some lengths to encourage urban tree planting but does not mention street trees. Nevertheless, there is some indication that several of the early walks or promenades did effectively become very similar to streets lined with trees. While most tree-lined walks remained relatively open in nature, some became quite heavily developed along one or both sides, particularly with shops offering luxury goods or refreshment (Borsay 1986, 129–30). In 1706, at the popular tree-lined Gravel Walks in Bath, a row of new houses was begun on their south side and a pavement was laid with large flat stones. While these walks were still pedestrian areas, they could be described as some of the earliest streets lined with trees. Loudon (1835a, 646) was later to define public walks as promenades or roads among trees.

Continental influences on street trees

Some of the few eighteenth century street plantings that did take place in London and other major cities were encouraged initially by a continental trend, although not one directly connected with trees. It was prompted by interest in playing a new popular game, *palemail*, which had been introduced from the continent (Lawrence 2006, 32). This involved hitting a ball with a mallet in a manner that was similar to modern croquet. Trees were planted simply for shade and to mark the sides of the course. When these areas were not being used for the game they functioned as shady promenades that were a popular haunt of the urban upper and middle classes. The game of *palemail* originally appeared in Paris and as it became fashionable was adopted elsewhere. In London, the game was a popular amusement in the reign of Charles II. Originally, it was played on the site of the street that still bears its name, Pall Mall. Rows of elms were planted on either side of the street but as the coach traffic and the nuisance of dust increased, Charles II had a new mall, now called The Mall, planted inside the northern edge of the park in the 1660s (Strutt 1810, 103) (Figure 54). This was generally open to the public as long as they behaved themselves (Lawrence 2006, 33). After the game fell out of favour later in the seventeenth century, the long allées of trees were used exclusively as pedestrian promenades. By the eighteenth century the terms *mail* and *mall* were often used for promenades that were not covered with grass or associated with any games.

By the middle of the seventeenth century recreational carriage promenades or *cours* were becoming popular in many European cities and London was no exception (Lawrence 2006, 34). This was another urban feature inspired by garden allées, transformed into roadways for pleasure riding by the rich. Usually lined with trees, the first of these was established in the 1630s when The Ring was planted in the east end of Hyde Park under Charles I. During the Commonwealth it became rather dilapidated but was then renovated back to its former condition under Charles II (Lawrence 2006, 37). It appears likely that any planting of this type would have comprised mainly native trees together with some of the early introduced species such as common lime (*Tilia x europaea*) and horse chestnut (*Aesculus hippocastanum*). In the late nineteenth century, the planting around the Ring was notable for some large elms trees which provided shade and shelter for the spectators to watch the coaches driving around (Amherst 1907, 29).

A mall or *cours* added something new to the British urban landscape. They were recreational areas outside garden walls that were generally accessible to the

FIGURE 54. The Mall is another famous thoroughfare and avenue of plane trees in London that runs from Buckingham Palace to Admiralty Arch. It began in the 1660s as a replacement venue for the playing of the popular game of *pailmail* (or pall mall). Over the centuries the trees have often been decorated with flags and bunting on major royal and civic occasions.

elite in society (Lawrence 1988, 361). They formed part of the urban scene rather than being restricted to a semi-private garden or country estate. The *cours* was especially important because it transformed the garden allée into a place for vehicles, albeit one not yet integrated into a city's street system.

Despite the virtual absence of trees from British streets in the seventeenth and eighteenth centuries, by the eighteenth century they were a more common sight in some other European cities (Lawrence 2006, 43). Some leading European authorities on urban landscaping were now actively promoting formal plantings of street trees where they were not already established. Johann Peter Willebrand, a Danish architect working in Germany, was one of these. In his influential work *Grundriß einer schönen Stadt* (plan of a beautiful city), Willebrand (1775, section 93) highlights the prestige value of trees in front of houses but warns against them being planted too close to the house where they could offer a hiding place for thieves or trap moisture that could damage the building fabric. Willebrand also gave recommendations for species of tree suitable for this purpose and this mainly featured large forest-type trees such as lime, horse chestnut, spruce and fir. While a movement to plant trees in streets was gaining ground on the Continent, this was not yet evident in Britain.

Treeless streets in the eighteenth century

Streets today are regarded as a particularly difficult environment for urban trees and this was also the case some three hundred years ago. For several centuries, if there were any street trees at all, they were located in the roadway (Lawrence 2006, 8). There was no pavement or kerb to provide protection and any trees were completely exposed to whatever came along the roadway. Most streets had no separation of pedestrian from vehicular traffic until at least the eighteenth century and often much later. For this reason street trees were regarded as an unnecessary obstruction and planting was generally discouraged.

To accommodate increases in vehicle and pedestrian traffic the width of some roads was expanded but rather than encourage tree planting this was to have a negative impact on other urban greenspace. Although town gardening increased in popularity during the eighteenth century, this invariably did not include the provision of front gardens (Longstaffe-Gowan 2001, 58). The presence of the road at the front of the house severely restricted the space available for this. Front gardens were only occasionally included in more expensive housing towards the periphery of cities such as London, Bristol and Edinburgh. Some of these front gardens contained small trees which contributed to the generally pleasant and leafy appearance of the street. Over the course of the century many of these front gardens and their trees were lost due to increased building or road widening. With no front gardens and mostly treeless streets, many residents valued a view out of their front windows of a garden or square to offer some natural vista.

The turning point in urban road improvement in Britain was the first Westminster Paving Act of 1762, followed by other Acts for London and elsewhere (Porter 2000, 152). Previously, it had been the obligation of householders to keep the streets in front of their houses in good repair. Now this series of parliamentary acts authorised towns and boroughs to raise taxes to pay for improvements in paving, drainage, lighting and the removal of obstructions. Paving commissioners were appointed with paid staff, gutters were built on either side of the road and in the main street Purbeck paving stones replaced pebbles. Other road improvements included convex carriageways and underground drains. Among other provisions of the 1762 Act was a requirement that that the major streets in Westminster should be provided with separate footpaths (Lawrence 2006, 86). This was accomplished mostly by erecting posts of wood or stone to separate the pedestrian zone on each side from the space reserved for horses and vehicles in the centre. While these were not uncommon by then, this was the first law requiring them to be widely used in a city. The addition of footpaths transformed street use for pedestrians who could now stroll along them undisturbed by vehicles and animals. While this improvement had no immediate impact on the planting of trees, it would provide a suitable place in the urban streetscape for trees in the nineteenth century. The essential conditions for tree survival in streets had been created with the footpath or pavement space providing a planting site with improved drainage and some protection from soil compaction and injury. Further advances were made in London with the Metropolitan Paving Act of 1817 that permitted the various paving authorities to extend their boundaries to fill in the gaps that lay between them (Hart 1959, 65). It also gave them, as local authorities, the power to acquire land for street widening and extension (Edwards 1898, 11). The London Act was followed by similar legislation for other urban areas.

While the various Paving Acts had created suitable conditions where trees might now be planted in streets, there seemed little interest in this prospect among the wider urban population and some outright opposition from some supposedly enlightened minds. For example, the author John Stewart defined the city in opposition to the country and insisted that its identity should not be compromised by such ineffectual and anomalous rural reminders as street trees (Longstaffe-Gowan 2001, 208). He was certainly not supportive of the concept of *rus in urbe* (the countryside in the city) that was preoccupying the minds of many other Enlightenment intellectuals. In his influential book *Critical Observations on the Buildings and Improvements of London*, Stewart states:

> The rus in urbe is a preposterous idea at best; a garden in a street is not less absurd than a street in a garden; and he that wishes to have a row of trees before his door in town, betrays almost as false a taste as he that would build a row of houses for an avenue to his seat in the country.
>
> Stewart, 1771, 14

The Regency era witnessed one of the largest developments in London for many years, the construction of Regent Street and Regent's Park with its attendant terraces and villas (see Chapter 4). However, no trees were planted along the new thoroughfare of Regent Street (Lawrence 2006, 182). These were reserved instead for the Park and the private gardens of the villas. Despite the fact that Regent Street did not have any trees lining its route, its irregular path through the existing urban landscape was thought by some to represent an urban adaptation of the design principles of the picturesque. The idea that the urban landscape was now considered in these aesthetic terms was itself a significant development. Many other major urban schemes of the time also excluded the planting of trees along their streets (Edwards 1898). There were only a few exceptions to this, most notably in London with a row of trees fronting a new terrace development near Blackfriars Bridge and in Oxford with a row of trees in St Giles Street. Despite the lack of more street tree planting, many new developments and the redesign of existing streets had involved features that would enable planting to occur later.

The improvement in the structure of British streets was now followed by various other efforts to improve the physical condition of cities (Hunt 2004). This included street lighting, systematic house numbering and regular mail deliveries, water supply and distribution systems and regular waste disposal systems. It is interesting to note that the British example in road construction and street amenities were widely admired and later adopted in other parts of

Europe (Lawrence 1988, 370). However, it would be some time before the British embraced the continental idea of planting street trees in any significant numbers. The British continued their preference for locating urban trees mainly in residential squares, crescents and pleasure gardens.

The trend towards privatization of the urban landscape with the urban enclosure movement in the mid-eighteenth century was widespread at the beginning of the nineteenth century and now also affected many streets (Atkins 1993, 268). Throughout the eighteenth century and first half of the nineteenth century numerous streets in London and other major cities had barriers to prevent non-residents, 'undesirables' and through traffic from entering. It was not until the late nineteenth century that concerted public efforts led to municipal acts to remove them and free all public streets to true public access.

New residential areas and street trees

As many British cities grew in population during the nineteenth century, they also grew in size (Burnett 1986, 4–7). This new mainly residential development was outside the existing urban core and became known as the suburbs. These newer suburban areas were generally less densely settled than the older sections of towns and cities. This was due largely to the presence of more greenspace in the wealthier middle class residential suburbs, mainly in the form of individual gardens. There was also more treecover than the old neighbourhoods due to planting of trees in the private gardens and along the side of some of the new roads. It also appears likely that as suburbia expanded into what was previously countryside, some tree-lined country roads subsequently became tree-lined suburban streets. For the vast majority of working class families in the established parts of the city, their homes had no front garden and just a yard at the back, so garden trees were out of the question (Roger 2000, 236–44). Almost invariably their streets of tenements or terraced houses were entirely treeless. Furthermore, those less fortunate residents would not have been able to visit those greener suburban neighbourhoods as access to many was severely restricted throughout much of the Victorian era (Atkins 1993).

Other forms of urban landscape developed during the nineteenth century were those in the model towns. Generally these were far more spacious and greener than most of the older urban settlements and many of them had plenty of trees planted along their streets (see Chapter 8).

Victorian boulevards and avenues

By the mid-nineteenth century, Paris led the way with the development of street trees along some of its major routes as other European cities tried to emulate its example (Lawrence 1988, 355). The terms *avenue* and *boulevard* became widely adopted to refer to these wide tree-lined streets that formed a prominent and distinctive element of the street system in Paris. The avenue originated as a French Baroque landscape feature involving a straight route lined with trees or large shrubs along each side which prolonged the garden *allée* out into the private park and even beyond (Hussey 1967, 15). The French word *boulevard* had originally referred to the flat part of a rampart. Several earlier Parisian grand boulevards had actually been built on top of the remnants of the old city walls and the more recent outer ring that was pieced together in the 1830s and 1840s (Lawrence 2006, 238). The word *boulevard* acquired its modern meaning when applied to new streets forced through the dense neighbourhoods of central Paris by Haussmann and his lieutenants (Jacobs *et al.* 2002, 76–81). It is ironic that the magnificent lines of large mature trees that now adorn the Paris boulevards were the result of an urban planning initiative that had highlighted the need for wide avenues to facilitate military movement and discourage the formation of barricades.

By the mid-eighteenth century only a few well-known streets in major British cities such as London, Oxford and Edinburgh had been planted with trees, although there were often more street trees in the new suburbs. Some prominent people from horticulture and landscape were now calling for a more continental approach to improving the urban landscape that included the provision of street trees. William Robinson, the influential Victorian horticulturist had lavished much praise on the Parisian boulevards in his book *The Parks, Promenades and Gardens of Paris* (Robinson 1869) (Figure 55). He was also enthusiastic about the Parisian's use of the plane as a street tree and urged its wide use in British cities. He was highly critical of some existing street tree planting, particularly in London. He remarked: "I can imagine nothing more calculated to bring town-gardening into disrepute than such a specimen of planting as that in The Mall in St James's Park. Had the Plane been planted it would have made a noble

FIGURE 55. When William Robinson visited Paris in 1867 he was hugely impressed with the magnificent tree-lined boulevards that had recently been created by Baron von Haussmann for Napoleon III. On his return he argued strongly that British cities should adopt a similarly bold approach to street tree planting. This engraving shows the Boulevard du Temple in the 1860s and is taken from Robinson's book *The Parks, Promenades and Gardens of Paris* (Robinson 1869).

avenue – the Elm now forms a miserable one" (Robinson 1869, 166). Those responsible for the trees must have agreed with Robinson because it was not long before the elms were replaced with planes and The Mall has since become world-famous as an historic and spectacular avenue.

Arguments in favour of street trees not only focused on their aesthetic value but increasingly on their health benefits. As well as providing much needed shade from the summer sunshine, street trees were also thought to purify the air by removing harmful elements from the 'miasmas', a form of noxious or 'bad' air, believed as late as the 1850s to cause diseases such as cholera (Lawrence 1988, 371). Despite the compelling arguments for street trees, many members of the public remained quite resistant to this trend. For example, back in 1824 William Trench MP had planned to include tree-lined promenades in his proposal for a major new built development along the Thames in London (Barker and Hyde 1982, 65). This was vigorously opposed by riparian property owners and shopkeepers, which was sufficient to prevent the project and it was not until the 1860s that the Thames was embanked.

The idea of having a grand style of planting trees along city streets, such as in Paris, did eventually take root in Britain. When the tree-lined boulevard finally made its belated appearance, it was in the new neighbourhoods of villa suburbia (Lawrence 2006, 242). As early as 1851, the Margaretta Terrace neighbourhood of Chelsea had a tree-lined avenue at its centre, reportedly admired by Prince Albert, who became an enthusiastic supporter of the idea. The first major works in central London were the Victoria Embankment along the north side of the Thames in the 1860s (Figure 56) and construction of the Chelsea Embankment and the piercing of Northumberland Avenue between the Thames and Trafalgar Square in the 1870s (Porter 1998). The tremendous care taken to ensure the survival of trees on Northumberland Avenue was described by Percy J. Edwards, Clerk of the Improvements Committee:

> To secure the well-being of the trees, pits were formed and filled with proper soil, and a footway surrounding the trees was covered with an open grating to admit the rain and air to the soil, and to enable it to be stirred and kept loose on the surface. The grating and footway were supported independently by girders over the tree pits, so as to prevent the settlement of the paving and the hardening of the ground around the roots of the trees. Plane trees were selected as most suitable for the atmosphere of the metropolis.
>
> Edwards, 1898, 58

While this standard of work was already typical of Paris and some other continental cities, it was all rather new in Britain, as Edwards notes:

> In designing the Embankments an endeavour had been made to render them not only useful, but agreeable, by giving some architectural embellishments to the wall and its accessories, laying out the surplus ground as ornamental gardens and planting trees on either side of the road, in imitation of the Boulevards of Paris, a feature somewhat novel in this country. When the whole length of the road is completed from Blackfriars to Battersea, and fringed with building worthy of the site, it is

FIGURE 56. Some of the first major plantings of street trees in central London were along the newly created Victoria Embankment in late 1860s on the north side of the River Thames. The plane trees on the pavement close to the riverside not only added a sense of grandeur to the route but also provided a pleasant prospect for pedestrians. This photo was taken around 1900 when the trees were still quite young (Mawson 1911).

probable that it will scarcely be surpassed as an agreeable promenade for both foot and carriage traffic. The ample width of the road with its continuous avenue of trees, flanked on one side by the river and on the other by ornamental grounds and handsome buildings, will form a thoroughfare not unworthy of the great capital. The crowds which throng the existing embankment on fine summer Sundays afford proof that its advantages are fully appreciated by the public.

Edwards, 1898, 129

The Public Health Act of 1875 gave local authorities powers to control housing conditions in their district, which also included the specifications for new streets and street improvements, thus raising the possibility of establishing street trees in the future (Burnett 1986, 158–9). However, it was not until the latter part of the nineteenth century that urban authorities formally acquired powers to plant trees in highways under section 43 of the Public Health Acts Amendment Act 1890 (Mynors 2002, 180). This legislation was particularly welcome as many urban authorities had become increasingly cautious about planting any street trees since Lewes Corporation had been convicted at Sussex Assizes in 1886 for causing a nuisance by planting trees on a public highway (Pettigrew 1937, 182). The move towards giving local authorities powers to plant street trees had been facilitated in part by the 1888 Local Government Act that passed responsibility for main roads to County and County Borough Councils. By the end of the century, the planting of trees along many streets had become routine (Edwards 1898). There was also general agreement that this trend in urban landscaping was beneficial to the health of the community and enhanced the visual amenity of streets and neighbourhoods. In the suburbs of London, piecemeal development of private estates led to groups of streets laid out with detached and semi-detached houses. The species most frequently planted as street trees in these areas were planes and limes. According to Harold Dyos (1961, 188) in his study of the Victorian London suburb of Camberwell, the species of trees planted along the streets could vary with the social class of a neighbourhood's residents. He noted the following pattern in Camberwell in the last decades of the nineteenth century: "The choice of trees, too, had its social overtones: planes and horse chestnuts for the wide avenues and lofty mansions of the well-to-do; limes, laburnums and acacias for the middle incomes; unadorned macadam for the wage-earners." The social divide in terms of publicly-owned trees that can be witnessed today in many of Britain's urban forests began with the earliest street tree plantings. The wealthier middle class neighbourhoods with their broader streets tended to have more trees and of larger-growing species, while the poor working class neighbourhoods often had no street trees at all.

Although many urban streets were now being planted with trees, the width of the streets was often considerably less than that in continental cities such as Paris (Edwards 1962, 42). This included the vast areas of 'bye-law' streets with their terraced housing set out in a rigid grid pattern that became a feature of many Victorian towns. As a result, the space available in these endless miles of narrow British urban streets was usually insufficient to plant medium or large-growing trees. Nevertheless, this did not dissuade the highway authorities from planting innumerable planes and limes, which were favoured for their tolerance of the smoky and polluted air that pervaded many of Britain's large cities. Many of these large-growing trees would inevitably become a problem in future years when they outgrew these confined spaces.

In the wider urban environment an increasing number of new exotic species were being planted. This had been encouraged by the founding of many botanic gardens in the early nineteenth century which were being planted up with more and more exotic species of trees collected from distant parts of the world (Elliott *et al.* 2011, 67). These exotic trees were now becoming common in parks and private gardens and by the mid-nineteenth century some of them became popular as street trees. However, the range of exotic species planted in streets was generally more limited than those in parks, due to the more demanding growing conditions.

By the end of the nineteenth century, British perspectives on the planting of trees in cities continued to be significantly influenced by continental ideas. While there was now widespread acceptance in the British planning profession that trees had an important role in urban landscapes, there was still plenty of debate about how that could be accomplished. A powerful voice among designers and planners of the age was that of Joseph Stübben, an influential planner from Cologne who was frequently consulted by other cities. As well as being an internationally recognised expert in the field of planning, he also wrote some major texts, in particular his widely used manual on urban planning. In a public lecture in 1885 entitled 'Practical and Aesthetic Principles for the Laying Out of Cities', Stübben (1885) set out many of his recommendations for urban planning and this included plenty of detailed specifications on street tree plantings, such as the distances between trees and distances from various elements of urban development and infrastructure. He strongly advocated the planting of trees in rows, not just at the sides of the road but also, where possible, in the central reservation of dual carriageways.

By 1900, however, the aesthetic of tree-lined streets laid out in geometric order was being criticised by some European authorities as being as too regimented (Lawrence 2006, 258). The most vocal opponent of the Haussmann-Stübben tradition was Camillo Sitte, an Austrian architect now regarded as a pioneer in urban planning. His major work *City Planning according to Artistic Principles*, published in 1889, raised issues that are still regarded as contentious in urban planning. Sitte (1889, 176) stated "All tree-lined streets are tedious but no city can do completely without them…" He had particularly disdain for the boulevards of Paris, saying that the trees would have been better planted in a few parks instead. He believed that rigid adherence to symmetry in the tree planting gave no consideration to the healthy growth of the trees, to the light or to the surrounding cityscape. While some British professionals found sympathy with Sitte's view, others were adamantly opposed. The garden city movement led by Ebenezer Howard had an entirely different perspective on tree-lined boulevards and these featured prominently in his vision for the garden city (Howard 1898, 14–6) (see Chapter 8). Howard also regarded the planted sections of boulevards, avenues and streets as 'in the nature of a park', which says much about his perception of the role of these thoroughfares.

In the early 1900s, Thomas Mawson, the eminent landscape architect and town planner, was a particularly strong advocate of the creation of wide and impressive boulevards in the style of Paris. An example of his bold and imaginative approach was his proposed scheme for the Grand Boulevard in Dunfermline, Scotland, that would terminate at the town's Guildhall (Mawson 1911, 250) (Figure 57). This would comprise three roadways and two avenues, giving a total width of one hundred and fifty feet. If the scheme had been undertaken as Mawson intended, he believed this would have created the finest boulevard in Britain. Nevertheless, throughout his distinguished career he was responsible for many successful urban park and street tree planting schemes. The scale of Mawson's vision for impressive boulevards in our towns and cities is typified by the range of tree species he recommended for street planting, which are listed in an appendix in his classic work *Civic Art* (Mawson 1911, 355). Of over 30 trees listed, the majority are large-growing forest-type trees that would undoubtedly make a major impact on the urban landscape when planted as formal and extensive avenues.

It would be difficult to overestimate the remarkable achievements of the Victorian and Edwardian eras in planting trees in many of the streets of British towns and cities. The enormous contribution that was made to greening the urban environment has left us with a legacy today of many fine mature street trees. While we might now question the choice of species for some of the more narrow streets, that does not detract from the sheer scale of what was achieved

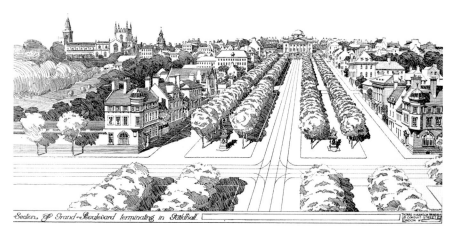

FIGURE 57. Thomas
Mawson's proposed
scheme for the
Grand Boulevard in
Dunfermline, Scotland,
terminating at the
Guildhall. He was a
strong advocate of the
creation of wide and
impressive boulevards
in the style of Paris.
Mawson also admired
the French use of public
sculpture to enhance
the grandeur of their
boulevards and added
some statues to his own
scheme (Mawson 1911).

and the commitment to civic values that drove it. Furthermore, all those street trees were planted without the use of many of the specialist planting products and equipment that many professionals regard as so necessary today.

Conflicts with built development and urban infrastructure

The advent of motorised transport on Britain's roads had a dramatic impact on all aspects of urban life. Some forms of motorised transport had been present since 1801 when Richard Trevithick ran a full-sized stream-driven vehicle on the road in Camborne (Lay 1992, 137). These types of vehicle steadily became popular over the next few decades as improvements were made to their construction and performance. However, public concern at these large, speedy and potentially dangerous vehicles resulted in the passing through Parliament of the Locomotive Act in 1865. This required self-propelled vehicles to be proceeded by a man on foot waving a red flag and blowing a horn. This effectively stifled automobile development in Britain for the rest of the nineteenth century and ensured that efforts at developing mass transit focused on the railways. The law was only fully repealed in 1896.

By the start of the twentieth century the automobile industry in Britain was expanding rapidly and many vehicles were also being imported from Western Europe (Lay 1992, 156–9). This was soon followed by the mass production of lorries for commercial and industrial use. The increases in vehicle numbers and speeds precipitated some fundamental changes in road construction and layout and led to a rapid expansion in Britain's road network. The construction of new roads also gave rise to new opportunities to plant trees, although the extent to which this was undertaken varied considerably. It depended largely on the motivation of the highway authority to commit funding for this but also on the opportunities to plant trees offered by the road design. Roads with wide grass verges were often well planted, although sometimes the choice of small ornamental species did not make full use of the space available. Roundabouts, the first of which was in Letchworth Garden City in 1909, were also becoming popular both for new and existing roads. Unfortunately, they were generally not much planted or the planting design was poor (Wells 1970, 301).

In the 1890s and 1900s, electric trams had been introduced into several major British cities and this rapidly became a popular mode of transport (Lay 1992; 134; Taylor and Green 2001). This greatly restricted the space for the crowns of street trees along these tram routes, particular from the overhead cables that carried the electricity. After World War II when planners saw trams as old fashioned, inflexible and a hindrance to the free flow of traffic, tramways began to disappear from British cities. The removal of the track was sometimes an opportunity for more extensive highway tree planting. In Birmingham, for example, the trams used to run along the central reservation of Bristol Road but when the tramway closed in 1952, the reservation was planted up with a long avenue of deciduous and coniferous trees (Figure 58).

The introduction of larger vehicles such as lorries and buses necessitated some radical pruning or planting restriction for many roadside trees. The advent of the motorised double-decked bus in 1923, especially in densely built-up areas with large mature street trees, caused significant difficulties. Many existing trees had to be pruned drastically so their crowns were lifted clear of the top deck and new plantings often had to be set back some distance from the kerb (Balfour 1935, 167). However, the precise positioning of new tree planting in the pavement was still a matter of debate. While some highway engineers preferred tree planting at the back line of the pavement, partly to give greater clearance

FIGURE 58. This central reservation on the Bristol Road, Birmingham, is the site of a former tramway. When the tramway closed in 1952, the opportunity was taken to plant up the reservation with a long avenue of both deciduous and coniferous trees, adding an attractive landscape feature to this main traffic route

PHOTO: SUE GRIFFITHS

for vehicles, others still regarded the correct position to be within a foot or so of the kerb (Pettigrew 1937, 183).

As the volume of road traffic increased it became clear that the presence of any roadside trees could also have a negative impact on driving conditions, particularly in inclement weather. Roads soaked by rain were slow to dry out and frosty roads slow to melt when shaded by nearby trees. Fallen leaves in autumn, combined with wet or frosty conditions could make the road surface even more treacherous for drivers. The truth of this was brought home in dramatic fashion to many arboriculturists in 1930 when Ernest Wilson, the great plant collector and world-renown authority on trees, was killed with his wife in Massachusetts, USA, by their car skidding from this cause (Balfour 1935, 167).

In the early years of the twentieth century, professional and popular opinion continued to be divided on the value or otherwise of planting trees in streets. Frederick Balfour was an eminent arboriculturist, a Fellow of the Linnaean Society and served on the Council of the Royal Horticultural Society (Cotton 1945, 358). In a paper presented in 1934 to a meeting of the Institution of Municipal and County Engineers, Balfour gave an account of the current knowledge regarding the planting and care of roadside trees (Balfour 1935). He sets out clearly many of the arguments regarding their perception as 'asset or liability' that we would recognise today. He was certainly not an advocate of planting large forest-type trees in many streets, generally favouring small ornamentals. His opinions have echoes in our own time with current fears for a proliferation of so-called 'lollipop landscapes'.

> It is patent to anyone who drives along the Chelsea Embankment and on countless other planted London thoroughfares that it is little less than an outrage on the owners of house property that light and view should be denied them by the close proximity of rows of planes, the heavy foliage of which reached their windows. In such situations crabs, cherries, laburnums of other flowering trees of low stature are what the situation demands.
>
> Balfour, 1935, 165

The typical urban street in Britain was now becoming a very crowded place. This did not just relate to the volume of traffic or pedestrians. The pavements were also becoming crowded with the addition of street furniture, the collective term for objects and pieces of equipment installed on streets for various purposes. This included traffic signs, traffic bollards and barriers, traffic lights, post boxes, street lighting, telephone boxes, streetlamps, bus and tram stops, taxi stands, benches, waste bins, public lavatories, fountains, watering troughs and memorials. Under the pavement was a growing mass of pipes and wires for utilities such as electricity, telephone, gas, water and sewage. Finding room for even a small number of street trees, particularly large-growing species, was becoming an increasingly difficult task. Where trees were already present, the potential for conflict with this street furniture and utility services was often very high (Balfour 1935, 167).

As well as often conflicting with the demands of built development, there was also recognition that street trees in their exposed position were themselves particularly prone to damage from different agencies. This could arise from a variety of sources such as damage to the bark or branches by vehicles, pollution in the root zone, compaction of the soil and, increasingly, vandalism (see Chapter 3). Balfour (1935, 184) reports on an example of major vandalism to scarlet oaks recently planted on Kingston by-pass "at the expense of several hundred pounds". In the first year, he states that, "no less than 10 per cent were broken off by passers-by and the culprits were by no means only youthful persons".

Lack of arboricultural expertise

In the 1930s there was also growing concern at the lack of specific arboricultural expertise on the part of local authorities when it came to caring for publicly owned trees. While the planting and maintenance of street trees was usually the responsibility of the highways department, the work involved was invariably carried out by the staff of the parks department where such a department existed (Pettigrew 1937, 182). Regardless of any involvement by parks staff, decisions about where and when to plant the trees, as well as the provision of funding for this, were still the concern of the Highways Committee and its engineers. The engineers often had no formal training in arboriculture to equip them for even this limited role. In terms of the parks department staff, their arboricultural skills also tended to be limited, particularly in terms of maintaining mature trees. When the pruning of street trees became necessary to reduce conflicts with built development or ensure public safety, the standard of routine maintenance was often very poor. Balfour highlighted this problem of a general lack of arboricultural expertise in his usual unequivocal fashion:

> The pruning of street and roadside trees is all too often left by councils to a committee who may be eminently able to deal with engineering problems but who have not an iota of knowledge of how trees should be treated or, indeed, any clear idea of what they should ultimately look like. In some of the larger cities and London boroughs men are employed to take charge of street trees well qualified and expert in their art. There are, however, many glaring exceptions, and too often the care of trees is regarded by those responsible for roads as a side issue of little or no importance.
>
> Balfour, 1935, 173

Many of those responsible for street and highway trees at that time often seemed unaware of some of the advances in reconciling their potential conflicts with urban infrastructure that had already been made by professionals in the USA. In 1929, a major American text was published entitled *Roadside Development* that focused on the planting, maintenance and management of roadside trees in both urban and rural situations (Bennett 1929). The author, Jesse Merle Bennett, had gained much experience as Superintendent of Parks and Forestry at Wayne

County in Michigan. As the title of the book was just 'roadside development' and it was not published in Britain, this probably ensured it was not read by the relevant local authority staff.

Local authority planting and the role of the RBA

In 1925, the Roads Improvement Act was passed and this had a substantial impact on the planting of roadside trees and shrubs (Wells 1970, 295). For the first time local authorities were empowered to acquire highway marginal land for the purposes of planting and amenity. With the great programme of arterial road construction that was then underway a new chapter opened up on highway planting.

Initially, local authorities with their lack of specialist knowledge found they were ill-equipped to meet this new task and their early efforts were largely unsatisfactory (Wells 1970, 295). However, help was soon at hand in the form of the Roads Beautifying Association (RBA). Formed in 1928 by Dr Wilfred Fox, a dermatologist with an interest in the environment, this voluntary organisation was to play a leading role in promoting and advising on roadside planting over the next three decades (*ibid.*, 296). Through a personal contact Fox was able to enlist support for his campaign for highway planting from the Editor of the *Daily Express* newspaper. The Editor was also a personal friend of the then Minister of Transport and a meeting with him and Fox was arranged. As a result of this, the Minister invited Fox to assemble a voluntary organisation of horticultural experts for the purpose of advising local authorities on the planting and preservation of roadside trees. From the outset, the RBA's influential supporters emphasised the public benefit of its advisory role:

> The cost of roadside planting is comparatively slight – possibly one-hundredth part of the expense of building a new arterial road – and the outlay can be reduced by consultation with experts, whose advice will prevent a repetition of errors committed in the past. To place such advice at the free disposal of local authorities and their officers is one of the main purposes of the Roads Beautifying Association, whose committees include some of the leading horticultural experts in Great Britain. Their guidance is often needed, not only in the most advantageous utilisation of familiar wayside trees, but in the introduction of ornamental and flowering species which have hitherto been neglected.
>
> Bressey 1930, v

In the early days, expert advice was offered free of charge to local authorities by the RBA and its acceptance encouraged by the Ministry of Transport. The organisation's first technical committee included prominent horticulturists of the day, a number of whom had aristocratic backgrounds. The RBA also gained the services of William Jackson Bean, recently retired as Curator of Kew Gardens, who became horticultural advisor to the RBA, a post he retained until shortly before his death in 1947. Bean's recommendations for the selection of species for planting on urban roads reflected his knowledge and admiration

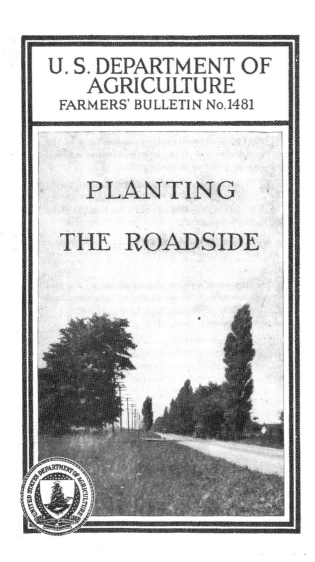

U. S. DEPARTMENT OF AGRICULTURE

FARMERS' BULLETIN No.1481

PLANTING

THE ROADSIDE

FIGURE 59. Information and illustrations from this booklet by the United States Department of Agriculture, issued in 1926, were used by the Roads Beautifying Association (RBA) in its own book *Roadside Planting* published in 1930 (USDA 1926).

of a wide range of ornamental trees (Bean 1929).

In 1930, the RBA's advice was detailed in a book called *Roadside Planting* (RBA 1930). It was directed mainly at local authorities, many of which were now submitting their five year programmes for road works to the Ministry of Transport. The early part of the book included technical advice on location, planting and aftercare. Some of this was actually a repetition of advice, including diagrams, from the United States Department of Agriculture, indicating that some American publications on this topic had reached Britain (Mulford 1921 and 1926) (Figure 59). Much of the book contained lists of species suitable for planting in various locations and for different purposes. When dealing with urban and suburban areas, which were the main concern of the RBA, exotic trees of striking foliage and flower were freely introduced. This included a huge variety of trees and shrubs, many of which were uncommon exotics at that time. For rural roads, the choice was mainly native trees or cultivars of these.

In deciding what tree species to recommend in different planting schemes, the RBA's advice was determined largely by safety considerations (Wells 1970, 301). For obvious reasons trees with brittle wood such as poplar and willow were not encouraged. Also, trees with large and persistent leaves such as London Plane and Sycamore were usually absent from planting designs because of supposed problems with leaf fall. In areas of dense built development, trees with extensive and vigorous roots systems were avoided for fear that these could block drains and damage pavements and building foundations. In general, all fruit trees were discouraged because of the supposed nuisance that would be caused by falling and rotting fruit. The type of roads dealt with by the RBA in the early days of its history were usually by-passes around towns and villages, link roads between towns and road-widening schemes, all generally urban in character (Figure 60). In the first eight years of

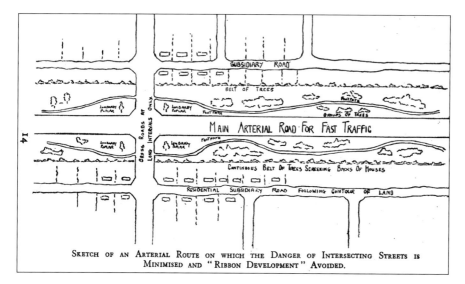

SKETCH OF AN ARTERIAL ROUTE ON WHICH THE DANGER OF INTERSECTING STREETS IS MINIMISED AND "RIBBON DEVELOPMENT" AVOIDED.

FIGURE 60. This plan by the Roads Beautifying Association (RBA) shows how careful landscaping with belts of trees and shrubs by the side of a main arterial route can avoid the danger of intersecting streets and 'ribbon development'. This is actually a version of the American 'parkway' concept, although the RBA book makes no reference to that (RBA 1930).

work over 300 miles (483 km) of road were inspected and some 50,000 trees recommended for planting.

In an extension of the influence of the garden cities movement (see Chapter 8), many 'parkways' were built that were well-planted arterial roads linking city and commercial centres with suburbs and residential areas (O'Reilly 2013, 125). Princess Parkway at Wythenshawe in south Manchester opened in 1932 and was the first of its kind in Britain. The aim of the parkway was to provide a major corridor for free-flowing traffic that was segregated from nearby housing and minor roads by attractively landscaped greenspace on both sides, extensively planted with trees and shrubs. Essentially a landscaped dual carriageway, it created attractive vistas leading off from the road in different directions which it was hoped would stimulating public interest in nature.

In 1937, the passing of the Trunk Roads Act was a significant event in the administration of Britain's roads (Wells 1970, 299). Some 4,500 miles (7242 km) of trunk road were transferred from local authority control to the jurisdiction of the Ministry of Transport. Dual-carriageway roads, which had previously been confined to a few urban areas, now became quite common in towns and cities, particularly as main arterial roads and around the urban fringe. The Act also signalled a new phase in the history of the RBA. In 1938, it was appointed as advisor on trunk road planting to the Ministry of Transport. Between 30 and 40 trunk road plantings were designed by the RBA, of which 12 were carried out before the Second World War.

The increase in dual-carriageway roads required a new form of planting to establish a natural screen in the central reserve strip to cut out headlight dazzle at night (Wells 1970, 299–300). The Ministry issued precise specifications for this in terms of height, length of gaps and clearance from major intersections. To be effective throughout the year, this type of planting required a high proportion of evergreens for opaqueness in winter. On narrow central reservations trees and shrubs with a wide spread were avoided as well as species that developed thick and robust stems which might be dangerous in the event of a high-speed crash. Forest trees in general were discouraged on central reservations on safety grounds and also because of heavy leaf fall, lack of room for root systems and large trunks close to the highway if the width of the reservation was reduced. On the recommendation of the RBA, the planting here was often just long sweeps of one species. These would then have breaks of varying lengths, sometime set with tall trees, to break the monotony of otherwise continuous low planting.

Landscape architecture and the modern road

During the 1940s, the Institute of Landscape Architects pushed for the involvement of its members in the landscaping and planting of all future roads (Merriman 2006, 81). Prominent landscape architects criticised the tendency of local authorities to plant ornamental trees and shrubs which they believed would interrupt the flow of the landscape and distract drivers travelling at speed.

In the journal of the Institute of Landscape Architects in 1939, leading landscape architect Brenda Colvin criticised the prevailing British obsession with trying to 'beautify the road', arguing that planting must be used to knit the highway into the landscape (Colvin 1939). Although Colvin does not name those who she thinks are doing the misplanting, contemporary readers may have guessed she was referring to the work of the RBA (Merriman 2006, 82). It had produced planting schemes for many of the new bypasses and arterial roads constructed during the interwar years but Colvin was not impressed with its use of exotic trees and shrubs in these situations. Colvin also stated in her influential book *Land and Landscape* that beautiful modern roads would only result from a more fundamental approach to landscape than the largely horticultural approach adopted by the RBA (Colvin 1948).

In truth, the landscape profession's criticism focused more on new roads in rural situations than on streets in towns and cities. However, it was also clear that landscape architects increasingly viewed themselves as the arbiters of good landscape design for roads, wherever they may be, and that included tree planting. In Colvin's 1947 book *Trees for Town and Country* she has two distinct categories for trees on the 'streets' and on 'roadsides' and declares that trees suitable for streets, where she lists predominantly exotic trees, should not normally be used for planting along main roads (Colvin 1947, 7).

In 1955, the government announced the establishment of its Advisory Committee on the Landscape Treatment of Trunk Roads, commonly known as the Landscape Advisory Committee (Merriman 2006, 87). Membership of this included Colvin, representing the Landscape Institute, and other prominent professionals and specialists. It was chaired by Sir David Bowes-Lyon, President of the Royal Horticultural Society. While the committee comprised some leading landscape architects together with horticultural and forestry experts, there was nobody specifically identified as an arboriculturist.

In 1960, Colvin's friend and fellow landscape architect Sylvia Crowe provided a more extensive discussion of their approach to tree planting on roads in her book *The Landscape of Roads* (Crowe 1960). After the publication of Crowe's book there was much interest in this subject. In 1961, the Ministry of Transport eventually appointed a landscape architect, Michael Porter, but this was too late for the first sections of the M1 (Merriman 2006, 88). The growth of interest in the landscaping of new and existing roads that had occurred since Brenda Colvin's first pronouncements on the topic was demonstrated by the excellent attendance and lively discussions at the 'Roads in the Landscape' conference held in 1967 at Keele University (Anon 1967).

Other post-war Initiatives

Following the Second World War, the Ministry of Transport formed its own department for trunk road planting and appointed its own committee of distinguished volunteers to advise on the landscape treatment of motorways and trunk roads (Wells 1970, 305). The RBA continued for several years to be fully occupied in the planting of other roads and on special schemes such as the Worcester Plan and Crawley New Town. When the Department of the Environment and county authorities accepted full responsibility for the landscaping of highways the RBA's role diminished and it finally ceased to operate in 1965. At the same time the Ministry of Transport was giving advice on tree planting for trunk roads, the subject of tree planting in smaller roads and streets in urban and suburban areas was being well covered by a circular issued by the Ministry of Town and Country Planning (Anon 1946). In this circular were lists of trees annotated to show their size at maturity, soil requirements and their relative tolerance to smoke and exposure.

Encouraged by the pioneering work of the RBA, other non-government organisations were now engaged in promoting the planting and care of street and highway trees. The Council for the Preservation of Rural England was one of the more prominent. In 1948, its Sheffield and Peak District Branch published a pamphlet entitled *Trees in Towns: A Road in Sheffield* which was a passionate and erudite plea for better maintenance and management of the city's street trees (CPRE 1948). Another pamphlet was produced by the Bournville Village Trust describing its experience and expertise in roadside planting (Salter 1953).

A major urban planning initiative that was to lead to thousands more street trees was the development of the New Towns (Morris 1997, 98) (see Chapter 8). These were designated and developed in England, Wales and Scotland between 1946 and 1970. While the overall success of these pioneering urban settlements is still widely debated, there is no doubt this initiative involved the creation of many highly functional and innovative green landscapes. The new roads and streets that were part of these new towns were also planted with plenty of trees.

In the immediate post-war years, the legacy of some Victorian street tree plantings began to cause problems for local authorities. Many of the planes and limes planted in narrow residential streets were now outgrowing their situation. The trees were generating an increasing number of complaints from residents about the blocking of light, interference with utility wires, cracked and lifted pavements and other problems. An immediate solution was to pollard the trees, a process that involved the removal of the large diameter branches to reduce the height and spread of the tree considerably and then regularly pruning the regrowth to maintain it this way. Although often effective in reducing the problems, this was an intensive and expensive form of management that many people regarded as unsightly (Pearce 1961, 47). As far back as 1835, no less a horticultural authority than Loudon had stated, "Pollarded trees may be considered in most cases as injurious deformities" (Loudon 1835b, 1143).

One notable authority on highway trees in the post-war years was Don Wells (Honour 1977). After the Second World War, Wells was employed by the Ministry of Transport to promote and advise on the planting of trees and shrubs on new roads. At this time he was also appointed as an advisor for the RBA. He wrote extensively on the subject of highway trees in a way that mostly emphasised their aesthetic contribution to the urban landscape (Wells 1954 and 1963). Wells was quite cautious about roadside planting and did not recommend tree planting in verges less than 10 ft (3 m) in width, something which he recognised would preclude countless miles of verges lining many dual carriageways. In the early part of his career Wells regarded roadside planting as "a highly specialised branch of horticulture and one which has not, unfortunately, received the attention it deserves" (Wells 1954, 41). However, in his later years he came to recognise the specialist role of arboriculture, playing a pivotal role in the founding of the Arboricultural Association in 1964 and becoming its first Chairman.

A brief mention should be given to the development of motorways in Britain and their associated tree planting as many are located in and around urban areas. This began with the opening of the Preston Bypass (later part of the M6) in 1958 and in 1959 the initial sections of the MI, Britain's first inter-urban motorway (Lay 1992, 321). Landscaping policy for these motorways was formulated by the government's Landscape Advisory Committee, now chaired by Sir George Taylor, formerly the Director of the Royal Botanic Gardens, Kew (Dunball 1972, 42). Work on the ground was often directed by landscape architects, with other professionals with a more horticultural approach also playing an important role. Sir Geoffrey Jellicoe, possibly the most well-known landscape architect of his generation, had an early and special interest in the landscape design of motorways (Jellicoe 1958). Another influential figure who specialized in tree planting on both motorways and trunk roads was Anthony Dunball who for many years in the 1960s and 70s was Horticultural Advisor to the Ministry of Transport. In 1964, he was a member of the inaugural committee of the Arboricultural Association and continued to play a significant role in the organisations for several years to come. Dunball (1968 and 1972) was also responsible for writing some influential papers on the topic of tree planting on motorways and trunk roads.

Although not a specifically urban phenomenon, mention should be made of the anti-roads protests that received an enormous amount of media coverage in the 1990s (McKay 1996, 127–58). Many of the new roads were bypasses around urban areas intended to relieve the congestion in various towns and cities. In an effort to halt and reverse the government's extensive new roads programme, a protest movement developed that consistently highlighted the loss of trees and woodlands that the construction involved. Scenes of protesters being forcibly removed from the trees to enable contractors to move in with their bulldozers and chainsaws became a regular feature of the nation's television news. While the moment did not win any individual actions, the huge cost of policing the protests undoubtedly influenced the government's future transport policy.

Suburban streets

The growth of suburbia that had continued into the twentieth century entered a massive phase of expansion in the period between the First and Second World Wars (Burnett 1986). In the 1950s, suburban expansion gathered pace again, although more regulated by the establishment of greenbelts. In larger cities such as London, these suburbs now include formerly separate towns and villages that had gradually been absorbed due to the city's growth and expansion.

Immediately after the Second World War, the planting of small ornamental street trees became very fashionable with local authorities over vast areas of suburbia, a trend that had begun before the war (Figure 61). Many of these suburban streets had grass verges that could easily accommodate a significant amount of tree planting. Mile after mile of ornamental cherries, pears, apples, hawthorn, whitebeam and similar trees adorned these suburban streets with a show of spectacular but often gaudy colour for a couple of weeks in the year. Even where quite large trees could be planted, it was often fashionable to favour these small ornamentals. Eventually, the establishment of these types of trees on streets throughout suburbia became so extensive it provoked a negative reaction among many professionals and also members of the public. There was another factor which prompted a rethink of this planting policy. Many of these species were susceptible to a disease called fireblight that had been first recorded in Britain in 1957 (Burdekin 1981, 75–6). The extensive planting of susceptible species as street trees throughout suburbia had encouraged the rapid spread of the disease and highlighted the need for greater biodiversity to maintain the resilience of the tree population against attack from deadly pathogens. During the 1960s, 70s, and even later, the often scarce resources of many local authority tree sections had to be diverted into extensive programmes of sanitation felling (see Chapter 3).

The influence of modern arboriculture and urban forestry

From the 1970s, the establishment of many tree officer posts in local authorities had a radical impact on the management of urban trees in Britain. There had also been some remarkable advances in the development of arboricultural techniques and equipment over the previous two decades (Bridgeman 1976). An equally significant impact was felt with the growth of urban forestry ideas and practice, a concept originating in North America (Johnston 1997a and 1997b) (see Chapters 1 and 2). All these new developments had a particularly significant impact on the management of street trees in Britain.

From the 1970s, partly encouraged by North American practice, some tree officers began to experiment with planting a much wider range of species as street trees. Ginkgo (*Ginkgo biloba*), dawn redwood (*Metasequoia glyptostroboides*), Italian alder (*Alnus cordata*) and other previously untried species began to appear in urban streets (Mitchell 1989). Some tree officers had undoubtedly been encouraged to try these unusual species by college tutors during their arboricultural education. To meet this growing demand for more unusual street trees British commercial tree nurseries started to stock a much wide range of species. Also prompted by North American practice, they began to offer a range of trees specially bred for street conditions. Following tree breeding programmes, which began in the United States in the 1970s, nurseries could now offer a selection of 'tailor-made' street trees (Santamour *et al.* 1976). These had been specially developed with qualities that made them ideally suited as street trees and they soon became popular in local authority planting schemes. At the same time, some tree officers were coming under pressure from conservationists to actually limit the range of trees planted in urban streets by focusing on planting mainly 'native' trees. An example of this was in the aftermath of the 1987 'Hurricane' when the London Wildlife Trust demanded assurances that 60 per cent of the street trees lost in London would be replaced with 'native' trees (Johnston 1991, 137). Most tree officers were irritated by this inappropriate demand and ignored it.

In the early 1970s, many urban local authorities tried to regrow the crowns of their pollarded street trees, often planes and limes, in an attempt to give them a more attractive and natural appearance (Brown 1972, 36) (Figure 62). This change in pruning policy was often prompted by lobbying from local amenity societies and residents associations that viewed pollarding as an unsightly practice and much the same as 'lopping'. Once the tree crowns had been allowed to regrow to a limited extent, they were then kept from getting any larger by regular crown reductions. Unfortunately, the resulting crowns were often unstable due to extensive decay in the pollard points. When high winds occurred many trees would suffer from branches splitting out, causing a danger to people, property and vehicles. A gradual programme of replacement was often considered the only long-term solution to the problems of these previously pollarded street trees. As forest-type trees were removed, they were replaced with smaller growing species

such as cherry, whitebeam and hawthorn. However, the felling of these mature street trees frequently led to protests by residents who saw their leafy treescape being replaced by small newly-planted trees that had little landscape impact. Some residents were also conscious of the reduction in the value of their properties resulting from the felling of the mature trees. Trying to implement a long-term replacement programme for these large-growing mature trees that have outgrown our older and narrower streets continues to pose a management headache for many tree officers (Condron 2005). Furthermore, trying to retain large-growing trees in residential streets where these trees are an appropriate species is proving a real challenge for tree officers in an increasingly risk-averse society (see Chapter 3).

It is interesting to note that throughout the history of street trees in Britain, there has been little enthusiasm for the shaping of trees in a manner often undertaken on the Continent. While the pruning of street tree crowns into round or square shapes continues to be popular in countries such as France and Italy, this had never really been fashionable or widely practiced in Britain. A factor in this might be the same public attitudes about the 'unnatural' appearance of trees that condemns pollarding, although topiary in gardens appears to be another matter.

The 1970s and '80s witnessed the introduction into Britain of a wide range of new equipment and technology for urban tree management. Peter Bridgeman's book *Tree Surgery*, published in 1976, gives a good account of the new arboricultural tools, equipment and large machinery that had recently become available (Bridgeman 1976). While much of this had applications in many types of arboricultural work, some of the large machinery was particularly useful when working on street trees. This heavy machinery had often been initially developed in the United States, although as it became popular here some British companies began to manufacture their own versions. Hydraulic or aerial platforms enabled tree workers to access the crown of the tree without having to use a rope and harness. When working systematically along an avenue of street trees and undertaking tasks such as reducing overhanging branches, the use of a platform could increase the speed and efficiency of this work. When the branches had been removed, they could be feed into a brushwood cutter that would reduce them to wood chip. These wood chips would take up less than one-tenth of the space of the original branches and thus reduce transport costs as well as being a recycled product with a number of uses. When street trees are felled, the stumps have to be removed so they do not cause an obstruction on the pavement. Large machines called stump grinders can be positioned over the stump and literally grind or chip away at this until its height is reduced to below the level of the pavement. The shallow hole can then be backfilled and the surface of the pavement reinstated.

From the early 1980s, the introduction of computerised technology into tree management in Britain has also been responsible for introducing many new practices in the management of street and highway trees (Bickmore and Hall 1983). For example, some local authorities had previously recorded details of their street trees on card index systems, as an aid to management. Nowadays,

FIGURE 61. In the 1950s and '60s, it became popular for local authorities to plant vast numbers of small ornamental trees along roadsides, particularly in suburban locations. Endless miles of flowering cherries and similar trees were used, which gave a riot of colour for perhaps two weeks of the year. Often, the locations in which they were planted could have accommodated much larger and more long-lived trees, such as with this grass verge on a Liverpool housing estate.

FIGURE 62. These plane trees, probably planted in the late Edwardian era, have been subject to regular maintenance over the years to keep them from outgrowing their situation. Initially, they were most likely pollarded on a very regular basis but in more recent years the crowns have been allowed to regrow for a few years before they are pollarded again. These trees in Liverpool appear to be quite a successful example of this management practice.

most operate computerised systems that not only keep an inventory of their street trees, along with other trees and woodland, but also include various management functions, enabling a more planned, systematic and integrated approach to urban tree management (Britt and Johnston 2008, 193). If local authorities have the necessary funding and expertise to monitor, maintain and manage their street tree populations efficiently and effectively, these trees can be a vital element of the whole urban forest.

References

Amherst, A. (1907) *London Parks and Gardens*. Writing as the Hon. Mrs Evelyn Cecil. A. Constable and Co: London.

Anon (1946) *Tree Planting in Road and Streets in Urban and Suburban Areas*. Circular No. 24 issued by the Ministry of Town and Country Planning, 14 May, 1946. HMSO: London.

Anon (1967) *Roads in the Landscape*. Conference papers and report of discussions, July 17–20 1967. Contributed by the Ministry of Transport and British Road Federation. The University of Keele: Staffordshire.

Atkins. P. J. (1993) How the West End was won: the struggle to remove street barriers in Victorian London. *Journal of Historical Geography*, Volume 19(3), 265–277.

Balfour, F. R. S. (1935) The Planting and After Care of Roadside Trees. *Quarterly Journal of Forestry* 29, 163–188.

Barker, F. and Hyde, R. (1982) *London as it Might have Been*. John Murray: London.

Bean, W. J. (1929) The Planting of Roads. *The New Flora and Silva* 1(4), 247–252.

Bennett, J. M. (1929) *Roadside Development*. The Macmillan Company: New York.

Bickmore, C. J. and Hall, T. H. R. (1983) *Computerisation of Tree Inventories*. A. B. Academic Publishers: Berkhamsted.

Borsay, P. (1986) The Rise of the Promenade: the Social and Cultural Use of Space in the English Provincial Town *c.* 1660–1800. *Journal for Eighteenth-Century Studies* 9(2), 125–140.

Bressey, C. H. (1930) Foreword by C. H. Bressey, Chief Engineer, Roads Department, Ministry of Transport. In: *Roadside Planting*; by 'RBA' (Roads Beautifying Association). Country Life: London.

Bridgeman, P. H. (1976) *Tree Surgery: A Complete Guide*. David and Charles: Newton Abbot.

Britt, C. and Johnston, M. (2008) *Trees in Towns II: A New Survey of Urban Trees in England and their Condition and Management*. Department for Communities and Local Government: London.

Brown, G. E. (1972) *The Pruning of Trees, Shrubs and Conifers*. Faber and Faber: London.

Burdekin, D. (1981) Tree Diseases and Disorders. In: Coulston, B and Stansfield, K. (eds) *Trees in Towns: Maintenance and Management*. The Architectural Press: London.

Burnett, J. (1986) *A Social History of Housing 1815–1985*. Second edition. Routledge: London and New York.

Colvin, B. (1939) Roadside Planting in Country Districts. *Landscape and Garden* 6, 86.

Colvin, B. (1947) *Trees for Town and Country*. Lund Humphries: London.

Colvin, B. (1948) *Land and Landscape*. John Murray: London.

Condron, S. (2005) They Have Stood Proudly for 130 years. Now the Compensation Culture could fell 4,500 Lime Trees. *Daily Mail*, Thursday 24 March, 39.

Cook, M. (1676) *The Manner of Raising, Ordering, and Improving Forest-Trees: Also, How to Plant, Make and Keep Woods, Walks, Avenues, Lawns, Hedges, etc.* Peter Parker at the Leg and Star: London.

Cotton, A. D. (1945) Mr. F. R. S. Balfour C.V.O. *Nature*, 24 March 1945, No. 3934, Vol. 155, 357–8.

CPRE (1948) *Town Trees: A Road in Sheffield.* Council for the Preservation of Rural England, Sheffield and Peak District Branch: Sheffield.

Crowe, S. (1960) *The Landscape of Roads.* Architectural Press: London.

Dunball, A. P. (1968) The Practical Problems of Motorway Planting. *Arboricultural Association Journal* 1 (7), 179–186.

Dunball, A. P. (1972) Landscape Treatment of Trunk Roads and Motorways. *Arboricultural Association Journal*, 2(2), 38–43.

Dyos, H. J. (1961) *Victorian Suburb: A Study of the Growth of Camberwell.* Leicester University Press: Leicester.

Edwards, P. J. (1898) *History of London Street Improvements, 1855–1897.* London County Council: London.

Edwards, P. (1962) *Trees in the English Landscape.* G. Bell and Sons: London.

Elliott, P. A., Watkins, C. and Daniels, S. (2011) *The British Arboretum: Trees, Science and Culture in the Nineteenth Century.* Pickering and Chatto: London.

Evelyn, J. (1901) *The Diary of John Evelyn.* Edited in 1901 from the original manuscript by William Bray in two volumes. Volume 1. M. Walter Dunne: New York and London.

Fry, A. W. (2003) *Road and Way: An Analysis of These Expressions in the Highways and Related Acts of Parliament c.1500 to 1929.* Published privately: Alresford. Available at: http://www.bbtrust.org.uk/misc-items/roadway.pdf (accessed 3.6.2014).

Hart, W. O. (1959) Local Government in London. *Journal of the Society of Public Teachers of Law.* New Series 5(2) (December), 62–76.

Honour, D. R. (1977) Donald Vernon Wells. *Arboricultural Journal* 3(2), 72–73.

Howard, E. (1898) *Tomorrow: A Peaceful Path to Real Reform.* Swan Sonnenschein and Company: London.

Hunt, T. (2004) *Building Jerusalem: The Rise and Fall of the Victorian City.* Weindenfeld and Nicolson: London.

Hussey, C. (1967) *English Gardens and Landscapes 1700–1750.* Country Life: London.

Jacobs, A. B., Macdonald, E. and Rofé, Y. (2002) *The Boulevard Book: History, Evolution, Design of Multiway Boulevards.* The MIT Press: Cambridge, MA.

Jellicoe, G. A. (1958) Motorways: their landscaping, design and appearance. *Journal of the Town Planning Institute* 44, 274–283.

Johnston, M. (1997a) The Early Development of Urban Forestry in Britain: Part I. *Arboricultural Journal* 21, 107–126.

Johnston, M. (1997b) The Early Development of Urban Forestry in Britain: Part II.*Arboricultural Journal* 21, 317–330.

Johnston, M. (1991) The Forest of London: I – Planting an Idea. *Arboricultural Journal* 15, 127–143.

Lawrence, H. W. (1988) Origins of the Tree-lined Boulevard. *The Geographical Review* 78 (4), 355–378.

Lawrence, H. W. (2006) *City Trees: A Historical Geography from the Renaissance through the Nineteenth Century.* University of Virginia Press: Charlottesville and London.

Lay, M. G. (1992) *Ways of the World: A History of the World's Roads and the Vehicles that Used Them.* Rutgers University Press: New Brunswick, NJ.

Longstaffe-Gowan, T. (2001) *The London Town Garden 1740–1840.* Paul Mellon Centre for Studies in British Art: London.

Loudon, J. C. (1835a) Remarks on Laying out Public Gardens and Promenades. *Gardener's Magazine* 11, 644–59.

Loudon, J. C. (1835b) *Encyclopaedia of Gardening, Comprising the Theory and Practice of Horticulture, Floriculture, Arboriculture and Landscape-gardening*. Longman, Rees, Orme, Brown, Green and Longmans: London.

McKay, G. (1996) *Senseless Acts of Beauty: Cultures of Resistance Since the Sixties*. Verso: London.

Mawson, T. H. (1911) *Civic Art: Studies in Town Planning, Parks, Boulevards and Open Spaces*. B. T. Batsford: London.

Merriman, P. (2006) A New Look at the English Landscape: Landscape Architecture, Movement and the Aesthetics of Motorways in Early Postwar Britain. *Cultural Geographies* 13, 78–105.

Mitchell, A. (1989) The Plant Hunters and their Effect on the Introduction of Exotic species to the Urban Environment. In Chaplin, J. (ed.) *Celebration of Trees: Silver Jubilee Conference Proceedings*. Arboricultural Association: Ampfield

Morris, E. S. (1997) *British Town Planning and Urban Design: Principles and Policies*. Addison Wesley Longman: Harlow.

Mulford, F. Ll. (1921) *Planting and Care of Street Trees*. Farmers' Bulletin No. 1209. United States Department of Agriculture: Washington, DC.

Mulford, F. Ll. (1926) *Planting the Roadside*. Farmers' Bulletin No. 1481. United States Department of Agriculture: Washington, DC.

Mynors, C. (2002) *The Law of Trees, Forests and Hedgerows*. Sweet and Maxwell: London.

Newcomen, T. G. (1951) Pre-Roman Roads in Britain. *Contractors' Record and Municipal Engineering*. 14 and 21 (Feb) 11–16, 28.

O'Reilly, C. (2013) "We Have Gone Recreation Mad": The Consumption of Leisure and Popular Entertainment in Municipal Public Parks in Early Twentieth Century Britain. *International Journal of Regional and Local History* 8(2), 112–128.

Pearce, S. A. (1961) *Ornamental Trees for Garden and Roadside Planting*. W. H. and L. Collingridge: London.

Pettigrew, W. W. (1937) *Municipal Parks: Layout, Management and Administration*. The Journal of Park Administration: London.

Porter, D. (1998) *The Thames Embankment: Environment, Technology, and Society in Victorian London*. University of Ackron Press: Ohio.

Porter, R. (2000) London: *A Social History*. Penguin Books: London.

RBA (1930) *Roadside Planting*; by 'R. B. A'. (Roads Beautifying Association). Country Life: London.

RBA (1935) *Seventh Report of the Roads Beautifying Association, October 1933–March 1935*. Roads Beautifying Association: London.

Robinson, W. (1869) *The Parks, Promenades and Gardens of Paris, Described and Considered in Relation to the Wants of Our Cities*. John Murray: London.

Roger, R. (2000) Slums and Suburbs: The Persistence of Residential Apartheid. In Waller, P. (ed.) *The English Urban Landscape*. Oxford University Press: Oxford.

Salter, R. G. (1953) *Roadside Tree Planting in Urban Areas*. Bournville Village Trust, Bournville: Birmingham.

Santamour, F. S., Gerhold, H. D. and Little, S. (1976) *Better Trees for Metropolitan Landscapes*. Symposium Proceedings. USDA Forest Service General Technical Report E-22. Upper Darby: PA.

Sitte, C. (1889) *City Planning According to Artistic Principles*. Translated in 1965 by George R. Collins and Christiane Crasemann Collins. Columbia University Studies in Art History and Archaeology, No. 2. Phaidon: London.

Stewart, J. (1771) *Critical Observations on the Buildings and Improvements of London*. J. Dodsley: London.

Strutt, J. (1810) *Sports and Pastimes of the People of England*. Second edition. T. Bensley, Bolt Court, Fleet Street: London.

Stübben, J. (1885) *Practical and Aesthetic Principles for the Laying Out of Cities*. English translation by W. H. Searles and published in 1893. Transactions of the American Society of Civil Engineers. Available at: http://www.library.cornell.edu/Reps/DOCS/ stubb_85.htm (accessed 2.6.2014).

Taylor, S. and Green, O. (2001) *The Moving Metropolis: The History of London's Transport Since 1800*. Laurence King Publishing: London.

Wells, D. V. (1954) Trees and Highways. In Morling, R. J. (ed.) *Trees in Towns*. The Estates Gazette: London.

Wells, D. V. (1963) Trees and Highways. In Morling, R. J. (ed.) *Trees, Including Preservation, Planting, Law, Highways*. The Estates Gazette: London.

Wells, D. V. (1970) History of the Roads Beautifying Association. *Arboricultural Association Journal* 1(11), 295–306.

Willebrand, J. P. (1775) *Grundriß einer schönen Stadt* (Plan for a beautiful city). Published by the author: Hamburg and Leipzig. Available at: http://www.cloud-cuckoo.net/ openarchive/Autoren/Willebrandt/Willebrandt1775.htm (accessed 2.5.2014).

Trees in Other Urban Greenspaces

The contribution to our urban forests over the centuries by trees in private gardens, public parks and streets, has been supplemented by tree cover in other forms of urban greenspace. Some of these spaces, such as churchyards and the grounds of ancient universities, date back many hundreds of years. Others, such as golf courses and roof gardens, are relatively recent introductions into the pattern of greenspace in Britain. In this chapter we take a brief look at the history of trees and woodlands in some of these other elements of the urban realm.

Churchyards and ecclesiastical properties

The presence of a churchyard around the main ecclesiastical building has been a common feature of Christian sites of worship in Britain since the enclosure of land around churches began about 750 (Swanton 1958, 19). These have always been sacred spaces, primarily for the burial of the dead, and valued as pleasant landscapes for quiet contemplation and reflection. Churches and their churchyards, sometimes called burial grounds, tend to be located at the centre of communities rather than on their periphery (Rugg 2000, 265). For that reason they are often in close proximity to other built development even when located in rural villages. The sites of churchyards also tend to be quite small in size and the popular term 'God's acre' is often an accurate description of their physical scale. It would be hard to overestimate the importance of trees to churchyards. They invariably contribute most to the design of those landscapes and by their grace and disposition they provide dignity and beauty to the churchyard (Cocke 2012, 101). Throughout most of their history, churchyards in towns and cities have generally had a greater density of treecover than most other urban greenspaces and have often been the location for ancient trees, particularly yew (Figure 63).

The churchyard yew is a relic of pre-Christian and Pagan times that has been incorporated into the Christian tradition, along with the association of its evergreen foliage with immortality (Cornish 1946, 17–8). In medieval times churchyard yews were a source of revenue, the branches being sold for longbows and arrows (*ibid.*, 38). As all parts of the yew, except the flesh of the berries, are poisonous both to people and animals, churchyards have customarily been enclosed with boundary fences and gates to exclude animals and young children.

In the seventeenth century when the major towns and cities had very few public open spaces, it was often the churchyards of the many parish churches that provided some nearby greenspace (Harding 1990, 51–2). However, many of these were tiny and encroachment of various kinds was commonplace. The use of the phrase 'green churchyard' in many parish records to describe their churchyard implies that these were well-endowed with trees and shrubs, and where the phrase does not appear the churchyard was probably paved or gravelled. In the eighteenth century, some greener churchyards were laid out as public walks, as at St Mary's in Painswick, Gloucestershire, and St Philip's in Birmingham (Borsay 2013, 54). The churchyard at Painswick has long been famous for its yew trees with over 100 magnificent clipped specimens thought to have been planted nearly 300 years ago (Bailey 1987, 33).

In the early nineteenth century, urban churchyards and burial grounds were becoming increasingly overcrowded with the growth of urban populations (Conway 1991, 215). This overcrowding also led to the loss of some trees in cemeteries in an effort to create more burial space. The Burial Act 1853 allowed overcrowded churchyards to be closed and for the prohibition of new burial grounds if there was a health risk. The next decade saw the closure of many urban churchyards around the country. As no provision was made for the maintenance of these closed grounds, they gradually fell into disrepair and decay. Because of the general lack of urban greenspace, some public-spirited individuals and reforming organisations began to lobby for the conversion of many of these disused burial grounds into open space for recreation. Initially, there was some resistance to the idea of "children romping about in the churchyard and turning somersaults on the graves" (Hardwicke 1877, 513). Despite some public disquiet, the creation of gardens and open spaces out of churchyards and burial grounds grew as the importance of accessible greenspace was increasingly recognised (Conway 1991, 219). Although the transformation of these sites did not add significantly to the total area of open space in many towns and cities, their amenity value was often considerable as they tended to be in densely populated districts.

As well as churchyards, other ecclesiastical properties in towns and cities have also made an important contribution to urban greenspace over the centuries. In Chapter 4 we mentioned the role of monastic gardens in medieval times, while recognising that their use of trees as ornamental features was likely to have been limited. In the seventeenth and eighteenth century, the grounds of some sumptuous church properties were to become famous for their gardens and tree collections. The Bishop's Palace at St Davids in Wales dates from the fourteenth century and the area to the south of the palace was originally laid out as formal gardens with some fine trees (O'Malley 1997). The Bishop's Palace at Ely in Cambridgeshire was initially built in the fifteenth century, although little of this survives. In the grounds, which now belong to an independent school, is one of the oldest and largest plane trees in Britain, planted by Bishop Gunning in 1680 (Stokes and Rodger 2004, 97). Following the Reformation and the dissolution of the religious houses in the 1530s, some properties and open spaces belonging to the Church became available in urban centres (Willes 2014, 18). However, these were usually snapped up by the rich and powerful and were especially prized if they had attractive gardens.

Lambeth Palace has been the London residence of the Archbishops of Canterbury for nearly 800 hundred years (MacLeod 1972, 102–3). Its private garden has been in existence since the twelfth century and is thought to be the oldest continuously cultivated garden in London. In 1901, Archbishop Frederick Temple gave nine acres of land from the east side of the garden on an indefinite lease to the people of Lambeth to form Archbishop's Park (Amherst 1907, 307) and this continues to have some magnificent trees.

The garden at Fulham Palace, the other ecclesiastical palace of London, has a remarkable history of fine and rare trees (Amherst 1907, 308–9). From the eighth century until very recently, the palace was the home of the Bishops of London and several who have held this office have shown great interest in the gardens, particularly Bishops Grindal and Compton. Grindal introduced the tamarisk and was regarded as one of the foremost gardeners of his age. Unfortunately, Bishop Aylmer, who succeeded Grindal, undid much of his work and was accused of cutting down his trees, then some 35 years old. The most significant contribution to the arboricultural fame of the gardens was made by Henry Compton, who was Bishop of London from 1675 until his death in 1713 (Morris 1991). Over many years, Compton built up an unrivalled collection of rare trees and shrubs, many of them from North America where John Bannister was engaged in plant collecting for the Bishop. These introductions included

FIGURE 63. For hundreds of years before the advent of public parks it was the town and village churchyards that represented some of the most accessible trees and greenspace for those residents without gardens. This is the famous 'bleeding yew' at the parish church of Nevern, West Wales, which leaks red sap.

Liquidambar styraciflua, *Liriodendron tulipifera*, *Magnolia virginiana*, *Acer negundo*, *Quercus ilex*, *Quercus suber* and *Juglans nigra*. The fame of the gardens spread and visitors (including John Evelyn in 1681) came to Fulham Palace to study and admire the trees and the many exotics plants in the stovehouses. The high level of horticultural maintenance was due to an experienced team of gardeners, one of whom was George London who went on to be a founding partner in the famous nursery of London and Wise at Brompton Park. When Compton died, his successor took no interest in his rare plants, choosing to remove many of them to make more room for fruit and vegetables. Nevertheless, the Kensington nursery of Robert Furber and the Fulham nursery of Christopher Gray are known to have brought plants from the garden. In 1975, after years of neglect, the London Borough of Hammersmith and Fulham embarked on an ambitious plan to restore the palace and recreate the garden.

Early development of the cemeteries movement

By the early nineteenth century, the state of many urban churchyards and burial grounds throughout Britain was generating widespread public concern (Curl 2000, 73). Shocking reports appeared in newspapers that used lurid phrases to describe their overcrowded and dilapidated condition, such as 'dangerous masses of corruption' and 'injurious to the living'. They were regarded as major contributing factors to 'atmospheric impurity' because of the foul 'miasmas' which escaped from the seething corruption of graves, and this was thought to be one of the causes of outbreaks of cholera and other diseases. It was believed

FIGURE 64. The Père-Lachaise cemetery in Paris, opened in 1804, was one of the main inspirations for the garden cemetery movement in Britain. This wonderful Elysian landscape made a dramatic contrast to the monotonous, dilapidated and increasingly treeless landscapes of British burial grounds of the early nineteenth century.

that trees and shrubs would help to absorb these harmful gases and generally improve public health. In the 1830s and '40s, with mortality rates in cities at horrific levels, there was also a growing clamour to defeat overcrowding in burial grounds by establishing new cemeteries outside city boundaries. These ideas were to come together in the concept of the 'garden cemetery' and prompt the development of a cemetery movement in Britain that proposed to locate new attractively landscaped burial grounds on the outskirts of towns and cities (Rutherford 2013a, 10). In contrast to churchyards and many burial grounds, cemeteries are principally secular spaces where ownership is almost always by local authorities or private sector concerns (Rugg 2000, 261–4). They are usually multidenominational and serve the whole community but may sometime belong exclusively to a single denomination.

Much of the inspiration for the design of these new garden cemeteries came from one existing example in Paris, the Cimetière du Père-Lachaise, opened in 1804 (Etlin 1984; Curl 2000, 70) (Figure 64). This was built on a picturesque area of hilly ground with axial avenues and winding paths, together with plenty of trees and shrubs along the routes and between the artistic graves and monuments. This wonderful Elysian landscape where nature and art were joined together made a dramatic contrast to the monotonous, dilapidated and increasingly treeless landscapes of British burial grounds. The carriageways and main paths had their own distinct allées of different tree species and there were several thickly planted bosquets. By the 1830s, the cemetery had becomes so famous that to see this was *de rigueur* for any new visitor to Paris. Nonetheless, the aesthetics of Père-Lachaise were based on sound economics as this was a commercial venture with the burial plots for sale at a range of prices, reflecting their size and location within the cemetery.

Liverpool was among the first British cities to establish a garden cemetery. In 1829, St James's Cemetery was opened as a commercial venture on the site of an exhausted quarry occupying 12 acres (4.8 ha) at the cost of £21,000 raised through public subscription (Rutherford 2013a, 13). The landscape design, modelled on Père-Lachaise, was a major factor in attracting customers and the cemetery was later described by Nikolaus Pevsner, the architectural historian, as the most romantic in England. By the 1830s, the idea of new landscaped cemeteries in the urban fringe was being considered by civic leaders in many towns and cities (*ibid.*, 14–5). In response, further commercial cemeteries were established on a business model that was later to be used for municipal cemeteries. Among the cities to gain cemeteries as this time were Birmingham, Newcastle, Sheffield, Nottingham and Manchester. The Glasgow Necropolis opened in 1832 as the first major cemetery in Scotland.

Meanwhile, London was lagging behind much of the rest of Britain and its first proper cemetery was not opened until 1832 when the Kensal Green Cemetery was created (Rutherford 2013a, 16–8). After that, there was a 'wait and see' attitude to the creation of more cemeteries until it became apparent that many cemetery companies were paying good dividends (Curl 2000,

83). It was another five years before the next venture in London, the South Metropolitan Cemetery in West Norwood (1837), which was for many years the most fashionable London cemetery south of the river. There followed Highgate Cemetery (1839), Abney Park (1840), Nunhead (1840), Brompton (1840) and Tower Hamlets (1841). Together these new cemeteries became known as the 'Magnificent Seven' and when they were finally completed London had at last secured adequate provision for burial space.

Most Victorian cemeteries were built in the second half of the nineteenth century, with a great burst of construction around the 1850s (Rutherford 2013a, 31). The second cholera epidemic of 1848–9 gave considerable impetus to this. A series of Acts were passed by Parliament which became known as the Burial Acts, many of which specifically enabled individual cemeteries to be built in various towns and cities. It was also with the Burial Acts of 1850 and 1852 that local authorities began to get extensively involved in creating and managing cemeteries (Elliott 1986, 52). There was invariably a strong element of civic pride involved in driving forward these proposals and not a little competition between towns.

For the many reformers in Victorian society garden cemeteries were not simply repositories for the dead. It was believed they should adopt a similar role to public parks in having a moral and 'improving' dimension, promoting good manners and taste and acting as educational and soothing places for the resort of relatives (Rutherford 2013a, 29). In the view of John Claudius Loudon (1843, 13) they "might become a school of instruction in architecture, sculpture, landscape-gardening, arboriculture, botany, and in those important parts of general gardening, neatness, order and high keeping." Furthermore, through the text and artwork on their gravestones and monuments, cemeteries should also serve as the repository of historical records or a 'living history library' in a similar manner to that performed by churchyards over the centuries.

Trees and design in the garden cemetery

A number of cemeteries were established on hilly sites, as had Père-Lachaise in Paris, and this gave economic as well as visual advantages (Rutherford 2013a, 18–9). This land often had little value for much else and therefore the sites were relatively cheap to buy. They were sometimes former quarries, such as at St James's in Liverpool and Key Hill in Birmingham, where the workings had become exhausted or uneconomic. At the same time, steeply sloping sites, such as those at Highgate in London and the Glasgow Necropolis, provided interesting relief and spectacular views over their respective cities. In other sites on more level ground curved paths led through informal lawns destined for graves and monuments and planted with ornamental and native trees. Some cemeteries, such as Gravesend in Kent and Arnos Vale in Bristol, were created on the site of earlier gardens and incorporated previous landscaping. Arnos Vale (then known as the Bristol General Cemetery) was especially fortunate in being formed out of a pleasant country estate with plenty of mature deciduous trees (Jones 2007, 159). Even when there was no previous landscaping, some designers were very conscious of the value of any mature trees on the site. When the Stoke Cemetery was developed in the 1880s, following a design by Edward Milner, all the mature trees on the property were left undisturbed "and they helped to redeem much of that appearance of newness...associated with young planting" (Milner 1890, 99) (Figure 65).

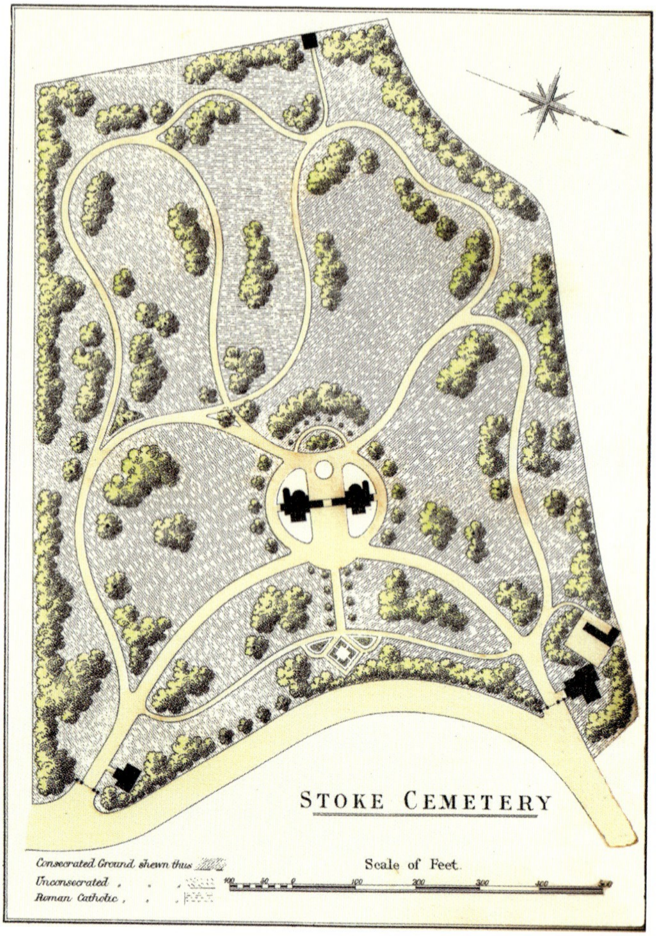

Most of the notable designers of cemeteries were landscapers or architects or a combination of both. Many were also involved in the laying out of public parks and the similarities between their work on parks and cemeteries are often clear to see. They included individuals such as Joseph Paxton, Edward Kemp, William Barron, Edward Milner and later Thomas Mawson. Other landscape designers focused specifically on cemeteries, such as William Gay and Stephen Geary. One name stands out as having an exceptional influence on the overall design and planting of the Victorian garden cemetery: John Claudius Loudon. In 1828, Loudon began

FIGURE 65. Edward Milner's landscape plan for the Stoke Cemetery developed in the 1880s. All large trees already on the site that had amenity value were retained to give the landscape a mature appearance from the start. Note the legend in the bottom left-hand corner that indicates how the cemetery space was divided into areas of consecrated ground, unconsecrated ground and a section for Roman Catholics (Milner 1890).

his campaign to promote decent cemeteries and graveyards as Editor of his own *Gardener's Magazine*, which was to culminate in a series of articles (Curl 2000, 74). In 1843, he incorporated these articles into his seminal work on the topic entitled *On the Laying Out, Planting, and Managing of Cemeteries* (Loudon 1843). It was one of the most exhaustive books on cemeteries ever written and was to have a lasting impact on how these were laid out (Figure 66).

Loudon was critical of all cemetery design of the early Victorian era as he felt this was concerned too much with grandiose monuments and picturesque landscape "too much in the style of the common pleasure-ground" (Loudon 1843, 69) (Figures 67 and 68). In his own approach to cemeteries, Loudon was keen to make the most efficient utilisation of the burial space available as well as make them appropriate landscapes. To this end he had much to say on their design, with particularly reference to the use of trees and shrubs. For the layout of the burial plots he favoured a rectangular grid system, connected by a hierarchy of straight or occasionally curved drives and pedestrian paths. Along each side of the main roads, rows of trees would be planted parallel to the road

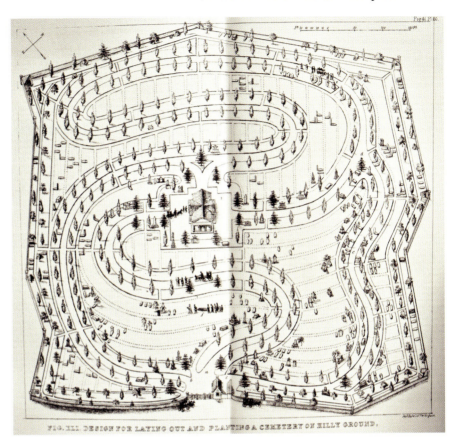

FIGURE 66. Loudon's design for laying out and planting a cemetery on hilly ground. Much of the tree planting is along the side of the main routes and around the periphery of the cemetery. The plan is taken from his book *On the Laying Out, Planting, and Managing of Cemeteries* (Loudon 1843).

and at regular distances. Along the centre of the beds adapted for double rows of graves, trees and shrubs would be planted at regular distances and these could be removed or replanted as new graves were required. In terms of the overall design of the cemetery landscape, Loudon declared:

> On the introduction of trees and shrubs into cemeteries very much of their ornamental effect is dependent; but too many trees and shrubs impede the free circulation of air and the drying effect of the sun. They ought not, as we think, to be introduced in masses to the interior of the cemetery, nor in strips or belts around its margins, unless under very particular circumstances. Every mode of introducing trees and shrubs that is identical to that practiced in planting parks and pleasure-grounds is to be avoided, as tending to confound the character and expression of scenes which are, or ought to be, essentially distinct.
>
> Loudon, 1843, 20

In terms of the individual species of trees and their form, Loudon also had some quite specific requirements:

> We would not, in the case of cemeteries on low or level ground, plant trees which produce bulky heads; but confine ourselves chiefly to kinds having narrow conical shapes, like the cypress, the form of which not only produces little shade or shelter, but has been associated with places of burial for time immemorial. Almost all the

kinds should be evergreen and of dark foliage; because the variety produced by deciduous and flowering trees is not favourable to the expression of either solemnity or grandeur. Along most of the gravel walks we would plant for the most part only fastigiate shrubs, such as the Irish yew, Irish and Swedish juniper.

Loudon, 1843, 20–1

Loudon also excluded all weeping varieties of trees, despite their long association with ancient burials, because they were of "such marked and peculiar forms", although he had no objection if families selected them for individual graves (Loudon 1843, 20–1). However, at the junction of roads, or at the intersections of the squares where this mode of division had been adopted, trees of a strikingly different kind should be planted. This would help to emphasise these junctions when viewed from a distance.

Most of the designers of the new cemeteries seemed to agree that trees provided the essential landscape structure and gave some clothing to otherwise stark strips of lawn that were awaiting future graves and monuments. To achieve this, impressive avenues were a popular planting arrangement and a number of evergreen species were favoured, such as holm oak, holly, cedars, Irish yew and monkey puzzle (*Araucaria araucana*). Following its introduction in 1853, the giant sequoia (Wellingtonia for the Victorians) was used frequently because of its impressive stature, rapid growth and relatively compact crown. For the main avenue of cemeteries, Loudon favoured various species of pine and cypress as well as the Greek juniper (*Juniperus excelsa*), although if planting conditions were unfavourable then the red cedar (*Thuja plicata*) or common spruce (*Picea abies*) (Loudon 1843, 21). At Brandwood End Cemetery in Birmingham, one of the later Victorian cemeteries opened in 1899, there are notable avenues comprising Scots pine and cypress trees and across the centre of the site one particularly fine and imposing avenue of giant sequoia (Figure 69).

With regard to the use of other plants in cemetery design, there was a sharp difference of opinion among designers on the presence of flowers. As usual, Loudon led the way in this debate, relating it to the cultivation of beds and any other part of the grounds. He declared:

> The planting of flowers in cemeteries is very general, not only in the margin of masses and belts, and in beds as in pleasure-grounds, but on graves. For our own particular taste, we would have no flowers at all, nor any portion of the ground within a cemetery that had the appearance of being dug or otherwise moved for the purpose of cultivation. A state of quiet and repose is an important ingredient in the passive sublime; and moving the soil for the purpose of culture, even over a grave, is destructive of repose.

Loudon, 1843, 21

In contrast to flowers and other herbaceous plants that required much attention and expense, trees and shrubs usually required little maintenance once established, thus reducing the overall extent of maintenance activity undertaken by the gardeners. However, just as with public parks, bedding displays proved a popular attraction for visitors and Loudon's views placed him at odds with

FIGURES 67 and 68. Loudon contrasted the 'pleasure ground' style of cemetery planting (67), which he disliked, with his much preferred 'cemetery' style (68) that used plenty of conifers and owed a lot to his 'gardenesque' approach to landscaping. The cemetery shown is the South Metropolitan at Norwood, Surrey, completed in 1837. The engravings are taken from his book *On the Laying Out, Planting, and Managing of Cemeteries* (Loudon 1843).

FIGURE 69. This impressive avenue of giant sequoia is located at the Brandwood End Cemetery, Birmingham, opened in 1899. Avenues of exotic conifers, including quite recent introductions from the west coast of North America, were a frequent addition to the landscape of the Victorian cemetery.

many reformers, landscape designers and the owners and superintendents of cemeteries.

One Victorian cemetery that deserves a special mention for its trees is the Abney Park Cemetery in Stoke Newington. This was one of London's 'Magnificent Seven' and opened in 1840 as the first wholly nondenominational garden cemetery in Europe (Curl 2000, 100–8). The site was fortunate in already having some lush planting and the cemetery company wisely decided to retain as much of this as possible. According to George Collison, one of the promoters of the cemetery, the presence of many sizable and beautiful trees was a major attraction of the site, providing a mature look to the landscape lacking in many other new cemeteries. In addition to the existing treecover, it was the new plantings of trees and shrubs that were to radically transform the landscape and it ensure its reputation as a pioneering example of the garden cemetery. Abney Park was laid out as an extensive arboretum, created in part by George Loddiges of the celebrated Loddiges nursery in Hackney, which also supplied the wonderful selection of trees and shrubs.

There was much emphasis at Abney Park on producing an educational landscape within the cemetery grounds, just as with any other arboretum. Its 2,500 different species and varieties of trees from all over the world were labelled and arranged around the perimeter in alphabetic order to make them easier to locate. There was also an arboretum catalogue produced by Collison listing all the trees and shrubs together with their botanic details and information on cultivation, which was available to visitors as they walked through the grounds. The overall landscape design was a simplified version of Loudon's 'gardenesque' approach, although there was no mound planting. Loudon himself was suitable impressed with the entire venture and describe Abney Park as "the most highly ornamented cemetery in the neighbourhood of London" (Loudon 1843, 22).

In the 1970s and '80s, many Victorian cemeteries were suffering from serious neglect and decay, the same scenario that was befalling many Victorian public parks. The difficulties encountered in trying to secure the eventual restoration of Arnos Vale Cemetery have been documented by Owain Jones (2007). The difficulties experienced at Highgate Cemetery are particularly interesting as they highlight some of the major conflicts in management that can threaten the restoration of historic cemeteries. According to James Stevens Curl (2000, 95), the respected architectural historian, a Friends Group was established in 1975 and together with the Highgate Cemetery Trust took over the management of the western part of the site. As a result, from 1976 until 1983, the emphasis was on managing the cemetery as woodland. It was not until an architect was appointed to examine the condition of the buildings that their desperate condition was noticed. Until then, the woodland enthusiasts had insisted that the ubiquitous ivy was 'harmless' to the monuments, although it was actually doing great damage. However, the 'ecological' position adopted in the management policy had banned the use of chemical herbicides in maintaining the grounds. As a result, nature ran riot. Only recently has a more balanced approach been adopted. Fortunately, a number of those threatened historic cemeteries have now been saved and restored thanks to the determination of local residents, often with support from the local authority and the Heritage Lottery Fund.

Crematoria and woodland burial

The late nineteenth century saw a movement that sought to establish crematoria in Britain, buildings where the bodies of the dead are burned, or cremated, as part of a funeral ceremony (Jupp 2006). With the problems associated with overcrowded and dilapidated burial grounds, cremation was viewed by many reform-minded people as a necessary sanitary measure and precaution against the spread of disease. It would also reduce the expense of funerals, spare mourners the necessity of standing exposed to the weather during interment, and prevent the theft of bodies for medical research. After much public debate and religious opposition, the first official cremation in Britain took place at Woking Crematorium in 1885.

One landscape designer with a particular interest in crematoria was William Robinson, who by the late nineteenth century had established himself as an authority on all matters horticultural. In 1880, he published *God's Acre Beautiful or The Cemeteries of The Future*, in which he applied his gardening aesthetic to urban churchyards and cemeteries (Robinson 1880). As a vocal campaigner for the advantages of cremation over burial, he was instrumental in the founding of Golders Green Crematorium, the first to be opened in London in 1902 (Allan 1982, 129). His design for the crematorium's gardens was at odds with Loudon's views on the landscape design of cemeteries that had held sway for many decades. This was not simply because of the presence of flowers, the wide expanses of lawn and the absence of graves and monuments, although these were the more obvious differences. More fundamentally, the underlying philosophy of Robinson's landscape design had moved away completely from Loudon's essentially gardenesque approach (see Chapter 4).

Considering how many neglected cemeteries reverted to overgrown woodland in the last few decades of the twentieth century, it is interesting to note the recent growth of interest in woodland burials in Britain. While this has only attracted interest since the 1970s, the idea has echoes in the distant past of many cultures and also reflects some of the ideals of the garden cemetery movement (Wienrich and Speyer 2003). Woodland burial plots are set among trees and wildflowers and families can chose to bury or scatter the ashes of their loved ones within the peaceful grounds. If the body is buried it should be interned unembalmed in a biodegradable coffin. Instead of a traditional headstone, the plots are marked with the planting of a memorial tree. While a number of woodland burial sites have been established in the urban fringe, their landscape is essentially rural as a requirement of a natural setting. Some local authorities have now included woodlands groves in municipal cemeteries where relatives can sponsor a commemorative tree planting and scatter ashes on that spot.

Urban botanical gardens

As well as containing plants from all over the world, botanical gardens invariably have fine collections of trees and shrubs, sometime located in discrete arboretums or pinetums. Although these botanic gardens may initially have been situated in the urban fringe or even the countryside, with urban expansion over the centuries many have long been an integral part of our urban greenspace. As such, they have provided attractive landscapes that could often be enjoyed by a wider circle of people than just their academic staff, students and gardeners.

While these botanic gardens were initially privately owned, often by the universities, they did function to some extent as semi-public landscapes.

One of these earliest plant collections of note in Britain was not a formal botanical garden but the private endeavour of a dedicated individual. Friar Henry Daniel's fourteenth century garden at Bow in London, in which he grew 252 different kinds of plants, has been described as possible the first early botanic garden in Europe (Keiser 1996; Hobhouse 2002, 117). While Daniel's principal interest was in herbal medicine, there is evidence from his own herbal that his garden contained a range of trees and shrubs.

The first true botanic garden was established in Italy in 1543 at the University of Pisa (Oldfield 2007, 11). Other Italian universities quickly followed suit and gardens were created at Padova (1545), Firenze (1545) and Bologna (1547). These very early botanic gardens were purely for the academic study of medicinal plants. In the sixteenth and seventeenth century botanic gardens in Europe experienced a change of usage with the beginnings of the age of exploration and international trade. Instead of focusing primarily on medicine, much wider scientific, economic and even aesthetic objectives gained increasing importance.

The University of Oxford Botanic Garden was the first to be established in Britain, founded in 1621 as a physic garden with a mission to promote learning and the glory of God (Hyams and MacQuitty 1969, 102–3). Always a very small garden close to the heart of the city, it still manages to accommodate a remarkable number of trees, some of great age and rarity. The oldest tree to be seen in the garden today is an English yew, planted in 1645 (Oldfield 2007, 13). Oxford was followed in 1670 by the Royal Botanic Gardens Edinburgh, also originally founded as a physic garden to grow medicinal plants (Hyams and MacQuitty 1969, 44–8). This grew in size and statute over many years when in 1820 the Regius Keeper, Robert Graham, asked the Principal Gardener, William MacNab, to organise the moving of its plant collection, including many mature trees, to a new site. This massive undertaking confirmed the soundness of MacNab's pioneering technique for moving large trees. The exercise took three years to complete and used specially designed machinery that MacNab had invented. The botanic gardens at Edinburgh have allowed public access for many decades and continue to be a popular and beautiful open space in the heart of the city.

Three more botanic gardens were established by institutions in Britain in the seventeenth and eighteenth century (Ballard 2003, 11–13). These were Chelsea Physic Garden (1673), Glasgow (1705) and Cambridge (1760). Then, in the first fifty years of the nineteenth century a further seventeen botanic gardens were founded. The impetus for this came from a dramatic increase in plant introductions which were then flooding into Britain and from a desire by the founders to emulate the earlier institutions. The first of these was Liverpool Gardens which opened in 1802, followed by other large towns and cities such as Hull (1812), Manchester (1831), Birmingham (1832), Bath (1834), Sheffield (1836) and Leeds (1840). Many of these gardens were located in rapidly expanding industrial centres and were often created thanks to generous private donations and subscriptions. In the early nineteenth century, before the establishment of public parks, these subscription botanic gardens provided a vital recreational and educational resource that was especially appreciated by the expanding middle class.

Despite their relatively small size, the Liverpool and Hull botanic gardens both had impressive tree collections (Elliott, *et al.* 2011, 65–7). William Roscoe, the designer and one of the benefactors of the five-acre Liverpool garden, believed that public institutions were especially able to plant and preserve trees, providing the continuity, skills and knowledge necessary for their study and exploitation. To this end, part of the garden featured an extensive collection of labelled trees and shrubs from around the world, reflecting Liverpool's international maritime links. In the 1830s, the garden was relocated and the Wavertree Botanic Garden is now a popular public park managed by Liverpool City Council. At Hull, rare trees were placed throughout the garden providing the local gentry with an opportunity to inspect these before deciding what to plant on their country estates. The Hull garden also helped inspire Peter Watson's (1824) *Dendrologia Britannica*, one of the most important arboricultural treatise of the early eighteenth century and an inspiration for Loudon's *Arboretum Britannicum*.

The Manchester Botanic Garden opened in 1831 and, after a chequered history that included national fame and financial disaster, effectively ceased to exist in 1908 (Brooks 2011). It seems remarkable that such a prestigious horticultural and botanical institution could achieve such recognition in its time and yet be almost forgotten today. Fortunately, the Birmingham Botanical Gardens that opened in 1832 fared much better (Ballard 2003) (Figure 70). This was laid out by Loudon who prepared a plan for the 16-acre (6 ha) site at Edgbaston and although there has been some important improvements with the addition of modern amenities, the overall appearance of the gardens has changed little. As might be expected of Loudon, the planting plan included a wonderful selection of trees and shrubs, all detailed in the catalogue of plants produced in 1836 (*ibid.*, 131–47). Over the years, the gardens have trained many talented individuals, most notably the eminent arboriculturist and plant collector, E. H. Wilson, who undertook his training there from 1893–97.

Opening in 1836, Sheffield Botanical Gardens was another subscription garden that was designed by the leading landscape designer Robert Marnock (Woustra 2007). Loudon visited the gardens in 1839 and commented favourably on all aspects, especially the collection of hardy trees and shrubs in the arboretum and fruticetum, which in his view was so arranged to show them at their best. Sheffield has been another botanical garden to experience difficulties periodically over its lifetime (Hunter 2007). In 1897, falling income, competition from the new free parks and proposals to build residential development posed a major threat to its future. Now in the twenty-first century, the future looks much brighter with a major restoration programme just completed with a substantial grant from the Heritage Lottery Fund.

In addition to the institutional botanic gardens founded in the eighteenth and nineteenth century, certain private individuals also laid out botanic gardens. The most famous of these was the Royal Garden at Kew, established by the Princess Augusta in the late 1750s (Paterson 2008). In 1840, the gardens at Kew were adopted as the national botanical institution with the establishment of Royal Botanic Gardens (RBG), Kew. Over some 250 years, Kew has built its reputation as one of the world's leading botanical institutions and centre of horticultural education and research. In terms of the actual gardens, its remarkable tree collection dominates its landscape and, together with the magnificent glasshouses, are the features most fondly remembered by visitors. Throughout the 1840s and '50s, extensive tree planting bolstered the newly established arboretum and pinetum. By the 1870s, the pinetum alone held over 1000 trees, due to the many new introductions from the west coast of North America (*ibid.*, 157). Unfortunately, Victorian London's polluted air severely damaged many of Kew's conifers or at least stunted their growth. Eventually, an alternative site for conifers became available when the National Conifer Collection (now the National Pinetum) was set up in 1924. This was established amid clean rural air at Bedgebury in East Sussex, with support from the Forestry Commission that owned the land (*ibid.*, 186).

Some other gardens in London were initiatives of what is now known as the Royal Horticultural Society (RHS) (Elliott 2004, 59–75). In 1816, the Society had announced that it had no intention of establishing a 'public garden'. Over the next few years, however, the increasing quantities of plant material it was receiving prompted it to rent a garden site in Kensington that was sufficient for the immediate needs of plant storage. By the middle of the 1820s the Kensington site was becoming cramped and in 1821 a more permanent garden was leased from the Duke of Devonshire at Chiswick. This was established as an experimental garden and by the end of the 1820s there was no significant rival to Cheswick that could offer the same facilities or programmes. At that time, there were no public parks and its closest rivals were the small botanic gardens at Liverpool and Hull. The extent of its tree and shrub collection was especially impressive. This included not only an orchard area of many types of fruit trees but also an extensive arboretum, laid out initially as a collection of tree and shrub beds intermixed with some scattered trees. Loudon was critical of this design and declared he could see neither 'beauty nor fitness' in any part of the plan. Much of the initial tree planting at Chiswick had been very dense, with the intention of thinning this out by half as it matured. Unfortunately, this did not happen as planned and by 1850 the overcrowding of trees in the arboretum was described as 'a forest scene'. A drastic programme of thinning was finally undertaken, followed by extensive replanting. In 1861, the RHS developed a new garden at South Kensington, mainly because it wanted to be closer to central London where its shows could compete more successfully

FIGURE 70 *(above)*. Birmingham Botanical Gardens were designed by Loudon and opened in 1832. The gardens are on a 16-acre (6.5 ha) site at Edgbaston just two miles from the city centre. This view shows the terrace outside the main buildings and glasshouses.

FIGURE 71 *(right)*. One of the ancient sweet chestnut trees (*Castanea sativa*) on the course of the Edgbaston Golf Club, located near the centre of Birmingham. The original landscape was designed by Capability Brown in 1776 for the Gough Calthorpe family who lived at Edgbaston Hall, now used by as the club house.

PHOTO: SUE GRIFFITHS

with its rivals, namely the Royal Botanical Society's garden at Regent's Park and the new public park at Crystal Palace. The RHS garden at Kensington was landscaped by William Andrews Nesfield, who had previously worked on designs for the RBG Kew. The site was cleared of its existing trees and a great many mature trees were transplanted there from Chiswick and other sources, including some donated by Prince Albert. The style of the garden represented the culmination of the Italian garden in Britain and its influence was immediate and widespread. However, within a few years of its opening, complaints began to be made about the lack of shelter and especially about the problems of air pollution with 'miserable-looking, soot-begrimed trees'. Part of the problem was the general lack of mature tree cover, leaving the site too open. Attempts were made to rectify this that including planting many more trees and creating groves. During the latter part of the nineteenth century, the garden underwent various changes in its design and its fortunes until it finally closed in 1882. The Chiswick garden was also closed in 1905 after the RHS had moved its headquarters to its new garden at Wisley in rural Surrey.

The introduction and extent of wider public access to these botanic gardens varied considerably with different institutions. For example, in 1820 requests from members of the public to visit RBG Kew were quite unusual and when accommodated the visitors were escorted around the gardens by staff. By 1861 annual visitor numbers had swelled to over 500,000 and the gardens were one of the capital's major attractions (Paterson 2008, 139). By the end of the nineteenth century, full public access had become the custom in most of the major botanic gardens.

University, college and school grounds

Many of the older universities had always had fine ornamental gardens and picturesque parkland surrounding their academic buildings, which were for the enjoyment of staff and students as well as the visiting public. The colleges at Oxford, Cambridge and some other ancient academic institutions prided themselves in their immaculately kept gardens and were usually keen to show these off to visitors of discerning taste. During the seventeenth century, the first provincial public walks appear to have been planted by Oxford and Cambridge colleges (Borsay 1986, 126). In the 1850s, to the benefit of the people of Mid-Victorian Oxford which had no urban park at that time, the university greatly extended its area of parkland and opened this to public access. It purchased a total of 91 acres (37 ha) of land from Merton College, ostensibly to provide a site for a museum, but was able to use the rest of the land for sport and recreation (Steane 2004, 88–9). James Bateman, the creator of the gardens at Biddulph Grange, submitted a design for the new Oxford University Parks and despite some subsequent modification the layout still remains much as Bateman intended. Over many years, the parks have built up a superb collection of fine mature trees that are much appreciated for their beauty and as objects for study.

Leicester University has an accumulation of fabulous Arts and Crafts gardens, which were formerly the private gardens of a society of successful industrialists (Brown 1999, 214). These gardens contain a fine collection of mature trees, both native and exotic. Yet another university that has accumulated an impressive tree collection is Nottingham. The University Park is laid out largely in the English landscape style but this also includes a number of discrete gardens with their own arboreal gems.

Of all the university campuses in Britain, the University of Exeter has one of the most outstanding tree collections and this only a few miles from the city centre (Caldwell and Proctor 1969). The beautiful estate of some 300 acres (121 ha) contains a marvellous range of fine mature trees, shrubs and other plants. A substantial part of the estate was initially in the private hands of the Thornton West family who had the grounds of their mansion landscaped in the second half of the nineteenth century by the famous nursery firm of Veitch. A key feature of this was the arboretum and pinetum containing specimens of trees that Veitch had sourced from all over the world. Due to a decline in the fortunes of the owners, the estate was in a neglected state almost to the point of being derelict when it was taken over by the university in 1922. The university has always been very conscious of its magnificent heritage of trees and shrubs and has subsequently maintained this to a high standard as a major attraction for students, staff and visitors.

Just as some universities have contributed much to our urban treecover over the centuries, so also have some schools (Mitchell 1974, 404). This applies particularly to those schools from the independent sector located in and around our towns and cities. These include a number of Britain's old public schools that have always had extensive grounds and fine trees, while other independent schools may have been founded in former eighteenth and nineteenth century houses and estates and inherited a fine tree collection from their gardens or pleasure grounds.

Hospitals, asylums and therapeutic landscapes

Gardens have a long association with medical and therapeutic institutions. In ancient Greece, Hippocrates used his garden for the rehabilitation and treatment of his patients, something that reflected his belief in the power of nature to keep life in balance. In medieval Britain, monastic infirmaries invariably had gardens for the cultivation of herbs and scented plants for medicinal purposes. These gardens were also beneficial for the sick and the convalescent and provided a natural extension of the infirmary space (Rawcliffe 2008, 15). At St Giles' Hospital in Norwich, the surrounding landscape with its trees, gardens and orchards was utilised in many ways, both economically and in the treatments. The landscape not only provided food, fuel and medicinal plants but also engendered a sense of spiritual and psychological well-being (Rawcliffe 1999, 51). As the medical profession became more involved with hospitals towards the end of the eighteenth century, doctors began to suggest they should be purpose-built (Hickman 2013, 17). Gardens in some form were increasingly considered a part of that, with their therapeutic role focusing on their ability to provide fresh air and allow opportunities for exercise (*ibid.*, 119).

With the advent of the Victorian period, hospitals of all types were to undergo significant development, both structurally and clinically in their approach to medicine and treatments. For example, there was an increasing awareness that the hospital itself could be a dangerous place as a source of disease, often full of 'miasmas' or 'bad air' (Hickman 2013, 126). Better ventilation was part of the response to that and this included promoting a pavilion design for wards and the use of gardens. For many general hospitals in urban areas, finding space for a garden of any size was often difficult. By the end of the Victorian era, purpose-built sanatoria were being constructed specifically for the treatment of tuberculosis, where exposing the patient to fresh air and a pleasant view was a vital part of the treatment. Consequently, these were in quite rural locations and surrounded with attractive gardens. Gertrude Jekyll ventured into therapeutic landscape design when she provided planting plans for the private King Edward VII Sanatorium at Midhurst, Sussex (*ibid.*, 174–8). This had magnificent pine woodland, a common feature of tuberculosis sanatoria which marked them out from other types of hospital landscape. In the past few decades there has been much emphasis on the provision of gardens and attractive landscapes for general hospitals. This was prompted by Robert Ulrich's landmark research that found that post-surgical patients with a view of trees in full foliage versus patients with a view of a brick wall had shorter post-operative hospital stays, required less medication, and experienced few post-surgical complications (Ulrich 1984).

Of the various hospitals developed during the Victorian era, asylums were especially notable for their extensive landscapes with an emphasis on the use of trees and shrubs. From the mid-nineteenth century it became common for patients with mental illness or disability to be treated in purpose-built therapeutic estates known as asylums (Rutherford 2005, 61). The Lunatic Act of 1845 had forced counties to provide publicly-funded treatment for pauper lunatics. By the time of the First World War, there were 102 asylums in England and Wales with a total of nearly 109,000 patients (Rutherford 2013b, 6). Most were located in the urban fringe of major towns and cities that were their main service or catchment areas. London eventually had 20 public asylums, averaging more than 2000 patients each.

The asylum was a distinct landscape type with its design based on private asylum buildings and landscape developed in the eighteenth century, using models such as Brislington House, Bristol (Hickman 2005). Whether they were public institutions for paupers or private asylums for the middle class, the style was based largely on the classic English landscape park and garden. This model was adopted because it addressed the needs of an extensive building complex, which required ornamental grounds and an element of agricultural self-sufficiency. The landscape of the asylum was an integral part of the therapeutic regime, reflecting the 'moral therapy' approach to mental disorder that centred on placing the patient in a carefully designed relaxing environment which minimised the use of restraints and encouraged self-discipline (Hickman 2013, 25–6). Prominent landscape features included ornamented drives, avenues, parkland, pleasure grounds and kitchen gardens (Rutherford 2005, 63). The main physical difference between the country house and the asylum estate was the introduction of closed exercise yards, or airing courts, next to the main asylum buildings. The airing courts had an ornamental layout of lawns, paths and often borders with a pleasant view out that was intended to calm and cheer the patients. The boundaries were either fenced, walled or ha-has were used in reversed form to ensure the patients benefited from the views but could not escape.

The grounds of asylums were laid out by professional landscape designers (Rutherford 2005). Although there is no evidence of work by any of the 'superstars' of the time, such as Loudon, Paxton and Nesfield, some other well-known figures did get involved, such as Robert Marnock, Edward Milner, Henry Milner and Alexander McKenzie. One designer stands out as a specialist in this field: the horticulturist Robert Lloyd, Head Gardener at the Brookwood Asylum, who undertook several commissions. William Goldring also emerged as a professional freelance designer who also had an asylum specialism. As many of these landscape designers had substantial experience of laying out public parks and cemeteries, it is not surprising that the planting schemes for asylums should feature a similar range of trees and shrubs, with the usual emphasis on evergreens. Tree planting often occurred at a relatively early stage in the construction of the asylum, although sometimes this was left until after the opening to be undertaken by male patients as a therapeutic activity that also had the advantage of reduced cost (*ibid.*, 74).

In the latter part of the twentieth century, many of these asylums either closed or evolved into modern psychiatric hospitals (Rutherford 2013b, 51). Of those that evolved, the fundamental structure of their buildings remained largely the same but the standard of maintenance and management of their landscapes declined. In the past few decades many of those remaining large psychiatric hospitals have themselves closed due to developments in medication, the opening of specialist psychiatric units in general hospitals and instigation of 'care in the community' regimes. The sites of these former asylums have since been redeveloped, often as new housing estates, although some of their magnificent trees have been retained.

Seaside resorts

Related to the topic of therapeutic landscapes are the spa towns and seaside resorts that emerged in the eighteenth century. A spa town is a specialist resort situated around a mineral spa which people visit to 'take the waters' and sometimes to bathe for its supposed health benefits (Borsay 1989, 31). Although some locations were used in Roman times, they came to the fore after the Restoration and particularly in the early 1700s. The city of Bath soon emerged as the leader in spa resorts, followed by other locations around England such as Buxton in Derbyshire, Leamington Spa in Warwickshire and Tunbridge Wells in Kent. Other examples were Strathpeffer in Scotland and Builth Wells in Wales. With the spa towns becoming increasingly fashionable, considerable attention was given to creating a green and pleasant landscape that complemented the splendid architecture of their prominent buildings. As these landscapes were not significantly different from other fashionable towns that were not spa resorts, we will not focus on them here. By contrast, seaside resorts have tended to have treecover and landscapes with a quite distinct character, largely by virtual of their coastal location.

Sea-bathing was practiced in Kent and Lancashire as early the 1720s and by the mid-eighteenth century was becoming common in several early resorts (Brodie and Winter 2007, 11). Visitors were initially just a few wealthy people in search of cures for their ailments through the supposed beneficial effects of the fresh sea air and cold water bathing. Early seaside attractions often included tree-lined promenades or walks along the seafront where visitors could take in the bracing sea air. Ladies Walk at Liverpool was a typical example (Borsay 2013, 56–7). In 1750, this was reported as being a very fine location, commanding views over the sea and divided into three parts by narrow strips of grass and two rows of trees. The sea view and the beauty of the natural landscape were considered an essential part of the visitor experience.

By the end of the eighteenth century, there was a network of resorts across Britain catering for a range of tastes and pockets (Brodie and Winter 2007, 11). These often developed around small existing settlements but others were entire new ventures. Initially, they were created by wealthy landowners and entrepreneurs, who built new residential properties often in the form of squares or crescents with communal gardens (*ibid.*, 65–6). For example, Kemp Town in Brighton was a residential estate started in 1823 by the politician Thomas Read Kemp, with gardens designed by Henry Phillips, the well-known local landscape gardener and horticulturist (Coats 1971, 3).

From the early nineteenth century, the motivation for people to visit the seaside evolved to become less about promoting their health and wellbeing and more about enjoying a range of leisure and entertainment opportunities. Commercial pleasure gardens were created, similar to those in other towns and cities, including seven which opened in and around Brighton before 1840 (Berry 2000, 225). With the advent of the Victorian era and the growth of local government, public finances were also used to increase the visitor attractions of the resort, with the building of piers, the laying out of public parks and gardens and the planting of street trees (Brodie and Winter 2007, 32). A popular landscape feature was the promenade running along the top of the sea wall providing visitors with a healthy, bracing place to walk and socialise (*ibid.*, 36). These were often the location of formal gardens or mini-parks, usually in the form of long relatively narrow rectangular beds, whose shrubs and bedding plants were carefully chosen to be colourful yet robust enough to withstand storms and tolerate salt sea spray. Photographs of these promenades from Victorian and Edwardian times suggest that trees were not a common feature (Hannavy 2003). The arrival of the motor car in the early decades of the twentieth century saw many of these promenades eventually transformed into busy seafront roads and their gardens converted to car parks (Brodie and Winter 2007, 61)

After the First World War, local authorities in seaside resorts maintained their interest in creating public parks (Cherry *et al.* 1993, 316). For example, in 1922 Blackpool Corporation requested Thomas Mawson, the eminent landscape architect, to prepare plans for a new 280 acre (113 ha) town park, Stanley Park, with peripheral residential areas. The work led to his involvement in the new South Shore extensions, including Ashton Marine park, which stretched along the sea front to the borough of St Anne's, and covered a total of 127 acres (51 ha), including the promenade and a housing estate. Mawson was then invited to submit a scheme for the whole of the Borough. Mawson was also employed by the other resort towns of Hastings and St Leonards on the south-east coast, and Weston-super-Mare on the Bristol Channel.

Horticultural and arboricultural literature in the nineteenth century makes little mention of the ornamental use of trees and shrubs in seaside locations. Even the enlarged edition of Loudon's *Encyclopaedia of Gardening* has virtually nothing to say on the subject (Loudon 1835). While William Ablett's 1880 book *English Trees and Tree-Planting* has a chapter on 'sea-side planting', this refers to forestry plantations and shelterbelts and not ornamental planting (Ablett 1880, 404–13) However, with the enormous popularity of the seaside in Edwardian times this situation changed. To meet the demand for specialist knowledge about the cultivation of ornamental trees and shrubs in seaside locations, a growing number of books and articles on the subject were published (Gaut 1907; Webster 1918). These gave lists of tree and shrub species suitable for both structural and ornamental planting in coastal areas. In more recent years, palm-like trees and shrubs have become a popular choice, with species such as cabbage palm (*Cordyline australis*) and Chusan palm (*Trachycarpus fortunei*), to give the resort something of a subtropical or 'Riviera' look. Lots of colourful bedding displays have also been a traditional feature of British seaside resorts.

There has always been quite fierce competition between seaside resorts in the extent and splendour of their horticultural displays and landscape features. When the British Tourist Society launched its 'Britain in Bloom' competition in 1963, an entry category was created for coastal towns and seaside resorts. The competition is now held under the auspices of the Royal Horticultural Society (Elliott 2004, 351).

Golf courses

Golf courses in and around towns and cities are another landscape form that has contributed much tree cover to our urban forests. Ever since Edwardian times when the game of golf became popular with the working class, the number of golf courses in Britain has grown at a remarkable rate (Cousins 1975, 86–93). A recent survey has indicated that a very large proportion of these are now located in and around urban centres (De Castella 2013).

The basic landscape of the golf course, with its broad expanses of lawn plus clumps and belts of trees to separate fairways and offer a backdrop to greens, has obvious similarities with the classic English landscape (Elliott 1986, 242). It is not surprising that a number of former eighteenth and nineteenth century estates have been converted into golf courses. A good example is Edgbaston Hall near Birmingham, formerly the home of the Gough Calthorpe family. In 1776, Sir Henry Gough commissioned Capability Brown to lay out the park with much of his work focusing on avenues and stands of trees (Stroud 1975, 224). This is now leased by the Calthorpe family to the private Edgbaston Golf Club that has used the land for their course since 1936. This outstanding landscape just two miles from the city centre has some fine ancient sweet chestnuts (*Castanea sativa*) and other veteran trees (Figure 71). Another example of a notable landscape partly converted to a private golf course is Cassiobury Park in Hertfordshire, initially laid out in the seventeenth century by Moses Cook for the Earl of Essex and praised by John Evelyn (Lasdun 1991, 188).

As golf became more popular among the working class, local authorities developed municipal golf courses to meet the growing demand of their urban population. As with many private clubs, some of these courses were converted from the former estates of aristocrats and wealthy industrialists that they had recently purchased for the public. Others were carved out of areas of existing municipal parks as local authorities attempted to expand their range of recreation facilities. An example was Heaton Park in Manchester, when part of this was opened as the city's first municipal course in 1911 (O'Reilly 2013, 146). It covered 140 acres (57 ha) and much of the impetus behind its establishment was due to other cities making similar provision in their public parks. At the opening ceremony, the Lord Mayor expressed the hope that the working class would use the course and that they might "find the game well within their means" (Anon 1911, 3). At a cost of one shilling for the first round of golf, it was not likely to be the case. One golfer commented that the difficulty posed by the course would deter those who were beginners and that the facility was therefore more suited to those who were already members of other, more expensive, courses elsewhere. Despite this rather shaky start, municipal golf in Manchester eventually flourished as many more courses were established.

The conversion of parts of public parks into municipal golf courses has not always met with the approval of local residents, particularly those who do not play golf. In some respects the similarities with the English landscape park can be seen to go further than simply the style of the landscape. Just as the country estates of the aristocracy and wealthy industrialists were landscapes of exclusion, so too are most golf courses as they can only be enjoyed by club members or their guests. In the case of municipal golf courses, there may be objections when a public park freely enjoyed by all then becomes an exclusive landscape for the benefit of a select group of people.

Roof gardens

We tend not to think of roof gardens in an historical context or in terms of mature trees. However, that would be a mistake. One of the earliest British references to urban roof gardens can be found in Thomas Fairchild's early eighteenth century work *The City Gardener* when he talks of growing current trees "even upon the Leads on the Tops of Houses amidst the Chimneys" (Fairchild 1722, 57). According to Fairchild they can be kept successfully in pots or cases if attention is given to adequate watering. One well-documented roof garden from the nineteenth century belonged to Elizabeth Kent and was set high above St Paul's Churchyard, where her stepfather ran his bookseller's business (Willes 2014, 163). In her book *Flora Domestica, or, the portable Flower-Garden*, published in 1823, she wrote of how she managed to grow flowers, shrubs and even small trees in pots (Kent 1823). She may well have inspired Charles Dickens to include the roof garden of Mr Riah, the Jewish money-lender, in his novel *Our Mutual Friend* (Willes 2014, 164).

The 1920s and '30s saw the heyday of the roof garden in London and these splendid creations attracted national attention that helped promote other roof gardens in the provinces. First, there was the roof garden at Selfridge's store in Oxford Street, undoubtedly the place to be seen in the 1920s (Anon 2011). Crowds would ascend on the top of the building to meet with friends, watch fashion shows and even play a round of crazy golf. As well as lawns, herbaceous borders and shrubs, there were also some trees, although these were clipped evergreens and kept quite small. Although the Selfridges building itself survived the Second World War comparatively unscathed, the roof garden was destroyed in the Blitz and never re-opened to the public again until major redevelopment in 2009.

The most famous London roof garden of the 1930s was on top of the Derry and Tom's store in High Street Kensington (MacLeod 1972, 285–7). The gardens were designed by the landscape architect Ralph Hancock and opened in 1938 as a spectacular novelty to attract people to the store. Its three themed gardens covering a total of 1.5 acres (0.6 ha) have changed little over the years. The Spanish garden is based very loosely on the Alhambra and has a distinct Moorish flavour (Figure 72). The Tudor Garden is filled with evergreen shrubs surrounded by fragrant lilies, roses, lavender and plenty of trailing wisteria. The most surprising of the three is the English Woodland, a small woodland garden where a meandering stream flows through the grove of trees. This is best

FIGURE 72. The Spanish Garden, one of three themed gardens at The Roof Gardens, Kensington, originally called the Derry and Toms Roof Garden and opened in 1938. In the tranquillity of this beautiful garden it is hard to imagine you are 100 feet (30 m) above High Street Kensington, one of the busiest roads in central London.

PHOTO: THE ROOF GARDENS

seen in the spring months, when thousands of narcissus, crocus, muscari and anemones burst into life. In addition to these fabulous landscapes, what makes Derry and Tom's roof garden so extraordinary is the trees. There are around 125 of these, with 50 of them in the woodland garden, including some quite large oaks planted some 75 years ago when the garden was constructed. These mature trees grow in just 5 ft (1.5 m) of soil. In the Second World War a bomb damaged the Spanish Garden and one landed in the Woodland Garden but did not explode. Other roof gardens in London were not so fortunate, either destroyed in the Blitz like Selfridge's or neglected over the war years and later abandoned.

One of the most notable roof gardens created in the provinces was at Harvey's store in Guildford (Brown 1999, 309). Designed by the landscape architect, Sir Geoffrey Jellicoe, this opened in 1956 and continues today. Although the garden has a few shrubby trees, the emphasis is on flowers and water. Despite their obvious commercial attractions, there has been no ongoing tradition of roof gardens in Britain. While 'green roofs' have been popular recently, these are primarily for environmental and conservation objectives, rather than as amenity landscapes. However, roof gardens with plenty of trees could soon be a prominent feature of towns and cities in Britain, as the demands on urban space increase and architectural and engineering solutions become more imaginative.

References

Ablett, W. H. (1880) *English Trees and Tree-planting*. Smith, Elder and Co: London.

Allan, M. (1982) *William Robinson 1838–1935: Father of the English Flower Garden*. Faber and Faber: London.

Amherst, A. (1907) *London Parks and Gardens*. Writing as the Hon. Mrs Evelyn Cecil. A. Constable and Co: London.

Anon (1911) Municipal Golf. *Manchester Courier*, 8 September, 1911, 3.

Anon (2011) Boating Lake with a View! Selfridges Opens Rooftop to Visitors for the First Time Since WWII. *Daily Mail*, 22 July 2011. Available at: http://www.dailymail.co.uk/travel/article-2017623/Selfridges-opens-rooftop-reveal-lake-cocktail-bar.html (accessed 25 May 2014).

Bailey, B. (1987) *Churchyards of England and Wales*. Robert Hale: London.

Ballard, P. (2003) *An Oasis of Delight: The History of Birmingham Botanic Gardens*. Revised edition. Brewin Books: Studley.

Berry, S. (2000) Pleasure Gardens in Georgian and Regency Seaside Resorts: Brighton, 1750–1840. *Garden History*, 222–230.

Borsay, P. (1986) The Rise of the Promenade: the Social and Cultural Use of Space in the English Provincial Town *c.* 1660–1800. *Journal for Eighteenth-Century Studies* 9(2), 125–140.

Borsay, P. (2013) Pleasure Gardens and Urban Culture in the Long Eighteenth Century. In Conlin, J. (ed.) *The Pleasure Garden, from Vauxhall to Coney Island*. University of Pennsylvania Press: Philadelphia.

Brodie, A. and Winter, G. (2007) *England's Seaside Resorts*. English Heritage: Swindon.

Brooks, A. (2011) *'A Veritable Eden' – The Manchester Botanic Garden: A History*. Windgather Press: Oxford.

Brown, J. (1999) *The Pursuit of Paradise: A Social History of Gardens and Gardening*. Harper Collins: London.

Caldwell, J. and Proctor, M. C. F. (1969) *The Grounds and Gardens of the University of Exeter*. University of Exeter: Exeter.

Cherry, G. E., Jordan, H., and Kafkoula, K. (1993) Gardens, Civic Art and Town Planning: The Work of Thomas H. Mawson (1861–1933). *Planning Perspective* 8(3), 307–332.

Coats, M. (1971) A Forgotten Gardener: Henry Phillips, 1779–1840. *The Garden History Society Newsletter*, No. 14 (Sep. 1), 2–4.

Cocke, T. (2012) *The Churchyards Handbook*. Fourth edition. Church House Publishing: London.

Conway, H. (1991) *People's Parks: The Design and Development of Victorian Parks in Britain*. Cambridge University Press: Cambridge.

Cornish, V. (1946) *The Churchyard Yew and Immortality*. Frederick Muller: London.

Cousins, G. (1975) *Golf in Britain: A Social History From the Beginnings to the Present Day*. Routledge and Kegan Paul: London.

Curl, J. S. (2000) *The Victorian Celebration of Death*. Sutton Publishing: Stroud.

De Castella, T. (2013) How Much of the UK is Covered in Golf Courses? *BBC Magazine*, 24 December, 2014. British Broadcasting Corporation: London. Available at: http://www.bbc.co.uk/news/magazine-24378868 (accessed 30 May 2014).

Elliott, B. (1986) *Victorian Gardens*. B. T. Batsford: London.

Elliott, B. (2004) *The Royal Horticultural Society: A History 1804–2004*. Phillimore: Chichester.

Elliott, P. A., Watkins, C. and Daniels, S. (2011) *The British Arboretum: Trees, Science and Culture in the Nineteenth Century*. Pickering and Chatto: London.

Etlin, R. A. (1984) Père Lachaise and the Garden Cemetery. *The Journal of Garden History* 4(3), 211–222.

Fairchild, T. (1722) *The City Gardener*. T. Woodward and J. Peele: London.

Gaut, A. (1907) *Seaside Planting of Trees and Shrubs*. Country Life: London.

Hannavy, J. (2003) *The English Seaside in Victorian and Edwardian Times*. A Shire History in Camera book. Shire publications: Princes Risborough.

Harding, V. (1990) Gardens and Open Space in Tudor and Early Stuart London. In Galinou, M., *London's Pride: The Glorious History of the Capital's Gardens*: Anaya Publishers: London.

Hardwicke, W. (1877) House Accommodation and Open Space. *Transactions of the National Association for the Promotion of Social Science*, 513.

Hickman, C. (2005) The Picturesque at Brislington House, Bristol: the Role of Landscape in Relation to the Treatment of Mental Illness in the Early Nineteenth-century Asylum. *Garden History*, 47–60.

Hickman, C. (2013) *Therapeutic Landscapes: A History of English Hospital Gardens Since 1800*. Manchester University Press: Manchester.

Hobhouse, P. (2002) *The Story of Gardening*. Dorling Kindersley: London.

Hunter, A. (2007) *Sheffield Botanical Gardens: People, Plants and Pavilions*. Friends of the Botanical Gardens: Sheffield.

Hyams, E. and MacQuitty, W. (1969) *Great Botanical Gardens of the World*. Macmillan: New York.

Jones, O. (2007) Arnos Vale Cemetery and the Lively Materialities of Trees in Place. *Garden History*, 149–171.

Jupp, P. C. (2006) *From Dust to Ashes: Cremation and the British Way of Death*. Palgrave Macmillan: Basingstoke.

Keiser, G. R. (1996) Through a Fourteenth-Century Gardener's Eyes: Henry Daniel's Herbal. *The Chaucer Review*, 58–75.

Kent, E. (1823) *Flora Domestica, or, the Portable Flower-Garden*. Printed for Taylor and Hessey: London.

Lasdun, S. (1991) *The English Park: Royal, Private and Public*. Andre Deutsch: London.

Loudon, J. C. (1835) *Encyclopaedia of Gardening, Comprising the Theory and Practice of Horticulture, Floriculture, Arboriculture and Landscape-gardening*. A new edition. Longman, Rees, Orme, Brown, Green and Longmans: London.

Loudon, J. C. (1843) *On the Laying Out, Planting, and Managing of Cemeteries, and on the improvement of Churchyards*. Longman, Brown, Green and Longmans: London.

MacLeod, D. (1972) *The Gardener's London*. Gerald Duckworth: London.

Milner, H. E. (1890) *The Art and Practice of Landscape Gardening*. Published by The Author and Simpkin, Marshall, Hamilton, Kent and Co: London.

Mitchell, A. (1974) *A Field Guide to the Trees of Britain and Northern Europe*. Collins: London.

Morris, S. (1991) Legacy of a Bishop: The Trees and Shrubs of Fulham Palace Gardens Introduced 1675–1713. *Garden History*, 47–59.

Oldfield, S. (2007) *Great Botanic Gardens of the World*. New Holland Publishers Ltd: London.

O'Malley, B. B. (1997) *A Pilgrim's Manual: St. Davids*. Canterbury Press: Norwich.

O'Reilly, C. (2013) From 'the people' to 'the citizen': the emergence of the Edwardian municipal park in Manchester, 1902–1912. *Urban History* 40(01), 136–155.

Paterson, A. (2008) *The Gardens at Kew*. Frances Lincoln: London.

Rawcliffe, C. (1999) *Medicine for the Soul: The Life, Death and Resurrection of an English Medieval Hospital, St Giles's, Norwich, c. 1249–1550*. Alan Sutton Publishing: Stroud.

Rawcliffe, C. (2008). 'Delectable Sightes and Fragrant Smelles': Gardens and Health in Late Medieval and Early Modern England. *Garden History*, 3–21.

Robinson, W. (1880) *God's Acre Beautiful: or, The Cemeteries of the Future*. Garden Office: London

Rugg, J. (2000) Defining the Place of Burial: What Makes a Cemetery a Cemetery? *Mortality* 5(3), 259–275.

Rutherford, S. (2005) Landscapers for the Mind: English Asylum Designers, 1845–1914. *Garden History*, 61–86.

Rutherford, S. (2013a) *The Victorian Cemetery*. Shire Publications: Oxford.

Rutherford, S. (2013b) *The Victorian Asylum*. Shire Publications: Oxford.

Steane, J. (2004) The Oxford University Parks: the First Fifty Years. *Garden History*, 87–100.

Stokes, J. and Rodger, D. (2004) *The Heritage Trees of Britain and Northern Ireland*. Constable: London.

Stroud, D. (1975) *Capability Brown*. Faber and Faber: London

Swanton, E. W. (1958) *The Yew Trees of England*. Langham Herald Press: Farnham and Haslemere.

Ulrich, Roger S. (1984) View through a window may influence recovery from surgery. *Science*. New Series 224(4647), 420–421.

Watson, P. W. (1824) *Dendrologia Britannica, Or Trees and Shrubs That Will Live in the Open Air of Britain Throughout the Year*. Printed for the author by John and Arthur Arch: Cornhill.

Webster, A. D. (1918) Seaside Planting: For Shelter, Ornament and Profit. T. Fisher Unwin: London.

Wienrich, S. and Speyer, J. (eds) (2003) *The Natural Death Handbook*. Fourth revised edition. Rider: London.

Willes, M. (2014) *The Gardens of the British Working Class*. Yale University Press: New Haven and London.

Woudstra, J. (2007) Robert Marnock and the Creation of the Sheffield Botanical and Horticultural Gardens, 1834–40. *Garden History*, 2–36.

8

Visions of Urban Green

....

Throughout our history there have always been a few far-sighted individuals who have conjured up visions of British towns and cities in a golden age in the future. Instead of the invariable negative reality of an urban existence in their own age, they have not only dreamt of a green and pleasant urban future but described this in detail. Furthermore, not only have they often urged their fellow citizens to turn those visions into reality, they have also played a leading role themselves in creating these new settlements. In this final chapter we explore the extent to which these visionary ideas and practical initiatives have embraced urban trees and woodland and highlight some of their innovative landscape and arboricultural practice.

Early Utopian communities and ideas

Some notable early texts inspired visions of the future with fictional descriptions of harmonious and prosperous places, such as Sir Thomas More's book *Utopia* first published in Latin in 1516 (More 1895). However, it was not until the dawn of the Industrial Revolution that any significant attempts were made to create new planned settlements based on visionary ideas. The Moravian settlement at Fairfield near Manchester (1783–85), the capital of early industrialism, was one of the first of these (Creese 1966, 6–8). The 'Fairfield Square Settlement' was a pedestrian village and although contemporary pictures show quite a lot of open space, this was devoid of trees until hawthorn and ash were planted much later in 1848. Undoubtedly the most socially innovative of the new settlements was New Lanark in Scotland, developed by Robert Owen (Morris 1997, 37). New Lanark was a cotton manufacturing village taken over by Owen in 1799 and subsequently governed as a community on paternalistic lines. The dwellings and gardens were grouped around a large open space and were separated by the roadway from the workshops and factories.

In 1829, John Claudius Loudon wrote an article for *Gardener's Magazine* entitled *Hints on Breathing Places for the Metropolis* (Loudon 1829). This was in response to the threatened enclosure of Hampstead Heath and in support of the growing public opposition to this (Simo 1981, 187). In his article Loudon sets out his general plan to preserve not only the Heath but also thousands of areas of undeveloped land in and around London. The essence of the plan was a series of concentric green belts or 'country zones', alternating with town zones, to surround London at one mile intervals. Loudon's ideal capital city would include a radial and concentric network of street and transport networks at surface level and a corresponding underground network of utility services. As might be expected from Loudon, this idyllic metropolis would also have a wealth of trees and public greenspace. For the plan to have been implemented it would have required a massive restructuring of governmental processes and this never happened (*ibid.*, 188).

Owen's reforming efforts and Loudon's visionary plans had little impact on the urban scene in the early part of the nineteenth century. As the Industrial Revolution gathered pace, urban expansion continued at a relentless rate with much poor-quality housing thrown up by developers (Gauldie 1974). The over-riding consideration of factory owners was the maximisation of profit and in pursuit of that there was scant concern for the welfare of their workforce. In the mid-nineteenth century, thanks to the efforts of a few enlightened industrialists, a more compassionate, humane and productive approach was pioneered. This took the form of the creation of model or industrial villages.

Model or industrial villages

The first model or industrial villages were clustered in the wool and worsted manufacturing centres of the West Riding of Yorkshire and were the initiative of a handful of wealthy industrialists (Creese 1966, 13–5). Three families were involved – the Salts, the Akroyds and the Crossleys – that had industrial, political and religious aspirations in common (*ibid.*, 20). As well as having genuine concerns about the welfare of factory workers, their motivation was also political with growing trepidation among the ruling class about the impact of the Luddites, the French Revolution and growth of radical ideas. Because these new settlements were conceived and largely executed by one man, the factory owner, there was no delay or need for any persuasion in building them.

The first of the model villages was Copley in Yorkshire where Colonel Akroyd and his family firm had purchased the mill estate in 1844 and built a second mill in 1846 (Creese 1966, 22–4). The model houses in the form of back-to-back dwellings went up during 1849–53. While there was little space at the rear, garden allotments ran along the front of the properties, kept tidy at company expense. Annual flower and vegetable shows were organised that were well-supported by the workers and their families.

A far more influential and ambitious model village than Copley was Saltaire, built near Bradford by Sir Titus Salt during 1848–63 (Jackson *et al.* 2010). This took its name from its founder and from the River Aire that ran past the woollen mill. The village eventually housed all Salt's extensive workforce in quite high-density but high-quality housing. The density of the development did not allow for much in the way of open space or gardens (Creese 1966, 31). While many of the supervisory workers had small front gardens most of the other houses did not and because of the back-to-back nature of the housing all properties just had a small yard but no rear garden (Figure 73). To compensate for this and to encourage self-sufficiency among his workers, Salt allowed an extensive area along the side of the mill to be used as allotments and this included many fruit trees (Figure 74). There were no significant plantings of street trees. Those recreational greenspaces that did exist in the central part of the village were modest setbacks in front of the Institute and the school and the Alexander quadrangle, around which 45 almshouses for the aged and retired were grouped. These areas included some amenity trees. There was also a sizable amount of greenspace and some fine trees around the Congregational Church, which Salt and his family attended. In true mid-nineteenth century style, the major area of public open space was concentrated in the 14-acre (5.7 ha) park across the River Aire from the houses and factory. This has always had plenty of trees and ornamental landscape features and is now known as Roberts Park. The importance of Saltaire in the history of town planning is now recognised with its designation in 2001 as a UNESCO World Heritage site.

Akroydon Model Village in Halifax was the second venture of Colonel Akroyd and work on this began in 1861 (Creese 1966, 40). The settlement's central park, known as The Square, was located within a quadrangle of houses and was a step towards the single garden that was prophetic of some later garden city developments. Although this had some trees planted around its periphery, it was mainly open lawn with the Victoria Cross monument at its centre, dedicated to Queen Victoria (Figure 75). The West Hill Park Estate was another development in Halifax that began in 1863 (*ibid.*, 46–48). This was the project of John Crossley the Younger, although the inspiration is said to have come largely from Colonel Akroyd. A few streets away and earlier in 1857, the People's Park had been completed, given to the people of Halifax by local carpet manufacturer Sir Francis Crossley and adjoining his mansion at Belle Vue and his almshouses of 1855 (*ibid.*, 48–50). The landscape was designed by Joseph Paxton and Edward Milner and they took care to conceal the crowded town of Halifax behind trees and mounds, while opening up views out to the distant moor.

Bedford Park

Bedford Park in West London is often considered the world's first garden suburb, although it was not built in the cooperative manner like some later developments of that name. In 1875, Jonathan T. Carr acquired 24 acres (9.7 ha) of land in Chiswick adjoining an old Georgian mansion known as Bedford House (Creese 1966, 87–90). The owner had been Dr John Lindley, Curator of the RHS Gardens at Chiswick, and the plan was to create an attractive residential estate that would also save Lindley's extensive tree collection, something that a less imaginative development by speculative builders would destroy. This was achieved through a truly innovative scheme that represented the first attempt to build moderately-priced homes in a vernacular style for the aspirational middle class (Binns 2013, 61).

FIGURE 73. The model village of Saltaire, near Bradford, was built by Sir Titus Salt during 1848–63. The village eventually housed all Salt's extensive workforce in quite high-density but high-quality housing. The density of the development did not allow for much in the way of open space or gardens. Some of the supervisory workers were fortunate in having small front gardens but most did not allow for any tree planting.

FIGURE 74. To compensate for the lack of communal open space elsewhere and to encourage self-sufficiency among his workers, Sir Titus Salt allowed an extensive area along the side of the mill to be used for allotments. As well as growing vegetables, various types of fruit tree were also popular. This area continues today to provide local people with space for allotments and fruit trees.

The visual impact of the Bedford Park setting and its abrupt contrast with the more conventional suburbs of the time was immediately obvious (Creese 1966, 88–90). This was an estate of 'pretty houses dotted among trees', where the streets were not on a typical block or grid pattern but followed the natural

FIGURE 75. Akroydon Model Village in Halifax was the second venture of Colonel Akroyd and work on this began 1861. The settlement's central park, known as The Square, was located within a quadrangle of houses and was a step towards the single garden that was prophetic of some later garden city developments. Although this had some trees planted around its periphery, it was mainly open lawn with the Victoria Cross monument at its centre, dedicated to Queen Victoria.

features of the tree collection and landscape. Most of the houses were semi-detached and in the Queen Anne revival style, with generous gardens planted with apple, pear and plum trees. Along the roads, in addition to Lindley's trees, there were limes, poplars and especially willows. What harmonised the disparate elements of Bedford Park was the new and revolutionary consciousness of space brought alive by light filtering through the trees. There was a quality of luminosity that suggested a watercolour sketch or the work of the French impressionist painters. This artistic image of the Park was reinforced by its liberal-minded residents who helped shape its public image as Arts and Crafts or Pre-Raphaelite 'aesthetic colony' (*ibid.*, 100).

Port Sunlight and Bournville

In contrast to the genteel and middle class Bedford Park, two late nineteenth century industrial villages epitomised the social and economic benefits of attractive housing for workers in a landscaped setting (Rutherford 2014, 17). These were Port Sunlight on the Wirral and Bournville in Birmingham.

William Hesketh Lever, later Lord Leverhulme, founded Port Sunlight in 1888 for the factory workers of his adjacent palm oil soapworks in the Wirral (Hubbard and Shippobottom 2012, 1). The name of the new settlement was taken from his best-selling product, the world's first packaged soap for laundry and general household use. While most of the later garden communities followed the gentle roll of the countryside, this was not the case at Port Sunlight, which was relatively low, flat, and deeply penetrated by tidal wash (Creese 1966, 109–10). The Dell was the first area occupied and this had low density housing but with old-fashioned service alleys, while in the larger blocks of housing the central area was filled with allotment gardens. Many of the houses had space at the front which Lever was keen to keep unobstructed in a continuous frontage along the street, often referred to as the 'American open front' system. However, this system largely failed, as it did later in many other settlements in Britain, because the tenants enclosed their front yards with hedges to protect what they planted from dogs, cats and children (*ibid.*, 117) (Figure 76). Lever sometimes found it necessary to take over these front gardens and maintain them at company expense because the tenants occasionally used them as chicken runs or dumping grounds. Port Sunlight was also experimental in wider aspects of town planning in being one of the first industrial villages to depart from the grid pattern layout and emphasise the amenity setting of the homes (Rutherford 2014, 18). When Lever engaged Thomas Mawson, the renowned planner and landscape architect, to assist the student Ernest Prestwick to prepare plans for the redevelopment and expansion of Port Sunlight this resulted in a bold and spectacular scheme for its central area (Mawson 1911, 278–87). Through his visits to the United States, Mawson had been influenced by the American Beaux Arts style and City Beautiful movement and he used formal Beaux-Arts-style tree-lined boulevards to unite the overall design (Creese 1966, 133–5). In the core of the village was The Causeway, a beautifully planned and wide tree-lined boulevard with Christ Church at one end. A second major boulevard known as The Diamond, which intersects with The Causeway, was laid out in 1910 as the central boulevard of the replanned village. This also has grand avenues of trees and terminates at its northern end with the Lady Lever Art Gallery, a magnificent building opened in 1922 (Figures 77 and 78).

The model village of Bournville, founded by George Cadbury in 1895, was not meant to be an exclusively company settlement like Port Sunlight (Miller 2010, 10). Up to half of the housing was available to non-Cadbury workers, which muted company paternalism and promoted social integration. The layout resembled a low-density suburb, with a central village green, shopping parade and nearby community buildings (Figure 79). Great attention was paid to house design, the provision of open space and environmental conditions as a whole. As part of this, there was an emphasis on large gardens and irregular street patterns which led Bournville to develop the cul-de-sac and the crescent, elements of planning arrangements that were later to become typical of garden suburb (Morris 1997, 40). The specification for its individual roads was similar to Port Sunlight, comprising an 18 ft (5.5 m) carriageway with a grass verge and path of 6 ft (1.8 m) each with a setback amounting to 20 ft (6.1 m) (Creese 1966, 119). In contrast to the street tree planting at Bedford Park and much of Port Sunlight, which favoured forest-type trees, there was a preference for smaller and more exotic trees at Bournville, such as whitebeam, thorn, Japanese crab and cherries, almond, mountain ash, silver birch and laburnum (*ibid.*, 123) (Figure 80). To emphasise the significance of the trees and reinforce their contribution to neighbourhood identity, streets were often named after the trees planted in them. Much of Bournville's reputation as a green and pleasant village has been due to its attractive roadside trees and in the 1950s their design, selection, planting and management was promoted as a model for other urban areas (Salter 1953).

The provision of public and private open space at Bournville, and its arrangement, was as important as the buildings (Willes 2014, 290). Cadbury felt that a large garden around even the most mundane house was especially important and this single plot of residential green for all tenants was a major innovation for working class housing. Not only did gardens provide an attractive amenity but the growing of fruit and vegetables also promoted self-sufficiency. In addition for Cadbury, who was a committed Quaker, the recreation and physical exercise of gardening might also encourage his workers to refrain from alcoholic drink. The idea behind the layout of the gardens was given in a small book entitled *The Model Village* by Alexander Harvey, the architect who had designed the cottages (Harvey 1905). The plot was covered with lawn that had flowerbeds nearest the house followed by a vegetable patch and fruit trees at the end of the plot. To give each family a good start, the Village Trust made the paths, laid the lawn, rough dug the ground and planted the fruit trees, shrubs and climbers (*ibid.*, 24). Each garden was provided with eight apple and pear trees, assorted according to the soil conditions, and a range of more shrubby fruits. These were generally planted at the end of the rear garden and when springtime came the blossom running along the garden boundaries made a wonderful sight. One or two forest trees were also planted to frame the building, together with thorn hedges to divide the cottages. The choice of climbers was determined by the suitability of the soil and the aspect. To encourage high standards of horticulture and to promote self-sufficiency, Cadbury employees were offered the opportunity to receive instructions in gardening from a professional trained at Kew (Simo 1988, 260). Another reason for the success of the gardens at Bournville was a clause in the tenancy agreement requiring high standards of neatness and beauty (Creese 1966, 117).

Bournville was, and still is, a very pleasant place to live and raise a family. The generous-sized gardens, tree-lined roads, parks and recreation grounds gave the Cadbury workers and other tenants living conditions that were far superior to workers anywhere else. However, the importance of both Bournville and Port Sunlight in the history of working class housing should not be overstated (Gauldie 1974, 193–4). While other industrialists of the time praised the efforts of Lever and Cadbury, they did not copy them and most neglected to provide any housing at all for their workers. These two pioneering settlements were much more important in educating public opinion and influencing future town planning. The fact that they were followed by the Garden Cities gave them real significance.

Howard and the Garden City Movement

Towards the end of the Victorian era some prominent thinkers, artists and designers, such as John Ruskin and William Morris, had spoken out against the

FIGURE 76. At Port Sunlight in the Wirral, Lever was keen to keep the front gardens unobstructed in a continuous frontage along the street, often referred to as the 'American open front' system. However, this system largely failed at Port Sunlight, as it did later in many other settlements in Britain, because the tenants enclosed their front yards with hedges to protect what they planted from dogs, cats and children. This row of houses has retained its open frontage.

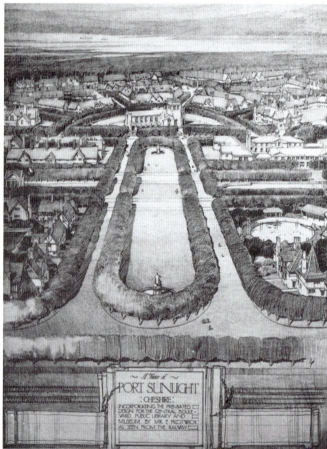

FIGURE 77. Through his visits to the United States, Thomas Mawson had been influenced by the American Beaux Arts style and City Beautiful movement and he used formal Beaux-Arts-style tree-lined boulevards at Port Sunlight to unite the overall design. In the core of the village is The Causeway, a beautifully planned and wide tree-lined boulevard with Christ Church at one end (Mawson 1911).

FIGURE 78. A second major boulevard at Port Sunlight is known as The Diamond, which intersects with The Causeway, and was laid out in 1910 as the central boulevard of the replanned village. This also has grand avenues of trees with gardens in the centre and terminates at its northern end with the Lady Lever Art Gallery, the final large building at the centre of Port Sunlight.

FIGURE 79. The model village of Bournville was founded by George Cadbury in 1895 for the workers at his cocoa and chocolate factory. The layout resembled a low-density suburb, arranged around a central green that was typical of the traditional English village, and which is pictured here. On one side of the green was a shopping parade and there were community buildings nearby.

FIGURE 80. In contrast to the street tree planting at Bedford Park and much of Port Sunlight, which favoured forest-type trees, there was a preference here at Bournville for smaller and more exotic trees, such as whitebeam, thorn, Japanese crab and cherries, almond, mountain ash, silver birch and laburnum.

industrial squalor and cultural monotony of the age. Some authors published works that graphically highlighted the grim Victorian conditions or gave a vision of what might be possible in the future. In his book *News from Nowhere*, Morris (1890) painted a Utopian picture of London in the twenty-first century as a green and pleasant place, a transformation driven mainly by a movement of people back to the country. The novels of Charles Dickens conveyed a grim picture of the conditions for working people in the industrial city. Richard Jefferies's novel *After London* described how its hero escapes the apocalyptic collapse of the polluted industrial city to find a post-disaster Utopia as wild nature takes over again (Jefferies 1895).

The model villages of Port Sunlight and Bournville had pointed a way forward to a brighter, greener, urban future – but not much else had happened. Life for the vast majority of people in the Victorian industrial city was a depressing, dull and monotonous existence. Repressive economic and political conditions ensured that efforts by the working class to organise and affect genuine change were slow to make progress and often frustrated (Morton 1938, 432–9). Social and cultural progress was also drained by the devouring greed of industrial development. While growing numbers of the middle class were becoming concerned about the employment and living condition of working people, there was very little action. What was urgently needed was a catalyst that could draw together some of these like-minded theories and people and harness this towards some real action on the ground (Rutherford 2014, 25).

Ebenezer Howard was born in London in 1850 to relatively comfortable middle class parents. He had no special education in town planning, having left school by the age of 15, drifting between jobs and then moving to the United States and working on a farm in Nebraska (Clark 2003, 88). On his return to England in 1876, he was employed as a parliamentary reporter and this sharpened his awareness of the great social problems of the age. During that time he read widely and mingled with socialists, anarchists and other nonconformist freethinkers, and became friends with the socialists Sidney and Beatrice Webb and George Bernard Shaw. Howard was particularly concerned about the steady migration of people from the countryside into the already overcrowded towns and cities. His philosophy was simple – he viewed town life as offering economic benefits and social opportunities, while country life offered all the human benefits. His idea was to create a community that offered the best of both town and country life, to be called a Garden City. This basic idea was to be encapsulated later in his now famous diagram of The Three Magnets, which skilfully summarised his concept of 'joyous union' between town and country (Figure 81).

Howard only wrote one publication in his life but it transpired to be one of the most influential texts ever written on town planning and urban reform (Parsons and Schuyler 2002). Published in 1898 as *To-Morrow: A Peaceful Path to Real Reform*, it was significantly revised in 1902 as *Garden Cities of To-morrow*, the title by which it is now commonly known (Howard 1898). In Lewis Mumford's introduction to the 1976 edition of the book, he identified the significant elements of Howard's proposals as: (a) the permanent ownership of land by the municipality with leasing to private concerns; (b) the resultant recouping of unearned increment by the municipality rather than private landowners; (c) a sufficient diversity of activities, including social institutions; (d) industry; (e) agriculture to make the garden city fairly independent; (f) the use of a Green Belt for agriculture and to restrict the growth of the city; (g) a limit on the population to a planned size; and (h) further growth in new communities to be arranged as a 'Social City' (Howard 1976, 34).

Municipal control of the land was the key to Howard's scheme (Morris 1997, 49). Initially, this would be acquired by a private corporation that would hold it in trust for the future residents. The town's revenue was to be used for the benefit of the townspeople with the accrued money to be spent on the creation and maintenance of all public works. One of the reasons for the later success of the garden city movement was Howard's description of this financial and administrative process in great detail. Arranging the municipal ownership of land in this way allowed the implementation of a comprehensive town plan. Within that plan, land-use zoning was a key feature.

The entire area covered by the plan would be 6,000 acres (2428 ha) and the garden city itself, which would be built near the centre of this, would cover 1,000 acres (405 ha). The plan of the ideal garden city would be laid out in circular form measuring nearly 0.75 miles (1.2 km) from centre to circumference. Howard gives the following description of the town itself:

> Six magnificent boulevards – each 120 ft wide – traverse the city from centre to circumference, dividing it into six equal parts or wards. In the centre is a circular space of 185 yards in diameter, and containing about five and a half acres, laid out as a beautiful and well-watered garden; and surrounding this garden, each standing in its own ample grounds, are the larger public buildings – town hall, principal concert and lecture hall, theatre, library, museum, picture-gallery, and hospital.
>
> Howard, 1898, 14

The rest of the large space would be a public park over 145 acres (59 ha), which included recreation grounds within easy access for everyone. Running around this Central Park (except where it was intersected by the boulevards) was a wide glass corridor called the 'Crystal Palace'. This would function in a similar manner to a modern shopping and commercial arcade, together with exhibition areas and a Winter Garden, and provide cover for residents and visitors in wet weather.

Trees and greenspace featured to a great extent in Howard's plan (Figure 82). He states that all the roads of the garden city would be lined with trees and then adds:

> Walking still towards the outskirts of the town, we come upon 'Grand Avenue'. This Avenue is fully entitled to bear its name, for it is 420 feet wide, and forming a belt of green upwards of three miles long, divides that part of the town that lies outside Central Park into two belts.
>
> Howard, 1898, 15

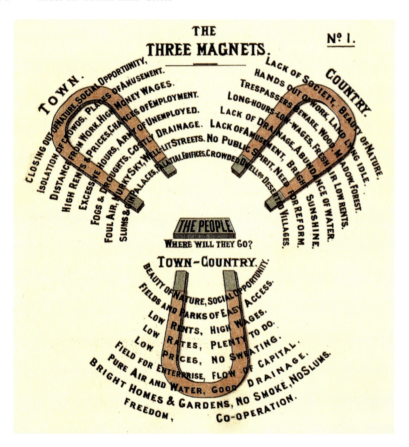

FIGURE 81. Ebenezer Howard's philosophy was simple – he viewed town life as offering economic benefits and social opportunities, while country life offered all the human benefits. His idea was to create a community that offered the best of both town and country life, to be called a Garden City. This basic idea was to be encapsulated later in his now famous diagram of The Three Magnets, which skilfully summarised his concept of 'joyous union' between town and country (Howard 1898).

This Grand Avenue really constituted an additional park of 115 acres (47 ha) which was within 240 yards (219 m) of the furthest removed inhabitant. Later in his book when he discusses the nature of roads and streets, Howard's view of the function of these as both transport corridors and additional greenspace is clearly evident:

> Experts will also not forget that the cost of the road sites is elsewhere provided for. In considering the question of the actual sufficiency of the estimate they will also remember that of the boulevards one-half and of the streets and avenues one-third, may be regarded as in the nature of a park, and the cost of laying out and maintenance of these portions of the roads is dealt with under the head 'Parks'.
>
> Howard, 1898, 53

Perhaps Howard's most striking and realistic physical proposal was the Green Belt, a band of open land around the garden city (Morris 1997, 50). First, it could function as a source of large-scale open space that was easily accessible from the city. Secondly, it could serve as a location for agriculture and other space-consuming activities. Thirdly, the Green Belt could act as a device for planning control made possible by the municipal ownership of land. In particular, it could be used to limit the physical growth of the city to the desired size of 30,000 people. Howard's solution to urban growth beyond this

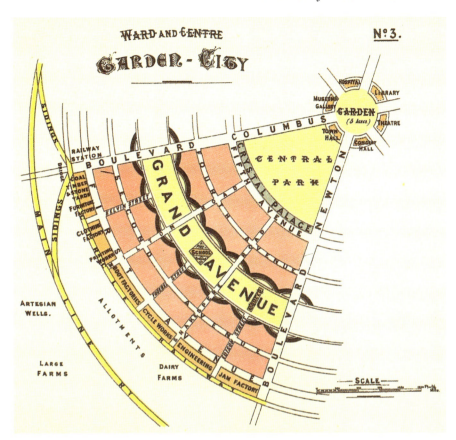

FIGURE 82. Trees and greenspace featured to a great extent in Howard's plan for his garden city. There would be six magnificent boulevards traversing the city and dividing it into six equal parts or wards. In the centre was a small circular space laid out as a beautiful garden. Surrounding this garden, each standing in its own ample grounds, were the larger public buildings. Also in this inner area was Central Park, a large public park within easy access for everyone. In addition there was the circular Grand Avenue forming a wide belt of greenspace, dividing that part of the town that was outside Central Park into two belts of housing (Howard 1898).

population limit was to envisage a group of Garden Cities (*ibid.*, 51). He called these 'Social Cities' where a group of garden cities would be grouped around a 'Central City'. This would have a larger population some 58,000. Although the cities would be close enough to have ties with each other and enjoy supporting services from the Central City, each city would preserve its own green belt. Residents would enjoy living in the relative countryside while benefiting from the advantages of the main city through rapid transit systems. The idea of the 'Social City' was never realised, although the later concept of satellite cities developed from this and eventually reappeared in the New Towns concept.

Howard's 1898 book with his vision of the garden city attracted much attention, both positive and negative. Most importantly, in 1899 it drew together a small group of influential people to form the Garden City Association (later the Town and Country Planning Association) that mobilised like-minded people keen to finance and participate in this social experiment (Clarke 2003, 94). The Association held its first conference in 1901 at Bournville, hosted by George Cadbury, and second conference in 1902 at Port Sunlight, hosted by Lever (Miller 2010, 13).

While visionaries like William Morris and Ebenezer Howard had their dreams of a bright new urban future, it took two remarkable individuals from the next generation to help these dreams come true (Creese 1966, 158). These were Barry Parker and Raymond Unwin, both architects and town planners who came together in 1896 to form a partnership, with a particular interest in housing and garden city community design (Miller 2010, 13). Unwin's briefing paper on garden city housing, delivered at the 1901 Bournville conference, led to a commission for a plan for New Earwick, near York, which was to become the testing ground for garden city design.

In 1901, Joseph Rowntree, another Quaker chocolate manufacturer, purchased the estate of New Earswick near his coca works, three miles northeast of York (Creese 1966, 191). The earliest sector of 28 houses was mapped out and built in 1902–3 by Parker and Unwin, while the older half of the settlement was built later in 1919. The Rowntrees refrained from selling their houses to the tenants, because of the Cadbury's unfortunate experience at Bournville with rising values and speculative turnover (*ibid.*, 192).While many of the houses in New Earswick were quite plain, they had large gardens and there was plenty of attractively landscaped communal space (Rutherford 2014, 23). The streets were planted extensively with trees, where the identifying trees for each street followed the earlier Bournville practice with names such as Chestnut Grove, Poplar Grove and Sycamore Avenue (Trinder 1982, 252).

The newer half of New Earswick also contained some of the best example of the cul-de-sac device which Parker and Unwin used to get around the awkwardness of irregular sites (Creese 1966, 195). This not only provided additional greenspace, often in the form of a distinct 'green' in the centre of the cul-de-sac, but the enclosed arrangement of the housing also acted as a buffer against the dust and noise of vehicles on the main roads. The cul-de-sac was to become a hallmark of Parker and Unwin work and a typical feature of the garden city, the garden suburbs and many of the more conventional residential suburbs. Parker and Unwin were to have enormous influence over many aspects of town planning, but perhaps their greatest legacy was to give countless thousands of working class families a garden of their own, often for the first time.

Letchworth

The garden city idea became reality in 1903 with the establishment of the first settlement at Letchworth, 30 miles (48 km) from London (Anon 1935, 9). This began with the formation of a company called First Garden City Ltd in 1903 which initially purchased 3826 acres (1548 ha) of agricultural land in the three adjacent villages of Letchworth, Willian and Norton. The site met the need for good communications being close to the old Great North Road (now the A1 motorway) and on the London Kings Cross to Cambridge rail route. A competition to determine the layout and character of the garden city was won by Barry Parker and Raymond Unwin, whose plan was adopted in 1904. Howard himself was closely involved in the implementation of the plan.

The most characteristic feature of Letchworth was the very open layout of the roads and houses. Together with the extensive planting of trees, shrubs and

FIGURE 83. Letchworth in Hertfordshire was Britain's first garden city, founded in 1903. The extensive plantings of trees, shrubs and hedges gave the whole town a park-like appearance befitting the term 'garden city'. This photograph taken in 1935 shows an avenue of ornamental trees underplanted with shrubs creating a delightful pedestrian approach to the shopping district (Anon 1935).

hedges, this gave the whole town a park-like appearance befitting the term 'garden city' (Miller 2010, 22) (Figure 83). Parker and Unwin designed the town and its housing around a Beaux-Arts-style formal axial road network focused on Broadway, a broad tree-lined spinal approach road, which opened into a formal central square (Rutherford 2014, 38). Much of the housing was low-density and developed around several 'village greens'.

Howard was anxious to avoid any crowded housing developments, so minimum lot sizes were 29 ft × 100 ft (9 × 30.5 m) (Creese 1966, 206–7). Frontages were later expanded up to 40 ft (12.2 m). Parker and Unwin established a general rule that no more than one sixth of the site should be covered with buildings. The precise density of housing per acre was a reflection of the cost of individual houses but never greater than 12 per acre for the cheapest houses. The dwellings were positioned on the plot to command the sunniest aspect and most pleasant prospect available, instead of merely aligning them with the street. Both Parker and Unwin were aware of the value of trees in built development (Creese 1966, 207). In giving advice to young planners, Parker urged them to do their best not to cut down a single tree. He was enormously proud of the fact that the building of Letchworth had only involved the destruction of one tree. Furthermore, care had been taken to ensure that existing trees and woodland of amenity value were incorporated into their urban landscape schemes (Anon 1935, 20). In 1905, Letchworth golf course was constructed in parkland formerly belonging to the Manor House of Letchworth (*ibid.*, 24). A substantial part of the existing parkland was finely wooded with many mature trees and much of this was incorporated into the golf course design. Norton Common on the northern side of the town had extensive scrubby woodland over its 60 acres (24 ha) and this was acquired by First Garden City Ltd in 1904 (*ibid.*, 24). It was then taken over by the Urban District Council in 1922 and developed as a public park with sports and recreational facilities, although still retaining some important semi-natural and wooded areas. A completely new public park, Howard Park and Garden, was placed (1904–11) in a residential area close to the civic centre, and its serpentine lines contrasted nicely with the formality of Broadway.

Many new trees were also planted along roads with the innovation of narrow grass verges along their roadside specifically for tree planting (Creese 1966, 229). In a scheme reminiscent of Bournville, each road had its own species of tree (45 in all) as part of a campaign to promote a sense of place and greater appreciation of the trees. Unwin observed:

> The Japanese have special holidays to celebrate the flowering times of certain trees; and even the English workman might be tempted to vary his route home, if in one street he would find the earliest blossoming trees, in another the first spring green, and in a third the last bright colours of autumn.
>
> Unwin, 1904, 3

In Broadway, a double avenue of lime trees was used along this major street to give it identity and stature (Creese 1966, 208). At the end of Broadway was the first traffic roundabout to be built in Britain, although for some reason this was not planted with any trees. Elsewhere in the civic centre, Lombardy poplars were planted to define the building outlines in Central Square, although these were felled recently when the square was remodelled as Broadway Gardens in 2003 (Miller 2010, 22).

The trees, hedges and grass verges of Letchworth furnished a living and spatial screen for the houses and family life, which Parker and Unwin considered paramount (Creese 1966, 208–9). However, there has been some criticism made of the landscaping programme at Letchworth which believes that eventually nature swung out of balance and became something of a burden. The trees, shrubs and flowers were planted quickly, while the buildings lagged behind. This was especially noticeable around the central square of the town. By the 1950s, many older residents were complaining regularly that the trees were 'overgrown' and 'robbing' them of light and views.

It is important to remember that while Letchworth later came under the control of a local authority, it started out as a private sector development – but not one driven by the generosity of a single benefactor (Gauldie 1974, 204–5). By abandoning private philanthropy, as followed by the garden village, Howard to some extent deprived his garden city of the immediate architectural orchestration that made the earlier efforts harmonious. The garden city builders could not impose their wills on the community as effectively as the old-time industrialists, either in terms of planning or architecture. As a consequence, the amount of greenspace for the community also fell below the standard set by Howard and the ring of agricultural land around the central area was significantly reduced.

Letchworth remained the sole example of a garden city until the development of Welwyn Garden City after the First World War. In the meantime, work continued on various garden suburbs and villages.

Hampstead and other garden suburbs

Garden suburbs and villages became more prevalent than garden cities because they were easier to establish at a smaller scale and were more commercially viable for developers (Rutherford 2014, 49). While these attractive and often exclusive garden suburbs were clearly inspired by Howard's garden city, they were not entirely in harmony with its ideals.

The most notable example of this British town planning phenomenon is Hampstead Garden Suburb founded in North London in 1907 (Creese 1966, 220–2). This started as an effort to save a portion of the fast disappearing landscape around London. By the end of the nineteenth century, the rapidly advancing sprawl of the capital had made its way around to the northern side of Hampstead Heath, which was now under threat from speculative development. In an effort to counter that, Henrietta Barnett, who already had a reputation as a social reformer, proposed the building of Hampstead Garden Suburb. In 1906, Barnett set up the Hampstead Garden Suburb Trust Ltd, which purchased 243 acres of land from Eton College for the scheme and appointed Raymond Unwin as its architect. The basic aim of the new suburb was to furnish a home for the working man for a 2*d* fare from London on the tube (*ibid.*, 226). What was 'common to all', natural beauty, would then be made 'enjoyable to all' through open spaces, green gardens, and tree-planted streets. Barnett wanted to reform the suburb as it then existed by integrating all classes within it.

While Raymond Unwin was responsible for the overall design of Hampstead Garden Suburb, the architect Edwin Lutyens was responsible for its central square (Creese 1966, 230–1). This was located at the highest point in the development and, somewhat appropriately, was reserved for houses of worship and learning. If the planning arrangement and density at Letchworth was too loose, Hampstead was in some places overly organised (*ibid.*, 242–4). Unwin went to some lengths to avoid any regular, predictable layout for the roads and neighbourhoods. He had a strong dislike of the monotony of the English 'bye-law' street and his offsets, focal points, curves and angles produced in the Hampstead streets were deliberately designed to avoid that, and also to discourage traffic.

Unwin's overall design for the garden suburb was careful to take into account its existing natural features, making sure to retain significant areas of woodland, ancient hedgerows and mature oaks (Rutherford 2014, 50). Big Wood and Little Wood were two important patches of woodland that had been part of some early forest in the area dating back over 1,000 years. Both were leased from the Ecclesiastical Commissioners and preserved as woodland with public access when the suburb was extended in 1911. Extensive new landscaping and tree planting was also undertaken throughout the development with every road lined with trees (Figure 84). As well as having houses of high quality and outstanding

FIGURE 84. Hampstead Garden Suburb was founded in North London in 1907 and these roadside plane trees were planted at an early stage in its development. However, for some reason they have since been quite severely pruned even though they are situated at some distance from the properties.

architecture, the residents were fortunate in having generous garden spaces, both front and back. Two fruit trees were planted in every back garden before any residents moved in. Like Lever in Port Sunlight, Barnett was attracted by the uniform open front system rather than separate individual front gardens (Creese 1966, 227). While a few open fronts were achieved at Hampstead, these were not favoured by the residents and generally the system was not used. Hedges were preferred to walls as garden boundaries. There was a limit to the height of garden hedges and a measuring stick was used to check that this was not being exceeded. The rule was to enable neighbours to chat to each other over the hedge, thus encouraging social contact and promoting good neighbourliness.

While Barnett's original intention was for Hampstead Garden Suburb to have residents of all classes, with particular emphasis on working class families, this has not transpired. Today, the suburb is one of the most exclusive and expensive places to live in the whole of Britain. A search of the internet will reveal a list of its current 'notable residents' that includes television personalities, film actors, rock stars, authors and composers.

Another garden suburb in London, Brentham, actually predates Hampstead and was the first garden suburb to be built on co-partnership principles (Rutherford 2014, 53). Co-partnership management schemes gave residents greater equality and influence in the running of their suburb (*ibid.*, 22). Tenants were made joint owners of the houses they occupied, along with outside financiers or developers, with the estate managed by an elected committee of shareholders. Brentham Garden Suburb in Ealing was founded in 1901 by the great promoter of the co-partnership movement, Henry Vivian (*ibid.*, 53–7). The relatively small suburb began with housing on a conventional pattern in a tight layout. In 1907, Ealing Tenants Limited, the progressive cooperative representing the tenants, appointed Unwin to take forward the development of their suburb. This second stage had the typical Parker and Unwin spacious garden suburb plan, with the retention of mature trees and plenty of new tree planting along winding roads. Surprisingly, there was no ornamental park, only a small green in front of the imposing Institute building, which was a social and sports club for the residents. Instead, five acres of additional gardens in seven plots were enclosed by back gardens, used mainly as allotments but also as grassy spaces, and reached by narrow privet-hedged paths linking the rows of houses.

Throughout the first half of the twentieth century many more garden suburbs were developed in Britain (Rutherford 2014, 57–9). Perhaps the most outstanding example in Wales was Rhiwbina Garden Village, Glamorgan, founded in 1912. In Scotland, the first garden suburb was the Glasgow (now Westerton) Garden Suburb in Bearsden. Overseas, the concept of garden suburbs was embraced with enthusiasm in many countries, particularly in the British Colonies. (*ibid.*, 63)

Welwyn Garden City and Rosyth

In 1919, soon after the end of the First World War, those promoting the garden city concept were concerned at the lack of action in creating another English initiative (Miller 2010, 31). There was disappointment with the government's neutral stance on garden cities compared to the generous grants and compulsion for local authority housing, despite this being encouraged to develop along 'garden city' lines. These developments had been prompted by the impact of the Tudor Walters Report on legislation and working class housing, published by the Local Government Board in 1918 (Rutherford 2014, 65). This had been much influenced by Unwin who by then had been appointed as a government official (Creese 1966, 256).

As a result of a personal initiative by Howard that was not part of any government plan, another garden city initiative was founded in 1920 in the form of Welwyn Garden City, located in Hertfordshire (Morris 1997, 52). It aimed to have a population of 50,000, although it grew rather slowly in the first fifteen years. Welwyn has eventually proved to be successful in many respects. Although very close to London, it has retained its own identity and 85 per cent of its residents still work in the town.

The layout of Welwyn was masterminded by Louis de Soissons, a French-Canadian architect, with Howard closely involved (Rutherford 2014, 42–3). Although the site was quartered by railways, a grand focal Beaux-Arts layout was planned around two formal axes. The main one was Parkway, the impressive and equally scenic equivalent of Letchworth's Broadway, which comprised a great formal boulevard with a double avenue of trees. The Parkway terminated at its north end in The Campus, a semi-circular public space surrounded by civic buildings. A number of other ornamental tree-lined boulevards linked the different buildings in the civic centre. Overall, landscaping was one of the highlights of Welwyn Garden City, especially the broad expanses and sweeping vistas of Parkway which surprised and impressed many visitors (Miller 2010, 35).

The third and only Scottish garden city was established during the First World War (Chalkley and Shiach 2005). Rosyth Garden City on the Firth of Forth was built to serve the Admiralty's workforce and their families in the Royal Navy Dockyard that had opened in 1915 (Rutherford 2014, 44). Rosyth's layout and houses reflected the precedents set in England and adopted in the Glasgow Garden suburb in 1912 (Rutherford 2014, 44). They also echoed the general principles established at Bournville and promoted by Parker and Unwin with picturesque cottage-style houses arranged at low density in both terraces and semi-detached pairs. Front gardens were hedged with privet, holly and beech, linked by broad, tree-lined streets. Generous rear gardens were supplemented by plenty of communal greenspace, including a wide greenbelt around the town.

Wythenshawe

A major inter-war municipal housing project started at Wythenshawe in the 1920s which was intended initially to be another garden city (Deakin 1989). This was planned by the Corporation of Manchester to provide new housing for families being moved out of the slums and squalor of industrial Manchester. In 1920, the Wythenshawe district was identified by Patrick Abercrombie, the eminent town planner, as the only undeveloped land suitable for building close to Manchester and recommended building a satellite town, separated from the city by a green belt (Miller 2010, 80).

Wythenshawe Hall and parkland was bought in 1926 by Shena and Ernest Simon, wealthy local politicians, who presented the house and its 250 acre (101 ha) park to the City Corporation (O'Reilly, C. 2013, 123). This was 'to be kept forever as an open space for the people of Manchester' and specifically intended for the recreational use of people living on the newly built Wythenshawe housing estate. Prior to its purchase by the Simons, Wythenshawe was an ancient country estate that had descended through the Tatton family from the late 1300s and the name itself comes from Old English meaning 'willow woodland' (Deakin 1989, 1–17). The Tatton family also owned a vast amount of other land in the area until this was purchased by Manchester Corporation, also in 1926, to turn into a massive new housing development.

The overall design of Wythenshawe was undertaken by Barry Parker, this time without Raymond Unwin, and it was to be his last and largest work (1927–41) (Creese 1966, 255). Although the project had the misfortune of being started at a time of national economic depression, it nevertheless had the political and financial weight of Manchester behind it. By 1935, it had already outgrown both Letchworth and Welwyn, testimony to the swift municipalisation of the garden city idea. Its proposed population was almost twice these, at around 90,000.

Wythenshawe has been described as one of the most complete municipal experiments in garden city design ever undertaken (Miller 2010, 80–2). Parker's plan certainly attracted much praise at the time with Lewis Mumford, the eminent American sociologist-planner, regarding his plan as a bold updating of Howard's garden city concept. It specified a hierarchy of streets and residential neighbourhoods with community facilities, a town centre, industrial zones, open spaces and a peripheral green belt. Most revolutionary were the main high-speed transport arteries, the parkways – reflecting Parker's enthusiasm for American innovations and advanced practice. He had visited the United States to attend conferences on urban planning and had been particularly inspired by the parkway system of Chicago (Creese 1966, 261).

Princess Parkway, the main parkway at Wythenshawe, was the first of its kind in Britain and its bold scale and distinct environment ensured it stood out from the rest of the town's development (Creese 1966, 261–3). The essential purpose of a parkway is to provide a major corridor for free-flowing traffic that is segregated from nearby housing and minor roads by attractively landscaped greenspace. The first section of Princess Parkway to Altrincham Road was officially opened in 1932 and its high-quality landscaping and overall design was greatly admired by both professionals and locals (Deakin 1989, 49). The nearby houses were 150 ft (46 m) back from the parkway and limited vehicle access from side streets occurred approximately every quarter of a mile (0.4 km) (Creese 1966, 261–3). There were four lanes of traffic and on either side of this a broad verge planted with rows of trees and hedges. As well as the improvements in traffic flow through Wythenshawe, there were various supplementary benefits from the parkway. The belts of trees and dense shrubbery would not only act as a buffer against the dust, smell and noise of vehicles on the main road, but also be part of people's daily routines as 'pedestrian parkways', following the main streams of traffic but protected from them. The trees and shrubbery would also visually screen the houses from cars and boost residential values with green views.

Parker believed the concept of the parkway to be a refreshing alternative to the ubiquitous ribbon or strip development (Creese 1966, 262). It would eliminate the usual "shoddy houses, cheap shacks, petrol filling stations, garages, advertisement hordings, shabby tea-rooms and miserable shops" (Parker 1937, 19). In terms of traffic management, there would be free-flowing traffic, permanently open and clear of any parked cars. It is interesting to note that as a result of Parker's experience at Wythenshawe, the greenbelt in his philosophy was beginning to be elongated rather than circular because he felt that was more consonant with the velocity and direction of traffic (Creese 1966, 266). After the Second World War objections were raised that there was too much traffic passing through the garden city (*ibid.*, 263). Even more objections followed as Princess Parkway was extended out from Manchester beyond its first stopping point at Altrincham Road.

It was always intended to continue Princess Parkway south to Ringway, the new city airport (opened in 1938) and beyond (Miller 2010, 85). However, the *City of Manchester Plan 1945* recognised that the parkway would become a barrier, dividing rather than uniting Wythenshawe. Nevertheless, in 1969 work began on upgrading the parkway to motorway standard and the route was renamed the M56, part of a major motorway construction project eventually connecting Manchester and Cheshire. Some 50,000 trees and shrubs were sacrificed in the parkway upgrade, although this was compensated later by some additional planting (Deakin 1989, 152). For many people, what had been planned by Parker as a pioneering road renowned for its beautiful landscaping was now just another motorway.

Adjacent to Princess Parkway on its west side is Wythenshawe Park, which continues to be managed as a public park of 270 acres (109 ha). Parker's original plan had been careful to ensure the integrity of this valuable greenspace and to protect its existing trees and woodland (Miller 2010, 83). The park now has thirteen separate woodlands and many more trees have been planted as avenues and as individuals. Throughout the whole of the development of Wythenshawe existing trees and woodland of amenity value were protected, often by adjusting the layout of the buildings and hard infrastructure.

Parker and his co-workers at Wythenshawe always regarded it as a third garden city and in 1945 Unwin went as far as to praise it as the most perfect example of this (Rutherford 2014, 34). In reality it was always a garden suburb with an industrial zone. It is ironic that it has achieved fame as 'the world's largest council estate' rather than as the garden city that the planners intended (Deakin 1989, 113–28). A drive around today's Wythenshawe suggests that all may not be well with much of this vast expanse of working class housing. Indeed, the fate of its pioneering parkway could be seen as a microcosm of what has happened to much of this area.

The New Towns movement

The New Towns Programme of 1946 to 1970 was one of the most substantial periods of urban development in Britain (Morris 1997, 91; Alexander 2001). Whether the results of individual examples of new towns are admired or criticised, the sheer feat of creating 14 of these in the first wave of development was a remarkable post-war achievement. Britain received widespread international recognition for this pioneering work, which several other counties such Israel, the United States and China have subsequently imitated. Since the New Towns Act of 1946, 32 new towns have come into existence in Britain and Northern Ireland.

The new towns movement owes a considerable debt to the garden cities movement and in many respects the ideas of Howard and his followers were vindicated by the New Town Act 1946 (Alexander 2009, 53–64). The early experimental settlements of Letchworth in 1903 and Welwyn Garden City in 1920 provided tangible evidence that the concept could be realised (Morris 1997, 91). Although the idea was regularly debated between the wars, nothing was done. It was only after the Second World War that the devastation and urgent need for reconstruction promoted some real action on the ground. This began with the formation of the New Towns Committee, headed by Lord Reith, to investigate the feasibility of the idea. After much consultation and deliberation, the committee reported to government with a series of recommendations that set the parameters for any future programme. The Labour government elected in 1945 was sympathetic to the planners' vision for the new towns and it also conformed to their socialist belief that the state should play a greater role in production and development. Furthermore, emergency war powers still existed, including the control of building licences and material, which could help facilitate the project. The efficiency of the Civil Service at that time also meant the associated 'red-tape' could be kept to a minimum. This special set of circumstances came together and allowed the concept to be translated into legislation in the New Towns Act of 1946. This decreed that new town policy was to be implemented not by central government or the local authorities, but by individual and separate development agencies, the New Town Development Corporations, established specifically for the purpose of planning and building the new towns. These corporations were appointed and financed by government and given a degree of independence and special powers that the local authorities did not have.

Between 1946 and 1950, 14 new towns were designated, known as the first-generation New Towns (Morris 1997, 92). The first of these was Stevenage in Hertfordshire, designated in 1946. Eight were established in a ring around London and these were Bracknell, Crawley, Basildon, Hemel Hempstead, Stevenage, Harlow, Hatfield and Welwyn Garden City (first founded in 1920 as a garden city). These were intended to relieve congestion and pressure on housing in the capital. The other six provisional new towns were established to meet the special needs of regional decline. Of these, Peterlee, Newton Aycliffe, Cwmbran and Glenrothes were established to provide housing and new industry for declining mining communities. Corby, was established to provide housing for the rapidly growing local steelworks. East Kilbride aimed to provide employment and housing for the overspill population from Glasgow. The fifteenth New Town, Cumbernauld, was the only new town to be designated in the 1950s.

Each first-generation new town had a population target of about 50,000 people (Morris 1997, 92). This gave an acceptable level of density and a convenient relationship of housing to industry, the town centre and the countryside. The industrial and residential districts were placed in separate zones, surrounding a geographically central town centre. The residential districts were based on the concept of the neighbourhood unit, usually of several thousand people, with a primary school, a few shops, a pub and a community centre. They were given a physical identity by main roads and mini-green belts separating each other. The vast majority of the housing was low-rise, which was actually cheaper to build at the time than high-rise blocks.

The first-generation new towns placed considerable emphasis on pleasant landscaping (Morris 1997, 96). Hemel Hempstead, Crawley and Glenrothes were considered to be particularly outstanding examples with good hard and soft landscaping in town centres and careful choice of trees and shrubs in housing areas. True to Howard's vision for the garden cities, all the first-generation new towns had green belts and many incorporated mini-green belts surrounding neighbourhoods and town centres respectively within the town. Harlow is a classic example of the use of green belts. Howard's hope that the garden city would unify town and country also meant that new town housing usually had an abundance of greenspace in public places (Alexander 2001, 74). In the case of Harlow this fitted into the landscape such that it really did feel like a town in the countryside and at times as if one had left the town entirely.

After Cumbernauld in 1956, the government suspended the new towns programme and embarked on what is known as the expanded towns programme (Alexander 2001, 41–51). This involved the substantial expansion of some existing towns to accommodate the overspill population from the cities. It was not regarded by government as particularly successful and was shelved in favour of more new towns, generally known as the second generation. This comprised a second wave (1961–64) of several new towns, followed by a third and final wave (1967–70) involving several more. Of the 32 new towns designated in Britain and Northern Ireland, not all were completed as originally intended.

Trees at Crawley, Warrington and Milton Keynes

The landscapes of the new towns were generally quite varied in style and there were some quite distinct approaches, particularly with regard to trees and woodlands. In this section we look briefly at three new towns in terms of their management approach or distinct challenges they faced relating to trees. Some of the information given is based on the author's personal experience, both at the time and more recently. The situations described will have relevance not only to other new towns but also for other towns and cities in Britain.

Crawley

Crawley in West Sussex was designated as one of the first new towns in 1947 and since 1974 has come under the jurisdiction of Crawley Borough Council (Gwynne 1990, 155–7). The 5,920 acres (2,396 ha) of land set aside for the new town was predominantly open countryside in a part of the country that was still relatively well-wooded and with plenty of fine individual trees, especially in the hedgerows. From an early stage the planners and landscape architects were keen to retain as much as possible of the existing mature treescape. This would help to give a feeling of maturity to the new landscape while the extensive tree plantings became established. The overall landscape at Crawley is now regarded as one of the best examples in the new towns (Morris 1997, 96).

Despite the general success of the landscape plan, retaining a significant number of large mature trees that had previously been located in farmland did prove very difficult. Many were native English oaks, some at least 200 years old, and they suddenly found themselves incorporated into new urban and suburban scenes. While a substantial number were retained in the various neighbourhood 'greens', many were also retained in the roadside verges of housing estates or even by the side of busy streets in the city centre. Although these roadside oaks seemed initially to have coped with the transition fairly well, by the late 1960s many were showing signs of stress. Small dead branches started to become very noticeable in the tree crowns and after several more years this dieback steadily progressed until the trees became 'stag-headed', a condition where large dead branches have the appearance of deer antlers sticking out of what is left of the foliage. The trees did not appear to be suffering from any pest or disease and the most likely cause of the decline was said to be a build-up of abiotic stress factors resulting from disruption to the rooting zone in the initial development process. Rather than fell the trees immediately, a programme of drastic pruning was instituted where the major branches were reduced leaving the trees resembling coat-stands. This was intended as a 'kill or cure' treatment that hopefully would have a positive outcome by 'shocking' the tree into producing vigorous new growth that could then be trained into a new tree crown. Unfortunately, the trees invariable died and had to be removed, including some by the author in his job as a tree surgeon. While the efforts to retain the mature oak trees often ended in failure, Crawley should be congratulated for at least trying to incorporate these magnificent trees into its new town landscape.

Warrington

Warrington in Cheshire was designated in 1968 in the third wave of new towns. Historically this Saxon town had been located in Lancashire and its urbanisation had coincided with the Industrial Revolution (Crosby 2002). Much of Warrington's expansion as a new town occurred on the site of the former Royal Ordnance Factory site at Risley. There were considerable challenges in reclaiming this large derelict military establishment and a bold approach was devised for the landscape restoration and conservation of areas of ecological importance (Scott 1991, 24).

In a radical departure from traditional horticulture-led landscape practices, much of the new landscape at Warrington was inspired by nature and influenced by forestry practices, wildlife conservation and the desire to create a multifunctional landscape (Scott 1991, 24). To help achieve this, the plan set out to create a series of linked woodland belts and naturalistic spaces. Planting began in 1974 and was completed in the early 1990s. The landscape planning policy aimed to commence planting of the new woodland belts three to six years before adjoining housing areas were occupied with the objective of creating a 'green' and sheltered environment for early residents. The new woodland was established using predominantly native species and involved a technique where all the woodland species, including trees and other plants, were planted at the outset. By using a mixture of fast-growing 'nurse' species and slow-growing climax species, dense woodland cover was established rapidly. After a closed canopy had been obtained, maintenance operations were minimal involving mainly seasonal coppicing and thinning.

The landscape at Warrington received several awards and in the 1980s was held up as a model for the 'ecological approach' to urban landscape design (Ruff and Tregay 1982), In contrast, many residents have not been so enthusiastic, particularly in its early stages of development. When the author visited some of the new housing estates in the late 1980s, one of the major concerns of residents was the 'wild' and dense nature of the woodland so close to their homes. Many expressed the wish that the landscape had a more ornamental character, similar to that in other new housing developments. Comparable views were echoed recently in a formal survey of residents in the Birchwood district using a postal questionnaire and semi-structured interviews (Jorgensen, *et al.* 2007). This revealed a very mixed reaction from residents, with both positive and negative feelings towards Warrington's 'trees and greenery'. While some regarded the woodlands as among their favourite places, others regarded them with fear as places where they could become victims of crime and intimidation. Women felt particularly vulnerable in this respect. Many residents contrasted their wooded landscape with other municipal landscapes elsewhere and felt that those colourful and well-tended landscapes had the ability to act as signs of a caring community. In another visit to Warrington in 2014, the author was struck by the considerable change in some areas of the original landscape, particular that close to the housing. This had now developed a more horticultural character with the addition of ornamental trees and shrubs (Figure 85).

Milton Keynes

Milton Keynes in Buckinghamshire was designated in 1967 as the only green-field 'new city' and was planned for a population of 250,000 to anticipate the considerable growth in the South East (Morris 1997, 117–9). It is widely considered the most successful of all the new towns and is unlike the others in a number of ways, not least in its overall landscape plan.

The intention was that the city should be greener than the surrounding countryside and in order to achieve that the parks and open spaces were the starting point of the layout. Several linear parks were created that ran right through the urban area, often following the path of existing water courses and food plains. The town-wide park system eventually occupied 20 per cent of the land and was linked to the circulation system for pedestrians, cyclists and motorists. While some new towns such as Runcorn were planned around their mass transit system, Milton Keynes was planned for cars and other vehicles (Morris 1997, 118). The low-density neighbourhoods were separated with dual carriageways for high-speed traffic and the extensive landscaping and tree planting was used to shield the housing from the increased traffic noise (Alexander 2001, 74).

What is especially interesting about the landscape at Milton Keynes has been its emphasis on trees. The original design concept aimed to create the visual impression of 'a city in a forest' and the city's foresters and landscapers planted millions of trees from its own nursery in Newlands (Walker 1981). The extent of

FIGURE 85. In a radical departure from traditional horticulture-led practices, much of the landscape at Warrington New Town was inspired by nature and influenced by forestry and wildlife conservation practice. This native Scots pine woodland on a housing estate at Birchwood was initially more overgrown and had a 'wild' appearance, raising concerns among many residents about crime and safety. In response to this the woodland has developed in recent years into a more open landscape that includes some ornamental planting.

tree planting has been quite extraordinary and by 2006 the urban area had 20 million trees. There had been some challenges along the way, especially when the drought of 1976 laid waste to 200,000 newly-planted trees and shrubs (Bendixson and Platt 1992, 181). Nevertheless, the rapid replacement of these losses ensured this was just a temporary setback.

A range of marketing strategies have been employed to attract businesses and residents to Milton Keynes and many of these have focused on promoting the city's 'green' image (Bendixson and Platt 1992, 8). Furthermore, that 'green' image has often emphasised the extensive tree cover throughout the city. In the 1970s, the author recalls seeing television advertisements urging people to "come and live and work in Milton Keynes – City of Trees".

Milton Keynes has also developed an innovative approach to the governance of its parks and trees that has been studied and admired by other parks agencies around the world. Following the winding up of the original Development Corporation in 1992 its major parks and greenspace were transferred to the Milton Keynes Park Trust (now The Parks Trust). This an independent charity that now own and cares for up to 5,000 acres (2,023 ha) of river valleys, woodlands, lakesides, parks and 80 miles (129 km) of landscaped areas alongside the main roads – about 25 per cent of the new city area. The aim of this transfer was to create an agency that was independent of the local authority which would be able to resist future pressure to build on the parks. The Trust was endowed with a portfolio of commercial properties, the income of which pays for the upkeep of the greenspaces. This has ensured that spending on parks is protected or 'ring fenced' and does not have to compete with other local authority priorities.

Impact of the new town landscapes

There is still much debate about the success or otherwise of the new towns as places to live and raise a family. Some have been more successful than others and to live in the worst parts of some less successful examples can be a very bleak experience. In this concluding section we are not concerned with wider socio-economic issues but focus on the impact of the new town landscapes.

There has been some criticism of the location of the new towns in often previously 'unspoilt' countryside and on their subsequent impact on surrounding rural areas. However, it should be remembered that they were intended partly as an alternative to the dormitory suburbs that were sprawling out from many towns and cities. It could be argued that if the new towns had not been built, the likely impact of the continued spread of largely unplanned urban areas into the countryside would have been far more devastating.

As would be expected, the impact of the new town landscapes on the residents who live there varies enormously between different towns and different socio-economic groups. Although there is no firm evidence, it is thought that the level of satisfaction has been quite high, especially among residents in the first wave of new towns and particularly with the greenspace in their own neighbourhood. This may be due in part to the comparatively low housing densities of the early new towns that allowed for private gardens of a reasonable size (Pitt 1972, 139). For many residents, particular the older people who had come from inner-city areas, this was the first time they had ever had their own garden. Whether they chose to plant a tree in this or whether there was already a tree there, it is impossible to say. It is interesting to note that in a government-sponsored social survey of new towns residents in 1969, where over 90 per cent had a garden, the most frequently requested improvement was a larger garden. As we have seen throughout history, larger private gardens tend to encourage more urban trees.

The innovative nature of the parks and greenspace in many new towns has had a significant impact on the horticultural and landscape industry in Britain. It almost certainly had a major impact on how the concept of the public park has changed from the idea of discrete individual parks and recreation grounds to a much broader perception of parks, in all their many forms, as part of a town or city's parks system. Relevant professionals now refer to urban parks systems and this wider perspective was encouraged by the town planning approach to urban greenspace that was a major element in planning the new towns. It may also have encouraged some local authority parks departments to develop a more integrated approach to the management of their urban forest.

The sheer scale of the landscapes being created in the new towns provided a major boost to the horticultural and landscape industries in the immediate post-war era. Apart from those established in the new towns, there were very few new parks created in the last half of the twentieth century (Lasdun 1991, 190). The high-profile nature of the new towns ensured that these attracted some of the most respected landscape architects and planners of the time. For example,

Sylvia Crowe was appointed as a consultant for Harlow and Basildon, and she contributed to the master plans for Warrington and Washington, while Geoffrey Jellicoe was involved in drawing up the initial plans at Hemel Hempstead (Conway 2000, 127). In their early years the parks departments of many new towns also established a national reputation for the high standard of their work (Pitt 1972, 141). This enabled them to attract high-calibre horticultural and landscape staff, which in turn helped them to maintain their reputation.

It is impossible to make any general predictions about how the landscapes of the new towns might develop in the future. Each is now under the control of its own local authority and there is no overarching national plan. The new towns are now continually evolving, just like other towns in Britain. In that respect they are not like the model villages, garden suburbs, and to a lesser extent the garden cities, where efforts are actively made to preserve their essential character, not least for its heritage value. Some new towns have already seen dramatic changes to elements of their landscape, for better or worse, and others are going through phases of renewal. There will also undoubtedly be new initiatives to come that will represent the twenty-first century equivalent of those early visions of a greener urban future.

References

Alexander, A. (2001) *Britain's New Towns: Garden Cities to Sustainable Communities.* Routledge: London.

Anon (1935) *Letchworth: The Well-Planned Town.* Silver Jubilee souvenir, 1910–1935. First Garden City: Letchworth.

Bendixson, T. and Platt, J. (1992) *Milton Keynes: Image and Reality.* Granta Editions: Cambridge.

Binns, S. (2013) *The Aesthetics of Utopia: Saltaire, Akroydon and Bedford Park,* Spire Books: Reading.

Chalkley, L. and Shiach, M. (eds) (2005) *Rosyth: Garden City and Royal Dockyard.* Rosyth Garden City Millennium Project: Rosyth.

Clark, B. (2003) Ebenezer Howard and the Marriage of Town and Country: An Introduction to Howard's Garden Cities of To-morrow (Selections). *Organization and Environment* 16(1), 87–97.

Conway, H. (2000) Everyday Landscapes: Public Parks from 1930 to 2000. *Garden History,* 117–134.

Creese, W. (1966) *The Search for Environment: The Garden City: Before and After.* Yale University Press: New Haven.

Crosby, A. (2002) *A History of Warrington.* Phillimore: Chichester.

Deakin, D. (1989) *Wythenshawe: The Story of a Garden City.* Phillimore and Co Ltd: Chichester.

Gauldie, E. (1974) *Cruel Habitations: History of Working Class Housing, 1780–1918.* Allen and Unwin: London.

Gwynne, P. (1990) *A History of Crawley.* Phillimore: Chichester.

Harvey, A. W. (1906) *The Model Village and its Cottages: Bournville.* B. T. Batsford Ltd: London.

Howard, E. (1898) *To-Morrow: A Peaceful Path to Real Reform.* Swan Sonnenschein and Co. Ltd: London.

Howard, E. (1976) *Garden Cities of Tomorrow*. Edited by Frederick Osborn with an Introduction by Lewis Mumford. Faber and Faber: London.

Hubbard, E. and Shippobottom, M. (2012) *A Guide to Port Sunlight Village*. Second edition. University of Liverpool Press: Liverpool.

Jackson, N., Lintonbon, J. and Staples, B. (2010) *Saltaire: The Making of a Model Town*. Spire Books: Reading.

Jorgensen, A., Hitchmough, J. and Dunnett, N. (2007) Woodland as a Setting for Housing-appreciation and Fear and the Contribution to Residential Satisfaction and Place Identity in Warrington New Town, UK. *Landscape and Urban Planning* 79(3), 273–287.

Loudon, J. C. (1929) Hints on Breathing Places for the Metropolis, and for Country Towns and Villages, on fixed Principles. *Gardener's Magazine* V, 686–90.

Mawson, T. H. (1911) *Civic Art: Studies in Town Planning, Parks, Boulevards and Open Spaces*. B. T. Batsford: London.

Miller, M. (2010) *English Garden Cities: An Introduction*. English Heritage: Swindon.

More, T. (1895) *The Utopia of Sir Thomas More*. In Latin from the Edition of March 1518 and in English from the First Edition of Ralph Robyson's Translation in 1551. Oxford at the Clarendon Press: Oxford.

Morris, E. S. (1997) *British Town Planning and Urban Design: Principles and Policies*. Addison Wesley Longmans Ltd: Harlow.

Morris, W. (1890) *News from Nowhere (or an Epoch of Rest)*. Roberts Brothers: Boston

Morton, A. L. (1938) *A People's History of England*. Victor Gollancz: London.

O'Reilly, C. (2013) "We Have Gone Recreation Mad": The Consumption of Leisure and Popular Entertainment in Municipal Public Parks in Early Twentieth Century Britain. *International Journal of Regional and Local History* 8(2), 112–128.

Parker, B. (1937) Site Planning at New Earswick. *Town Planning Review*, February 1937, 19.

Parsons, K. C. and Schuyler, D. (eds) (2002) *From Garden City to Green City: the Legacy of Ebenezer Howard*. John Hopkins University Press; Baltimore, MD.

Pitt, G. (1972) A consumer's view. In: Evans, H. (ed.) *New Towns: The British Experience*. Charles Knight: London.

Richard J. (1895) *After London; Or, Wild England*. Cassell and Company: London.

Ruff, A. R. and Tregay, R. (eds) (1982) *An Ecological Approach to Urban Landscape Design*. Occasional Paper Number 8. Department of Town and Country Planning, University of Manchester: Manchester.

Rutherford, S. (2014) *Garden Cities*. Shire Publications: Oxford.

Salter, R. G. (1953) *Roadside Tree Planting in Urban Areas*. Bournville Village Trust, Bournville: Birmingham.

Scott, D. (1991) The Greening of Warrington. *Landscape Design*, 24–25.

Simo, M. L. (1981) John Claudius Loudon: on Planning and Design for the Garden Metropolis. *Garden History* 9(2), 184–201.

Simo, M. L. (1988) *Loudon and the Landscape: From Country Seat to Metropolis*. Yale University Press: New Haven and London.

Trinder, B. (1982) *The Making of the Industrial Landscape*. J. M. Dent and Sons Ltd: London.

Unwin, R. (1904) *The Improvement of Towns*. Paper Read at the Conference of the National Union of Women Workers of Great Britain and Ireland. November 8, 1904, 3.

Walker, D. (1981) *The Architecture and Planning of Milton Keynes*. Architectural Press: London.

Willes, M. (2014) *The Gardens of the British Working Class*. Yale University Press: New Haven and London.

Index

Numbers in italics denote pages with illustrations